CHINA'S NEW DIPLOMACY

Rethinking Asia and International Relations

Series Editor
Emilian Kavalski, University of Western Sydney, Australia

This series seeks to provide thoughtful consideration both of the growing prominence of Asian actors on the global stage and the changes in the study and practice of world affairs that they provoke. It intends to offer a comprehensive parallel assessment of the full spectrum of Asian states, organisations, and regions and their impact on the dynamics of global politics.

The series seeks to encourage conversation on:

- What rules, norms, and strategic cultures are likely to dominate international life in the "Asian Century";
- How will global problems be reframed and addressed by a "rising Asia";
- Which institutions, actors, and states are likely to provide leadership during such "shifts to the East";
- Whether there is something distinctly "Asian" about the emerging patterns of global politics.

Such comprehensive engagement not only aims to offer a critical assessment of the actual and prospective roles of Asian actors, but also seeks to rethink the concepts, practices, and frameworks of analysis of world politics.

This series invites proposals for interdisciplinary research monographs undertaking comparative studies of Asian actors and their impact on the current patterns and likely future trajectories of international relations. Furthermore, it offers a platform for pioneering explorations of the ongoing transformations in global politics as a result of Asia's increasing centrality to the patterns and practices of world affairs.

China's New Diplomacy

Rationale, Strategies and Significance

ZHIQUN ZHU
Bucknell University, USA

ASHGATE

Published by
Ashgate Publishing Limited
Wey Court East
Union Road
Farnham
Surrey, GU9 7PT
England

Ashgate Publishing Company
110 Cherry Street
Suite 3-1
Burlington, VT 05401-3818
USA

www.ashgate.com

British Library Cataloguing in Publication Data
A catalogue record for this book is available from the British Library

The Library of Congress has cataloged the printed edition as follows:
Zhu, Zhiqun.
China's new diplomacy : rationale, strategies and significance / by Zhiqun Zhu.
   pages cm. – (Rethinking Asia and international relations)
   Includes bibliographical references and index.
   ISBN 978-1-4724-1368-0 (hardback) – ISBN 978-1-4094-5292-8 (pbk.) – ISBN 978-1-4094-5293-5 (ebook) – ISBN 978-1-4724-0729-0 (epub) 1. China–Foreign relations–1976- I. Title.
   DS779.27.Z489 2013
   327.51–dc23

                                                                        2013003102

ISBN 9781472413680 (hbk)
ISBN 9781409452928 (pbk)
ISBN 9781409452935 (ebk – PDF)
ISBN 9781472407290 (ePUB – PDF)

MIX
Paper from
responsible sources
FSC
www.fsc.org   FSC® C013985

Printed in the United Kingdom by Henry Ling Limited, at the Dorset Press, Dorchester, DT1 1HD

Contents

Foreword

On October 1, 2009, in a grand ceremony on the Tiananmen Square in Beijing, the People's Republic of China celebrated the 60th anniversary of its founding. By then, China had become the third largest economy (next to the United States and Japan) and the largest trading nation in the world. In 2010 China overtook Japan to become the second largest economy in the world. Since China's economy is expected to continue its high growth in the coming years and the US economy is likely to grow at a slow pace, barring major man-made or natural disasters, China's aggregate economy may be surpassing that of the United States within a decade or so.

Whereas China has been generally referred to as New China since October 1, 1949, there has been no widely accepted term for China since its reform and open policies started at the end of 1978. The official term used by the Chinese authorities is a tongue-twister in itself and refers only to the beginning event of the past 30 plus years: "Since the third plenary session of the 11th central committee of the Communist Party of China," which was convened in the fall of 1978 in Beijing.

I have coined a new term, "New New China," to refer to the post-1978 China. The towering figure of New New China is the late paramount leader Deng Xiaoping, for whom I had the great honor of working as an English interpreter in the 1980s. Deng's policy decisions, both for domestic economic and political reforms as well as for China's foreign policies, still constitute the foundation of Chinese policies today. However, with Deng Xiaoping phasing out of the public view after 1992 and with his eventual passing away in 1997, the baton was passed to the third generation of the PRC leadership headed by President Jiang Zemin and Premier Zhu Rongji, and since 2002, to the fourth generation of the PRC leadership headed by President Hu Jintao and Premier Wen Jiabao. In November 2012, the Chinese Communist Party elected a new leadership headed by Xi Jinping and Li Keqiang, who have vowed to deepen reform and opening up in the years ahead.

While the focus of China's efforts over the past 30 plus years has been on domestic economic reform and reconstruction, China's diplomacy has played a crucially important role in creating and maintaining an international environment and China's constructive relations with other countries as well as its position in the international order most suitable for achieving its policy priorities. China's desire for world peace is both an end in itself and a means to achieve its objective of economic development and peaceful rise in the world. Without a generally peaceful and stable international order, China's economic development would have been out of the question.

Therefore, China's diplomacy and domestic economic reconstruction are very much intertwined with each other. In a sense, China's diplomacy is mandated to serve its overall economic development, and its growing economic prowess has enabled China to become a more active and constructive participant in international diplomacy. Furthermore, since many hot issues in China have an important international dimension, the interrelations between major Chinese domestic affairs and China's diplomacy cannot be overemphasized. To learn about China's new diplomacy is essential in achieving a better understanding of today's world as well as today's China.

Professor Zhiqun Zhu's new book is an extremely timely and authoritative narrative and a top-notch scholarly analysis of the practices and implications of Chinese diplomacy since the early 1990s. Comprehensive in the scope of study, Professor Zhu sheds an illuminating light on the complex and multifaceted diplomatic activities and initiatives of China and their underlying rationale and philosophy. Only a serious scholar with deep knowledge of Chinese foreign and domestic policies can produce such an excellent piece.

With China fast becoming an increasingly key global player, I sincerely hope Professor Zhu's book will help the readers to understand better what China is up to globally today as well as the future trend of China's diplomacy. Professor Zhu's well-written work is a useful handbook, a thought-provoking text, and an indispensable guide for understanding China's diplomacy.

Victor Zhikai Gao, J.D. (Yale)
Former English interpreter for Deng Xiaoping
Director, China National Association of International Studies

August 2013
Beijing, China

Acknowledgements

Many colleagues and friends have helped in the process of writing and revising this book. I wish to express my heart-felt thanks to the following individuals for their invaluable support and help: Dave Benjamin, Gang Chen, Robert Dayley, John Doces, Wenping He, Doug Hecock, Hochul Lee, Mingjiang Li, Guoli Liu, Yawei Liu, Tony Massoud, Eduardo Daniel Oviedo, Jim Rice, Paul Rodell, Dingli Shen, Swaran Singh, Paige Johnson Tan, Thomas Ward, Yongjin Zhang, Quansheng Zhao, and Zhu Lumin. They either read part of the original manuscript and offered insightful comments and suggestions or shared their thoughts with me at different stages during my preparation for this book. I thank Jenny Clegg, Willy Lam, and David Shambaugh for endorsing the first edition, and Willy Lam, David Shambaugh and Zheng Yongnian for the second edition. However, these individuals are not responsible for any errors in the book.

I wish to thank Professor Zheng Yongnian in particular for offering visiting fellowships to me to do research at the East Asian Institute (EAI) of National University of Singapore during the summers of 2010 and 2012. EAI is a premier research institution for East Asian studies, with exceptional strength in Chinese domestic and foreign affairs. I learned a great deal from EAI researchers as well as other visiting scholars during my tenures there. I was extremely impressed by the expertise and diligence of these colleagues, many of whom would spend weekends and holidays working in their offices. The conversations during Tuesday morning meetings, lunch hours, and EAI seminars were a great source of inspiration for me.

Victor (Zhikai) Gao (J.D., Yale), a Director of China National Association of International Studies and an International Councillor of Asia Society, graciously agreed to read the original manuscript and write a foreword. Mr. Gao worked for the Chinese Foreign Ministry and the United Nations between 1983 and 1989. Most notably, he was an English interpreter for the late Chinese leader Deng Xiaoping. His first-hand experience in Chinese diplomacy makes him uniquely qualified to write the foreword for this book. I'm truly grateful to him.

At Bucknell University in Pennsylvania, I wish to thank my colleagues at Political Science Department, International Relations Department and East Asian Studies Department for their encouragement and support. I also want to thank the University and the College of Arts and Sciences for generous research support. My students from various classes I have taught over the years read some of the chapters and helped me clarify my thoughts as I was writing and updating the book. Many of them have stayed in touch with me after graduation. Their strong interest in China has helped me sustain my research activities.

At Ashgate, Kirstin Howgate, Publisher of Politics and International Relations, played a crucial role in this book's publication. She saw immediately the value in my original proposal and sample chapters and decided promptly to publish the book. Three years later, she continues to have confidence in me and this project. I appreciate her decision to publish this paperback and updated edition of the book and to include it as a title in the new "Rethinking Asia and International Relations" series. Margaret Younger, Assistant Editor of Politics and International Relations, Carolyn Court and Jude Chillman, Editorial Administrators, and Nicole Norman, Administrative Assistant for Marketing, also helped greatly before the book entered the production stage. Matt Irving, my desk editor, did a marvelous job to ensure that everything went smoothly in the production process. I'm really grateful for all the help I've received from the superb Ashgate staff.

The book was first published in April 2010. It has been thoroughly updated to reflect the most recent developments in China's relations with the developing world. With an expanded bibliography, the new edition also contains "Questions for Discussion" at the end of each chapter, making it pedagogically friendly to use as a textbook. This paperback has benefited from several reviews of the first edition, particularly those published by *The China Journal* and *East Asian Integration Studies.*

As usual, my family has been extremely patient and supportive during the writing and revision of this book. I often worked late into the night and my wife Amanda (Zhimin) was always there for me. I know my children Julia, Sophia and Matthew are very proud of their Chinese heritage. This book is dedicated to them. I hope they will be well-prepared for the challenges in the fast-changing 21st century, in which China will be a key player.

Zhiqun Zhu, PhD
John D. and Catherine T. MacArthur Chair in East Asian Politics
Associate Professor of Political Science and International Relations
Bucknell University
Lewisburg, Pennsylvania

August 2013

List of Abbreviations

ADB	Asian Development Bank
ADS	Approved Destination Status
AEW&C	Airborne Early Warning and Control
AICHR	ASEAN Inter-Governmental Commission on Human Rights
ANU	Australian National University
APEC	Asia-Pacific Economic Cooperation
APT	ASEAN Plus Three
ARF	ASEAN Regional Forum
ASEAN	Association of Southeast Asian Nations
AU	African Union
BCM	Billion Cubic Meters
BFA	Boao Forum for Asia
BOC	Bank of China
BRIC	Brazil, Russia, India and China
BRICS	Brazil, Russia, India, China and South Africa
CAFTA	China-ASEAN Free Trade Agreement
CASS	Chinese Academy of Social Sciences
CCP	Chinese Communist Party
CCTV	China Central Television
CMCC	China Mobile Communications Corporation
CNOOC	China National Offshore Oil Corporation
CNPC	China National Petroleum Corporation
CPPCC	Chinese People's Political Consultative Conference
CRI	China Radio International
CRS	Congressional Research Service
DFID	Department for International Development
DPP	Democratic Progressive Party
DRC	Democratic Republic of Congo
ECFA	Economic Cooperation Framework Agreement
ECLAC	(United Nations) Economic Commission for Latin America and the Caribbean
EEZ	Exclusive Economic Zone
ESPO	East Siberia-Pacific Ocean

FAS	Free Associated States
FDI	Foreign Direct Investment
FMF	Foreign Military Financing
FTA	Free Trade Agreement
G-8	Group of 8
G-20	Group of 20
GCC	Gulf Cooperation Council
GDP	Gross Domestic Product
GMS	Greater Mekong Subregion
Hanban	Office of Chinese Language Council International (国家汉办)
IADB	Inter-American Development Bank
IAEA	International Atomic Energy Agency
ICBC	Industrial and Commercial Bank of China
IMF	International Monetary Fund
KMT	*Kuomintang* (Nationalist Party)
LNG	Liquefied Natural Gas
MDC	Movement for Democratic Change
MEND	Movement for the Emancipation of the Niger Delta
MOGE	Myanmar Oil and Gas Enterprise
NATO	North Atlantic Treaty Organization
NBN	National Broadband Network
NDU	National Defense University
NEA	National Energy Administration
NEPAD	New Partnership for Africa's Development
NGO	Non-Governmental Organization
NPC	National People's Congress
OAS	Organization of American States
ODA	Official Development Assistance
OIC	Organization of Islamic Conference
ONGC	Oil and National Gas Corporation
PetroChina	PetroChina Company Limited
PICL	Pacific Island Conference of Leaders
PIF	Pacific Islands Forum
PLA	People's Liberation Army
PME	Professional Military Education

PNG	Papua New Guinea
PRC	People's Republic of China
ROC	Republic of China (Taiwan)
ROK	Republic of Korea (South Korea)
SANA	Syrian Arab News Agency
SCO	Shanghai Cooperation Organization
SED	Strategic and Economic Dialogue
SEZ	Special Economic Zone
Sinopec	China Petroleum & Chemical Corporation
SPTO	South Pacific Tourism Organization
TICAD	Tokyo International Conference on African Development
TMD	Theater Missile Defense
TPP	Trans-Pacific Partnership
UAE	United Arab Emirates
UN	United Nations
USAFRICOM	United States African Command
USPACOM	United States Pacific Command
UWA	University of Western Australia
VLCC	Very Large Crude Carriers
VOA	Voice of America
WHA	World Health Assembly
WHO	World Health Organization
WMD	Weapons of Mass Destruction
WTO	World Trade Organization
WUC	World Uyghur Congress
WWII	World War II
ZTE	Zhongxing Telecommunication Equipment Company Limited

Chapter 1

China's New Diplomacy Since the Early 1990s: An Introduction

Chinese diplomacy has undergone several major transformations since the early 1990s. Immediately following the Tiananmen Square incident in the spring of 1989 when the pro-democracy student movement was crushed by the Chinese government, major Western powers imposed economic, trade, political and other sanctions on Beijing.

To break out of the diplomatic isolation, China attempted to improve and strengthen relations with its Asian neighbors first. Vice Premier and Foreign Minister Qian Qichen, once nicknamed the "godfather of contemporary Chinese diplomacy," masterminded these efforts. This "good neighbor diplomacy" (*mulin waijiao* 睦邻外交) worked successfully. As a result, relations between China and the ten-member Association of Southeast Asian Nations (ASEAN) greatly improved. This was significant given the fact that many of these nations remained firmly anti-communist not long ago. Even disputes over the controversial South China Sea were temporarily shelved, making way for closer economic and political cooperation. China–Japan relations were also strengthened. In 1990 Japan became the first major power to lift economic sanctions against China and resume economic and political dialogues with Beijing. In October 1992 China welcomed Emperor Akihito and Empress Michiko to Beijing, signalling restoration and expansion of Sino-Japanese relations. The Republic of Korea (ROK or South Korea), partially due to its own *nordpolitik* policy, normalized and established diplomatic relations with Beijing in 1992 and severed formal ties with Taiwan which it had maintained since the Chinese civil war separated Taiwan from mainland China in 1949.

By the mid-1990s, as Chinese economic power continued to grow and as China became more self-confident, talks of "revitalizing the Chinese nation" (*zhenxing zhonghua* 振兴中华) had become prevalent inside China. Increasingly the Chinese government and the Chinese public began to consider China as one of the great powers in the world. Built upon its successful "good neighbor diplomacy," China refocused on big powers in its foreign relations. Chinese leaders started to travel to major capitals and invited their foreign counterparts to visit Beijing. Most notably, this "great power diplomacy" (*daguo waijiao* 大国外交) resulted in President Jiang Zemin and President Bill Clinton's exchange of visits in 1997 and 1998. As a symbol of China's growing importance in the global economy, China was eventually admitted into the World Trade

Organization (WTO) at the beginning of the new century, after some 13 years of tough negotiations with the United States.[1]

China desires a world order that is peaceful and conducive to continued economic growth and stability at home. It seeks international cooperation to achieve policy objectives. China's foreign exchange reserve reached over $2 trillion in April 2009 and over $3 trillion in March 2011, much larger than that of any other country. This, together with the fact that China has fared much better than most other major economies since the global economic downturn in 2008, makes it possible for China to continue to expand trade and investment and enhance its political influence in every corner of the world.

In the first three decades of the People's Republic of China (PRC)'s history (1949–1979), energy concerns were only a minor factor in Beijing's national security and strategic assessment. China's own oil fields, such as Daqing in the Northeast that was first discovered in 1959, had produced enough oil to keep China self-reliant. Since the end of the 1970s when China reopened its door to the Western world and adopted economic reform policies, the Chinese economy has been expanding at an average of 10 percent annual growth rate. This rapid expansion requires enormous resources, especially energy and raw materials. Since the mid-1990s China has been seeking oil and other energy and natural resources in Africa, the Middle East, Latin America, Central Asia, the South Pacific, Southeast Asia and elsewhere. This new "energy diplomacy" (*nengyuan waijiao* 能源外交) has become a key component of Chinese foreign policy in the new century since energy security has become essential for China to achieve its strategic goal of quadrupling its gross domestic product (GDP) from 2000 to 2020.

At the beginning of the 2000s nearly two thirds of China's energy still came from coal, and over four fifths of its electricity was created by burning coal. In 2007, China mined 2.5 billion metric tons of coal, equivalent to 46 percent of total world production—more than the United States, the EU, and Japan combined.[2] More than 40 percent of China's rail capacity was devoted to transporting coal across the country. In 2007 China became a net importer of coal. It can still meet about 90 percent of its overall energy demand with domestic supply. This is projected to be near 80 percent in 2020.[3] China will strive to meet its energy needs mainly through domestic supply. On the other hand, it will take an active part in energy cooperation with other countries.

---

1   For a discussion of major debates in the United States over China's WTO membership and its implications for US–China relations, see Zhiqun Zhu, "To Support or Not to Support: The American Debate on China's WTO Membership," *Journal of Chinese Political Science*, Vol. 6, No. 2 (Fall 2000), pp. 77–101.

2   "Coal Use in China," *Freeman Report*, Center for Strategic & International Studies (CSIS), Washington, DC, June 2009.

3   Xuecheng Liu, "China's Energy Security and Its Grand Strategy," Policy Analysis Brief, *The Stanley Foundation*, September 2006.

Until the early 1990s, China was still an oil exporter. That changed permanently in 1993 when it became a net oil importer. Though the global economic crisis slowed down China's demand for energy, the Chinese economy, helped by government stimulus packages to expand domestic consumption, had shown signs of recovery by early 2009, and energy needs are expected to grow in the years ahead. Oil now accounts for just about 19 percent of China's energy needs, but China's oil demand is predicted to more than double by 2030 to over 16 million barrels a day, according to the International Energy Agency, as more Chinese rise from poverty, move out of villages and buy cars. The number of vehicles in China rose sevenfold between 1990 and 2006, to 37 million. In 2009 China surpassed the US to become the world's biggest automobile market, selling a total of 13.6 million vehicles, compared with 10.4 million sold in the US. The streets of major Chinese cities are crammed with cars driven by the new middle class. China is adding cars at such a rate that by 2030 it could have as many as 300 million vehicles.[4] If that happens, by then China and the world will be in a dire situation unless renewable energies are developed.

In the several years after it became a net oil importer in 1993, China's oil imports were increasing by 10 million tons yearly. By 2003, the annual increase reached 20 million tons. In 2007 China's total oil imports reached 197 million tons, with 45 percent of the crude oil coming from the Middle East, 32.5 percent from Africa, and 3.5 percent from the Asia and Pacific region.[5] (See Table 1.1). Given that several major oil exporters in the Middle East and Africa are politically unstable, China diversified the sources of its oil imports, with increased attention to Central Asia, Russia, Latin America, Southeast Asia, and the South Pacific. Top Chinese oil companies—China National Petroleum Corporation (CNPC), China National Offshore Oil Corporation (CNOOC), and China Petroleum & Chemical Corporation (Sinopec)—have been very active in acquiring exploration rights from Mauritania and Angola to Azerbaijan and Kazakhstan, and Chinese oil

Table 1.1   Top oil exporters to China: 2006–2010

Ranking Year	1	2	3	4	5	6
2006	Angola	Saudi Arabia	Iran	Russia	Oman	Equatorial Guinea
2007	Saudi Arabia	Angola	Iran	Russia	Oman	Sudan
2008	Saudi Arabia	Angola	Iran	Oman	Russia	Sudan
2009	Saudi Arabia	Iran	Angola	Russia	Oman	Sudan
2010	Saudi Arabia	Angola	Iran	Oman	Russia	Sudan

Source: The General Administration of Customs of China (http://english.customs.gov.cn), various years.

---

4   Jad Mouawad, "The Big Thirst," *The New York Times*, April 20, 2008.
5   "China's Oil Imports in 2007 Close to 200 Million Tons," *Xinhua*, March 3, 2008.

workers are becoming a growing presence in the Middle East, Africa, Central Asia, and Latin America.

China's efforts to snatch oil and gas and other resources from the developing world and expand its influence there have triggered intense competition between China and other powers. For example, Sri Lanka's Mannar Basin is believed to hold vast reserves of oil and gas and has attracted foreign companies to compete in exploration. Sri Lanka has divided the Basin into nine areas so that different foreign companies, including those from China and India, can explore there. However, India is reportedly working with the Sri Lankan government to prevent Chinese companies from entering the region since China's presence may pose "national security challenge" to India.[6] India also plans to open a new four-lane motorway to allow traders and tourists to drive from its eastern state of Assam into Myanmar, Thailand and, eventually, Cambodia and Vietnam.[7] The United States, Japan, and South Korea, among others, have also strengthened their relations with South and Southeast Asian countries. South Korean President Lee Myung-bak visited Myanmar in May 2012 to discuss economic cooperation, becoming the first ROK president to do so since 1983. In April 2012, Japan announced that it would write off $3.7 billion debt owed by Myanmar. The United States, Japan and South Korea will also work together to build more power plants for Myanmar.

To deal with the worsening energy issues and ensure the sustainable and steady development of the national economy, China's inter-ministerial National Energy Administration (NEA) began operation in July 2008. According to *Xinhua*, China's official news agency, the new institution consists of nine departments, with 112 personnel. Its main responsibilities include drafting energy development strategies, proposing reform advice, implementing management of energy sectors, putting forward policies of exploring new energy and carrying out international cooperation, among others.[8] In 2005 China also began work on a strategic oil reserve in coastal Zhejiang province that would allow the country to operate without imports for as long as three months.[9]

Seeking and preserving energy is not the only objective of China's new diplomacy. China has multilayered interests and manifold purposes in each of the regions where it has conducted active diplomacy. It is looking for new markets for its consumer products. Chinese firms are beginning to invest in overseas markets and purchase foreign assets. For example, Chinese companies have been purchasing and investing in Africa since the turn of the century. Between 2005 and

---

6   "India Wants to Prevent China from Exploring Sri Lankan Gas Field," *VOA News* (Chinese), March 15, 2012.

7   "India to Open Superhighway to Myanmar, Thailand," *Today (Singapore)*, May 30, 2012.

8   "China National Energy Administration Commences Operation," *Xinhua*, July 29, 2008.

9   Peter S. Goodman, "Big Shift in China's Oil Policy," *The Washington Post*, July 15, 2005.

2006, Chinese investment in Africa jumped from $6.2 billion to $12 billion.[10] In October 2007 China's largest bank, the Industrial and Commercial Bank of China (ICBC), purchased a 20 percent stake in Standard Bank, South Africa's largest bank by assets and earnings, for $5.5 billion, representing the largest foreign direct investment (FDI) in South Africa by then. Chinese investment in Africa is projected to increase to $50 billion by 2015.

In addition, the Chinese government has been promoting a new national image as a responsible, friendly and peaceful player in international affairs. As part of the "going out" (*zou chu qu* 走出去) strategy, major Chinese media groups have all expanded their overseas services, especially "the big four" — Xinhua, China Central Television (CCTV), China Radio International, and China Daily. Some provincial-level media such as those from Shanghai, Guangdong and Chongqing have also bolstered their overseas presence.

By September 2009, CCTV had set up six channels to broadcast news globally in English, French, Spanish, Arabic, Russian and Chinese around the clock to counter the perceived distorted coverage of China by foreign media. It is conducting new economic and cultural diplomacy around the world. In early 2012, both CCTV Africa and CCTV America went on air. CCTV America selected 100 journalists from China, with 40 of them sending dispatches in Mandarin to 42 channels back home, and 60 others producing business and newsmagazine shows for the new English-language channel in Washington.[11] Like other states, China uses its growing soft power to win foreign friends and gain international influence.

China attempts to enhance and exercise its soft poweer by establishing Confucius Institutes around the globe.[12] The Confucius Institute is a non-profit public institution which aims at promoting Chinese language and culture and supporting Chinese teaching internationally. Normally a Chinese institution of higher learning will partner with a counterpart abroad to jointly operate the Confucius Institute locally. The headquarters in Beijing, the Office of Chinese Language Council International or *Hanban* (汉办), offers financial and teaching support to these institutions abroad. Chinese language instructors have been dispatched and books have been sent to many of these Institutes. By October 2010, nearly 700 Confucius Institutes and Confucius Classrooms had been established

---

10   Zheng Yuwen, "China's Investment in Africa and Concerns from the United States, Europe and Africa," *Voice of America (VOA) Chinese*, April 21, 2008.

11   "The New Guys on the Campaign Bus," *Bloomberg BusinessWeek*, October 8–14, 2012: pp. 36–7.

12   "Soft power" refers to a country's ability to win the hearts and minds of others through attraction and persuasion rather than the "hard power" of coercion and punishment. The term was coined by Harvard University professor Joseph Nye in a 1990 book, *Bound to Lead: The Changing Nature of American Power*. He further developed the concept in his other books such as *Soft Power: The Means to Success in World Politics* (PublicAffairs, 2005) and *The Powers to Lead* (Oxford University Press, 2008).

in 96 countries.[13] China's Ministry of Education estimated that in 2010 there were approximately 100 million non-Chinese worldwide learning Chinese as a foreign language. *Hanban* aims to establish 1,000 Confucius Institutes by 2020. Meanwhile, foreign students are flocking to China to study. By the end of 2012, the total number of foreign students in China had reached over 310,000.

Very significantly, the new diplomacy is no longer monopolized by the Chinese government; the public is increasingly involved in the process. Public diplomacy (*gonggong waijiao* 公共外交), whose tools include cultural and educational exchanges, business links, tourism, sports, and other people-to-people contacts, has greatly expanded between China and other countries. As a supplement to formal state-to-state diplomacy, public diplomacy has been instrumental in China's efforts to create and present a friendly image abroad. Sending medical teams (*yiliaodui* 医疗队) to work abroad has traditionally been part of China's public diplomacy. China sent its first medical aid team to Algeria in 1963. As of the end of 2008, China had sent more than 20,000 medical workers abroad, helping 260 million patients in 69 countries and regions across the world.[14]

The good neighbor diplomacy, great power diplomacy, energy diplomacy, and public diplomacy are all means to achieve the PRC's major foreign-policy objectives, intended to help develop China into a major economic, political, cultural and military power by the mid-21st century. In an attempt to better understand China's new diplomacy, this book will focus on three fundamental questions:

- *Why* has China practiced new diplomacy since the early 1990s?
- *How* has China implemented its new diplomacy?
- *What* are the implications for international political economy?

The first question deals with various motivations behind China's new diplomacy; the second one looks at specific Chinese strategies in achieving its diplomatic objectives; and the third one addresses the impact of Chinese new diplomacy on international politics and economics.

The overarching theme of the book is that China's new diplomacy has been chiefly motivated by the need to secure energy and commodity resources, to search for new markets for Chinese exports and investment, to isolate Taiwan internationally, and to project China's image as a responsible and peaceful power. To achieve these multiple purposes, China has employed a variety of strategies such as summit diplomacy, no political strings attached in trade and aid (except its insistence on the "one-China" policy), avoiding confrontation with existing powers, and active participation by the Chinese public. The book argues that while some of China's practices such as those in Sudan remain controversial, overall China's

---

13   For a complete list of the Confucius Institutes worldwide, refer to *Hanban*'s website at http://www.chinese.cn/college/globalColleges.htm.
14   "Senior Leader Hails Chinese Medical Assistance in Foreign Countries," *Xinhua*, December 6, 2008.

new diplomacy has been successful. The increasingly sophisticated Chinese diplomacy has been largely benevolent, presenting more opportunities than threat to developing countries and to the Western countries that were traditionally—and remain—the dominant outside powers of the developing world. China's new diplomacy also raises issues such as sustainable development and growth model in international political economy.

Main Features of China's New Diplomacy

To achieve its foreign-policy objectives, China has adjusted its diplomatic, political, and economic strategies. At the beginning of China's reform era which started in 1978, the prevailing strategy was "bringing in" or *yin jin lai* (引进来). China enthusiastically attracted FDI, especially from overseas Chinese who remained emotionally attached to their ancestral homeland. It established four Special Economic Zones (SEZs) in 1980 in southern China near Hong Kong, Taiwan and Southeast Asia where the majority of the Chinese diasporas live. The Chinese diasporas have provided the largest chunk of external investment into the Chinese mainland from the very beginning of China's reform era. Eventually China opened up the whole coastal region to foreign investment and trade.

Since the late 1990s, particularly after China became a member of the WTO in 2001, China has been more deeply integrated into the international political economy. A new strategy in the 21st century is "going out" or *zou chu qu* (走出去). China has been actively seeking oil and other energy deals around the world; Chinese companies have started to invest overseas, including purchasing foreign assets. Backed up by a huge foreign exchange reserve, China has been confidently reaching out to every corner of the globe. As well-known China scholar Harry Harding has remarked, China, much like what Japan did in the 1980s, is now in a position to make major investments and purchases in the United States, not just developing nations. Those investments include strategic and iconic ones, such as oil and automobiles respectively.[15]

From Passive to More Active Diplomacy

With growing political and economic strength, China has become more actively involved in international political economy. As Wu Jianmin, a senior diplomat and former President of the China Foreign Affairs University, has observed, China is moving from "responsive diplomacy" (*fanying shi waijiao* 反应式外交) to "proactive diplomacy" (*zhudong shi waijiao* 主动式外交) at the beginning of the 21st century.[16]

---

15 "China Goes Global: Implications for the United States," The Gramercy Round, *The National Interest*, September/October 2006, p. 58.

16 *China Youth Daily* (*Zhongguo Qingnian Bao*), February 18, 2004.

As an old saying goes, the nail that sticks out gets pounded down. For a long time, China had tried to avoid being such a nail. The late paramount leader Deng Xiaoping (1904–1997) concluded that China should keep a low profile and never take the lead in international affairs; instead, it needed to focus on domestic growth. This strategy was necessary at the early stage of China's development. Without being too heavily involved in external affairs, China was able to concentrate on economic development, yielding a double-digit growth rate during much of the 1980s and 1990s.

Those days are gone. After President Jiang Zemin, Premier Zhu Rongji and their colleagues gradually restored China's position in post-Tiananmen world politics and economics and improved relations with great powers in the 1990s, China became more active in regional and international affairs. The Hu Jintao—Wen Jiabao leadership that assumed power in 2002 walked a new path in diplomacy: take the lead if needed. China no longer shies away from international responsibilities.

Indeed, since the beginning of the 21st century, China has demonstrated leadership in several international arenas. In 2003 China initiated the Six-Party talks over North Korea's nuclear program, involving the United States, Japan, South Korea, North Korea, and Russia. Through several rounds of tough negotiations and talks, the six parties finally reached an agreement in Beijing in February 2007 to dismantle North Korea's nuclear program. In June 2008 North Korea blew up the cooling tower of its Yongbyon nuclear reactor and handed over to the United States a long-awaited declaration of its nuclear activities. In July 2008 US Secretary of State Condoleezza Rice and North Korean Foreign Minister Pak Ui-chun met for the first time at the multilateral disarmament talks in Singapore. The United States ultimately removed North Korea from the list of terror-sponsoring countries in October 2008, although the task of verifying North Korea's de-nuclearization remains difficult.

There was no breakthrough in US–North Korea relations during the first term of the Barack Obama administration. Instead, North Korea defied international pressures and launched a long-range missile (or a satellite as it claimed) in April 2009 and conducted the second nuclear test in May 2009. In December 2012 it launched a long-range rocket and in February 2013 it conducted a nuclear test, further complicating de-nuclearization of the Korean Peninsula. Though China joined other members at the United Nations Security Council in condemning North Korea's adventurism, it also urged restraint on all parties concerned and prodded North Korea to return to the negotiation table. Whenever a crisis occurs on the Korean Peninsula, even the United States looks up to China for leadership. China is expected to continue to play the leadership role in the long process of North Korea's de-nuclearization.

Officially China maintains an independent foreign and defense policy, but since the mid-1990s China has actively participated in selective multilateral political, economic and other organizations. For example, China, together with Russia, has been promoting economic, political, and military cooperation with Central Asian nations. The Shanghai Cooperation Organization (SCO), an intergovernmental political and economic cooperation organization, was founded on June 14, 2001 by the leaders of China, Russia, Kazakhstan, Kyrgyzstan, Tajikistan and Uzbekistan. The SCO was created on the basis of The Shanghai Five, a group originally created on April 26, 1996 with the signing of the *Treaty on Deepening Military Trust in Border Regions* in Shanghai by the heads of state of Kazakhstan, the PRC, Kyrgyzstan, Russia and Tajikistan. Though the declaration on the establishment of the SCO contained a statement that it is "not an alliance directed against other states and regions and it adheres to the principle of openness," some observers believe that one of the original purposes of the SCO was to serve as a counterbalance to NATO and the United States and in particular to avoid conflicts that would allow the United States to intervene in areas near both Russia and China. Others believe that the organization was formed as a direct response to the theater missile defense (TMD) systems by the United States. The SCO members have increased cooperation in energy and have conducted joint military exercises since 2002. Of particular interest to the West were the first ever joint military exercises between China and Russia in 2005 and the "Peace Mission 2007" military exercises among SCO members. Russia and China have conducted more rounds of joint military drills since 2009, including the first-ever naval exercises in the Yellow Sea in April 2012.

China has also been active diplomatically in other regions. Partially to deflect Western criticism that it had not done enough to help end conflicts in Sudan's Darfur region, China appointed a special envoy to Sudan in 2006 as part of its efforts to broker a peace deal between the Sudanese government and rebel groups. China has also named special envoys to the Middle East and Southeast Asia to promote relations with these regions and to get more actively involved in helping resolve controversial issues such as the Israeli–Arab conflict and Iran's nuclear program.

To present its image as a peacefully rising and responsible power, China has published a set of white papers to publicize its policies on a wide range of issues such as human rights, Taiwan, Tibet, national defense, and democracy in China. It has also established a multilevel public relations system, with speakspersons explaining China's foreign and domestic policies to foreign journalists at the central government level (primarily the State Council's Information Office), the ministerial level (Ministry of Foreign Affairs, Ministry of Defense, etc), and provincial level (such as Information Offices of Shanghai and Guangdong). In 2008 *Xinhua* announced its plan to launch a CNN-like news network to broadcast world and Chinese events around the clock. In April 2009 the English version of the popular newspaper *Global Times*, which is affiliated with the official *People's Daily*, was launched. According to its website, *Global Times* has more than 500 special correspondents and contributors posted around the world. It wants to show "how China is closely connected to global affairs" and present "the complexity and fascination of China to the world."[17] In July 2009 *Xinhua* started to provide English-language news broadcasts on the screens of supermarkets across Europe.

---

17   See *Global Times'* English website at http://en.huanqiu.com. "Global" can be translated as "huanqiu" in Chinese.

China's new, active diplomacy is sometimes perceived to be assertive especially in dealing with controversial issues, creating tensions with several of its neighbors. For example, in 2012 China reacted strongly to the Japanese government's "purchase" of Diaoyu/Senkaku islands by sending patrol ships and surveillance planes to the disputed area. And in November 2012 China issued a new passport containing a map of China that covers the whole South China Sea. How to mend relations with its neighbors such as the Philippines, Vietnam, India and Japan and how to improve China's international image have become a key foreign-policy challenge for the new leadership headed by Xi Jinping and Li Keqiang who came to office in 2012–13.

The Top-down Approach

Summit meetings and other forms of top-level exchanges are highly symbolic and often extremely effective in achieving foreign-policy goals. Before the 1970s, Chinese communist leaders were not frequent travelers internationally, partially due to the fact that the PRC did not have normal diplomatic relations with much of the Western world. Mao Zedong only ventured to the Soviet Union twice. Deng Xiaoping's most well-known travel was to the United States shortly after Beijing and Washington established diplomatic ties in January 1979. Deng studied in France as a young man, but he did not travel much as the supreme leader of the PRC after Mao's death.

China's leaders have become globetrotters since the early 1990s and have left their footprints in every region of the world. From Jiang Zemin and Zhu Rongji to Hu Jintao and Wen Jiabao and to Xi Jinping and Li Keqiang, many of these three generations of top leaders have engaged in frequent high-level diplomacy with countries near and far. For example, President Hu Jintao traveled to Africa six times between 1999 and 2009.

Chinese leaders' diplomatic activities have become more sophisticated now. For example, Xi Jinping's US trip in February 2012 included a brief stop at Muscatine, Iowa, a place he first visited in 1985 as a county official from Hebei Province. By visiting "old friends" there, Xi seemed to understand the importance of reaching out to ordinary people in America's heartland.

While maintaining good relations with other great powers, China pays particular attention to developing countries and has exchanged high-level visits with many of these countries. During their terms, President Hu and Premier Wen journeyed to many parts of Africa, the Middle East, Latin America, Southeast Asia, Central Asia, and the South Pacific. Likewise, leaders from developing nations have been welcomed to Beijing. Since the early 1990s, it has been a New Year ritual for the Chinese Foreign Minister to start his New Year international travel with visits to Africa first.

Beijing has become one of the most often visited capitals for foreign heads of state and heads of government in the new century. In 2006 alone, China hosted several major international conferences, attracting over 60 world leaders. In June that year, the SCO summit was held in Shanghai. In October, China hosted the China–ASEAN summit. In November, the summit of the China–Africa Forum was held in Beijing, attracting top leaders from all African nations that have diplomatic ties with China. And in December China hosted a multilateral energy conference.

Chinese leaders can be found now at many other international and multilateral venues such as the United Nations, the "ASEAN plus three" (APT, that is ASEAN plus China, Japan and ROK) Summit, ASEAN Regional Forum (ARF), the Davos World Economic Forum, Group of Eight (G-8) and Group of 20 (G-20) Summits, East Asia Summit, Boao Forum, and Euro-Asia Summit. This top-down approach demonstrates the Chinese leadership's determination to defend China's national interests and promote a confident and responsible image of China globally. Through a combination of growing economic clout and increasingly active diplomacy, China has established solid and productive relationships throughout Asia, Africa, Latin America, the Middle East, Central Asia and other parts of the world.

The Bottom-up Approach

Realizing that bilateral relations without participation and support of the public cannot be sustained, China has aggressively promoted cultural, educational, academic, business and other societal level exchanges with many countries around the world. The government is no longer the sole player in China's new diplomacy. Complementing the top-down approach, this bottom-up approach has brought China much closer to other countries, laying a solid foundation for expanding relations in the future. As a form of public diplomacy or citizen diplomacy, people-to-people exchanges have greatly expanded between China and the rest of the world.

To enhance its soft power, China is actively promoting the Chinese language and culture abroad by establishing the Confucius Institute around the world. On the other hand, China has made it easier for foreign students to travel to China. The Chinese government and dozens of Chinese universities have provided scholarships for international students.

Sports play a unique role in promoting friendship in international relations, as demonstrated by the "ping-pong diplomacy" of the early 1970s.[18] It was still inconceivable for Chinese athletes to play in professional sports teams abroad as late as the mid-1990s. But now China is exporting star athletes, including Houston Rockets' Yao Ming (2002–2011) and Manchester United's Sun Jihai (2002–2009). These stars, who have a large number of fans both in and outside China, serve as cultural ambassadors and help bring China closer to the outside world.

---

18   "Ping-pong diplomacy" refers to the exchange of ping-pong players of the United States and China in 1971 that helped improve relations between the two countries. American ping-pong players were invited to China in the absence of diplomatic relations between Beijing and Washington. The event marked a thaw in US–China relations that paved the way for a visit to Beijing by President Richard Nixon.

In the tradition of the "panda diplomacy" of the 1970s and 1980s, China has continued to use the cuddly and popular animals as friendship envoys to promote relations with key partners. For example, in September 2007 following President Hu Jintao's visit to Australia, China announced that two giant pandas would be loaned to the Adelaide Zoo in 2009 for ten years as a lasting reminder of the warm relations between Australia and China. Even in cross-Taiwan Strait relations, pandas have become special envoys. The Beijing government first offered two giant pandas to Taiwan in 2006 but the offer was rejected by the pro-independence government of Chen Shui-bian. After Kuomingtang (KMT)'s Ma Ying-jeou came to power in May 2008, cross-Taiwan Strait relations have significantly improved, and the two pandas, *Tuantuan* and *Yuanyuan*, arrived in Taiwan and made a new home at the Taipei Zoo in December 2008. The two pandas appeared to the excited public in Taipei during the Chinese New Year of 2009, creating quite a sensation among zoo-goers and generating much-needed goodwill across the Taiwan Strait.

In addition to academic, cultural, educational, sports, business and other exchanges, tourism can help improve international relations. To encourage the *nouveau riche* Chinese middle class to travel abroad, China has made dozens of countries "designated destinations" for Chinese tourists. Since the global economic downturn in 2008, such waves of Chinese tourists have been a very welcoming gesture to many businesses abroad. Already in many popular travel destinations, the Chinese language signs have been put up alongside the traditional English and Japanese ones.

Peaceful Rise or Peaceful Development

"Peaceful rise" (*heping jueqi* 和平崛起) is a phrase used by Chinese scholars and officials to describe China's foreign-policy approach in the early 21st century and to counter international fears about Beijing's growing economic and political might. China has shifted from the more aggressive policy of the 1970s and 1980s, when it was quite willing to use force, to a much more diplomatic and peaceful route of the 1990s and the early 21st century.

The term *heping jueqi* was first coined by Zheng Bijian, former Vice Principal of the Central Party School and longtime advisor to Chinese leadership, in a speech given at the Boao Forum for Asia (BFA) in late 2003. It was then reiterated by Premier Wen Jiabao at an ASEAN meeting as well as during his visit to the United States in 2004. Many of the ideas behind the effort to promote the concept of the peaceful rise of the PRC came from the new security concept, which was formulated by think tanks in the PRC in the mid-1990s.[19] Zheng pointed out that in the past, a rise of a new power often resulted in drastic changes to global political

---

19   For a useful discussion of peaceful development in China's foreign relations , see Sujian Guo (ed.), *China's Peaceful Rise in the 21st Century: Domestic and International Conditions* (Ashgate Publishing, August 2006).

structures, and even war. He believed that this was because these powers "chose the road of aggression and expansion, which will ultimately fail." Zheng stated that in today's new world, the PRC should and can instead develop peaceably, and in turn help to maintain a peaceful international environment.[20]

However, the term proved controversial in part because some observers thought the use of the word "rise" could fuel perceptions that China is a threat to the established order. China's "rise" implies that others will decline, at least in a relative sense, while "development" suggests that China's advance can bring others along. At the 2004 session of the BFA, President Hu used the phrase "peaceful development" (*heping fazhan* 和平发展), which has since been the preferred term by Chinese officials and scholars, although "peaceful rise" can still be heard. According to Shi Yinhong, a noted professor of international relations at Renmin University of China in Beijing, China's peaceful rise or peaceful development is all about its projection of soft power. A peaceful rise relies primarily on resources of non-military nature. These include economic power, foreign trade, diplomatic and cultural power and esteem from successful national development as well as persuasive power. The rise can be characterized as non-violent, gradually building and mutually beneficial. It is most unlikely to set off strong resistance, and while minimizing costs it generates results that are most likely to be "win for all."[21] The proposed establishment of 1,000 Confucius Institutes around the world, along with Chinese global trade and investment, has become an important component of China's soft power.

Before the mid-1990s, there was basically no transparency regarding the Chinese military. Now China publishes Defense White Papers regularly and has invited foreign military attachés and delegations to observe the People's Libration Army (PLA)'s regular exercises. The PLA has been offering annual courses for foreign officers and defense officials at the National Defense University (NDU) of China and hosting international symposia and seminars on international relations and Asia–Pacific security. To present a peaceful and responsible image, the PLA Navy has also been active in military diplomacy, including its first ever visit to Japan in November 2007 and its December 2008 unprecedented anti-piracy mission to the coast of Somalia.

In December 2008, the Chinese navy for the first time since the Ming Dynasty (1368–1644) sent its warships to Africa as part of international efforts against piracy on high seas near Somali. The international community generally welcomed China's naval mission. As another example of China's friendly military diplomacy, in April 2009 the PLA Navy marked the 60th anniversary of its founding with a display of fleet that featured 21 ships from 14 foreign countries including the United States and Russia. President Hu presided over the display and avowed that China would never seek hegemony and would strive to build a "harmonious ocean." In December

20   Zheng Bijian, "China's 'Peaceful Rise' to Great-Power Status," *Foreign Affairs*, Vol. 84, No. 5 (September/October 2005).

21   Shi Yinhong, "China's Peaceful Rise Is All About Soft Power," *China Daily*, June 16, 2007.

2012, when meeting with a group of foreign experts working in China, Xi Jinping reiterated China's peaceful intentions and claimed that China's development will benefit China and the world.

How to Understand China's New Diplomacy?

Most scholars would agree that national interests are the driving forces of a state's diplomacy. Interests have also been a key tool in analyzing a country's foreign policy.[22] A new analytical tool — influence — has featured prominently in studying China's new diplomacy. In addition to satisfying China's key economic interests, projecting its soft power around the world has become a new objective of Chinese diplomacy. China is attempting to grow peacefully, different from past rising powers that tended to disrupt the international system. How can a rising power like China develop peacefully? Will China's rise inevitably trigger a conflict with the United States? Chinese officials and scholars have embraced concepts such as peaceful development, a harmonious world, and responsible stakeholder. This new element in Chinese diplomacy is also consistent with President Hu Jintao's theory of *San He* ("the Three Harmonies"), which includes seeking peace in the world, reconciliation with Taiwan, and harmony in Chinese society.[23]

While China is playing an increasingly important role in international politics and economics, several questions remain unanswered regarding China's new diplomacy. For example, is China departing from its traditional foreign-policy based on the so-called *Five Principles of Peaceful Coexistence*?[24] Will China still invest heavily in

---

22   For a discussion of national interests and foreign policy in general, see, for example, Henry Kissinger, *Does America Need a Foreign Policy?: Toward a Diplomacy for the 21st Century* (Simon & Schuster, 2002); Karl K. Schonberg, *Pursuing the National Interest: Moments of Transition in Twentieth-Century American Foreign Policy* (Praeger Publishers, 2003); and Peter Trubowitz, *Defining the National Interest: Conflict and Change in American Foreign Policy* (University of Chicago Press, 1998).

For a discussion of national interests and Chinese diplomacy, see, for example, Bates Gill, *Rising Star: China's New Security Diplomacy* (Brookings Institution, 2007); Pobzeb Vang, *Five Principles of Chinese Foreign Policies* (AuthorHouse, 2008); and David Lampton, *The Making of Chinese Foreign and Security Policy in the Era of Reform* (Stanford University Press, 2001).

23   For a discussion of "the Three Harmonies," see Willy Lam, "Hu Jintao's 'Theory of the Three Harmonies,'" *China Brief*, Vol. 6, No. 1, The Jamestown Foundation, January 3, 2006.

24   The *Five Principles of Peaceful Coexistence* have been the PRC's guiding principles of foreign policy since the early 1950s. They were first put forth by Premier Zhou Enlai during Sino-Indian negotiations in 1953 on relations between the two countries with respect to Tibet. The Five Principles were formally written into the preface to the "Agreement Between the People's Republic of China and the Republic of India on Trade and Intercourse Between the Tibet Region of China and India" in 1954. The Five Principles

the developing regions if they lack resources that it desperately needs for domestic economic growth? And how can one explain China's new diplomacy theoretically?

Most people assume that China's diplomacy is simply driven by economic considerations. Are there any other motivations, in addition to the obvious need for energy and trade? What are the major strategies China has taken in implementing its new diplomacy? Does China have a grand strategy to compete with the United States around the world? This book suggests that there are other motivations which include promoting China's soft power around the world, isolating or competing with Taiwan diplomatically, and providing genuine assistance to developing nations. The author argues that despite some conflicting interests, the United States generally welcomes China's rise as a peaceful power. The two countries have many shared interests such as promoting peace in the Middle East, maintaining a nuclear free Korean Peninsula, fighting poverty in Africa, safeguarding the free passage of sea lanes, etcetera.

Despite repeated assurances from Chinese leaders that China will grow peacefully, why are some countries suspicious of China's intentions? Why do some people suggest that China's new diplomacy is detrimental to global development? As we will see in the following chapters, certain approaches of China to the developing world harm China's international image as a responsible great power and undercut its assurance strategy. For example, China's traditional "non-interference" policy in Sudan and Syria may have condoned bad governance and human rights abuses and has received strong criticism from many quarters.

International Relations theories provide a wide range of perspectives of foreign policy and diplomacy studies. Realism, liberalism, and constructivism are three major theories often used to interpret and analyze international affairs.[25] Which theory best explains China's new diplomacy? China emphasizes the enhancement of its "comprehensive national power" (*zonghe guoli* 综合国力) as a major objective of its foreign policy. Meanwhile, it is also embracing cultural power and endeavors to assure others that its development and rise to great power status will be steady and peaceful. If one focuses on the material motivations of China's policies, then realism may help understand why China is active abroad. If one looks at how China

---

were also contained in the 1954 joint communiqué issued by Premier Zhou Enlai and Prime Minister Jawaharlal Nehru. The Five Principles are:

1.   Mutual respect for each other's territorial integrity and sovereignty;
2.   Mutual non-aggression;
3.   Mutual non-interference in each other's internal affairs;
4.   Equality and mutual benefit; and
5.   Peaceful coexistence.

25   For an introduction to International Relations theories, see, for example, Robert Jackson and Georg Sorensen, *Introduction to International Relations: Theories and Approaches*, 3rd Edition (Oxford University Press, 2005); James Dougherty and Robert L. Pfaltzgraff, Jr., *Contending Theories of International Relations: A Comprehensive Survey*, 5th edition (Longman, 2009); and Paul R. Viotti and Mark V. Kauppi, *International Relations Theory*, 4th Edition (Prentice Hall, 2009).

is expanding its soft power and promoting cultural exchanges, maybe liberalism offers a good explanation. This book argues, however, that constructivism, with its emphasis on values, norms, identities and new concepts, can best explain the practice of China's new diplomacy and the challenges and problems associated with it.

Notable scholars on constructivism in International Relations include Nicholas Onuf, Alexander Wendt, Friedrich Kratochwil, John Ruggie, Richard Ashley, Emanuel Adler, Martha Finnemore, Kathryn Sikkink, and Peter Katzenstein. Wendt, in his 1992 article, "Anarchy is what states make of it: the social construction of power politics," popularized the term "constructivism" although Onuf first introduced it to the field of International Relations.[26] Constructivists argue that international norms and values are socially constructed. For Wendt, "anarchy" is a status constructed by states.[27] Norms help shape behaviors of states whose identities may change as a result of changing circumstances. States are self-interested but they continuously define what that means.

To build upon the Wendt thesis, one can propose that for China, "peace" is what states make of it. China's "peaceful rise" or "peaceful development" policy is a newly constructed concept in international politics. The rise of a new global power and the power transition associated with it used to lead to war in the international system.[28] China apparently wants to walk a different path. It is learning to become a great power that can develop peacefully. This is a completely new approach in international politics.

Since the early 1990s, China's diplomacy has gone through two distinct processes simultaneously, namely expansion (*kuozhan* 扩展) and reconstruction (*chongjian* 重建).[29] Geographically, China's foreign-policy interests have extended to regions near and far to cover both traditional and non-traditional policy issues. Along with the expansion of China's diplomacy, there is also the process of reconstruction. Old ideology and policies have been discarded, replaced by a more pragmatic and sophisticated approach to international affairs. Ideas about China's new identity in the world such as the concepts of peaceful rise/peaceful development, a harmonious world, and a responsible stakeholder have generated heated debates in China.

Time changes, so do norms and approaches. The constructivist theory also suggests that China is flexible and sometimes unpredictable in its new diplomacy. It will modify its strategies to maximize its national interests and improve its

---

26   Maja Zehfuss, *Constructivism in International Relations: The Politics of Reality* (Cambridge University Press, 2002), pp. 10–11.

27   Alexander Wendt, "Anarchy Is What States Make of It: The Social Construction of Power Politics," *International Organization*, 46 (1992), pp. 391–425.

28   For the original power transition theory, see A.F.K. Organski, *World Politics* (Alfred A. Knopf, 1958). For a discussion of the development of the theory and its application to China, see Zhiqun Zhu, *US-China Relations in the 21st Century: Power Transition and Peace* (London and New York: Routledge, 2006); and Steve Chan, *China, the US and the Power-Transition Theory: A Critique* (London and New York: Routledge, 2008).

29   Marc Lanteigne, *Chinese Foreign Policy: An Introduction* (London and New York: Routledge, 2009), pp. 150–53.

international image. Though China's overarching objectives have been consistent since the end of the Cold War, that is maintaining a peaceful regional and international environment and promoting domestic economic growth, the course of Chinese foreign policy in the post-Cold War period has been tortuous. China does not seem to have settled on a grand strategy in its foreign policy for the future. Perhaps Deng Xiaoping's motto "crossing the river while groping for the stones" best depicts China's cautious diplomatic approach. "Important developments inside China, such as leadership changes, debates, and economic and military modernization, have affected Chinese foreign policy, as have events outside China, most notably actions taken by the United States, Taiwan, Japan, and North Korea," observes veteran China scholar Robert Sutter.[30] To understand China's new diplomacy properly, one must be aware that China is pursuing a new identity while creating it. If it makes mistakes in the process, perhaps it is not intentional—making mistakes is part of the growing pain. China has moved into a more prominent role globally, faster than expected, and is still adjusting to that role.

More recently, some scholars including Joseph Nye and Ernest Wilson have developed the concept of "smart power," which combines elements of soft power and hard power to achieve a nation's foreign-policy goals. China has been considered as more successful than the United States under President George W. Bush in applying smart power effectively and efficiently.[31] China's December 2008 dispatch of warships to the area near the coast of Somali to counter piracy is often cited as a remarkable display of China's smart power. Obviously China is learning to project soft power globally in a smart way.

China's new diplomacy has achieved considerable success. Opinion polls in many countries reveal that China was viewed fairly favorably as a great power, even in countries considered as US allies such as Britain, South Korea and Australia. However, China's increasingly active diplomacy has generated some concerns and criticisms. Due to a host of reasons China's relations with a few of its neighbors such as Japan, the Philippines and Vietnam deteriorated after 2010. While most developing countries seem to welcome China's expanding trade and investment, some countries have raised eyebrows over China's growing influence around the world and its increasing military power. There has been resistance in some developing countries against Chinese trade and investment, which are believed to be crowding out local competitors. Nevertheless, most analysts would agree that China has gradually become an indispensable player in the international political economy of the 21st century.

---

30   Robert G. Sutter, *Chinese Foreign Relations: Power and Policy Since the Cold War* (Rowman & Littlefield Publishers, 2008), p. 11.

31   Wilson, Ernest J. III, "Hard Power, Soft Power, Smart Power," in Cowan, Geoffrey and Nicholoas J. Cull (eds) *Public Diplomacy in a Changing World*, The Annals of the American Academy of Political and Social Science, Vol. 616 (Thousand Oaks, CA: Sage Publications, March 2008), pp. 110–24. For more information about smart power, also see "Smart Power Initiative" on the website of CSIS at http://csis.org/program/smart-power-initiative.

Some people in the West, the United States in particular, are concerned that China's expanding clout around the world may be incrementally pushing the United States out of regional influence. They suggest that China may have perpetuated problems in the developing world such as lack of transparency in governance and human rights abuses. President Obama's "pivot to Asia" policy initiated in 2009 is widely viewed as America's efforts to counter China's growing influence. Can China assuage international concerns and learn to coexist with other powers in international political economy? How to reconcile its national interests and its international responsibility as an emerging power is a great challenge for China in the 21st century.

To a large extent, concerns and worries about China's rise are caused by poor transparency in China's military modernization program. Chinese military budget, though modest compared with that of the United States, has been growing at a double-digit rate since the end of the 1990s. In 2012 China commissioned its first refurbished aircraft carrier and tested landing and taking off of fighter jets from the carrier. To alleviate external concerns, China needs to do a better public relations job in explaining why it is necessary for China to increase its annual military budget and how it is going to use its growing power. Ultimately, the peaceful rise of China is not just a slogan; it will be judged by China's words and deeds. Since China's future is of great concern to many, the international community—especially the United States and China's immediate neighbors—has a huge stake in ensuring China's peaceful development.

The Structure of the Book

China's influence was historically limited to East Asia, but now global trade and communications have made its reach and impact being felt worldwide. The division of this book into chapters dealing with different regions of the developing world represents the author's efforts to analyze how China is diversifying its new diplomacy and reaching out to the global community. China's diplomacy in the developed world will be briefly mentioned but is not the focus of this book.

Until the early 2000s, China's view of the global energy map focused narrowly on the Middle East, which holds roughly two thirds of the world's oil. China paid special attention to Iraq and cultivated good relations with Saddam Hussein's government, hoping to develop some of Iraq's more promising reserves.[32] The American invasion of Iraq in 2003 frustrated China's plan, and both the Chinese government and Chinese companies realized that it would be too risky for China to rely on one or two oil production areas. Hence China's strategy of seeking oil and gas globally. While the Middle East remains China's major supplier of oil, since the early 2000s China has made major oil deals with countries in Africa, Latin America, Central Asia, and elsewhere in an effort to diversify energy sources. The

---

32   Peter S. Goodman, "Big Shift in China's Oil Policy," *The Washington Post*, July 15, 2005, p. D01.

chapters that follow will examine China's policies towards these regions, with emphasis on China's trade and investment and energy deals in these regions, its efforts to expand soft power abroad, its enduring competition with Taiwan, and its other strategic and diplomatic objectives.

This first chapter offers a general introduction of major characteristics of Chinese diplomacy since the early 1990s. It provides an observational and analytical framework for understanding China's new diplomacy in different parts of the world to be discussed in later chapters. What are the new features in China's diplomacy? How has the new diplomacy been implemented? What is the impact on international political economy? The overarching theme and main arguments are presented in this chapter and will be further discussed in later chapters.

Chapter 2 examines China's new diplomacy in Africa. African nations have been claimed to be China's brothers since their independence and the non-aligned movement in the 1950s and 1960s. How have China's relations with African nations developed? What are the factors that have helped maintain strong Chinese–African ties? How has China been promoting its new diplomatic objectives in Africa? What are the implications for political economy of China, Africa and the international community? Chapter 3 deals with China's diplomacy in the Middle East. Questions to be explored and discussed include: What are major objectives of Chinese diplomacy toward the Middle East? What has China been doing to achieve these objectives? What role does China play in the Middle East peace process? Why does China enjoy good relations with all countries in the region? How will China's presence in the Middle East challenge the interests of the United States, the dominant power in the region? And finally what is the future of China–Middle East relations?

Chapter 4 shifts attention to Latin America and examines China's diplomatic activities in the backyard of the United States. Once considered too distant, Latin American and Caribbean nations had not been China's foreign-policy priority. Why has Latin America become a sought-after region in the new Chinese diplomacy? And what is China doing to achieve its objectives there? How does it affect the US standing in the region and US–China relations? Chapter 5 focuses on China's relations with Central Asia and Russia. Traditionally the sphere of influence of Russia, Central Asia has attracted China's attention in recent years. What are China's interests there? How does China promote these interests? What common interests do China and Russia share in Central Asia? And where do they compete with each other?

Chapter 6 surveys China's diplomacy in the South Pacific region. Questions to be discussed include: How has China strengthened relations with Australia, New Zealand and small South Pacific nations? Why is China interested in these small island nations? What is the significance of China's involvement in the South Pacific region? Chapter 7 focuses on Sino-Southeast Asian Relations. As China's close neighbor, Southeast Asia is a barometer of Beijing's new diplomacy and how it is perceived abroad. This chapter will address the following questions: How have China's relations with Southeast Asia evolved? What does China want from Southeast Asian nations today? What are the problems and challenges facing China and Southeast Asia in their relations? What are Chinese strategies toward Southeast Asia? What is the significance of China's growing influence in the region?

Chapter 8 looks at various international responses to China's diplomatic activities in the developing world. Why are there mixed reactions from the international community? In particular, how do developing countries, the United States and its allies respond to China's rise and its active diplomacy? How do US and Chinese interests converge and diverge at the same time? Does the so-called "Beijing Consensus" challenge the "Washington Consensus"? And is China a neocolonial power? Chapter 9 summarizes the findings and further develops a framework based on social constructivism and "smart power" to observe and analyze China's diplomacy in the 21st century. Implications of China's new diplomacy on international political economy and future challenges facing China will be discussed. Policy recommendations will be offered to China on how it can deal with serious challenges ahead. There will also be discussions about how China and the United States can handle their complex relationship in the context of China's rise in the 21st century.

As the following chapters will demonstrate, in order to become a truly great power in the world, China, despite its diplomatic achievements, needs to be more responsible and sensitive in its foreign policy and contribute more to economic growth, good governance, progress in human rights, peace and security, and environmental protection in the world, especially the Asia–Pacific region. By tracing China's new diplomatic activities around the developing world, this book also challenges the "China threat" discourse and proposes that China's growing power and increased involvement in international affairs are essentially positive for China, its partners and international political economy. China's strong relationship with other developing countries is a potent example of successful South-South cooperation, which is extremely important and mutually beneficial today when much of the developed world is mired in economic or political troubles and unable or unwilling to help the developing world.

Questions for Discussion

1. How did China break out of the international isolation after the 1989 Tiananmen Square incident?
2. Why does China emphasize "peaceful rise" or "peaceful development" in its foreign relations? Is this slogan convincing?
3. What are the continuities and changes in China's diplomacy? What are the new elements in China's diplomacy since the early 1990s?
4. Is China's new diplomacy energy focused? Are there other driving forces behind China's new diplomacy?
5. Why have China's relations with some of its neighbors such as Japan and the Philippines deteriorated after 2010?
6. How can one understand China's new diplomacy theoretically?

Chapter 2
China and Africa

Background

Sino-African relations have a long history. About 600 years ago, Ming Dynasty (1368–1644) seafarers reportedly reached Africa's eastern shores and brought back a giraffe to satisfy the Chinese emperor's curiosity. Today Chinese vessels sail back and forth, bringing home much-needed oil, iron ore, timber, copper, cobalt, manganese, platinum, uranium, gold, silver, food products, and other commodities to satisfy the voracious appetite of a giant and still growing economy.

Contemporary Sino-African relations got on a good start in the 1950s shortly after the PRC was established. In 1956 Egypt became the first African country to establish diplomatic relations with Beijing. As African nations were achieving independence in the 1950s and 1960s, China offered moral and material support for their liberation movement. China also gave limited aid to them to build infrastructure as a way to counter US and Soviet influence in the region. In return, African countries stood by China as it attempted to achieve international recognition and enter the UN.

China pursued a political agenda in Africa in the 1960s and 1970s, supporting rebel movements and Maoist forces in competition with the Soviet Union. In the 1970s, in a mark of solidarity with newly independent African states, Chinese laborers — many of them poorer than Africans — came and toiled at ideologically driven projects such as the 1,160 mile Tanzam Railway linking Tanzania and Zambia in eastern Africa. They left when these projects were completed.

Over the past half century, China and Africa have supported each other in international affairs, and bilateral relations have grown steadily in every aspect. Chinese official aid to Africa has never stopped. By the mid-2000s, China had supported nearly 900 projects in Africa related to economic and social development, sent 16,000 medical care personnel to Africa, offered government scholarships for 50 African countries, and sent more than 3,000 officers and soldiers to carry out the UN peacekeeping missions in Africa.[1] Since China deployed its first medical team in 1964 at the invitation of the Algerian government, Chinese doctors have treated approximately 180 million African patients.[2] Chinese doctors who form the medical teams, or *yiliaodui* (医疗队), normally spend two years in-country, and many have served more than once.

---

1   "China's Aid to Africa 'Sincere,' 'Selfless,' African Trade Union Leaders Say," *The People's Daily*, September 14, 2006.

2   Drew Thompson, "China's Soft Power in Africa: From the 'Beijing Consensus' to Health Diplomacy," *China Brief*, Vol. 5, No. 21 (October 13, 2005), p. 3.

Yet Africa, a distant and poor land, remained a low priority for Chinese foreign policy for a long time. Only since the mid-1990s has China re-discovered Africa's economic and diplomatic values and begun large-scale investment and trade. The basis of Sino-African relations has evolved from politics and ideology in the 1960s and 1970s to economics and pragmatic cooperation today. Now, Chinese officials travel to Africa with contracts in their hands, accompanied by bankers and businesspeople, promoting commerce that raises China–Africa ties to a new level.

Africa has become the world's third largest oil-producing region, next only to the Middle East and Latin America. Oil production in Africa is predicted to double over the next 20 years while it stays flat or declines in much of the rest of the world.[3] Most African economies rely heavily on exports. Africa's abundant energy resources and oil production potential provide new trade and investment opportunities for energy hungry emerging economies such as China and India.

Despite profound changes in the world over the past 50 years, China–Africa relationship has progressed and is thriving with vitality. Since the mid-1990s, bilateral relations have turned a new page. Driven by tremendous domestic growth demand and backed up by its huge foreign exchange reserve, China is hunting for oil, gas and other energy and natural resources globally. Africa, with its bounty of raw materials, has become a major target of China's new, economy-centered diplomacy. China–Africa trade grew tremendously from less than $10 million in the 1980s to $10 billion in 2000. It jumped to $40 billion in 2005, 10 times that of 1995. In 2007 bilateral trade reached $73 billion, and the target of $100 billion was achieved in 2008, two years ahead of the expectation. China overtook the United States as Africa's top trading partner in 2009. Since then Sino-African trade has continued to grow, and in 2012 it totalled $200 billion (See Table 2.1).

China's leading energy companies—Sinopec, CNPC, and CNOOC—have inked oil contracts from Equatorial Guinea to Gabon, and from Algeria to Angola. China's foreign direct investment in Africa skyrocketed from under $100 million in 2003 to more than $12 billion in 2011. Chinatowns are springing up all over Africa to cater to the growing number of Chinese nationals working and living on the continent. According to Huang Zequan, vice chairman of the Chinese-African People's Friendship Association, there were about 550,000 Chinese nationals in Africa in 2008, compared with about 100,000 French citizens, and 70,000

Table 2.1   China–Africa trade: selected years (in billions of US dollars)

Year	1995	2000	2005	2007	2008	2010	2011	2012
Volume	4	10	40	73	107	127	166	200

Sources: The General Administration of Customs of China (http://english.customs.gov.cn), various years.

---

3   James Traub, "China's African Adventure," *The New York Times*, November 19, 2006.

Americans.[4] Some of the Chinese were sent there by their companies to build dams, roads, hospitals, and railroads. Others went to Africa in the hope of getting rich there.

China's approach to Africa, characterized by its "no political strings attached" financial and technical aid and its "non-interference" in other countries' internal affairs, is a source of both respect by African leaders and elites and criticism by some African people and Western nations concerned about governance and human rights issues on the continent.

Motivations Behind China's New Diplomacy in Africa

Africa as a Source of Energy and Natural Resources and an Export Market

Africa's growing market for inexpensive Chinese goods is alluring, as is cheap African labor to staff Chinese factories, but a top priority of China's diplomatic activities in Africa is to acquire energy and raw materials to fuel China's galloping economy. As the world's second largest consumer and importer of oil products, China is relentlessly searching for new sources of oil globally. China's fast-rising involvement with Africa grows out of its immense need for natural resources, in particular for imported oil, of which one third is already from Africa, compared with about 15 percent for the United States. China often uses infrastructure projects to sweeten oil and mining deals.

Angola is a top oil supplier for China. In 2006 it surpassed Saudi Arabia as China's largest supplier of crude oil, though it dropped to the number two position afterwards. In 2008 China–Angola trade rose to $25.3 billion, making Angola China's largest trade partner in Africa. In 2010 China bought about 45 percent of Angola's oil output. In July 2005 China reached an $800 million oil pact with Nigeria—Africa's leading oil producer, which agreed to provide 30,000 barrels of oil a day to China in the next five years.[5] In 2006 a state-owned Chinese company agreed to pump more than $2 billion into a major refinery in northern Nigeria in exchange for drilling rights in four sought-after oil blocks. In January 2006 Nigeria became the first African country to establish a "strategic partnership" with China. It is China's second largest trading partner in Africa, with bilateral trade reaching over $3 billion in 2006, an enormous increase from $384 million in 1998.[6] In 2006 China announced its plan to invest $267 million to establish the first phase of the Leikki Free Trade Zone in Lagos, the first of its kind China has constructed overseas. Trade between China and Nigeria exceeded $10 billion in 2008.

---

4 Serge Michel, "When China Met Africa," *Foreign Policy*, No. 166 (May/June, 2008), p. 41.

5 "A List of Major Fruits of China-Africa Trade," *BBC Chinese*, January 28, 2007.

6 Ian Taylor, "Sino-Nigerian Relations: FTZs, Textiles and Oil," *China Brief*, Vol. 7, No. 11 (May 30, 2007), p. 11.

China has actively encouraged its companies and citizens to invest and set up shop in Africa at a record pace. In Rwanda, Chinese companies have paved more than 80 percent of the main roads. In Nigeria, China is rebuilding the railroad network. In more than a dozen African countries, Chinese firms are rebuilding electricity grids and telephone networks. Chinese companies own one of Zambia's largest copper mines and run a major timber operation in Equatorial Guinea. In Lesotho, Chinese businessmen own and operate nearly half of all the supermarkets and a handful of textile companies.[7]

Huge energy deals have been signed between China and African countries recently. Sinopec signed a preliminary deal with Liberia to explore for oil and gas in the Western African state. Ghana's energy minister disclosed before the November 2006 China–Africa summit that his country was close to typing up a $600 million deal with China's Sino Hydro Corporation to build a 400 megawatt hydroelectric dam in north Ghana. Gabon also signed a $3 billion iron ore deal with China.[8] Crude oil exports from Sudan to China more than doubled from 2006 to 2007 to top 200,000 barrels a day, with official data showing that China now takes 40 percent of Sudan's total output. Sudan exported 10.31 million tons to China in 2007, or 113 percent above 2006, ranking as Beijing's sixth largest crude supplier.[9]

Oil is not the only commodity China is hunting for. For copper and cobalt, China looks to the Democratic Republic of Congo (DRC) and Zambia; for iron ore and platinum, South Africa. Gabon, Cameroon and Congo-Brazzaville supply it with timber. Several countries in west and central Africa sent cotton to its textile factories. Eighty-five percent of China's cobalt — a key component in cellphones, laptops, and batteries comes from the Republic of Congo, the DRC, and South Africa. More than one third of manganese used in China to manufacture steel comes from Africa.[10]

China has also turned its attention to Africa to meet its growing food demand. With over one fifth of the world's population but only 7 percent of its total arable land, China is beginning to feel the pressure of a potential food shortage. Due to land loss in the past three decades as a result of rapid industrialization, environmental damage and over planting, and dietary changes of Chinese from mainly rice and wheat to a variety of different foods, China has to import food products such as soybeans, beef, coffee, sugar, and potatoes. Africa, with its vast and sparsely populated fertile lands, offers China a solution to its rising food demand.[11] Chinese investment in Africa includes a large chunk in the continent's agricultural sector, which helps not only local farmers but also Chinese consumers.

---

7   Karby Leggett, "China Flexes Economic Muscle Throughout Burgeoning Africa," *The Wall Street Journal*, March 29, 2005.

8   "China Dangles Trade, Aid before Africa," *Reuters*, November 3, 2006.

9   "Sudan Doubles Crude Exports to China in 2007," *Sudan Tribune* www.sudantribune.com, January 22, 2008.

10   Danna Harman, "China Boosts African Economies, Offering a 'Second Opportunity,'" *The Christian Science Monitor*, June 25, 2007.

11   Loro Horta, "Food Security in Africa: China's New Rice Bowl," *China Brief*, Vol. 9, No. 11 (May 27, 2009), pp. 10–12.

Africa is also a lucrative market for China's weapons industry. Between 1996 and 2003, Chinese arms sales to Africa were second only to Russia's. In particular, China has developed close military ties with Zimbabwe, Sudan, and Ethiopia. China has developed good relations with both Ethiopia and Eritrea, which formally became independent from Ethiopia in 1993. China was reported to have sold weapons to both Ethiopia and Eritrea even though the two have engaged in border wars since 1998.[12] Most significantly, China was believed to be the largest supplier of arms to Sudan. Chinese-made tanks, fighter planes, bombers, helicopters, machine guns, and rocket-propelled grenades have been used in Sudan's civil war. In 2012 Chinese weapons accounted for 25 percent of Africa's arms imports and China sold weapons to 16 African countries. Some have raised questions about whether the Chinese foreign ministry has a grip on the reach of the country's influence in the arms industry beyond its borders since the PLA oversees China's arms exports. No matter how it defends its weapons sale policy, when its lethal wares wind up in conflict zones in violation of UN sanctions, one can argue that China is not playing a positive and responsible role.

Africa's Diplomatic and Strategic Values

Economic interests are just one motivation behind the active Chinese diplomacy in Africa. China became an oil importer in 1993, yet Sino-African relations have been developing steadily since the early 1950s. China's interaction with Africa, both past and present, is not limited only to resource-rich countries. So the quest for resources is not the only, nor the key, factor in China's engagement in Africa, observes a leading Chinese scholar on Africa.[13] In addition to burgeoning trade, Sino-African cooperation has expanded into other areas.

With 54 countries, Africa is the largest voting block at the UN and other international organizations. China's efforts in Africa are clearly aimed at safeguarding its political and diplomatic interests in international institutions, such as the UN Human Rights Commission, which was replaced by the Human Rights Council in 2006 with countries like Zimbabwe, Sudan, and Eritrea as its members. At every turn African countries have given China strong support in foiling anti-China motions introduced by some Western countries at the UN Human Rights Commission and helped China defeat many attempts by Taiwan to participate in the UN or to edge into the WHO and other international bodies. African countries also supported China in its bid to host the 2008 Olympics in Beijing and the 2010 World Expo in Shanghai. After China's accession into the WTO in 2001, China courted African countries intensely for recognition as a market economy. This

---

12   Joshua Eisenman and Joshua Kurlantzick, "China's Africa Strategy," *Current History*, May 2006, p. 222.

13   He Wenping, "The Balancing Act of China's Africa Policy," *China Security*, Vol. 3, No. 3 (Summer, 2007), p. 24.

is a crucial status for China as a WTO member, since it helps shield China from accusations of dumping.[14]

To prevent Taiwan's formal independence remains a top Chinese foreign-policy objective. The PRC insists that all other countries must follow the "one-China" principle and cannot adopt a "two Chinas" or "one-China, one Taiwan" policy. The PRC and Taiwan have competed fiercely for the loyalty of African nations since 1949. Africa used to be a stronghold of countries recognizing Taiwan. After gaining national independence, African nations established diplomatic ties with Beijing one after another. They offered valuable support to Beijing in the latter's effort to join the international community. In 1971 several African delegates reportedly danced at the UN general assembly floor to celebrate the PRC's admission into the UN, replacing Taiwan as the sole representative of China.

Since the 1990s, China's diplomatic offensive in Africa has further narrowed Taiwan's international space, partly because China has used its influence to convince African nations to switch their diplomatic recognition from Taipei to Beijing, and partly because several African countries such as Senegal made their own choices to maximize their national interests by allying with the PRC. After Beijing succeeded in converting Chad in August 2006 and Malawi in December 2007, only four countries in Africa (Burkina Faso, Gambia, Swaziland, and São Tomé and Príncipe) still maintained diplomatic ties with Taiwan.[15] As of 2013, Taiwan has formal relations with 23 countries around the world but maintains informal relations with dozens more (See Table 2.2). The PRC, on the other hand, has 172 diplomatic allies.

Table 2.2   Taiwan's diplomatic allies: as of August 2013

Africa	• Burkina Faso
	• Gambia
	• São Tomé and Príncipe
	• Swaziland
Europe	• Holy See
Latin America and the Caribbean	• Belize
	• Dominican Republic
	• El Salvador
	• Guatemala
	• Haiti
	• Honduras
	• Nicaragua
	• Panama
	• Paraguay
	• St. Christopher & Nevis
	• St. Lucia
	• St. Vincent & Grenadines
South Pacific	• Kiribati
	• Marshall Islands
	• Nauru
	• Palau
	• Solomon Islands
	• Tuvalu

Source: Ministry of Foreign Affairs, Republic of China (Taiwan) at http://www.mofa.gov.tw.

---

14   Denis M. Tull, "China's Engagement in Africa: Scope, Significance and Consequences," *Journal of Modern African Studies*, Vol. 44, No. 3 (2006), p. 467.

15   Additionally, Taiwan operates five quasi-official missions in Africa: one in Nigeria (Abuja), one in Libya (Tripoli), and three in South Africa (Pretoria, Cape Town, and Johannesburg).

On December 24, 2007, Malawi sent two ministers to Beijing to sign a memorandum of understanding to pave the way for launching official ties. To salvage the 41-year diplomatic relations with Malawi, Taipei immediately dispatched its Foreign Minister James Huang to Malawi on January 2, 2008. In a dramatic and perhaps unprecedented episode in diplomatic history, Huang was told that his visit had been cancelled while he was flying to the African country. According to Taiwan's Foreign Ministry, Malawi, which had initially welcomed the visit, informed Taiwan after Huang's plane had taken off that it was not a convenient time to receive Huang because "President Bingu wa Mutharika was still on holiday and Minister of Foreign Affairs Joyce Banda had left the capital because of an unforeseen incident."[16] To Taipei's great disappointment, on January 14, 2008, Malawi announced the establishment of diplomatic relations with Beijing while severing official ties with Taipei.

African leaders affirm their support for the "one-China" principle at nearly every official meeting with their Chinese counterparts. At the November 2006 Sino-Africa summit in Beijing, the 48 African countries present gave unanimous support to a declaration endorsing a one-China policy and China's peaceful reunification with Taiwan. Some countries went even further. Earlier in 2006, after Beijing passed the controversial anti-secession law regarding Taiwan, Ethiopia's national parliament adopted a resolution in support of Beijing's domestic law.

As an example of how Taiwan is an important factor in China's diplomacy in Africa, the Chinese ambassador in Lusaka suggested before the September 2006 Zambian presidential election that if Michael Sata—an opposition candidate who had criticized China's business practices in Zambia and who had advocated recognizing Taiwan as an independent state—were elected, Beijing might cut diplomatic relations with Zambia.[17] To Beijing's delight, Sata lost to the incumbent president, Levy Mwanawasa, who had close ties with China. After winning the presidential election in September 2011, Sata toned down his rhetoric against Beijing and vowed to continue the Zambian government's support for foreign investments. In fact, his first official appointment at the State House was with China's new ambassador Zhou Yuxiao.

Taipei and Beijing continue to woo African countries in their own ways. After Beijing hosted the first China–Africa Summit in November 2006, Taipei responded by hosting the first Taiwan-African Heads of State Summit with its African allies in September 2007. At the end of the one-day summit, leaders from Taiwan's then five diplomatic allies in Africa—Swaziland, Burkina Faso, Sao

---

16   "Malawi Cancels Visit by James Huang," *Taipei Times*, January 5, 2008, p. 1.

17   It was reported that Sata and the Taiwan government, through its embassy in Malawi, had a deal: Sata would defame China during the campaign in exchange for Taiwan's financial support. In February 2007, as Chinese President Hu Jintao was visiting Zambia, Taiwan rewarded Sata by inviting him to Taipei for meetings with senior Taiwan officials and discussing future cooperation. See "Claiming He Loves Taiwan, Sata Extorts Money from Taiwan," *Lianhe Zaobao* (Singapore), November 4, 2007.

Tome and Principe, Malawi and Gambia—issued a declaration in support of Taiwan's controversial bid to secure a seat at the UN.[18]

Since KMT's Ma Ying-jeou assumed the presidential office in Taipei in May 2008, cross-Taiwan Strait relations have drastically improved, and the two sides seemed to have reached a temporary "diplomatic truce," according to which, neither Beijing nor Taipei will take the initiative to snatch away the other's diplomatic allies. Ma and the KMT are supportive of closer ties with mainland China, though they are not in favor of reunification with China in the near future. As long as cross-Strait relations are stable, competition with Taiwan will decline as a motivation behind Beijing's diplomacy in Africa. To consolidate Taiwan's relations with its remaining allies, President Ma visited Burkina Faso, Gambia and Swaziland in April 2012.

Aside from Taiwan, China has other strategic considerations in Africa. For example, China has maintained a courteous relationship with the tiny West African archipelago nation Cape Verde since the two established diplomatic relations in April 1976. Cape Verde, with a population of 300,000, lacks natural resources that Beijing has sought elsewhere. Yet, due to its strategic location, close proximity to both Mediterranean Europe and West Africa, political stability and a well-educated population, Cape Verde is a country where China intends to create a special economic zone. As many as 2,000 Chinese nationals were living in Cape Verde, a former colony of Portugal, according to a 2006 Cape Verdian official estimate. The Chinese constitute one of the largest foreign communities now, second only to the Portuguese.[19] Unlike other African nations rich in raw materials, Cape Verde offers other possibilities, such as becoming a major commercial hub for Chinese goods and a launching pad for further Chinese political and economic expansion into West and North Africa as well as Mediterranean Europe. The fact that China was able to gain a preeminent position in a fairly wealthy and democratic country with no natural resources demonstrates that China's diplomacy is becoming more sophisticated, and the stereotypical view that China is in Africa just for raw materials is untrue.

China's Desire to Help African Countries to Develop

Very few African countries have succeeded by adopting the Western development models. China sees itself as offering something different from, and perhaps superior to, the standard Western prescription for African development. As a CSIS report suggested, China emerged from colonial encroachment, internal chaos, and economic destitution to achieve spectacular economic growth and infrastructure development. Chinese leaders and strategists believe China's historical experience

---

18   "Five African Allies Support Taiwan's UN Bid," *The China Post*, September 9, 2007.

19   Loro Horta, "The Changing Nature of Chinese Business in Africa: The Case of Cape Verde," *RSIS Commentaries*, S. Rajaratnam School of International Studies, Nanyang Technological University, Singapore, January 17, 2008.

and development model resonate powerfully with African counterparts, thereby creating a comparative advantage vis-à-vis the West.[20] African countries "have the panaceas of the World Bank and the IMF, and the experience of China. They can compare and choose the best," suggested Lu Shaye, China's ambassador to Senegal.[21]

Western countries have historically placed conditions on trade and aid. China gives fewer lectures and more practical help. In the 1990s, many African countries adopted the "Washington Consensus" of open markets, macroeconomic stability, trade liberalization, and more privatization, but these reforms have yet to improve the lives of most Africans, and many have grown disenchanted with the West. Chinese diplomacy in Africa has introduced competition of development models to the region. "For Africans it is quite a welcome change from the approach they get from Western governments that manages to be both patronizing and demeaning at the same time," remarked Duncan Green, head of research at Oxfam.[22] China's economic development model, dubbed the "Beijing Consensus" by scholars, essentially refutes Western notions of political liberalization as indispensable for sustained development. China has encouraged African nations to develop their own economies through trade and investment in infrastructure and social institutions, without dictating terms for political or economic reforms.

According to the Chinese government, China sincerely wants to help African countries to develop. At the November 2006 China–Africa summit, Beijing announced massive aid programs for Africa in the Action Plan, which included doubling aid to African countries from its 2006 level by 2009, providing $3 billion in preferential loans and $2 billion of export credits over the next three years, creating a $5 billion fund to encourage Chinese investment in Africa. In the next three years, China would train 15,000 African professionals, build 100 rural schools, ten hospitals and 30 anti-malaria clinics, send 300 youth volunteers, and double the number of scholarships given to African students to 4,000. According to the Action Plan, China would also send 100 senior experts on agriculture to Africa and set up ten agricultural demonstration sites in Africa. It would increase from 190 to over 440 the number of export items to China eligible for zero-tariff treatment from the least developed countries in Africa.

The growth of Chinese investment and aid outpaces its Western rivals. China is even investing heavily in politically unstable countries like Rwanda, where the immediate returns are murky at best. To facilitate its economic and other activities in Africa, China has opened more embassies in Africa than the United States has.[23] In 2006, which Beijing dubbed the "Year of Africa," Chinese companies spent more than $7 billion on the continent. In 2007 they invested an additional

---

20   Bates Gill, Chin-hao Huang, and J. Stephen Morrison, "China's Expanding Role in Africa: Implications for the United States," *CSIS*, January 2007, p. 5.

21   "China Makes Africa Its Business," *International Herald Tribune*, August 21, 2006.

22   Ibid.

23   Scott Johnson, "China's African Misadventures," *Newsweek*, November 24, 2007.

$4.5 billion on projects to build railroad lines, roads, hydroelectric plants and other operations, according to an August 2008 report by the World Bank.[24] At the November 2009 China–Africa summit in Egypt, Premier Wen pledged a loan of $10 billion to Africa over the following three years. Part of the loan will be used to develop clean energy in Africa.

At the July 2012 Forum on China–Africa Cooperation in Beijing, President Hu announced to offer another $20 billion in loans to African countries in the next three years, doubling the 2009 level. The Beijing summit was attended by leaders from 50 African states and international organizations including South Africa's Jacob Zuma and UN Secretary General Ban Ki-moon.

By the end of 2010, China's direct investment in Africa had reached $13 billion, with more than 2,000 Chinese enterprises having made investment in Africa. It is estimated that the number of Chinese citizens engaging in business or labor activities in African countries exceeds one million. Contrary to accusations that China is only interested in African oil and metals, China is offering aid and assistance to virtually every country in Africa — resource rich or not. The Chinese have been building roads, railways and airports in places where other foreign firms have feared to tread.

China has received tens of thousands African students in the past two decades. Many Chinese universities have established exchange programs with African institutions. In recent years, Chinese universities have also provided training to African government officials, business people, opinion leaders, diplomats, and medical professionals. Among others, the China Foreign Affairs University in Beijing has offered all-expenses paid training programs for young African diplomats.[25] Since 1990 China has participated in 12 UN peacekeeping missions in Africa. By the end of May 2006, China had sent 435 soldiers to Sudan as part of the UN peacekeeping efforts alone.[26] In November 2005 the forum on China–Africa education was held in Beijing. China vowed to double the number of African students enjoying Chinese government's scholarships within five years and train 1,000 education officials and teachers for African countries every year. At the 2012 China–Africa Forum in Beijing, China promised to provide 18,000 government scholarships for African students, to continue sending medical teams to Africa, and to increase investment in Africa's agriculture, manufacturing, and small to medium businesses.

Debt cancellation or debt relief is part of China's aid program to African nations. Effectively turning loans into grants, China has taken significant steps

---

24   Craig Simons, "China's Influence among African Nations Spurs Concerns," *The Atlanta Journal-Constitution*, November 30, 2008.

25   "China Wages Classroom Struggle to Win Friends in Africa," *The New York Times*, November 20, 2005.

26   "Zhongfei Guanxi Cheng Shang Xinshiji de Hangchuan (Sino-African Relations Taking Off in the New Century," *Xinhua*, September 15, 2006. At the end of 2006, China contributed peacekeepers to six of the seven current UN missions in Africa: Western Sahara, Democratic Republic of Congo, Ethiopia and Eritrea, Liberia, Sudan, and Cote d'Ivoire.

to cancel Africa's debt since 2000. It has waived over 10 billion yuan of loans for African nations.[27] In 2000 alone, it wrote off $1.2 billion in African debt, and in 2003 it forgave another $750 million. China has also provided medicine and medical equipment free of change to many African countries. It operates programs to jointly prevent and treat infectious diseases including malaria and AIDS. Ethiopia's Prime Minister, Meles Zenawi, described China as a key source of support as African nations try to reduce poverty. "China provides for Africa a source of successful development experience, technology transfer, trade and investment," said Zenawi in a speech.[28] As additional evidence that Chinese activities in Africa are meant to help African countries, China has invested in resource-deprived countries. For example, China is building a dam and a military hospital in Guinea-Bissau, a country with little industry, no oil, and few exports.

China is becoming a real partner for Sudan not only in the area of oil, infrastructure, industries and social services, but also in the development of agriculture which is the primary occupation of the majority of the Sudanese people. Agriculture is a vital sector in Sudan and many other African countries but never received adequate attention since these countries' independence. The involvement of China in African agriculture will be a very significant development especially in view of the hike in oil prices and the rising prices and scarcity of food in the world for the years to come.

As the financial and economic crises hit many countries including China in 2008, people wondered whether China would continue to keep its promise to help African nations. In meeting with visiting President of Angola José Eduardo dos Santos on December 19, 2008, Premier Wen Jiabao affirmed that China would implement the follow-up actions agreed upon during the 2006 Beijing Summit, and China would not reduce its aid to Africa despite the global financial crisis.[29] President Hu Jintao made similar promises during his trip to Africa in February 2009.

China's Efforts to Enhance Its Influence

China seems to understand the importance of soft power and has started to project it in Africa and elsewhere. In January 2006 China released its first African Policy Paper, which put forward its proposals for all-round cooperation with Africa based on equality and mutual benefits in various fields in the coming years. According to the Policy Paper, China seeks a new type of strategic partnership which respects African countries' independent choice of the road of development and which is premised on mutual benefit, reciprocity and common prosperity. China is boosting its aid and economic support to African countries with few strings at the same

---

27 "China's Influence in Africa Is Increasing in All Areas," *VOA Chinese*, October 19, 2006.

28 Quoted in "China Pledges $5 billion to Africa," *CNN*, November 6, 2006.

29 "China: No Less Aid to Africa Amid Financial Crisis," *Xinhua*, December 19, 2008.

time as Western countries and international financial institutions increasingly link aid disbursements in the developing world to good governance and anti-corruption initiatives. For some African countries, China is not just a new source of investment; it is also a useful counterweight to Western influence in the region.

Realizing the important role cultural exchange can play in bilateral relations, China has conducted educational exchange and cooperation programs with almost all African countries. The Chinese language is offered at many African schools now. Chinese universities have gone to Africa to directly recruit and offer scholarships for students in recent years. In June 2006, China donated $35 million to build the largest theater in Senegal, the largest cultural project it has been involved in Africa.[30]

China launched a communications satellite for Nigeria in 2007 and is planning to launch one for the Democratic Republic of Congo in the mid-2010s. China beat 21 other bidders for the $311 million contract to launch the satellite for Nigeria. The DRC only contacted China for the deal, which demonstrates China's reputation in satellite technology and launching. By 2012 China had been commissioned to launch over 30 satellites for foreign countries.

China also seeks to promote its culture in Africa. In December 2005 Africa's first Confucius Institute opened in Nairobi. According to a diplomat at the Chinese Embassy in South Africa, just a few years ago, nobody seemed to be interested in Chinese. Now in many public places, South Africans would greet the Chinese with *ni hao*.[31] China has dispatched hundreds of language teachers to feed a growing demand in Africa. By mid-2012, 31 Confucius Institutes and 5 Confucius Classrooms had been established in 26 African countries such as Rwanda, Cameroon, Egypt, South Africa, Madagascar, Togo, Benin, Botswana, and Mali.

China's influence can unmistakably be felt in Africa. Says Girma Biru, Ethiopia's Minister of Trade: "China has become our most reliable partner and there is a lot we can learn from Beijing, not just in economics but politics as well."[32] Chad, in a dramatic move, asked Chevron and a Malaysian oil company to withdraw their bid in 2006 in order to make way for a Chinese oil company.[33]

Military exchanges between China and Africa as part of the new diplomacy have become more frequent. China's military activities in Africa include presence of defense attachés, naval ship visits, professional training, and other missions to support military cooperation between the two sides. Chinese military delegations have visited every African country that recognizes China. The PLA maintains a growing military presence on the African continent, with estimates ranging from approximately 1,200 soldiers including Peacekeeping Operations forces to over

30   "A List of Major Fruits of China-Africa Trade," *BBC Chinese*, January 28, 2007.

31   "More African Countries Favor Confucius Institute," *Xinhua*, November 25, 2007.

32   Karby Leggett, "China Flexes Economic Muscle Throughout Burgeoning Africa," *The Wall Street Journal*, March 29, 2005.

33   "China's Influence in Africa is Increasing in All Areas," *VOA Chinese*, October 19, 2006.

5,000.[34] Egypt has received the highest number of visiting senior Chinese military groups. China and South Africa have held regular security consultations since 2003. At least 14 out of the 107 Chinese military attaché offices worldwide were in African countries. As of September 2009, out of the 100 countries that had military attachés in Beijing, 27 were African countries.[35]

Major Strategies of China's New Diplomacy in Africa

Highest-level Involvement

Except for Premier Zhou Enlai's ideology-tinged visits to Africa in the 1960s, past Chinese leaders seldom traveled to Africa. Visits by top leaders were few and far between—until now. Today Africa is high on China's foreign-policy agenda. Top Chinese leaders have frequently visited Africa since the late 1990s.

President Hu Jintao visited Africa six times between 1999 and 2009. In January and February 1999, when he was still Vice President, Hu paid his first visit to Africa, making stops at Madagascar, Ghana, Côte d'Ivoire, and South Africa. Two years later, he went to Uganda. Hu visited Egypt, Gabon, and Algeria in January and February 2004 within one year after he became the president. It is very rare for both the president and the prime minister of a country to visit the same region in the same year. Yet President Hu and Premier Wen paid separate visits to Africa in April and June 2006, covering a total of ten countries.[36] During Hu's visit to Kenya in April 2006, China and Kenya signed an agreement for licenses allowing CNOOC to explore for oil off the coast of Kenya. Barely eight months later, in his first overseas trip in 2007, Hu visited eight countries in Africa: Cameroon, Sudan, Namibia, South Africa, the Seychelles, Liberia, Zambia and Mozambique between January 30 and February 10. At every stop, President Hu announced new aid and investment programs for these African countries.

Partly to refute the charge that China is only interested in African resources, in February 2009 President Hu traveled to Mali, Senegal, Tanzania and Mauritius, which are not resource-rich or oil-producing countries. China has helped build schools, hospitals and other infrastructure projects in these countries. The Chinese leadership hopes to improve China's image abroad as a responsible and caring country. In March 2013, the newly installed President Xi Jinping visited Tanzania, Congo, and South Africa and attended the BRICS Leaders-Africa Dialogue Forum in Durban.

---

34   Susan M. Puska, "Resources, Security and Influence: The Role of the Military in China's Africa Strategy," *China Brief*, Vol. 7, No. 11 (May 30, 2007), p. 2.

35   Information from the website of Beijing Military Attaché Corps, available online at http://www.bjmac.org, accessed on September 5, 2009.

36   President Hu's trip took him to Morocco, Nigeria, and Kenya. Premier Wen's visit covered Egypt, Ghana, Congo, Angola, South Africa, Tanzania, and Uganda.

Other top Chinese leaders have traveled to Africa. In April 2002 Hu's predecessor Jiang Zemin visited three countries: Nigeria, Libya, and Tunisia. In June 2004, Vice President Zeng Qinghong traveled to Tunisia, Togo, Benin, and South Africa. In October and November 2004, NPC Chairman Wu Bangguo went to Kenya, Zimbabwe, Zambia, and Nigeria. In 2006, Vice President Zeng made another trip to Africa. In May 2007, Wu Bangguo visited Egypt, and in May 2011 he returned to Africa, with stops in Namibia, Angola and South Africa.

It has become a New Year ritual for the Chinese foreign minister to start his annual overseas visits in Africa since the early 1990s. For example, Foreign Minister Li Zhaoxing journeyed to Equatorial Guinea, Guinea-Bissau, Chad, Benin, Central African Republic, Eritrea and Mozambique from December 31 to January 8, 2007. His successor Yang Jiechi started a busy year of 2008 by visiting South Africa, the DRC, Burundi and Ethiopia from January 7 to January 11. In South Africa, Yang's visit coincided with the celebrations to mark the tenth anniversary of diplomatic relations between the two countries. In January 2009 Minister Yang visited Uganda, Rwanda, Malawi, and South Africa during his first overseas trip for 2009. In Uganda Yang signed agreements on foreign assistance totaling about $75 million. The two countries also discussed construction of a railway line from Uganda to neighboring southern Sudan. In Kigali, Yang dedicated a new building to house Rwanda's Foreign Ministry and attended an opening ceremony for the new Chinese Embassy.[37] Yang visited Malawi for the first time, which cut its official ties with Taiwan a year before. He wrapped up his Africa tour by returning to South Africa, China's major trading partner on the continent. China's commerce minister was on a separate tour of Africa at about the same time during Yang's visit, with stops in Kenya, Zambia, and Angola. Minister Yang began his 2011 and 2012 foreign trips again in Africa.

In November 2006 Beijing hosted a historic China–Africa summit, which was participated by 48 heads of state or government and over 500 delegates from Africa. The image of Beijing streets adorned with gigantic posters of giraffes and elephants as African leaders stepped out of limousines and into the Great Hall of the People at Tiananmen Square was a powerful one. The forum was a milestone in Chinese–African relations. Very few, if any, capitals outside Africa would be able to attract so many African leaders concurrently. "Anyone wanting to find an African leader this coming week will need to book a ticket to Beijing," a *Wall Street Journal* report remarked before the summit.[38] The Beijing Summit further boosted China–Africa cooperation by establishing the new China–Africa strategic partnership. The forum on China–Africa Cooperation, first launched in 2000, already held two ministerial conferences in Beijing and Addis Ababa. Top Chinese leaders, including Jiang Zemin, Hu Jintao, and Zhu Rongji, were all actively involved in the establishment of the forum.

---

37 "China's Foreign Minister Wrapping up Africa Tour," *VOA*, January 16, 2009.
38 "China Strengthens its Ties to Africa," *The Wall Street Journal*, October 28, 2006, p. 2.

In November 2008 NPC Chairman Wu Bangguo visited five African nations of Algeria, Gabon, Ethiopia, Madagascar and Seychelles. Wu also visited the African Union (AU) headquarters in Ethiopia's capital Addis Ababa. During Wu's visit, the construction of the new AU Conference Center officially started. The 25-story conference center complex, a gift from the Chinese government, will house a 2,500 capacity conference hall, 500 offices, a medium sized conference hall, meeting rooms, 30 caucus rooms, a 3,000 capacity multipurpose hall, an amphitheatre with 3,000 seats, a digital archive center and library, a medical center and numerous public spaces, among other features. AU Commission Chairperson Mr. Jean Ping hailed the new construction as a symbol of the strong cooperation and friendship between Africa and China.[39] The $200 million Chinese-build new AU headquarters was officially opened in January 2012 by Jia Qinglin, Chairman of Chinese People's Political Consultative Conference.

Aggressive and Creative Approaches

As a late entrant to the international market, China has little choice but to strike deals with countries that the West is unwilling or unprepared to conduct business with. In the late 1990s, for example, when Ethiopia went to war with neighboring Eritrea, the United States evacuated its Peace Corps volunteers, scaled back military aid and issued a security warning to US citizens and companies. In contrast, China saw the war as an opportunity to expand its influence. It dispatched even more diplomats, engineers, businesspeople and teachers to Ethiopia. Today, China's influence in Ethiopia is overwhelming. Most recently, China has begun exploring for oil and building at least one Ethiopian military installation.[40] Following the example of the Peace Corps program, China sent 12 "young volunteers" for the first time to Ethiopia in August 2005. After these members' successful six-month service in Ethiopia, this new program continued and expanded to other African countries.

Chinese oil companies have been aggressive in Africa in their search for partners. According to Iheanyi Ohiaeri, head of the business development for Nigeria's National Petroleum Corp., the Chinese call and email him everyday, seeking oil deals.[41] One analyst noted that the Chinese are adventurous in their business activities. Unlike American business people, who are generally risk-averse and spoiled in terms of the personal lifestyle they expect, the Chinese take economic risks for the prospect of gain, and Chinese workers will go and live anywhere. In contrast, American companies have had difficulty finding people to work in Africa.[42]

---

39   "Construction of New AU Conference Center Officially Begins," *African Press Organization*, November 11, 2008.

40   Karby Leggett, "China Flexes Economic Muscle Throughout Burgeoning Africa," *The Wall Street Journal*, March 29, 2005.

41   Vivienne Walt, "China's Appetite for African Oil Grows," *CNN Money*, February 8, 2006.

42   Dan Simpson, "China Woos Africa to Win Hearts and Markets," *The Toledo Blade*, November 8, 2006.

To assist Chinese commercial activities, the Chinese government has created the China Africa Business Council and the China Africa Cooperation Forum. In addition to inviting African officials and professionals to visit and be trained in China, China is sending professionals to Africa to train their counterparts. Today, hundreds of Chinese doctors are working in Africa, providing free equipment and drugs to help fight AIDS, malaria and other diseases. Several Chinese ministries, including Science and Technology, Agriculture, Commerce and Education, are working with African governments to train officials and develop human resources.

China's presence is strong in resource-rich countries like Nigeria, Angola and Sudan, but it is also growing in less obvious spots. In Sierra Leone, Chinese companies have built and renovated hotels and restaurants. In Mozambique, Chinese companies are investing in soybean processing and prawn production. In Senegal whose economy was long dominated by peanut farming, Chinese construction companies are working on roads, bridges, waterworks and other projects. At the July 2006 AU summit in Banjul, Gambia, the Chinese delegation dwarfed the ones sent by France, Britain and the United States.

China has adopted an aid-for oil strategy that has resulted in increasing supplies of oil from African countries. In several oil-rich countries, China has helped build roads, bridges, hospitals, power plants, and other infrastructure projects. In return, China has allowed these countries to pay the cost with oil. Africa, on the other hand, offers a largely untapped and underserved market for Chinese companies as they take steps toward becoming global players. For example, Huawei Technologies Co., China's leading telecommunications-equipment maker, has done a thriving business in Africa even as the company has struggled to penetrate more developed markets.

In October 2007 China's largest bank, ICBC, purchased a 20 percent stake in Standard Bank, South Africa's largest bank by assets and earnings. In a joint statement, ICBC said it views South Africa as an attractive market for investment, given its growth prospects, its sophisticated economic and well-regulated financial services infrastructure, as well as its rapidly growing banking customer base. As many of ICBC's large clients seek investments in Africa, the demand for cross-border financial services is accelerating. For ICBC, Standard Bank, with its market leading position in South Africa and a true pan-African footprint, represents the best organization with which it can partner.[43] After the 2007 purchase, Chinese bankers have quickly moved in to South Africa for a big buying spree in Africa and are examining potential targets in Africa's oil and gas, telecommunications, base metals and power sectors.

In the DRC, China used a $9 billion, multi-year project deal to build and upgrade the DRC's infrastructure in exchange for resources, especially copper and cobalt. The agreement was signed in early 2008 and approved by the DRC National Assembly in May 2008. The promised Chinese investment was more

---

43   "China Buys Into Standard Bank," *South Africa Information* www.southafrica.info, October 26, 2007.

than three times that of the DRC government's annual budget ($2.7 billion for 2007). Under the terms of the deal, the Export-Import Bank of China would help to develop the DRC's transportation system. In return, China would gain rights to extract 6.8 million tons of copper and 420,000 tons of cobalt, and the operations were to begin in 2013. By May 2008, 150 Chinese engineers and technicians were already in the DRC working on the joint ventures.[44]

No Conditions Attached

Following the tradition of its "non-interference" foreign policy, China is generally not interested in internal affairs of other countries. Other than an affirmation of the "one-China" policy, China attaches no political, economic, environmental or social conditions to its financial aid to Africa. According to Chinese Special Representative on African Affairs Liu Guijin, China's relations with Africa are based on three principles: equality, mutual benefit and mutual respect.[45] Chinese investment comes with no demands for making democratic reforms or promoting human rights. While Western countries have tried to impose a market economy and multiparty democracy on developing countries that are often not prepared, the Chinese are trying to separate politics from business. China's development model emphasizes political stability and economic growth first and foremost.

China has refused to back regular Western rebukes of African corruption and human rights abuses and threatened to block UN Security Council genocide charges against Sudan. A major reason is that China has huge interests in Sudan and has invested heavily in Sudan's oil industry. Thirteen of the 15 most important foreign companies in Sudan are Chinese, and more than 10,000 Chinese are working in Sudan's oil business.[46] In the five years since 2000, China had developed several oilfields, built a 930-mile (1,512 kilometer) pipeline, a refinery and a port.[47] Chinese companies have been pumping crude oil from Sudan's oilfields and sending it back to China's industrial centers.

To counter the charges that China puts oil interests above human rights and has not done enough to pressure the Sudanese government to end the civil war, a Chinese foreign ministry official pointed out that China was committed to playing a positive role in appropriately resolving the Darfur problem. China supported UN peacekeeping missions in Sudan and provided 40 million yuan of humanitarian aid to Darfur before the China–Africa summit in November 2006.[48] Others have

---

44   Wenran Jiang, "Chinese Inroads in DR Congo: A Chinese 'Marshall Plan' or Business"? *China Brief,* Vol. 9, No. 1, January 12, 2009, pp. 8–11.

45   "Chinese Envoy Briefs UN on China-Africa Relations," *Xinhua,* September 11, 2007.

46   "China's Expanding Interests in Africa," *World Politics Watch,* September 8, 2006.

47   "China's Oil Ties to Sudan Force it to Oppose Sanctions," *Sudan Tribune,* October 20, 2004.

48   See "Waijiaobu Buzhangzuli Tan Zhongfei Hezuo Luntan Beijing Fenghui (Assistant Minister of Foreign Affairs on China-Africa Forum's Beijing Summit)," *Xinhua,* October 27, 2006.

observed that Sudan's contribution to China's total energy needs is important but not strategic. Sudan accounts for only 5 to 7 percent of China's total oil imports, and less than one percent of China's total energy consumption.[49]

China has received international criticism for its policies elsewhere. In Angola, where China is the second largest oil customer after the United States, a $2 billion Chinese loan relieved the notoriously corrupt Luanda government of the need to improve transparency in the oil sector in order to secure funds from other donors.[50] Like in Sudan's case, China has been singled out for paying no attention to human rights violations in Angola. Not surprisingly, Angola is China's top crude oil supplier and one of its largest trade partners in Africa. By the end of 2007, China had extended $11 billion in loans to Angola, more than the World Bank.[51]

China is the largest foreign investor in Zimbabwe, where President Robert Mugabe's policies have impoverished the country and left millions homeless. When President Mugabe cracked down on the opposition in early 2007, Western countries condemned him but China remained silent. Zimbabwe doesn't have oil, but it is the world's second largest exporter of platinum, a key import for China's auto industry. Zimbabwe's gold, silver, and platinum resources have helped draw Beijing close to Mugabe. Mozambique is another firm supporter of China's independent foreign policy and regards China as one of its most important allies outside of Africa. Incidentally, the Ministry of Foreign Affairs building in Maputo was built with Chinese aid.

Nevertheless, the principle of "non-interference" does not mean that China rejects political and economic reforms or endorses human rights violations in Africa. China is careful to support African-led efforts to develop sound governance and sustainable development throughout the continent. For example, China has supported the New Partnership for Africa's Development (NEPAD), a consensus reached by 19 African nations to promote sustainable development, good governance, poverty reduction, and to stop the marginalization of African economies in an increasingly globalized world. China has also publicly called on Sudanese President Omar Hassan al-Bashir to step up efforts to resolve the bitter conflict in the Darfur region. In a meeting with Mr. Bashir in 2006, President Hu Jintao said that the Darfur matter had "reached a critical stage," and hoped the Sudanese government would maintain dialogue with all parties in the conflict, adjust its position, and improve the humanitarian situation in the region.[52]

---

49   J. Stephen Morrison, Testimony before the Subcommittee on Domestic and International Monetary Policy, Trade, and Technology, Committee on Financial Services, United States House of Representatives, "H.R. 180, Darfur Accountability and Divestment Act of 2007," Washington, DC, March 20, 2007.

50   "The Ugly Face of China's Presence in Africa," *Financial Times*, September 14, 2006, p. 13.

51   Scott Johnson, "China's African Misadventures," *Newsweek*, November 24, 2007.

52   "China Defends Decision to Invite Sudan, Zimbabwe to Africa Summit," *VOA*, November 3, 2006.

Reaching Out to Win African Hearts and Minds

Unlike former colonizers that treated Africa in a condescending way, China considers itself part of the developing world. The new strategic partnership with Africa is based on "political equality and mutual trust," says President Hu Jintao, and economic cooperation between China and Africa is "win-win."[53] During his visit to South Africa in February 2007, President Hu reached out to the youth and gave a talk at the University of Pretoria. He said, "China did not, does not, and will not impose its will or inequality on other countries, as well as do anything that would harm the African people."[54] Hu also announced that in the next three years, the Chinese government would invite 500 African youths, including university students, to visit China.

As part of the efforts to win Africa's hearts and minds, China proclaimed 2006 "the year of Africa" and pledged long-term investment in infrastructure and in training African workers. Chinese companies have built or agreed to build hospitals and railways in Angola, roads and bridges in Sudan and Kenya, dams in Ethiopia and Liberia, and telecommunications networks in Ghana and Zimbabwe, hotels and restaurants in Sierra Leone, along with scores of other projects in Africa. A Chinese contractor also renovated Kenya's Nairobi International Airport.[55] China pledged $4.5 million to AU's mission in Somalia in December 2011. China is also a major contributor to UN peacekeeping missions in Somalia, Burundi and Sudan.

When South Sudan gained independence in July 2011, China immediately recognized the new government while keeping close relations with Sudan. During South Sudanese President Salva Kiir's visit to Beijing in April 2012, China pledged $8 billion in development funds to South Sudan.[56] To help maintain stability in the newly independent country, China sent peacekeeping forces to South Sudan in December 2011. The Chinese state-owned CITIC Construction is building a new city of Kilamba Kiaxi near Luanda with a million new homes. The first phase, completed in December 2012, was able to provide housing for 120,000 Angolans, with associated schools, shops and parks.[57]

In an effort to develop cultural links, China is encouraging tourism in Africa. The government has approved 16 African countries as designated outbound destinations for Chinese tourists, including Ethiopia, Kenya, and Zimbabwe. The number of Chinese tourists to Africa rose to 110,000 in 2005, a 100 percent

---

53   "Win-Win Deals at China-Africa Summit," *Inter Press Service* (Johannesburg), November 6, 2006.

54   "Chinese President Addresses at University of Pretoria," *CCTV International*, February 8, 2007.

55   "China Pouring Money into African Infrastructure Projects," *McClatchy Newspapers*, September 13, 2006.

56   "South Sudan Criticizes China Diplomacy in Conflict," *Reuters*, May 1, 2012.

57   "China Is Building a New City—in Angola," *Week in China* (WiC 139), February 24, 2013.

increase over 2004.[58] China has actively promoted cultural exchanges with African nations. In 2004 an international arts festival with a focus on Africa was held in Beijing, attracting nine African arts groups and eight governmental delegations from Africa. In July 2004 China organized the "African Tour of Chinese Culture," which covered 16 countries.[59] State-run China Radio International launched its first overseas radio station in Kenya in January 2006 to provide 2 million Kenyans with 19 hours of daily programming in English, Swahili, and Chinese on major news from China and around the world, including China's exchanges with African countries.[60]

To facilitate growing trade and travel between China and Africa, China Southern Airlines launched the Beijing-Lagos route on January 1, 2007. With an intermediary stop in Dubai, this air service was the first ever to Africa by a Chinese airline. It not only promoted trade between China and Africa, but also made the China–Africa travel more convenient with Lagos International Airport's linkage to other parts of Africa and China Southern's coverage of major Chinese cities.

Implications

For the International Community

Close Sino-African ties are a successful example of "South-South" cooperation between developing countries in promoting their mutual development. As the largest developing nation and the largest developing continent respectively, China and Africa do not have any historical grievances against each other. Instead, they share a similar history of being victimized by Western powers. Both China and African nations have a strong desire to promote cooperation and take up new challenges of peace and development in the 21st century. Sino-African cooperation provides a significant lesson for other developing regions as to how they can help each other, other than simply relying on Western powers to be lifted out of poverty.

The international, primarily American and European, concerns about China's growing involvement in Africa has probably less to do with the competition over energy and resources, but more with China's new international behavior. China's practice of separating politics and business worries many people. China's willingness to deal with authoritarian regimes such as Sudan, Zimbabwe and Angola, to overlook corruption, and to ignore safety and human rights conditions may undermine democratic institutions and efforts to promote transparency and good governance in developing countries.

---

58   Eisenman and Kurlantzick, "China's Africa Strategy," pp. 219–24.
59   "Zhongfei Guanxi Cheng Shang Xinshiji de Hangchuan (Sino-African Relations Taking Off in the New Century)," *Xinhua*, September 15, 2006.
60   "China's First Overseas FM Radio Station in Kenya," *Xinhua*, January 27, 2006.

From China's perspective, China–Africa cooperation is "transparent, open and inclusive by nature," which will not hurt the interests of any third party, according to former Chinese State Councillor and former Foreign Minister Tang Jiaxuan.[61] Though there is no evidence that China is engaged in a strategic competition with the United States in Africa, the two countries have different interests in the region. They were clearly at odds over Sudan. The United States accused Sudan of carrying out genocide in the Darfur region, but China was reportedly to have sold weapons to the Sudanese government which used the weapons in the civil war. Chinese investment has helped Sudan become Africa's third largest oil producer. According to Chinese officials, China–Sudan bilateral trade hit $3 billion in 2006.[62]

Heavily embroiled in the Middle East since 9/11, the United States has paid scant attention to Africa. America's absence in Africa is "as noticeable and prominent as the Chinese presence," commented then Senator Barack Obama (D-Ill.) in 2006.[63] However, China imports much less oil from Africa than the United States or EU. According to former Chinese Commerce Minister Bo Xilai, in 2006, only 8.7 percent of Africa's oil exports went to China, while 36 percent went to Europe and 33 percent to the United States.[64] As both the United States and China try to diversify their energy sources, political, diplomatic and economic competition between them may intensify in the future.

Some US officials argue that China's diplomacy in Africa serves less as a threat and more as an opportunity for the United States. According to Michael Ranneberger, deputy assistant secretary in the US State Department's Bureau of African Affairs, "China's willingness to take on infrastructure projects can complement Western investment and assistance programs."[65] One of the biggest concerns of the United States is the spread of terrorism in Africa. Failed states, poverty and instability serve as the breeding grounds for future terrorists. The United States and other Western countries can work with China to eliminate these problems, as all have an interest in a stable Africa.

International fight against pirates also provides new opportunities to enhance cooperation and coordination between the US and Chinese militaries. Pirate activities have become extremely active off the African coast since the early 2000s. Vessels of many countries including China's have been frequently attacked by pirates on high seas. In 2008 alone, more than 100 ships were attacked by Somali pirates and over 240 sailors were held for ransom. A Chinese vessel carrying coal

---

61   "'China Threat' in Africa 'Unfounded,'" *The People's Daily*, October 24, 2006.

62   Morrison, Testimony before the Subcommittee on Domestic and International Monetary Policy, Trade, and Technology, March 20, 2007.

63   "China Pouring Money into African Infrastructure Projects," *McClatchy Newspapers*, September 13, 2006.

64   "Bo Xilai Refutes Claim That China Is Colonizing Africa," *Lianhe Zaobao* (Singapore), March 13, 2007. Bo became Party chief of Chongqing later and was dismissed from the Party on charges of corruption and other scandals in 2012.

65   "China's Expanding Interests in Africa," *World Politics Watch*, September 8, 2006.

and 25 crew was hijacked by Somali pirates in October 2009 and was held for over two months before being released with a reported ransom payment from China.

In December 2008 China sent two warships to the Gulf of Aden and the waters off the Somali coast to counter piracy and defend China's commercial ships passing through the region. The United States welcomed China's move and expressed its interest to cooperate with China. Admiral Timothy Keating, head of the US Pacific Command, held out hopes for a revival in military exchanges. "I hope the Chinese do (send ships to the Gulf of Aden) and we'll work closely with them," Keating told reporters during a briefing at the Foreign Press Center in Washington on December 18, 2008. "I think this could be a springboard for a resumption of dialogue between PLA forces and US Pacific Command forces," he said. China temporarily suspended military contacts with the United States in October 2008 in protest over US arms sales to Taiwan valued at $6.5 billion. Keating also said his command had been in touch with the PLA Navy to provide information as the latter prepared to deploy warships in the Gulf of Aden.[66]

China's energy deals and good relations with Sudan have complicated international efforts to stop what is called a state-sponsored genocide in the Darfur region. By not seriously pressuring Sudan to abide by UN resolutions and to end the Darfur conflict, China has been accused of behaving irresponsibly as a great power. Differences between China and Western democracies over human rights and sovereignty are obvious. In September 2004 the UN Security Council passed Resolution 1564, which condemned the mass killing of civilians in the Darfur region, but stopped short of imposing oil sanctions if Khartoum did not act to stop the killing. China abstained from the vote and threatened to veto any further move to impose sanctions.

However, China has adjusted its policy since 2007 when it appointed a special envoy on Sudan. To allay American and international concerns, President Hu publically asked the Sudanese government to work harder to bring more Darfur rebels into the peace process and give the UN a bigger role in solving the Darfur crisis during his two-day visit to Sudan in February 2007.[67] In Khartoum, President Hu said it was "imperative" to halt the deaths in Darfur. Partially due to China's lobbying efforts, Sudanese Foreign Minister Lam Akol announced during Hu's visit that Sudan was willing to see the mixed UN and AU force deployed in Darfur as soon as funding and troops were secured.[68] Apparently this was not enough for the United States. After President Hu's visit, US envoy to Sudan Andrew Natsios criticized China for failing to put more pressure on Sudan over Darfur.[69]

---

66   "Pirate War Could Revive US-China Military Ties: US Admiral," *AFP*, December 18, 2008.

67   "Chinese President Chides Sudan Leader," *Guardian Unlimited*, February 2, 2007.

68   "Hu to Sudan: Allow UN Bigger Darfur Role," *CNN International*, February 3, 2007.

69   "US Envoy to Sudan Critical of China," *Reuters*, February 9, 2007. Natsios, who visited China in January 2007, remarked then, "Our policy and the Chinese policy [on Darfur]

China's previous unwillingness to pressure the Sudanese government had generated appeals for a boycott of the 2008 Beijing Olympics. Several prominent figures, including Mia Farrow and Steven Spielberg, raised the idea of a boycott. Mia Farrow, a well-known Hollywood actress and a goodwill ambassador for the UN Children's Fund, started a campaign in March 2007 to label the 2008 Olympic Games the "Genocide Olympics" and called on corporate sponsors to publicly exhort China to do something about Darfur. Joining the chorus, 108 members of the US House of Representatives wrote a letter to the Chinese government in May 2007 warning that the Beijing Games could be spoiled unless China became more actively involved in stopping the violence in Sudan.[70] China deeply cares about its international image. Under international pressure, it has quietly pressed the Sudan government to cooperate with the UN and AU.

China has defended its Sudan policy and said that Beijing does not support the bloodshed. Liu Guijin, China's special envoy on Africa, said China made "huge efforts," often behind the scenes, to persuade the Sudanese government to accept the 26,000-strong AU-UN peacekeeping force for Darfur that was approved by the UN Security Council on July 31, 2007. According to Liu, China acted on many fronts to help Darfur, such as sending 300 engineers in October 2007 to lay the foundation for the joint UN-AU peacekeeping force. It also provided $10.6 million in humanitarian assistance and Chinese companies were working on projects to provide drinking water in southern and northern Darfur.[71]

While some activists and politicians have criticized China's role in Sudan, others have considered it to be constructive. China sponsored a humanitarian de-mining training course for Sudan in April and May 2008. About 20 military officers from north and south Sudan participated in the six weeks of training at the University of Science and Technology of PLA in Nanjing, Jiangsu Province. This was another concrete measure that China was actively taking part in international peacebuilding efforts; it also showed the Chinese government's firm support for national reconciliation in Sudan, its willingness and active attitude to help the African country's construction and development, according to a Chinese Foreign Ministry press release. China also donated detection and mine sweeping equipment to Sudan when the training was over. UN Undersecretary General for Peacekeeping Jean-Marie Guehenno praised China's "important and constructive

---

are closer than I realized they were, and I think the Chinese are going to play an increasingly important role in helping us to resolve this." *Agence France-Press*, January 12, 2007.

70   "In China, a Display of Resolve on Darfur," *The Washington Post*, September 16, 2007, p. A14.

71   "Chinese Envoy Offers to Mediate on Darfur," *The Associated Press*, September 11, 2007. However, just hours after a unit of some 130 Chinese army engineers flew into south Darfur's capital Nyala in late November 2007, the Justice and Equality Movement (JEM), a Darfur rebel force, said it would not allow the engineers onto land held by it. JEM accused Beijing of stoking the crisis by supporting the Sudanese government and of sucking oil out of Sudan. JEM did not rule out the possibility of attacking these engineers. See Andrew Heavens, "Darfur Rebels Reject Chinese Peacekeepers," *Reuters Africa*, November 24, 2007.

role" in helping ending the crisis on Darfur, and expressed his belief that China could use its influence and good relations with Sudan to help push forward the efforts in finding a political solution and a negotiated agreement on Darfur.[72]

China became the biggest buyer of South Sudan's oil after the latter seceded from Sudan in July 2011. Sudan and South Sudan have been arguing over oil transit fees, border demarcation, and citizenship, which may tip them back into war. China has major business and oil interests in both countries and has tried to maintain good relations with both. South Sudan's chief negotiator Pagan Amum complained that China had been too cautious and should play a more active role in helping defuse the conflict.[73]

In July 2005 Britain, backed by the United States and several other countries, led a UN Security Council briefing on Zimbabwe's slum demolition campaign in an effort to organize a formal debate in the General Assembly and possibly generate a punitive Security Council resolution. Meanwhile, Zimbabwean President Robert Mugabe visited Beijing, seeking financial assistance for his failing economy. Because of Beijing's strong support for Mugabe and opposition to Security Council action, the UN was unable to reach a consensus on further formal discussions of the issue.[74] When asked about China's investment in nations with records of human rights abuses—notably Sudan and the Central African Republic—former Chinese Foreign Minister Li Zhaoxing replied curtly: "Do you know what the meaning of human rights is? The basic meaning of human rights is survival—and development."[75] Differences on issues of human rights and sovereignty will remain between China and the West. The international response to Chinese activities in Africa will be mixed in the years ahead.

For African Countries

"I expect all of Africa will look at China's great transformation ... and identify new means by which we can support each other," said Ellen Johnson-Sirleaf, the Liberian president upon her arrival in Beijing for the China–Africa summit in November 2006.[76] Trade with and investment from China have become important contributors to economic growth in many African countries. Most governments in Africa appreciate China's assistance. Poor African consumers also enjoy the cheap Chinese goods. "The growth of China is a big blessing for us," said Francis Chigumta, a development expert at the University of Zambia. His words probably summarized the general feelings of many Africans.

72　"UN Official Praises China's Role on Darfar Issue," *Xinhua*, September 11, 2007.

73　"South Sudan Criticizes China Diplomacy in Conflict," *Reuters*, May 1, 2012.

74　Peter Brookes and Ji Hye Shin, "China's Influence in Africa: Implications for the United States," *The Heritage Foundation Backgrounder*, No. 1916, February 22, 2006.

75　Quoted in "China Courts Africa with Aid Projects," *The Associated Press*, January 4, 2007.

76　"African Leaders' Summit Promises to be Triumph of Diplomacy for Beijing," *Financial Times*, November 3, 2006, p. 2.

Growing Chinese influence is welcomed by African leaders, who see Beijing as a partner to help build their economies at a time when Europe and the United States are mired in economic turmoil. "China – its amazing re-emergence and its commitments for a win-win partnership with Africa – is one of the reasons for the beginning of the African renaissance," said Ethiopian Prime Minister Meles Zenawi when the China-funded new African Union headquarters was unveiled in January 2012. Despite criticisms of some Chinese policies in Africa, African officials insist that they are not being manipulated by China and that China–Africa relations are based on trade and development. "There are people who still consider Africans like children who can be easily manipulated. The good thing about this partnership is that it's give and take," said Faida Mitifu, the DRC's ambassador to the United States.[77]

Addressing the Shanghai National Accounting Institute on January 19, 2007, Harry G. Broadman, an economic adviser at the World Bank, remarked that China's trade with and investment in Africa present a significant opportunity for growth and integration of sub-Saharan nations into the global economy. China was helping Africa's economy diversify and China's reduction on tariffs for African goods had been particularly beneficial for the continent.[78] In South Africa, the foreign ministry issued a statement prior to President Hu's visit in February 2007. "China's resource and energy needs have certainly contributed to Africa's economic growth by boosting prices and exports from Africa and will continue to do so in the foreseeable future," it stated.

For Jose Cerqueira, an Angolan economist, China is welcome because it eschews what he sees as the IMF's ideological and condescending attitude. Others are pleased because China is ready to pass on some of its technology. It is, for example, helping Nigeria to launch a satellite into space. Some African officials, disillusioned with the Western development model, say that China gives them hope that poor countries can find their own path to development.[79] Indeed, when many developing countries in Africa have grown disenchanted with the "Washington Consensus," they show intense interest in learning from China. Nobel laureate Wangari Maathai, a Kenyan environmental activist who was the first African woman to win the Nobel Peace prize in 2004, suggested that cultural exchanges between China and Africa help Africans to have a better understanding of a fast-changing China, and China's development experience is significant for Africa.[80] For many African countries, China presents an opportunity to rebuild their stagnant economies and can be used as a lever to weaken the economic and political grip of former colonial powers and international financial institutions.

---

77   "Glitzy New AU Headquarters a Symbol of China-Africa Ties," *Reuters*, January 29, 2012.

78   Quoted in "Hu's Africa Visit to Build on Summit," *China Daily*, January 24, 2007.

79   "China in Africa: Never Too Late to Scramble," *The Economist*, October 28, 2006, p. 54.

80   "Striving for the New Strategic Partnership with Africa," *China Financial Times* (zhongguo jingji shibao), November 6, 2006.

While claims that China is planning to colonize Africa are spurious and overblown, the growing Chinese presence in Africa has been met with suspicion, and even resentment. One issue is that Chinese companies prefer to bring in their own workers as opposed to hiring locally. There have been talks of "Chinese invasion" and complaints that the Chinese are taking jobs and contracts away from the locals. Poor quality of some projects constructed by Chinese companies has created tensions between China and several African countries. For example, Marc Ravalomanana, President of Madagascar, reportedly refused to meet with a visiting Chinese leader in August 2006 to express his dissatisfaction with the shoddy Chinese-assisted projects and China's breach of agreements to build a cement factory and an international conference center. Only after the behind-scene mediation by a Hong Kong businessman did President Ravalomanana finally meet with Wu Guanzheng, a member of the Standing Committee of the CCP's Central Committee.[81]

Resentment is also starting to brew over some Chinese business practices in Africa. In August 2009 prosecutors in Namibia were investigating whether a Chinese company may have won a railroad-building contract through bribery. Another Chinese company was alleged to have paid bribes to win a contract to supply airport security scanners for Namibia. With huge investment pouring into Africa, China has sent thousands of workers to work on infrastructure and energy sectors in Africa. The locals who are employed by Chinese headmen often work in horrible conditions. Grass-roots resentment is perhaps strongest in Zambia, where disputes over wages and working conditions have roiled Chinese-run copper mines, resulting in riots and shootings. Trade unions have come out strongly against China's control of Zambia's economy. Anti-Chinese sentiment has mushroomed in Zambia since 2005, when an explosion at a Chinese-owned copper mine killed at least 46 workers and spawned complaints of unsafe working conditions and poor environmental practices.[82] In May 2012, Nigerian immigration officials arrested 45 Chinese nationals for alleged illegal textile trading in the northern city of Kano. The Chinese expatriates were found to be "scavenging in the market," which is hurting Nigeria's economy, said a Nigerian official.[83]

Chinese businesses have squeezed out some local competitors. Workers in Nigeria, South Africa, Angola and other countries have been upset by the loss of hundreds of thousands of jobs in the textile industry. There have been protests in South Africa and Zimbabwe against cheap clothing imported from China. South African trade unions have complained that Chinese textile imports are devastating South Africa's domestic industry, forcing the two governments

---

81   The story was carried in *Asia Week* (Chinese), reported by *Duowei News* (Chinese) on September 17, 2006.

82   "China's Influence in Africa Arouses Some Resistance," *The New York Times*, February 10, 2007.

83   "Nigeria Accuses Chinese Traders of 'Scavenging' in Kano, *BBC News*, May 22, 2012.

to sign a memorandum of understanding in 2006 aimed at restricting imports.[84] In April 2006, days after China agreed a \$4 billion infrastructure investment deal with Nigeria in return for preferential rights on four blocks in a coming oil acreage auction, the Movement for the Emancipation of the Niger Delta (MEND), a Nigerian militant group, warned Chinese companies to "stay well clear" of the oil-producing Niger delta or risk facing attack.

Zimbabwe and Sudan are perhaps China's most controversial partners on the continent. In April 2008 a Zimbabwe-bound Chinese vessel carrying arms arrived in South Africa among political crisis in Zimbabwe following presidential and parliamentary elections on March 29, 2008. President Robert Mugabe refused to publish the results of the elections several weeks after the elections. The Chinese ship, the *An Yue Jiang*, was carrying three million rounds of assault AK-47 rifle ammunition, 3,000 mortar rounds and 1,500 rocket-propelled grenades, according to its inventory, published by a South African newspaper.[85] The shipment, though ordered before Zimbabwe's elections, arrived at a sensitive time in the region. The United States became so concerned about the situation that its intelligence agencies tracked the vessel and its diplomats were instructed to press authorities in at least four nations—South Africa, Mozambique, Namibia and Angola—not to allow it to dock. The ship was earlier forced to leave the South African port of Durban after dock workers refused to unload it, amid concerns President Robert Mugabe might use the weapons to suppress his political opponents after disputed elections. Unable to dock elsewhere in the region, China, while insisting that the shipment constituted a normal military product trade between the two countries, eventually recalled the cargo. The Zimbabwe arms issue risks further harming China's reputation in Africa, where its aggressive business practices and support for authoritarian regimes have drawn increasing scrutiny.

African countries need China's trade and investment, but China is also creating political and social challenges for some of these countries. The fact that many African leaders support China does not mean that average Africans all benefit from China's investment and trade.

For China

China's aid and trade have undoubtedly helped many African countries to develop. Some Africans are beginning to see China as an exploitative major power supporting corrupt regimes in the same manner as Western imperial powers in the past. By shunning Western attempts to link aid and investment to human rights, environmental safeguards and the promotion of transparency in trade, China may be condoning abuses and corruption across the continent, hurting the continent in

---

84   "Chinese President in South Africa to Sign Trade Protocols," *CNN*, February 6, 2007.

85   "China Defends Zimbabwe Arms Shipment Headed for Angola," *AFP*, April 22, 2008.

the long term as well as its own image abroad. For some, China's Africa policy, although advertised as neutral and business friendly, is becoming as immoral as those of Western colonial powers. They claim that big Chinese banks have ignored the so-called "Equator Principles," a voluntary code of conduct pledging that projects financed by private bank lending meet certain social and environmental standards.[86]

Anger at China's presence has already been translated into violence in some parts of Africa, creating security problems for Chinese workers. In January 2007 five Chinese telecommunications workers were kidnapped by unidentified gunmen in Nigeria's southern Rivers State. Though they were eventually released unharmed two weeks later, the incident rang a safety alarm bell for tens of thousands of other Chinese workers and business people in Africa.

On 28th January, 2012, anti-government military force in Sudan kidnapped 29 Chinese workers engaging in infrastructure construction in South Kurdufan of Sudan. Only two days later, another 25 Chinese citizens were kidnapped by the Bedouins in Egypt. Though the hostages in the two snatches were set free soon, these consecutive events aroused concerns about the conditions of Chinese enterprises in Africa. These kidnappings of Chinese workers demonstrate that China can no longer depend on local security forces to protect its commercial interests. China may have to respond to security threats to Chinese property and personnel in the region by relying on its own military. The dilemma is if China sends ground forces to Africa, it may be creating the image of a threatening power.

China's economic and diplomatic approach toward Africa has been state-centric, which relies mainly on government-to-government relations. To protect China's national interests as well as individual safety, China needs to cultivate better relations with important local communities such as influential non-governmental organizations (NGOs), civic leaders and workers' unions.

Indeed, the Chinese in Africa have done a poor job in interacting with the local community. State-owned Chinese companies usually prohibit any type of fraternization or romantic relationships between their employees and local residents. Chinese workers essentially live in separate compounds from the locals, lacking opportunities to develop true and long-lasting friendship with them. If a worker becomes romantically involved with a local, he's quickly hustled back to China. Many Chinese managers believe that Africans and Chinese think differently.[87] Such racist stereotypes are common. It is rare to see Chinese and African workers at the same construction site go and drink beer together after work. Beijing could do more to promote understanding and trust between the peoples. Chinese residents in Africa must also avoid controversial practices related to bribery and counterfeiting.

Chinese presence and business practices in Africa provide an alternative development path for many African nations, but whether such a model is in the

---

86   "World Bank Chief Hits at China Lenders," *Financial Times*, October 24, 2006, p. 6.
87   Scott Johnson, "China's African Misadventures," *Newsweek*, November 24, 2007.

long-term interests of those nations and China itself is a question rarely asked in China. To become a responsible and well-respected re-emerging power in world politics, China has to move beyond commercial interests and help improve governance in Africa. Chinese commercial-driven policy towards Africa, with little interest in improving governance and human rights, undermines China's own efforts to be seen as a benign global power. Though China is not alone or the first in placing its national interests and growing demand for resources above the interests of others, its policies will be further scrutinized as it aims to become a great power in international political economy. If China continues to aid dictators and corrupt governments in Africa, it may lose its hard-earned credibility in Africa as a non-colonial state and a true friend. China's "non-interference" policy has enraged many human rights activists. Its arms sales to countries such as Sudan and Zimbabwe where states commit genocide and persecution of its citizens may have to be terminated.

It is encouraging that Beijing has become more actively involved in resolving the Darfur crisis since 2007. In April 2007 Beijing dispatched a senior foreign ministry official, Zhai Jun, to Sudan to push the Sudanese government to accept the United Nations peacekeeping force. By mid-2007 Sudan had decided to allow UN peacekeeping forces into the Darfur region. According to Susan Shirk, a political science professor at University of California, San Diego and a former deputy assistant secretary of state in the Clinton administration, China practices more mature diplomacy now and would adjust its policies if they face international repercussions, as in the case of Sudan. However, she also points out that China's influence in Sudan may have been overestimated by other countries.[88] Regardless, China has a long way to go to advance its growing interests in Africa and share more international responsibilities as a great power.

Concluding Remarks

Though the China–Africa relationship has a long history, the scale and scope of China's diplomatic activities have greatly expanded since the early 1990s. Managed well, China can significantly contribute to Africa's development; managed poorly, it may encourage bad governance and human rights violations.

To a great extent, the economic cooperation and trade between China and Africa are mutually beneficial. China's active diplomacy in Africa and its massive investment in Africa's infrastructure have played a positive role for African countries' economic growth. Africa's rich resources, huge potential market, and strategic value contribute to China's rise as an economic and political power. For many developing countries around the world, such kind of South-South cooperation is a useful alternative to heavy dependence on the West. As Paul Wolfowitz, former

---

88 "Analysis: China's Sudan Policy Seems to Have Changed," *VOA Chinese*, September 13, 2007.

President of the World Bank, commented that China, which helped over 500 million people escape poverty in the last 30 plus years, offers a valuable lesson for the 600 million people in sub-Saharan Africa who still struggle to find the path out of poverty.[89] Columbia University economist Jeffrey Sachs also remarked that "China gives fewer lectures and more practical help" to African countries.[90] But to avoid potential backlashes from its controversial practices, China must reconcile its national interests with global interests and do more to help improve good governance and human rights in Africa. China must actively engage local business, non-governmental and civil society sectors in order to enhance mutual understanding and improve its image among ordinary Africans.

China has integrated itself into the international political economy. In general, China's active participation in international political economy is good for China and many developing countries. China's political influence in the world will continue to grow corresponding to its expanding economic power. It is impossible and unwise for the United States or any other country to try to exclude China from Africa. China's thirst for energy poses a common development problem for the international community. Even without China, energy demands from India and other emerging markets are expected to jump up drastically in the next few decades. So for the international community, how to reduce the cost of modernization and improve development efficiency has become a serious challenge. Alternative energy sources such as ethanol, biomass, solar and wind power, and nuclear energy have to be used. In addition, the international community needs to pay more attention to energy conservation and the efficient use of energy. Western countries can also help China conserve energy, develop renewable energy, and become more energy efficient.

China's re-emergence as a great power will reshape the political and economic configurations of the contemporary world. Africa helps satisfy China's quest for resources, and untapped African markets serve as a magnet for Chinese manufactured goods. African countries are also rich terrains for Chinese investment, especially in infrastructure. China is not the only power that has expanded its activities in Africa. Brazil, for example, launched a charm offensive of aid and loans in the 2000s to project greater influence and propel trade in Africa. Brazil–Africa trade grew from $4.3 billion in 2002 to $27.6 billion in 2011. As president of Brazil, Lula da Silva made more than 10 trips to Africa from 2003 to 2010.[91]

The United States and China can work together in Africa from reducing poverty to ending civil conflicts, and from safeguarding energy security to combating infectious diseases. China is not involved in a zero-sum competition with the United States in Africa. The United States and China endorsed in principle a US–

89   Paul Wolfowitz, "China Has Valuable Lessons for Sub-Saharan Africa," *Financial Times*, October 30, 2006, p. 10.

90   "Chinese Take a Turn at Turning a Sub-Saharan Profit," *The New York Times*, August 18, 2006.

91   "Brazil Raises Its African Profile," *International Herald Tribune*, August 8, 2012, p. 2.

China subregional Africa dialogue in 2005, as part of the larger US–China strategic dialogue. The two sides should proceed to turn that commitment into practice sooner rather than later. What the United States can do now is to engage China and work together with other powers to ensure the rise of a peaceful and responsible China. On the other hand, China, in its trade with developing countries, must pay more attention to issues such as increasing transparency, enhancing governance, protecting the environment, and improving basic human rights in those countries. These are also in the long-term interests of China.

Questions for Discussion

1. How was China involved in Africa before the recent wave of new Chinese diplomacy?
2. What are Africa's values to China?
3. What are major strategies of China's new diplomacy in Africa?
4. How have African countries reacted to China's growing trade and influence there?
5. What are major problems in China's relations with African countries?
6. Is there a competition for resources and influence in Africa between China, the United States and other powers?

Chapter 3

China and the Middle East

This chapter examines Chinese diplomacy towards the Middle East since the early 1990s, with focus on China's efforts in obtaining energy, its military and security relations with Middle Eastern countries, and its fight against separatism and terrorism along its northwestern border. It also explores how Chinese activities in the Middle East affect US interests and US–China relations.

China's policy towards the Middle East has primarily been driven by economic interests so far. In early 2009, China overtook the United States as the world's largest exporter to the Middle East, marking an important milestone in what is a rapidly strengthening relationship between China and the Middle East. In 2010 China–Middle East trade volume reached $190 billion, much larger than the US–Middle East trade of $123 billion in the same year. In 2011, US–Middle East trade amounted to $153 billion, but China–Middle East trade already topped $120 billion within just the first half of that fiscal year.[1] According to Chinese Foreign Minister Yang Jiechi, the two sides plan to bring trade to $300 billion by 2014.[2] As its economic power continues to grow, China is expected to expand its political, diplomatic and cultural influence in the region.

The Middle East and China have been two areas of major US foreign-policy concern since the end of the Cold War. Why is China interested in the Middle East? How influential is China in the region? Where do America's and China's interests converge and diverge here? These are some important yet understudied issues. In addition to its strategic focus on great power relations and its traditional emphasis on relations with Asian neighbors, China has expanded diplomatic activities to other regions. The Middle East, once considered too distant for any significant economic and political investments, has become a newfound location to implement key objectives of China's new multidimensional diplomacy.

Like other countries, China's foreign-policy serves the nation's core interests. *The New York Times* columnist Thomas L. Friedman once succinctly summarized the two major objectives of Chinese foreign policy in the 21st century: unification with Taiwan and search for oil.[3] Both issues are of great concern to the United

---

1   Massoud Hayoun, "Is China Courting American Muslims"? *The National Interest*, July 30, 2012.

2   Yang Jiechi, "A Long-Term Friendship," *China Daily Asia Weekly*, June 1–7, 2012: p. 10.

3   In his talk "The World is Flat" given at Yale University on April 15, 2005 that this author attended, Thomas L. Friedman explained what China was doing in "a flat world" and why China was becoming more competitive globally.

States as well. In recent years, China and the United States have found more common ground on Taiwan, traditionally the most difficult and explosive issue between the two powers. With both China and the United States opposing *de jure* Taiwanese independence, the independence movement is unlikely to go very far in Taiwan, thus greatly easing tensions between the two great powers.[4] The return to power of the KMT in Taiwan after the 2008 elections brought to an end the pro-independence policy of the previous eight years under Chen Shui-bian. Relations across the Taiwan Strait have steadily improved. To a great extent, the traditional security issue regarding Taiwan has given way to energy and economy as the primary concern of US–China relations. China's hunger for energy and its active global hunt for oil are already creating a new and perhaps more intractable problem between the two powers.

Although China's current consumption of some seven million barrels of oil per day is about one third of America's usage of over 20 million barrels per day, China is becoming increasingly thirsty for energy from abroad as its economy continues to grow at a high rate. In 2003, China supplanted Japan to become the second largest oil consumer in the world behind the United States. The Daqing oilfield in Northeast China, which had produced enough oil to keep China self-sufficient after it was discovered in 1959, had become mature and unable to satisfy domestic needs. Since China became a net oil importer in 1993, Chinese leaders have considered developing relations with oil-rich countries, including oil producers in the Middle East, to be a diplomatic priority.

The increased emphasis on energy is indicative of a grand policy shift by China since the late 1990s. What concerns the United States most is that China not only seems to be competing for energy around the world, but is cozying up to some of the "problem states" such as Sudan, Iran and Venezuela, which may undermine America's global interests. Aware of its vulnerability on the energy front, China has attempted to diversify sources of energy supply. It has oil and other energy deals with many energy rich countries around the world including Sudan, Iran, Myanmar, Angola, Nigeria, Libya, Venezuela, Saudi Arabia, Mexico, Russia, Indonesia, Kazakhstan, Turkmenistan, and Canada.

This chapter, like others in the book, contends that so far, economic and strategic interests have largely driven China's new diplomacy, but with its growing strength China will continue to expand its presence and influence in the Middle East. Although China and the United States have their own separate interests in the region, the two countries share such common ground as fighting against terror, maintaining energy security, and promoting peaceful resolution of the Arab-Israeli conflict. Whether China and the United States can turn the Middle East into a new venue for cooperation in their joint efforts to advance international peace and development is an important issue to the two great powers as well as Middle Eastern countries.

---

4   Some scholars believe that due to political developments in Taiwan in recent years, the Taiwanese independence movement has lost its momentum. See Robert S. Ross, "Taiwan's Fading Independence Movement," *Foreign Affairs*, March/April 2006, pp. 141–8.

Chinese Objectives in the Middle East

Searching for Energy and Expanding Economic Cooperation

China's economic and political activities in the Middle East are part of its new global diplomacy. Different from its policies in the past that were often ideology-tinged, a key foreign-policy objective of China now is to secure energy to fuel its domestic growth.

The Middle East is China's largest oil supplier. According to the International Energy Agency, China's dependence on the Middle East will exceed 75 percent of its total oil imports by 2015.[5] Iran alone already accounts for over 11 percent of China's oil imports. In October 2004, Sinopec signed an agreement with Iran that could be worth as much as $70 billion—China's biggest energy deal yet with any major OPEC producer. China also committed to developing the giant Yadavaran oilfield in Iran and buying 250 million tons of liquefied natural gas (LNG) over the next 30 years; in return, Iran agreed to export to China 150,000 barrels of oil per day, at market prices, for 25 years.[6]

In December 2007 Sinopec and Iranian Petroleum Ministry officially signed the Yadavaran agreement. The Yadavaran deal called for the Chinese company to invest in developing the oilfield in two phases, with the first phase to produce 85,000 barrels per day to be carried out in four years and the second phase to produce another 100,000 barrels per day to be completed in another three years.[7] In addition to being a major source of energy, Iran is an important regional power, capable of playing a big role in the diplomatic balance in the Middle East, hence a highly valuable partner for China in its efforts to promote a multipolar world.

In response to US pressure, some European companies have cut their trade with Iran or withdrawn investment. Royal Dutch Shell and Repsol of Spain withdrew from Iran in 2007. In July 2008 French oil giant Total announced that it would pull out of a planned investment in a huge gas project in Iran's South Pars gas field.[8] As Western companies moved out, Chinese companies stepped in to fill the void and take over business, as has been the case in Africa. In March 2009 the Iranian government announced a $3.2 billion natural gas deal with China, according to which China would help in the development of the offshore South Pars field, believed to be part of the world's largest natural gas reservoir. Iranian state television quoted a senior government official as saying the deal with a Chinese consortium, announced two days after the Obama administration renewed US sanctions against

---

5   M.K. Bhadrakumar, "China's Middle East Journey via Jerusalem," *Asia Times Online*, January 16, 2007.

6   David Zweig and Bi Jianhai, "China's Global Hunt for Energy," *Foreign Affairs*, Vol. 84, No. 5 (September/October 2005), pp. 28–9.

7   "Reports: China Deals for Iran Oil," *CNN*, December 9, 2007.

8   Parris H. Chang, "China's Policy Toward Iran: Arms for Oil"? *China Brief*, Vol. 3, No. 21 (November 7, 2008), p. 10.

the Islamic Republic, would eventually include a European country as a partner.[9] Ironically, Western sanctions have forced Iran to seek business deals with Asian countries, which benefits both Iran and its Asian trade partners. Despite US pressure, India, China, and Japan remain Iran's largest oil export markets.

Iran's difficult relations with the West affect China's oil interests. Concerned about Iran's supply stability, China trimmed crude oil imports from Iran by 6,000 barrels per day for 2007. Meanwhile, China agreed to increase purchase of Saudi crude oil by about 44,000 barrels per day, which put Saudi Arabia above Angola as China's top oil supplier again.[10] Saudi Arabia currently supplies about 17 percent of China's total oil imports.[11] Since China and Saudi Arabia established diplomatic ties in 1990, bilateral relations have developed steadily, with increasing exchange of visits at different levels and expanding cooperation in various sectors. Except in 2006, Saudi Arabia has been China's largest oil supplier and has become China's largest trading partner in the Middle East. In 2008 two-way trade between China and Saudi Arabia amounted to $41.8 billion.[12] China imports more oil from Saudi Arabia than the United States does now. In 2012 Saudi oil giant Aramco teamed up with China's Sinopec to build a gigantic new oil refinery in the Red Sea port city of Yanbu that is scheduled to be fully operational by 2014. The $8.5 billion joint venture covers an area of about 5.2 million square meters. When completed, it will process 400,000 barrels of heavy crude oil per day. Aramco will hold a 62.5 percent stake in the plant while Sinopec will own the remaining 37.5 percent.

Iraq has been a top oil supplier to China. In 1997 the state-owned CNPC signed a deal with Saddam Hussein's government to develop the Ahdab oilfield. But work never started and Saddam-era contracts were no longer recognized in Baghdad after the 2003 US invasion. China opposed the US invasion of Iraq partly due to its substantial economic interests in Iraq. However, China quickly joined other major powers in the reconstruction of Iraq after the war. China pledged $25 million and agreed to forgive a large part of Iraq's debt. The Chinese embassy in Baghdad reopened less than two weeks after the transfer of authority to the Iraqi interim government in June 2004. Since the war, China has provided scholarships for Iraqi students to study in China, offered material assistance for Iraq's elections, and trained Iraqi diplomats at the China Foreign Affairs University in Beijing. As one analyst has observed, China's generosity was not motivated by sheer goodwill; China was hoping to gain access to the bidding processes on big oil and infrastructure projects.[13]

---

9   "Iran Signs $3.2 billion Natural Gas Deal with China," *Los Angeles Times*, March 15, 2009.

10   "China to Up 2007 Saudi Oil Imports to New High," *Reuters*, January 9, 2007. According to Chinese official statistics, in 2006 Angola surpassed Saudi Arabia to become China's largest oil supplier.

11   Bhadrakumar, "China's Middle East Journey via Jerusalem."

12   "Chinese President Meets Saudi Arabian King on Ties," *Xinhua*, February 10, 2009.

13   Yufeng Mao, "Beijing's Two-Pronged Iraq Policy," *China Brief*, Vol. 5, No. 12, (May 24, 2005), The Jamestown Foundation, Washington, DC.

China's support for the new Iraqi government quickly paid off. In early 2007 Iraq asked a Chinese oil company to review its drilling technique to develop the Ahdab oilfield. The two sides discussed the resumption of the Saddam Hussein-era agreement on the development of the Ahdab field. Iraqi President Jalal Talabani and Oil Minister Hussain al-Shahristani visited China in June 2007, accompanied by dozens of officials to revive the Ahdab negotiations. The upsurge in violence since 2003 has made Iraq less attractive to Western producers. Yet the new Baghdad government courted China because Chinese producers have been willing to invest in Angola, Sudan and other countries that are considered dangerous or politically isolated.[14] In August 2008 CNPC signed a $3 billion oil contract with Iraq. It is Iraq's first major oil deal with a foreign company since the fall of Saddam Hussein. It was also the first time in more than 35 years that Iraq has allowed foreign oil companies to do business inside its borders. The contract would allow the CNPC to develop an oilfield in southern Iraq's Wasit province for about 20 years, according to Iraq's Oil Ministry spokesman Assim Jihad.[15]

China has major oil deals with other Middle Eastern countries too. In 2006 Sinopec and Kuwait Petroleum Corp. agreed to build an oil refinery joint venture near the city of Nansha in Guangdong province. The $5 billion project, completed in 2010 with a 15-million-ton annual capacity, was then the biggest Sino-foreign joint venture in the petrochemical industry.

China and Syria signed an agreement to build a joint venture refinery in eastern Syria, expanding their cooperation to include oil processing during an April 2008 visit to Syria by Li Changchun, a member of the CCP's Politburo. The agreement called for CNPC to build a refinery with an annual capacity of 5 million tons (about 110,000 barrels a day), and CNPC was to shoulder 85 percent of the costs of the $1.5 billion project. This joint venture is also good for Syria since it has been seeking Chinese technology to increase output from its own oilfields and reduce its reliance on oil product imports.

Qatar is the world's largest producer and exporter of Liquefied Natural Gas (LNG) and third largest holder of natural gas reserves. It is an important source of China's LNG needs, satisfying around 20 percent of Chinese demand for LNG.[16] Qatargas and the China Natural Offshore Oil Corporation (CNOOC) signed a sales and purchase agreement in 2008 for Qatar to supply China with 2 million metric tons (m/t) of LNG annually over a 25-year period. The first shipment of Qatari LNG was delivered to China in October 2009.

China views the Middle East not only in terms of its value as a source of oil but also in the context of its huge potential as an oil services market and trade partner. By 2001 China had signed almost 3,000 contracts with all six Gulf Cooperation

---

14 "China and Iraq Plan to Resurrect Oil-field Deal Set in Hussein Era," *The Wall Street Journal*, October 30, 2006, p. A9

15 "Iraq Signs $3 billion Oil Deal with China," *CNN*, August 30, 2008.

16 Chris Zambelis, "China and Qatar Forge a New Era of Relations around High Finance," *China Brief*, The Jamestown Foundation, October 19, 2012.

Council (GCC) states for labor services worth $2.7 billion. In July 2004 the six GCC finance ministers visited China, where they signed a "Framework Agreement on Economic, Trade, Investment, and Technological Cooperation" with China and agreed to negotiate a China–GCC free trade zone.[17]

Since establishing diplomatic ties on November 1, 1984, the political, economic and trade relations between the UAE and China have evolved significantly in both scale and substance. Bilateral trade between the UAE and China recorded an impressive growth of 33 percent in the previous eight years reaching $20 billion in 2007. In 2007 China exported goods and services worth nearly $17 billion dollars to the UAE, of which nearly 70 percent were re-exported to other countries in the Middle East, Africa and even Europe.[18] Trade between the two countries hit $28 billion in 2008 before dipping to $21 billion in 2009 due to the global slowdown. With huge potentials for growth on both sides, it is predicted that the trade volume will top $100 billion by 2015.[19]

Chinese companies—especially construction, petroleum and petrochemical firms—are increasingly setting up their bases in the UAE, which is a strategic transit point for a huge market spanning from the Indian subcontinent to the African shores. There are more than 3,000 registered Chinese companies in the UAE. Dragon Mart, a supermarket vending low-priced Chinese products, is one of the important Chinese business establishments in the UAE. The Chinese Commodities and Trade Fairs, which are held throughout the UAE from Sharjah to Fujairah on a regular basis, have served as an effective forum to promote trade. Additionally, the increasing flow of Chinese manpower to the UAE surpassed the 200,000 mark in 2007, out of which only 30,000 were laborers, the rest being executives and businesspeople.[20]

In addition to state-owned oil companies, private Chinese companies are also looking for oil in the Middle East and elsewhere. The China International Petroleum Investment Union, a group that includes investors from China as well as Indonesia, Saudi Arabia, Kazakhstan and Singapore, has paid about $400 million for rights to four fields in Indonesia and two in the Middle East. The group, headed by Chinese oil entrepreneur Cui Xinsheng, hopes to sell the rights to China's big state-owned companies.[21] The economies of China and many Middle Eastern countries are complementary, so more future cooperation in trade and investment is expected.

---

17 Jin Liangxiang, "Energy First: China and the Middle East," *Middle East Quarterly*, Spring 2005. The Gulf Cooperation Council, set up in 1981, is composed of Saudi Arabia, Bahrain, Kuwait, Oman, Qatar and the United Arab Emirates (UAE).

18 Samir Ranjan Pradhan, "Dubai Inc. in China: A New Vista for Gulf-Asia Relations," *China Brief*, Vol. 8, No. 9, The Jamestown Foundation, April 28, 2008.

19 "China Trade with UAE Forecast to Top $100 bn," *The National*, June 1, 2010.

20 Ibid.

21 "Feeding China's Oil Thirst," *The Wall Street Journal*, January 2, 2007, p. A10.

Promoting Military and Strategic Cooperation

Another major interest of China in the Middle East is its arms trade and military cooperation with countries in the region. That China is both the recipient of advanced weapons from Israel and a traditional supplier of weapons to the Middle East may create serious security challenges to the United States and frustrate global non-proliferation efforts. Chinese weapons started to enter the Middle Eastern market as early as the 1970s with major buyers in Egypt, Iraq, Iran, and Saudi Arabia. However, since the early 1990s China has made tremendous improvements in its non-proliferation commitments. From 1999 to 2006, China ranked fifth among the leading suppliers of weapons to developing countries (behind the United States, Russia, United Kingdom, and France). The value of China's arms deliveries during the eight-year period totalled $5.8 billion, as compared to the $66.1 billion of the United States.[22]

While the United States and EU countries still maintain much of the Tiananmen-era sanctions to ban high-tech and military sales to China, Israel has become China's second largest advanced weapons supplier next only to Russia. China's interest in Israel's, and by proxy, in America's weapons, is always high. Despite its small size, Israel is an important investor in Chinese development projects and supplier of high-tech weapons. Prime Minister Benjamin Netanyahu once told Chinese visitors that "Israeli know-how is more valuable than Arab oil."[23]

Israel's arms sales to China have challenged US–Israel defense relations several times, especially its attempted sales of the Phalcon airborne early warning and control radar system and the planned upgrades of the Harpy unmanned aerial drone system in the late 1990s and early 2000s. The burgeoning relations between China and Israel have already had some effect on other policies. For example, in the Israeli–Palestinian conflict, China is taking a more balanced position now than its pro-Palestine stand in the past.

Israeli–Chinese relations started well at the very beginning. The Chinese press welcomed the establishment of the Jewish state in 1948, and Israel was one of the first countries to recognize the PRC after the latter's founding in 1949. The two countries would have established diplomatic relations in the early 1950s had Israel not been pressured by the United States and had China not readjusted its foreign policy following the Bandung Conference of Asian and African states.[24] Since the mid-1950s, the PRC had taken a strongly anti-Israel stance and eschewed bilateral contacts with Israel. Even trade with Israel was banned. After the Suez

---

22 Thomas Lum, et al. "Comparing Global Influence: China's and US Diplomacy, Foreign Aid, Trade, and Investment in the Developing World," Congressional Research Service, Washington, DC, August 15, 2008, p. 37.

23 Quoted in Barry Rubin, "China's Middle East Strategy," *Middle East Review of International Affairs*, Vol. 3, No.1 (March 1999).

24 Guang Pan, "China's Success in the Middle East," *Middle East Quarterly*, December 1997, http://www.meforum.org/article/373.

Canal crisis, Beijing denounced Israel as "the tool of imperialist policies," and all contacts between the two countries came to an end.[25]

China's policy reorientation towards Israel since the mid-1980s has clearly been driven by realism and pragmatism associated with its opening-up policy. An emerging superpower and an increasingly important player in the region, China's attitude toward the Israeli–Palestinian issue may influence the final resolution of the conflict. China both supports the concept of "land for peace" and recognizes the need for an independent Palestinian state. It also emphasizes the importance of guaranteeing Israel's security, a position the Chinese government has enunciated since the early 1990s.[26]

In the Israeli–Palestinian conflict, China does not want to be perceived as leaning toward either side. For example, after Hamas, a militant Islamic group, swept to victory over the long-dominant Fatah party in the January 2006 parliamentary elections in Palestine, the official Chinese response was mild and neutral compared to strong statements from the United States and EU countries that condemned Hamas' anti-Israel stance and demanded it to disarm. Consistent with its balanced approach, Chinese Foreign Ministry issued a statement that "welcomes the smooth completion of the election of the Palestinian Legislative Council;" meanwhile, China hopes "all Palestinian factions will maintain unity and solve the dispute with Israel through peaceful negotiations and political means."[27]

In the context of this "balance" policy, China–Israel relations have been warming up since the two countries finally established diplomatic relations in 1992.[28] The two countries began their trade relations long before 1992. Though the initial figures were quite modest, due to the constant and rapid growth in trade throughout the years, the bilateral trade surpassed $4 billion in 2007 and topped $8 billion in 2011. China plays a significant role in the contracted engineering market in the Middle East, with constructed projects valued at more than $1 billion, and more than 10,000 Chinese holding work permits in Israel's construction

---

25 Ibid.

26 China's position on the Middle East issue was summarized by Kong Quan, a Chinese Foreign Ministry spokesman, as follows: Israel's occupation of Arab territories should be ended in line with related UN resolutions and the legal rights and interests of the Palestinian people should be restored. Meanwhile, Israel's security should be ensured.

The "land for peace" principle should be respected. China opposes Israel's use of force and its violent actions against innocent civilians. China appeals the international community to focus more attention and efforts on the Middle East issue. The UN should play a bigger role in the settlement to the issue. See *Xinhua* news http://www.china.org.cn/english/FR/26692.htm, February 7, 2002.

27 "China Urges Hamas to Negotiate with Israel," *Reuters*, January 27, 2006.

28 Secret official contacts and exchanges between the two sides started in the early 1980s, leading to the establishment of semi-official China International Tourist Service in Israel and the Beijing Liaison Office of the Israel Academy of Sciences and Humanities in 1990. See E. Zev Sufott, *A China Diary: Towards the Establishment of China-Israel Diplomatic Relations* (London: Frank Cass, 1997).

and agricultural sectors.[29] To obtain hi-tech weapons from Israel is not the only incentive for China to develop close relations with the Jewish state. China figures that good relations with Israel would probably help its relations with the United States, given the special and close ties between Israel and the United States.

However, Israel and China infuriated each other in recent years—Israel canceled arms sales to China under US pressure, and China has warmed up to Iran, Israel's chief adversary. China and Israel traded military technology heavily for nearly a decade after 1992. The United States cut that cooperation short in 2000, when it pressured Israel to cancel its sale of sophisticated reconnaissance aircraft to China. The canceled deal angered China, cost Israel hundreds of millions of dollars and frayed ties between the two. In 2005, the United States persuaded Israel not to service spare parts for unmanned aircraft drones already sold to China, concerned that it would upgrade China's airborne anti-radar capability. Israel has since taken a wary approach to trade with China that could be deemed questionable by the US—limiting its exports of goods that could be seen as giving China a military advantage, including the state-of-the-art surveillance equipment and homeland security technologies that have made Israel a leader in that field.

Military relations began to improve after the 2011 exchange of visits by top military officials. Israeli Defense Minister Ehud Barak travelled to China in June 2011—the first visit of an Israeli defense minister in a decade. Two months later, Chen Bingde, Chief of the General Staff of the PLA visited Israel. A Chinese naval fleet visited Israel in August 2012 for the first time in history. And under the watchful eyes of Americans, the Chinese and Israeli navies conducted their first joint exercise.

Some experts suggest that China and Israel may try to "find loopholes" in US-imposed limits on Sino-Israeli military relations. Despite the restrictions, China is Israel's third largest trading partner, following the United States and Germany.[30]

Aside from military cooperation with Israel, China has also sold weapons to several countries in the Middle East.[31] China's alleged weapons sales to Iran, Iraq and Pakistan are most worrisome. China's record in weapons proliferation in the Middle East is a mixed one. Since China was found to have delivered 36 CSS-2 missiles and nine launchers to Saudi Arabia in 1988, there has been no documented evidence of transactions of a similar nature. Nor have there been credible reports of

---

29   "China Voices Concern About Business Interests in the Middle East," *China Daily*, April 10, 2002.

30   "Chinese Military Chief Visits Israel for First Time," *USA Today*, August 14, 2011.

31   In a typical Taiwan-PRC diplomatic competition, Taiwan was reportedly considering selling weapons to the UAE. The UAE has official relations with the PRC. Its diplomatic flirtation with Taiwan is not only irritating to Beijing but will also complicate the non-proliferation efforts in the region. According to Chinese language sources, former Taiwan President Chen Shui-bian stopped by the UAE on his way home after completing a visit to Central America at the end of September 2005. While in the UAE, Chen met with President Sheikh Zayed bin Sultan al-Nahayan's brother. See "Taiwan Plans to Sell Weapons to the UAE," *Duowei News* (Chinese), October 1, 2005.

sales by China of significant quantities of conventional arms to Saudi Arabia, Iraq, Iran or other countries since then. But there are still occasional reports in Western media of weapons or technology sales and transfers to the region by Chinese companies, although the Chinese government may have not authorized such deals.[32]

China's solid political and military ties with Egypt are sometimes contentious because of Egypt's pursuit of nuclear technology. Sino-Egyptian cooperation extends to military affairs in the form of regular high-level contacts between Beijing and Cairo. In response to Israel's powerful nuclear arsenal and Iran's weapons program, Egypt is often cited as a likely candidate to pursue its own nuclear option in the future. Egypt reportedly approached China and Russia in 2002 for assistance in the development of a nuclear reactor in Alexandria. China's history of weapons proliferation and nuclear cooperation in the region may portend closer ties with Egypt in this area, should Egypt adopt a course of action.[33]

China's growing involvement in the regional arms market has become a source of concern for American policy makers. However, since the mid-1990s, China has made tremendous improvements in its non-proliferation commitments. China is now a signatory to the Non-proliferation Treaty, both the Chemical and Biological Weapons conventions, as well as the Comprehensive Test Ban Treaty and the Missile Technology Control Regime. In addition, China's NPC has passed laws to administer export of both arms and military technologies.

For decades, China has conducted military training for developing countries in support of its arms sales or transfers to these countries. For example, in the 1980s and 1990s, the PLA Navy trained Pakistan's and Bangladesh's naval officers to maintain frigates and torpedo boats purchased from China. Besides economic aspects, defense cooperation between China and the UAE seems to be gaining strength recently. For the UAE, Chinese arms and ammunitions are inexpensive in comparison to Western imports, and such deals with China would not be perceived as a threat to its neighbors in general and Iran in particular.[34] Chinese expertise, especially in gathering military intelligence and defense software prowess, is of particular interest to the UAE.

Keeping the Restive Northwest Under Control

Unlike in Africa and other developing regions, China does not need to compete fiercely with Taiwan to win over diplomatic allies in the Middle East. By the time China established diplomatic relations with Saudi Arabia in July 1990 and with Israel in January 1992, China had built formal diplomatic ties with every country in the Middle East. Therefore China's major security concern in the Middle East is not competition

---

32   See for example, "China Calls on US to Stop Punishing Companies Accused on Proliferation," http://www.forbes.com, October 25, 2005.

33   "Down the River Nile: China Gains Influence in Egypt," *China Brief*, The Jamestown Foundation, October 25, 2005, p. 9.

34   Pradhan, "Dubai Inc. in China."

with Taiwan but its own northwestern front. A major pillar of China's Middle East policy is its fight against internal separatist movements linked to the Middle East.

While the United States has focused on weeding out global terrorist networks such as al-Qaeda in the Middle East, China is more interested in maintaining security by defeating radical separatists and terrorists within its borders. At least one such radical group was alleged to have received funds and training from al-Qaeda.[35] The July 2009 ethnic riot in Xinjiang and the subsequent al-Qaeda's vow to avenge the deaths of Uyghur Muslims killed during the unrest highlighted security challenges China faces from terrorism, separatism and extremism in the years ahead. In this largest ethnic riot between the minority Uyghurs and the majority Han Chinese since 1949, about 200 people were killed and thousands injured, most of whom were Han Chinese. The situation in Xinjiang remained volatile after the violence.

The Chinese government seeks diplomatic support from Muslim countries in the Middle East to cut off any financial, political, moral, or other support for radical groups. China's support for US actions in Afghanistan was in part a reflection of its own security concerns. The Taliban cooperated with al-Qaeda, which in turn supported the East Turkestan terrorist forces that threatened the stability of China's northwestern region. One major aim of the Shanghai Cooperation Organization (SCO) is also to stop terrorism from infiltrating into China from Central Asia and the Middle East.

China has serious security concerns along its northwestern border. China's political and intelligence support for US-led war against the Taliban after the 9/11 terrorist attacks is part of its own efforts to seek international and regional cooperation to crush the separatist movement in Xinjiang. China shares a 20-mile long border with Afghanistan. The Uyghurs in Xinjiang have preserved a distinct, non-Chinese ethnic identity. Radical separatists in Xinjiang have sparked riots, assassinations, and bombings since 1990. The East Turkestan Islamic Movement has sought to establish an Islamic Republic of East Turkestan in Xinjiang. According to Chinese official sources, between 1990 and 2001, East Turkestan terrorist groups staged more than 200 attacks in Xinjiang, killing 162 people, including local community leaders and religious personnel.[36]

The US Department of State labeled the East Turkestan Movement a terrorist group in 2002, but many in and outside the US government were concerned that China may tighten its ethnic policies in Xinjiang and other restive regions in the name of fighting terrorism and separatism. Nevertheless, China's determination to crush separatists provides an incentive for China to cooperate with the United States in the latter's war on terror in the Middle East.

In pursuing its avowed objective of becoming a major power while addressing its urgent domestic constraints such as its unstable west and strive for energy sources, China has redefined its engagement with the Gulf region. To protect

---

35 Chien-peng Chung, "China's 'War on Terror': September 11 and Uighur Separatism," *Foreign Affairs*, (July/August, 2002), pp. 8–12.

36 *The People's Daily* http://english.peopledaily.com.cn, January 25, 2002.

its lifeline energy-transport channels starting from the Middle East, China has expanded its naval power and gotten a foothold in the Indian Ocean by constructing the Gwadar Port in Pakistan. The UAE, as an Indian Ocean littoral state, is a natural strategic partner for China in its effort to make its presence felt as a power vis-à-vis other powers. Besides, the UAE's status as the most modern country in the Gulf region is not only a source of investment for the social, cultural and religious development of China's Muslim-dominated regions, but also allows it to act as an interlocutor in quelling possible independence movements in those regions.

Chinese Strategies in the Middle East

Highest-level Involvement

China attaches great importance to its relations with the Middle East now, which is reflected by the fact that Chinese engagement with the region involves leaders at the highest level. Frequent exchanges of high-level visits have pushed the relationship between China and many Middle Eastern countries to a new height.

Saudi Arabia has been a major oil supplier to China since the 1990s. Saudi Oil Minister Ali al-Naimi made at least six trips to China in 2004 and 2005.[37] King Abdullah bin abdul-Aziz's first official visit abroad, after succeeding his half-brother King Fahd to the throne in 2005, was to Asia; his first stop was China. The visit was also notable in that it was the first visit to China by a Saudi head of state since the two countries established diplomatic ties in 1990. A joint investment oil-refining project by Saudi Arabian and Chinese companies was put into production in Saudi Arabia in early 2006.

During the Saudi king's Beijing visit in January 2006, the two countries signed an agreement on oil, natural gas and mineral cooperation, in which Saudi Arabia promised to increase the annual oil and gas exports to China by 39 percent. As part of the agreement, a 100-million-ton crude oil storage facility was planned for construction in China's Hainan province.[38] In April 2006 President Hu Jintao visited Saudi Arabia. He toured East Province, Saudi Arabia's premier oil-producing region and became one of the few foreign leaders ever to address the Shura, the consultative council that advises the king and cabinet.[39] Hu's predecessor Jiang Zemin was the first Chinese head of state to visit Saudi Arabia in 1999.

---

37   John Calabrese, "Saudi Arabia and China Extend Ties Beyond Oil," *China Brief*, The Jamestown Foundation, September 27, 2005, pp. 3–4.

38   Jianjun Tu, "The Strategic Considerations of the Sino-Saudi Oil Deal," *China Brief*, Vol. 1, No. 4, The Jamestown Foundation, February 15, 2006.

39   "Avoiding Political Talk, Saudis and Chinese Build Trade," *The New York Times*, April 23, 2006.

From Saudi Arabia's perspective, China could be used as a valuable source of support as Riyadh continues on a path of cautious and selective economic liberalization while seeking to deflect US pressure in the area of political reform. The sometimes strained Saudi-US relations provide the opportunity for China to consolidate its relationship with the Saudis. China and Saudi Arabia signed a vocational training cooperation agreement between the two ministries of education in January 2006. Saudi Arabia also agreed to provide governmental loans to Aksu city of Xinjiang in infrastructure improvement project. For Saudi Arabia, maintaining good relations with the United States remains its key foreign-policy objective, given the long-standing economic and military ties between the two countries. Though China and Saudi Arabia are likely to expand their ties to other areas such as education, investment, and anti-terrorism, Saudi Arabia will need to strike a balance between the United States and China.

Shaykh Mohammed, Vice President and Prime Minister of the UAE and ruler of Dubai, visited China in March 2008 and met with Chinese President Hu Jintao, Premier Wen Jiabao and Vice President Xi Jinping. The entourage comprised of a who's who of Dubai Inc., the investment giant, led by Shaykh Mohammed, reflects the UAE's reinvigoration in recent years through proactive economic diplomacy in Asia. Apart from bolstering economic and commercial ties with China, this visit benefited the UAE in more than one way and the meetings "signified the symbolic rebirth of solidarity within the East, which could herald a new era in Gulf-Asia ties," commented one analyst.[40]

High-level visits between China and Israel have frequently been exchanged since 1992. Every Israeli president since Chaim Herzog has visited China. Prime ministers Yitzhak Rabin and Benjamin Netanyahu both visited Beijing during their terms. Chinese President Jiang Zemin visited Israel in 2000. In January 2007 Prime Minister Ehud Olmert visited Beijing to commemorate the 15th anniversary of China–Israel diplomatic ties and to seek China's support on the Iran nuclear issue.

Recognizing the huge potentials for synergizing complementarities, President Hu Jintao visited UAE and deliberated on various issues in January 2007. In April 2007 UAE Minister of Economy Shaykha Lubna Al Qassimi signed a memorandum of understanding (MOU) to set up a joint team tasked with boosting bilateral relations during a visit to China. Agreements on technological and scientific cooperation in the defense industry, higher education, health and other areas were also signed.

Iranian President Mahmoud Ahmadinejad flew to Beijing in September 2008 to attend the opening ceremony of the Paralympic Games. In Beijing, Mr Ahmadinejad met with President Hu, who said that China "respects Iran's right to the peaceful use of nuclear energy" and "adheres to the peaceful settlement of the Iran nuclear issue through dialogues and negotiations."[41] The two countries

---

40   Pradhan, "Dubai Inc. in China."
41   "China Calls for Peaceful Resolution of Nuclear Standoff," *Reuters*, September 6, 2008.

also agreed to boost the "strong and strategic" relations and expand the growing trade between the two countries which reached a record high of $30 billion by the end of 2008. The Chinese leader welcomed Iran's interest to join the SCO, saying an expert committee would be formed to consider the proposal of Iran, which already had an observer status at the SCO.[42] When the SCO convened a summit meeting in Tajikistan in August 2008, President Ahmadinejad was present and met with Chinese and Russian leaders. He attended the 2012 SCO summit in Beijing and discussed his country's disputed nuclear program with President Hu.

President Jiang Zemin made a state visit to Teheran in April 2002 to cement ties with Iran. When Teheran's subway was completed in February 2000, Chinese Foreign Minister Tang Jiaxuan was present for the opening ribbon-cutting ceremony. NPC Standing Committee chair Wu Bangguo visited Iran and met with President Ahmadinejad in September 2012 as part of his Asia–Pacific tour, which also took him to Myanmar, Sri Lanka, and Fiji.

In 2008 Chinese Vice Premier Li Keqiang visited Egypt and Kuwait. In his meeting with Emir of Kuwait Sheikh Sabah al-Ahmad al-Jaber al-Sabah, Li called on the two sides to promote high-level exchange based on equality and mutual benefit, political mutual trust as well as cooperation on trade. Bilateral trade volume between China and Kuwait reached $3.6 billion in 2007 and topped $10 billion in 2011.

President Hu Jintao began his 2009 foreign tours with a visit to Saudi Arabia in February, with a mission to strengthen economic and strategic ties between Riyadh and Beijing, especially in the oil and petrochemical sector. In Riyadh, King Abdullah held wide-ranging talks with President Hu. The two leaders called for a just and comprehensive Middle East peace settlement that would ensure the Palestinians an independent state. Hu's entourage included more than 125 high-ranking Chinese officials and businessmen including Foreign Minister Yang Jiechi, Minister of Commerce Chen Deming and Minister in charge of the National Development and Reform Commission Zhang Ping. "The visit of President Hu Jintao shows the great importance the Chinese leaders attach to the Sino-Saudi relations," said Chinese Ambassador Yang Honglin.[43]

After the magnitude-8.0 earthquake hit western China's Sichuan province and claimed nearly 90,000 lives in May 2008, King Abdullah became the biggest donor to China, offering a cash donation of $50 million and materials worth $10 million.[44] Twelve school children from Sichuan, survivors of the earthquake, traveled with President Hu to Saudi Arabia in February 2009 to thank the King and his people for their support and help. The two countries signed five bilateral agreements during Hu's visit, including cooperation in oil, gas and mining; in the field of

---

42   "Iran Seeks to Join Shanghai Cooperation Organization," *Teheran Times* www.teherantimes.com, September 7, 2008.

43   "Ghazanfar Ali Khan Chinese President Hu Jintao Meets Saudi Arabian King Abdullah in Riyadh," *Arab News*, February 11, 2009.

44   "Chinese President Meets Saudi Arabian King on Ties," *Xinhua*, February 10, 2009.

health; on quality inspection and standards of goods and services; a MOU to set up a chapter of King Abdulaziz Public Library in China and the Makkah railway project. President Hu also met with Secretary General of GCC Abdul Rahman Al-Attiyah to discuss cooperation between China and GCC member states.

In January 2012 Premier Wen Jiabao visited Saudi Arabia, the UAE and Qatar, marking the first visit by a Chinese premier to Saudi Arabia in over two decades and the first ever by a Chinese premier to the UAE and Qatar. During his visit, China and the UAE signed a multi-billion dollar currency swap deal that allows the central banks of the two countries to draw on the local currency to ease bilateral trade. Wen's visit to Qatar, in addition to reaching new accords on energy cooperation, also resulted in a series of agreements governing formal cooperation between the People's Bank of China and the Qatar Central Bank as well as between the China Banking Regulatory Commission and the Qatar Financial Center. Qatar has become one of the largest foreign investors in China's capital markets. Wen also met with the heads of the GCC and the Organization of the Islamic Conference (OIC) and attended the World Future Energy Summit and the China–Arab States Cooperation Forum.

Zhou Yongkang, a member of the CCP Politburo's standing committee, visited Afghanistan in September 2012, the first time by a Chinese leader since 1966. President Hamid Karzai, who visited Beijing in June 2012, said Afghanistan would like China to be more involved in its reconstruction efforts and expected China to play a bigger role in the peaceful development of Afghanistan and the region. Notably, since 2002 China's special envoys to the Middle East have frequently visited the Middle East to provide a sustained, high-level, and active Chinese presence in the region. (See Table 7.2.)

Public Diplomacy

Chinese–Middle Eastern ties have become so strong by the late 1990s that not knowing China's Middle East policies would mean not understanding Chinese diplomacy as a whole. Nor can one fully understand the Middle East without knowledge of that region's relations with China, claimed one scholar.[45] The strong relationship is a result of China's efforts to use both formal state-to-state diplomacy and public diplomacy or citizen diplomacy which promotes more extensive people-to-people exchanges.

Beijing's political and diplomatic pursuits in the Middle East have been underscored and reinforced by a clear trend of cultural, religious, educational, tourism, and other forms of societal exchanges between China and the Middle East. For instance, China has more than 23 million Muslims, and Chinese *hajj* pilgrims have traveled to Saudi Arabia every year since 1955; their number

---

45   For a historical survey of US–Middle East relations since 1949, see Guang Pan, "China's Success in the Middle East," *Middle East Quarterly*, December 1997.

regularly exceeded 6,000 in the 1990s, and by 2003 had ballooned to over 10,000.[46] Chinese state media reported that the China Islamic Association scheduled 82 charter flights to send more than 13,800 people to Saudi Arabia in 2012.

Chinese state-owned construction companies finished a railway allowing Muslims to travel between pilgrimage sites in Mecca and Medina in 2010 and broke ground in the construction of a monumental Grand Mosque of Algiers in 2012.[47] In 2012, about 8,000 Arab students were studying in China. Every year more than 1,000 Arab professionals from different sectors receive training in China. As religious and cultural exchanges widen, political and economic ties have also deepened.

China is involved extensively in many areas of economic development in the Middle East, and Chinese presence in the region is unmistakably glaring. For example, more than 100 Chinese state companies are working in Iran to help build infrastructure projects—highways, ports, shipyards, airports, dams, steel complexes and many other projects. A casual visitor to Teheran will be impressed by the supply of Chinese products in the supermarkets and department stores.

The China–Arab Cooperation Forum was first proposed in 2000 by the Arab League Foreign Ministers' Council. The Forum was officially established in January 2004 at a joint press conference with China's then Foreign Minister Li Zhaoxing and Arab League Secretary General Amr Moussa in Egypt. Since then, the China–Arab Cooperation Forum has held biannual ministerial meetings and other associated meetings. At the May 2008 third biannual ministerial Forum meeting in Bahrain, Chinese Foreign Minister Yang Jiechi said that "China and Arab states should make joint efforts to push for a new partnership and achieve peaceful and sustainable development."[48]

In Egypt, the most populous Arab country, China has been invited to participate in the joint development of the Suez Special Economic Zone.[49] China supports Egypt's strong interest in assuming the role of representing Africa and the Middle East alongside the five permanent members of the UN Security Council.

China is also projecting its soft power in the Middle East by promoting Chinese culture. In 2011, Chinese language courses were introduced into the academic curriculum in select Israeli elementary and high schools. The first Confucius Institute in the Middle East was established at St. Joseph University in Beirut, Lebanon in November 2006 to satisfy the growing demand for Chinese-

---

46   Quoted in John Calabrese, "Saudi Arabia and China Extend Ties beyond Oil," *China Brief*, Vol. 5, No. 20 (October 2005).

47   Massoud Hayoun, "Is China Courting American Muslims"? *The National Interest*, July 30, 2012.

48   "China's FM Makes Keynote Speech at China-Arab Forum in Manama," *Xinhua*, May 22, 2008.

49   "China, Egypt and the World," *Beijing Review* http://www.bjreview.com.cn, May 15, 2005.

learning.[50] The Confucius Institutes at Teheran University and Tel Aviv University officially opened in October and November 2007 respectively. The Amman TAG Confucius Institute was established in September 2008 as a cooperation of Talal Abu-Ghazaleh Organization in Jordan and Shenyang Normal University in China. As of late 2012, China had established 11 Confucius Institutes in the Middle East, and more are being planned, including one at Hebrew University in Jerusalem. Modeling on the American University in Cairo, China and Egypt have agreed to establish the Chinese University in Cairo, the first Chinese university in the Middle East. When Cairo University inaugurated its Chinese Department in 2004, China donated some 1,000 books and magazines. Like Saudi Arabia, Egypt often finds moral and political support from China on issues such as human rights and democratic reforms when censured by the United States or international organizations.

China's growing ties with the Middle East are also evident in the financial market. The Bank of China (BOC), China's central bank, was approved to set up a branch in Bahrain in 2004, the BOC's first overseas branch in the Middle East region.[51] The economic allure of China is impossible to ignore, which is perhaps nowhere more obvious than at Dragon Mart in the UAE. The 1.6 million-square-foot shopping complex, nearly three-quarters of a mile long, sprawls more or less in the shape of a dragon along the Dubai-Oman Highway. Inside, some 4,000 Chinese firms offer everything from children's toys and "Double Happiness" cigarettes to forklifts and heavy machinery. This may well be the largest Chinese trading hub outside mainland China.

In July 2009 China set up an Arabic-language TV channel to show the Middle East and North Africa the "real" China amid Chinese complaints that Western media often have distorted coverage of China. CCTV's Arabic channel broadcasts news, entertainment and cultural programs 24 hours a day. The new Arabic channel is accessible for nearly 300 million people in 22 Arabic-speaking countries. It represents the Chinese government's plan to promote its own viewpoints by encouraging state-controlled media organizations to go global. It's also part of the government's efforts to project its soft power around the world.

More Active Involvement in the Middle East Politics

Since the beginning of the 21st century, China has become more actively involved in the Israeli–Arab peace process. Perhaps as a most significant sign of China's deeper involvement in the region, in September 2002, Chinese Foreign Ministry declared to appoint a special envoy to the Middle East "at the request of several

---

50 "Zhongguo yu Zhongdong Guojia Hezuo Jinru Quanmian Fazhan Jieduan (China and Middle Eastern Countries' Cooperation Enter the Stage of Comprehensive Development)," *Xinhua*, December 18, 2006.

51 *The People's Daily* http://english.people.com.cn, April 20, 2004.

Arab states."[52] This was the first time that the Chinese government had appointed a special envoy on foreign affairs in a global region. Senior diplomat Wang Shijie was named the first envoy. Wang, a graduate of the China Foreign Affairs University, had rich experience in the Middle East and North Africa. Between 1990 and 1999, he served as the Chinese ambassador to Bahrain, Jordan, and Iran. Shortly after his appointment as the special envoy, Ambassador Wang visited Israel and all its neighbors and consulted with the special envoys of the Quartet: the United States, Russia, the EU, and the UN.

In April 2006 another senior diplomat Sun Bigan succeeded Wang to become the special envoy on the Middle East. Mr. Sun was previously Chinese ambassador to Saudi Arabia, Iraq, and Iran. China conducted a fresh series of shuttle diplomacy in 2009 to push for the peace process in the Middle East. In June 2009, Beijing's new special envoy to the Middle East Wu Sike traveled to Egypt, the Palestinian territories, Israel, Jordan, Syria, and Lebanon. In July and August 2009 he returned to the Middle East with visits to Algeria, Qatar, Syria and Iran. Wu said China was willing to help ease the tension in the Middle East, improve the relationship between Syria and the United States, and promote direct dialogues between Iran and the United States. When the Israeli–Palestine peace process and US–Iran relations stalemated, countries in the region welcomed China's active involvement.

On December 15, 2006, a symposium on the promotion of peace in the Middle East was held in Beijing. This was the first such international conference initiated and sponsored by Beijing that was attended by officials from both Israel and the Palestine authority. Chinese Foreign Minister Li Zhaoxing met with all participants during the conference. In 2006 Beijing also hosted Palestinian foreign minister and Hamas member Mahmoud Zahar. China has been active in UN activities related to the Middle East, ranging from pre-war arms inspections in Iraq to participation in the UN peacekeeping mission in Lebanon in 2005.

In addition to official activities, Chinese universities and think tanks have held academic events about the Middle East and China–Middle East relations. These institutions include Beijing University, Renmin University of China, Chinese Academy of Social Sciences (CASS), Fudan University, Shanghai International Studies University, and Shanghai Institute of International Studies.

The violence in Syria that started in early 2011 and left about 32,000 dead by the end of 2012 put China in the international limelight again. China has been criticized by some in the West and the Arab world for failing to take a stronger stance on the conflict in which Syrian rebels have been trying to oust President Bashar al-Assad. Although China's previous inaction was consistent with its traditional "non-interference" policy and its preference of political and diplomatic solution over military option, China took a more proactive role in late 2012. In November China issued a four-point proposal to head off an escalation of violence in Syria, including a phased, region-by-region ceasefire

---

52   Chinese Foreign Ministry news conference, September 17, 2002.

and the establishment of a transitional governing body. China has been keen to show that it is not taking sides and has urged the Syrian government to talk to the opposition and take steps to meet demands for political change. It also wants to demonstrate that it is a peaceful and responsible power in world politics.

Assessment

How Influential Is China in the Middle East?

According to Andy Xie, former chief economist at Morgan Stanley Asia, China's daily consumption of oil was expected to reach 14 million barrels soon, bringing Chinese oil consumption to US and European levels.[53] China may decide to produce more energy domestically, but its domestic production capacity is outdated and limited. It will have to import more from other parts of the world. China has two prevailing oil and gas strategies in the first two decades of the 21st century: increasing Middle East oil imports, and purchasing foreign oil properties.[54] This helps explain why Chinese companies have been purchasing oil assets globally since the beginning of the new century, including CNOOC's failed bid to buy the California-based oil company Unocal in the summer of 2005.[55]

The Middle East as a whole has become one of China's major trading partners. Being so late in entering the region—and having less to offer in economic or technological terms than the United States, Russia, Japan, and Europe—China must go after marginal or risky markets including Iran, Iraq, and Sudan where others cannot or will not go, supplying customers no one else will service with goods no one else will sell them.[56] For example, the China–Iran military relationship began during the Iran–Iraq war in the 1980s, when Iran was desperate for any supplies given US sanctions and Soviet reluctance to provide weapons.

In the long-running US–Iran nuclear row, large Western oil companies including Total, Royal Dutch Shell and Eni as well as Japanese companies have put their existing Iranian projects on hold and have avoided signing new deals with Iran. That has left Tehran with little option but to turn for help to countries that are not US allies, including China and Russia. For China Iran's pariah status was an opportunity to exploit a market that would otherwise not exist. China and Russia's unwillingness to further punish Tehran at the UN frustrate Western

---

53 "China and the Middle East," *AME Info* (http://www.ameinfo.com), September 5, 2004.

54 "China's Oil and Gas Import Strategies to 2020," Global Energy and Utilities Market Research, Washington, DC, April, 2001.

55 CNOOC eventually withdrew its bid due to fierce political opposition in Washington, DC. Members of Congress publicly opposed the Chinese bid on national security grounds.

56 Barry Rubin, "China's Middle East Strategy," *Middle East Review of International Affairs*, Vo. 3, No.1 (1999).

efforts to denuclearize Iran. As long as China needs Iran to help meet its huge energy demand, it is unlikely that China will join Western efforts to isolate Iran.

China's presence is largely perceived as non-ideological, economically oriented and pragmatic. Despite the fact that China has tremendously increased its presence in Middle Eastern politics and economics since the mid-1990s, there is little concern in the region that China's increasing status as a world power will constitute a threat. "Hegemony, domination, imperialism are associated with the United States and Europe. China is not seen that way," commented Sami Baroudi, a political scientist at Lebanese American University, "Arabs appreciate its economic might, but don't see it as a political threat."[57] In an interview with China's *People's Daily* in June 2004, Syrian President Bashar al-Assad said, "China is now a superpower and is very important after the absence of the Soviet Union. China's role has expanded across the world and has become more important especially for small countries including Syria."[58]

China's influence is steadily growing in the Middle East. In a 2011 release of the DC-based community-advocacy organization Arab American Institute (AAI) polling data from Morocco, Egypt, Lebanon, Jordan, Saudi Arabia and the UAE, all but Saudi Arabia had a more favorable opinion of China than of the United States. Morocco, Egypt, Jordan and the UAE had opinions of China five times higher, while Lebanon's opinion of China was three times higher than that of the United States.[59]

The Libyan crisis of 2011 illustrated the extent of Chinese involvement in the Middle East and Africa. As Libyan rebel forces and NATO warplanes worked to oust Muammar Gaddafi from power, China mobilized civilian and military aircraft along with foreign planes and ships to rescue 36,000 Chinese workers and return them safely to China. To protect ships ferrying Chinese workers from Libya, China also dispatched naval ships to the Mediterranean Sea off the Libyan coast for temporary assignment from their anti-piracy deployment off the Somali coast in the Gulf of Aden. In addition to demonstrating China's new power projection capabilities, the crisis revealed the risks of China's engagement in fragile regions.

In August 2012, two months after taking office as the first freely elected president of Egypt, Mohamed Morsi visited China. It was Morsi's first state visit outside the Middle East and Africa since becoming president, underscoring China's importance as one of five permanent members of the UN Security Council and as a vital source of trade and investment. China pledged $200 million in credit for the National Bank of Egypt and the two countries signed agreements on agriculture, telecommunications, the environment and other areas. Morsi was preceded to Beijing by a delegation of 80 Egyptian business leaders. The wealthy Chinese tourists are also expected to contribute to the recovery of Egypt's tourism industry.

---

57   Quoted in Wenran Jiang, "China's Growing Energy Relations with the Middle East," *China Brief*, Vol. 7, No. 14 (July 11, 2007), p. 13.

58   *Syrian Arab News Agency* (SANA), June 21, 2004.

59   The survey was conducted by Zogby International. The full report can be accessed at http://www.aaiusa.org/reports/arab-attitudes-2011/

China has been involved in Afghanistan's post-war reconstruction and peacebuilding. To prepare for the planned withdrawal of US-led NATO forces from Afghanistan in 2014, China began to train hundreds of Afghan police officers in 2012. In May 2004 China's UN mission raised a proposal to enhance the Iraqi government's power by setting a date for a US military withdrawal. Russia, France, and Germany supported China's proposal, which was reflected in the final text of UN Security Council Resolution 1546.[60] For China watchers, Beijing's actions were significant because China's Middle East policy had been passive in the past and China has seldom raised its own proposals on issues regarding the Middle East. One expects that China will play a bigger political and diplomatic role in the Middle East.

Nevertheless, China's influence in the Middle East is still limited and is overwhelmed by America's stronger ties with key players in the region. For example, Israel's relations with the United States seem more important than any other relations it has. Israel-US relations are built upon shared democratic values and common strategic interests. In the future, however, as Chinese–Israeli relations continue to strengthen, Israel risks finding itself between a rock and a hard place. Some have suggested that, for its own interests, Israel should explore the role of mediating differences between China and the United States.[61]

For some, China is still not a mature or trusted power yet. Analyst Abdel Moneim Said at the Al-Ahram Center for Strategic and Political Studies in Cairo commented that "China is giving two bad lessons to the Middle East. Number one: Violating human rights has nothing to do with development; you can have both. The second is that highly centralized political power does not mean necessarily an impediment for progress. ... Usually China is used as an example against local reformers."[62] Furthermore, American actions continue to determine the limits of Chinese activity in the Middle East. The US war in Iraq meant that China lost supplies from a 26-year oil production field contract it had signed with the Baghdad government in 1997.[63] Without a blue water navy, China remains uncomfortably dependent on US naval power to ensure the safety of its tankers to and from the Middle East.

The positions of China and many Middle Eastern countries on some key issues diverge, including on the uprisings in the Middle East and the crisis in Syria.

---

60 The Resolution begins with "The Security Council, welcoming the beginning of a new phrase in Iraq's transition to a democratically elected government, and looking forward to the end of the occupation and the assumption of full responsibility and authority by a fully sovereign and independent Interim Government of Iraq by June 30, 2004...."

61 See for example Shai Feldman, "China's Security: Implications for Israel," *Strategic Assessment*, Vol. 2, No. 4, Jaffee Center for Strategic Studies, Tel Aviv University, February 2000.

62 Peter Kenyon, "Political Factors Complicate China's Clout in Mideast," *National Public Radio* www.npr.org, All Things Considered, April 4, 2008.

63 "China and the Middle East," *AME Info* (http://www.ameinfo.com), September 5, 2004.

China's principled advocacy of non-intervention in other nations' internal affairs clashes with many regional countries' activist foreign policy and call for armed military intervention to oust the Syrian regime.

While China has penetrated into the Middle East on all fronts, the United States maintains the dominant external political, military and cultural actor in the Middle East. China's gain is not necessarily America's loss. For one thing, China cannot provide the security guarantees that the United States has to most of the countries in the region. But undoubtedly, countries in the region have become increasingly attracted by China's development and the opportunities it brings about. "We are in a Catholic marriage with America," said Omar Bahlaiwa, secretary general for the Committee for International Trade, a branch of the Saudi Chambers of Commerce, emphasizing that divorce is unthinkable. "But we are also Muslims—we can have more than one wife," he quickly added, referring to the importance and attractiveness of China.[64]

Following its traditional "non interference" policy, China does not meddle into internal affairs of other countries. China's growing influence in the Middle East is generally well received by countries in the region, and many Middle Eastern countries expect China to play a bigger role in regional issues. Increasingly Middle Eastern countries are beginning to turn to China for help in conflict resolution. For example, Egyptian Assistant Foreign Minister Ezzat Saad said that "China has become very much involved in the Middle East process and (Egypt) expects it to play a more active role."[65] Israeli President Moshe Katsav has also remarked that China has very good relations with both Israel and the Arab world. It can contribute positively to the relations between Israel and the Arab world.[66]

China seems ready to be playing a more constructive role in the Middle East peace process. In late October 2007 Beijing received two visitors from the Middle East: Israeli Foreign Minister Tzipi Livni and Jordan's King Abdullah II. Livni visited China in an effort to lobby Beijing for its support to impose tougher sanctions against Iran. Meanwhile, King Abdullah II urged China to take a more active role in helping broker peace in the Middle East. China's growing influence could speed up a resolution of the Israel-Palestinian conflict and other lingering regional tensions, Abdullah said at the start of a closed-door meeting with Chinese President Hu Jintao. He said he hoped for a stronger Chinese role because "you are always considered an honest broker and are very well-respected in our part of the world."[67] In May 2013 China simultaneously hosted Palestinian President

---

64 "Avoiding Political Talk, Saudis and Chinese Build Trade," *The New York Times*, April 23, 2006.

65 "China's Participation in Middle East Peace Process Welcomed: Egyptian Assistant FM," *The People's Daily*, November 23, 2004.

66 "Israeli President Expects China to Contribute More to Mideast Peace Process," *The People's Daily*, December 14, 2003.

67 "No Sign of Iran Sanction Breakthrough Following Israeli Foreign Minister's China Visit," *The Associated Press*, October 30, 2007.

Mahmoud Abbas and Israeli Prime Minister Benjamin Netanyahu. Either willingly or unwillingly, it seems that China is set to play a more prominent role in the Middle East peace process.

Implications for the United States

Comparatively speaking, the Middle East is more important to China than to the United States as an oil supplier. Three of the top four suppliers of oil to the United States are in the Western Hemisphere (Canada, Mexico, and Venezuela), which currently comprise over 48 percent of total US petroleum imports, and Saudi Arabia only supplies about 8 percent of total US demand.[68] The Middle East as a region has been China's largest supplier of oil since the early 1990s. In 1998 and 1999, for example, the import from there accounted for about 60 percent of the total Chinese oil imports,[69] though since 2000 China has attempted to diversify sources of energy and has increased imports from Africa, Latin America, Central Asia and other regions. Still, in 2004 more than 45 percent of China's oil imports came from the Middle East, with China's top three oil suppliers comprising Saudi Arabia, Oman, and Iran.[70] Given the global oil reserve and production pattern, the Middle East's status as China's leading oil supplier will unlikely change any time soon. If the US side can appreciate the Middle East's critical role for China's energy needs, perhaps it will understand why China has been actively engaged in the region. But if the United States perceives China's activities as threats to US interests, then the two great powers will be set on a collision course in the Middle East.

In fact, energy shortage is a challenge not just for China. In 2012, India vaulted to the top of the list of Iran's oil customers, overtaking China. Iran sells most of its oil exports in Asia, where China, India, Japan and South Korea are the biggest buyers. So as they continue to impose sanctions on Iran and punish those companies that do business with Iran, the United States and the EU have to address the energy needs of these economies.

There is no evidence suggesting that the Chinese engagement with the Middle East is designed to undermine US interests or to challenge US dominance in the region. On the one hand, China wants a peaceful and stable Middle East to ensure a steady source of oil and to avoid entanglement in the region's conflict. It focuses on trade and economic development and does not intend to undermine US interests in the region. On the other hand, China does not want to give up

---

68   Robert E. Ebel, "US Foreign Policy, Petroleum and the Middle East," testimony before the subcommittee on Near Eastern and Asian Affairs, US Senate Committee on Foreign Relations, 31 October, 2005.

69   Xiaojie Xu, "China and the Middle East: Cross-investment in the Energy Sector," *The Middle East Policy Council Journal*, Vol. 2, No. 3 (June 2000).

70   David Zweig and Bi Jianhai, "China's Global Hunt for Energy," *Foreign Affairs*, Vol. 84, No. 5 (September/October 2005), 28.

lucrative relationships with Iran and Iraq, or see a region so dominated by the United States that there is no room for a Chinese economic or diplomatic role. It is these competing Chinese interests and policies that contribute to the complication of US–China relations.

Increasing energy demand is drawing China into deeper involvement in politically volatile regions around the world. From the US perspective, China's foray into traditional America's spheres of influence—the Middle East, Latin America, and Africa—is a source of concern. Already, many conservative forces in the United States are debating what to do about this new type of "China threat." Strategically speaking, the United States is deeply uncomfortable with China's growing activities in regions where the United States has enjoyed a near monopoly on international influence since the end of the Cold War.

China and the United States have different interests in Iran. While Washington does not permit Iran to go nuclear, Beijing's attitude is more ambivalent. It appears that China supports Iran's right to peaceful nuclear technology but opposes it developing and possessing nuclear weapons. China has strong economic interests in Iran since Teheran is a top oil exporter to China. However, China is also trying not to confront the United States directly in the region. For example, despite its long-standing opposition, along with Russia's and India's, to UN sanctions on Iran for Iran's alleged nuclear program, China agreed with other four permanent members of the UN Security Council and Germany to report Iran to the Security Council over its nuclear program when Iran failed to account for its alleged nuclear activities to the International Atomic Energy Agency (IAEA) by March 2006.[71] During a meeting with visiting Israeli Prime Minister Ehud Olmert in January 2007, Chinese Premier Wen Jiabao was reported as saying that China opposed Iran having a nuclear arsenal.[72] Wen made a similar statement in Doha in January 2012. This was encouraging for Western countries in their efforts to prevent nuclear proliferation in the Middle East. Yet on other occasions, the Chinese government has suggested it does not oppose countries developing nuclear technology for peaceful purposes.

The United States has routinely renewed embargoes on doing industrial-scale business with Iran since the 1990s, even barring foreign companies that do more than $10 million a year of business with the Islamic Republic from operating in the US.[73] But many companies still do business with Iran, especially from the rapidly expanding Asian economic and political powerhouses of India and China and in countries with few commercial ties to the United States, such as Russia, which underscores the difficulty of using economic sanctions to pressure Tehran to bow to Washington's demands on its nuclear program. Without offering

---

71   "Iran to Be Reported to Security Council," *The Washington Post*, January 31, 2006.

72   "China Assures Israeli Prime Minister on Iranian Nuclear Bomb," *AFP*, January 10, 2007.

73   "Iran Signs $3.2 billion Natural Gas Deal with China," *Los Angeles Times*, March 15, 2009.

viable alternatives for Iran's trade partners, it will be difficult for the US to ask these countries such as China and India to curtail their oil imports from Iran. For Beijing, Iran also provides important diplomatic leverage over Washington. China's support for Iran serves as "a check against Washington in response to the US military presence in East Asia and its constellation of allies and partners surrounding Chinese territory," observed Chris Zambelis.[74]

China remains a relatively new player in the Middle Eastern oilfields and politics. For obvious economic and strategic reasons, China needs to maintain a good relationship with the United States, after all the US navy remains in control of the sea lanes for oil routes from the Persian Gulf to the Strait of Malacca, where about 80 percent of China's energy imports pass. As the United States pursues its fight against terrorism in the Middle East, China's involvement in the region, especially its close relations with countries hostile to America, may pose serious challenge to US interests. Would it be wise for the United States to counterbalance China's newfound influence in the Middle East? The answer is no. Despite Washington's concerns over China's outreach to the Middle East, the United States and China share several key interests in the region: seeking energy security, opposing terrorism, and supporting Arab–sraeli peace. And most importantly, both countries support a stable Middle East where their economic and strategic interests can be protected. The US–Chinese competition is clearly not built on the zero-sum model of the US–Soviet conflict during the Cold War. Today, China and the United States depend on each other for economic prosperity and international security. This interdependent relationship compels them to seek cooperation, not conflict. Furthermore, it is unlikely that the United States would succeed in finding countries in the region to support its opposition to Chinese influence.

China's global hunt for energy is clearly driven by its domestic growth needs. Though China is not engaged in a strategic or power competition with the United States in the Middle East, if its key interests are undermined by the United States, China may be forced to become more aggressive in its foreign policy such as being more proactive in its pursuit of oil from Iran and Sudan, which may pose a more serious challenge for the United States. CNOOC's bid to acquire Unocal in 2005, which eventually failed with strong opposition from US Congress, feeds the fear that the United States does not allow China equal and reliable access to the world's energy market. The growing threat of UN sanctions on Iran and Sudan, which between them supply some 20 percent of China's oil imports, puts Beijing in an awkward situation of having to choose between safeguarding its economic interests and protecting the country's international image. If oil imports from Iran were cut off by sanctions, China would be forced to extend its demand to other suppliers and look for oil elsewhere. Therefore, the United States has to work with China to give it a sense of energy security and shared interests in a stable energy market.

---

74   Chris Zambelis, "China's Persian Gulf Diplomacy Reflects Delicate Balancing Act," *China Brief*, Vol. XII, Issue 4 (February 21, 2012), p. 4.

Is there anything the United States can do to alleviate its own concerns and help overcome the energy shortage in China? Absolutely. For one thing, the United States can help China become more energy efficient. If China used its energy more efficiently, it would have less need to obtain oil from countries that the United States wishes to contain. The US–China Energy Efficiency Steering Committee was established as a result of the Protocol for Cooperation in the Fields of Energy Efficiency and Renewable Energy Technology Development and Utilization signed in February 1995 between US Department of Energy and China's State Science and Technology Commission. Such efforts should be further promoted.

The United States can also take a more positive step to collaborate with China in developing alternative energies. Nuclear energy and liquefied natural gas are two obvious options. With its advanced technology, the United States is well positioned to provide assistance to China in the fields of new energy and environmental protection. Cooperation with China on reducing oil dependency will benefit both countries. Furthermore, it will benefit the entire international community when developing countries are able to reduce the cost of modernization and improve development efficiency as a result of collaborating efforts between the United States and China.

Concluding Remarks

Long a bystander in Middle Eastern politics, China has become increasingly active, driven by its need for oil and gas, and its economic importance to the region has ballooned amid Europe's economic woes and the sluggish US recovery. There is a growing "China fever" in the Middle East. In addition to an increasing number of people in the region studying Chinese now, Middle Eastern investors who find it harder to conduct business in the West are increasingly sending their money east. Dubai-based DP World, for example, is now funding a half-billion dollar port project in China. Tens of billions of dollars' worth of oil projects are under way. Inexpensive Chinese cars are selling as fast as they arrive in Egypt, and, to the dismay of Egyptian craftspeople, most souvenirs now come with a "Made in China" sticker.[75] Step by step, China has increased its presence and expanded its influence in the Middle East since the 1990s. As its power continues to grow, China is likely and even expected to play a bigger role in Middle Eastern politics and economics.

The era of China's passive role in the Middle East is over. China's diplomatic and economic efforts in the Middle East have been largely successful; it maintains good relations with virtually every country in the region, ranging from America's close allies such as Israel and Saudi Arabia to intensely anti-American countries such as Iran. Though China's activities in the Middle East are commercially driven, it has become more involved in political, security and other issues, and

---

75   Kenyon, "Political Factors Complicate China's Clout in Mideast," April 4, 2008.

has enhanced soft power in the region. China has the potential and is expected to play a much larger political role in the Middle East especially in the Israeli–Arab conflict and the Iranian nuclear controversy. Maintaining good relations with all countries in the region, China can position itself as an honest broker on many issues. To become a more respectable growing power, China can and should take advantage of its good reputation in the region to do more to promote long-term peace between Israel and its Arab neighbors and to help resolve the stalemate in the Iran nuclear crisis and Syria's civil conflicts.

From the US perspective, China's involvement in the Middle Eastern political economy may have some negative and destabilizing effects. But the United States and China share many common goals in the region and there are prospects for cooperation between them on energy, peace, security, and other issues. Most significantly, the two countries have a common interest in the stability of the Middle East. It is premature to declare that the Middle East will become a new battleground for China and the United States to compete for power and control.

Many international and regional problems cannot be solved without cooperation between China and the United States. For the United States, paranoia about a coming China threat and a misguided policy based on this assumption will be the wrong choice. China is already heavily involved in Middle Eastern political economy. The US strategic calculations in the Middle East will have to take Chinese interests into consideration. It is impossible for the West to exclude or isolate China from the region. What the United States can do now is to actively engage China, address China's legitimate needs and concerns, and work with other powers to ensure the rise of a peaceful and responsible China in the future. Only by doing so can the two countries establish a constructive relationship and lay a solid foundation for future cooperation in international and regional affairs, including the Middle East issue.

Questions for Discussion

1. How does the Middle East serve China's geopolitical and geoeconomic interests?
2. Why does China seem to enjoy a more favourable view than the United States in many Middle Eastern countries? What is the implication?
3. How does China manage to maintain good relations with both Israel and Arab countries?
4. What challenges do Iran and Syria present to China and US–China relations?
5. How has China built up its influence in the Middle East? What can China do to play a bigger and more positive role in the region?

Chapter 4
China and Latin America

China–Latin America relations can be traced back to the Ming Dynasty (1368–1644).[1] China's silk, porcelain and cotton yarn were shipped to Mexico and Peru as early as the middle of the Ming Dynasty. The Latin America-oriented agricultural plants, such as corn, potato, peanut, sunflower, tomato and tobacco, made their way into China and have become China's popular agricultural products. There is also a claim that during a seafaring adventure some 600 years ago, the great Chinese sailor Zheng He and his fleet discovered the American continent 70 years earlier than Columbus.[2] But the first official ties between China and Latin American countries were established between the 1870s and 1900s, when China's last dynasty, the Qing Dynasty (1644–1911), forged diplomatic relations with Peru, Brazil, Mexico, Cuba and Panama.

Due to geographic distance and differences in language, history and culture, Latin America had not been on Beijing's list of foreign-policy priorities after the PRC was established in 1949, and bilateral contacts had been limited since most countries still maintained formal relations with the ROC that retreated to Taiwan. The PRC normalized diplomatic ties with most countries in the region in the 1970s and 1980s. It was during the 1990s that close cooperation between the two sides in various fields registered momentous growth. Since the beginning of the 21st century, China has practiced an active diplomacy towards Latin America. The two sides have enjoyed frequent high-level exchanges, strong economic and political ties and friendly cooperation in trade, science and technology, culture and education, and mutual support in international affairs. China published its first policy paper on Latin America in November 2008 to show its seriousness about the region.

---

1   Latin America refers to the territories in the Americas where the Spanish or Portuguese languages prevail: Mexico, most of Central and South America, Cuba, the Dominican Republic, Puerto Rico, and countries in the Caribbean. The term is often used, particularly in the United States, to refer to all of the Americas south of the United States, thus including (in addition to the above areas) English-speaking countries such as Belize, Jamaica, Barbados, Trinidad and Tobago, and the Bahamas. In this book, Latin America is used to cover all the 33 countries south of the United States. When discussing specific countries in the Caribbean, the term "Caribbean" is sometimes used.

2   Gavin Menzies, *1421: The Year China Discovered America* (Harper Perennial, 2004). Menzies, a former submarine commander in Britain's Royal Navy, claims that not only did the Chinese discover America first, but they also established a number of subsequently lost colonies in the Caribbean. He asserts that the Chinese circumnavigated the globe, desalinated water, and perfected the art of cartography. In fact, he believes that most of the renowned European explorers actually sailed with maps charted by the Chinese.

As part of its strategy to diversify energy sources and export markets, China has been purchasing oil, minerals and crops across the region while investing there. Trade between China and Latin America jumped from less than $3 billion in 1988 to over $240 billion in 2011. (See Table 4.1) Since China joined the WTO in 2001, Latin American exports to China have grown by more than 1,000 percent.[3] China aims to propel trade with the region to $400 billion by 2017.

Though the United States had dominated the regional economy and trade for decades after World War II, China is now the largest trade partner of major Latin American economies including Brazil, Argentina, Peru and Chile. Latin America's trade with China is still less than its trade with the United States or the EU, but the trend is clear and the jump is unrivaled.

According to UN figures, in 2007 nearly 40 percent of Chile's exports went to the Asia–Pacific region, mostly China. For Peru, the figure was 19 percent.[4] As a sign of its growing trade with the region, China has signed free trade agreements (FTAs) with several countries:

- Chile was the first non-Asian country to sign a FTA with China in 2005.
- Peru and China signed a FTA in 2008.
- Costa Rica and China signed a FTA in 2010.

China's rapid economic growth has created a dramatic increase in its demand for many raw materials and foodstuffs and has led it to look to Latin America as a source of key commodities. Seeking energy and raw materials has become a top objective of the new Chinese diplomacy in Latin America and the Caribbean. Latin America has huge potential as a major source of energy for emerging economies like China and India. Although China has tapped energy resources in Venezuela, Colombia, Ecuador and Peru and has begun to tap Argentina and Bolivia, there exists significant room for expansion, especially given that China still depends heavily on the Middle Eastern oil and wishes to diversify its oil imports.

China has increased investment in Latin America and the Caribbean, particularly in the fields of manufacturing, infrastructure, energy, minerals, agriculture and

Table 4.1   Sino-Latin American trade volume: selected years (in billions of US dollars)

Year	1988	1995	2000	2003	2005	2007	2008	2010	2011
Volume	2.8	6.1	13	26.8	50	102.6	143.4	178.9	241.5

Sources: 1) The General Administration of Customs of China (http://english.customs.gov.cn), various years. 2) *Xinhua, The Associated Press*, and *Reuters* reports, various years.

---

3   "Latin America: Exports to China Slowing Down," *VOXXI The Voice of Hispanic 21st Century* (www.voxxi.com), July 24, 2012.

4   James Painter, "China Deepens Latin America Ties," *BBC*, November 21, 2008.

tourism. Beijing has proposed establishing a China–Latin America cooperation forum to further enhance political mutual trust and strategic cooperation. China has diplomatic relations with 21 (of 33) Latin American countries. More recently, Beijing has been promoting the Chinese language and culture in the region as part of its soft power enhancing efforts.

Motivations Behind China's New Diplomacy in Latin America

Seeking Energy and Other Resources as well as Export and Investment Markets

China has identified Latin America as one of the three major regions (together with Russia/Central Asia and the Middle East/Africa) that may become China's key energy suppliers. Securing reliable access to petroleum products from Latin America is an important element of China's engagement in the region, especially with Venezuela, Brazil, Colombia, and Ecuador. In addition to oil, Chinese interests have included Chile's copper, Jamaican bauxite, Cuban nickel, Bolivia's tin as well as iron, asphalt, and soybeans from the region. China is the leading importer of Trinidadian asphalt, used to pave many Chinese highways and airport runways.

A founder of OPEC, Venezuela has one of the largest oil and natural gas reserves in the world. The country also has abundant resources in hydroelectricity, minerals, aquifers, agriculture, forestry, climate and soil diversity, and biodiversity in flora and fauna. China used to import only small quantities of oil from Venezuela while the United States absorbed two thirds of its oil exports. The major reason is that China lacks the refining technology needed to process Venezuela's heavy crude, but the potential cooperation between the two countries is enormous. In December 2004 President Hugo Chávez traveled to China to sign 19 cooperation agreements, including plans for Chinese investment in oil and gas exploration. CNPC, which already operates two Venezuelan oilfields, agreed to spend additional $400 million in developing Venezuelan oil and gas reserves.

The Jieyang (揭阳) refinery in Guangdong, the first of the three that will be built jointly by the two countries, began construction in April 2012. Venezuela is exploring plans to rebuild a pipeline to Panama to pump crude oil to the Pacific, where it would be loaded onto supertankers that are too big to use the Panama Canal. Venezuela and Colombia are also considering the construction of a pipeline across Colombia to carry Venezuelan hydrocarbons, which would then be shipped to Asia from Colombia's Pacific ports.

By 2011, Venezuela had increased its supply of crude oil and products to more than 422,000 barrels a day to China. The goal is to reach a daily supply of one million by 2014.[5] Bilateral trade exceeded $9 billion in 2008, from less than $200 million a decade ago. In 2011 it reached $18 billion and topped $23 billion in 2012.

---

5   "Energy Powering Close Bilateral Ties," *China Daily*, June 28, 2012: p. S3.

In September 2008 Chávez made his fifth trip to China since 1999. During his visit the two countries signed a dozen agreements, including one on doubling a joint investment fund to $12 billion and another on extending energy cooperation. Chávez said the two countries had agreed on plans for a fleet of four oil tankers and one refinery to process Venezuela's heavy crude oil.

As of 2012, a total of 460 official agreements have been signed between China and Venezuela, 98 percent of which have been finalized.[6] The Venezuela-China High Level Commission, founded by the two governments in 2001, is the mechanism in charge of following up on these agreements, which cover virtually every field of cooperation possible between the two countries. The two countries started their strategic partnership in 2001. It initially focused on two issues: energy and agriculture. Since then the partnership has evolved, becoming more complex and diversified.

Between 2007 and 2012, the China Development Bank lent Venezuela a total of $42.5 billion, which accounted for nearly a quarter of the bank's overseas loans.[7] The Chinese also built railways, daycare centers, housing, energy and agricultural projects for Venezuela. Loans from China helped Chavez to keep his promises to increase government spending to fuel economic growth, which apparently aided his re-election for the third time in 2012.

In 1960 Cuba became the first country in Latin America to recognize the PRC, but Fidel Castro's alignment with the Soviet Union during the Cold War strained his government's ties with Beijing. After the disintegration of the Soviet Union, China–Cuban relations greatly improved. In early 2005 the Cuba Oil Company Cubapetróleo signed a production contract with Sinopec to work in areas around the Cuban island believed to contain oil deposits. Economic and trade cooperation between the two countries have developed quickly, particularly after a two-day visit to Cuba by Chinese President Hu Jintao in November 2004, during which a number of bilateral cooperation agreements were signed. Trade between the two has burgeoned, growing from $590 million in 2004 to $1.8 billion in 2010, making China Cuba's second largest trading partner, next only to Venezuela. Major Chinese imports from Cuba include nickel and sugar. Since Cuba faces difficulty in drawing investment from the West, closer China–Cuba economic ties constitute strong support for its economic development.

Brazil and China are grouped together in the so-called BRICS (Brazil, Russia, India, China and South Africa) nations which have some of the most dynamic emerging markets today. Brazil and China established diplomatic relations in 1974, but trade boom has taken place only since the late 1990s. In 2002 China surpassed Japan as Brazil's largest trade partner in Asia, and in 2009 it overtook the US as Brazil's leading trade partner and its largest export market. In recent years Brazilians have made up one of the largest contingent of buyers at the biannual Canton Fair in China.

---

6 "Venezuela, China: 38 Years of Diplomatic Relations," *China Daily*, June 28, 2012: p. S1.

7 "Chavez's Most Helpful Campaign Aide: China," *Bloomberg BusinessWeek*, October 8–14, 2012: pp. 14–15.

According to Brazil's Ministry of Development, Industry and Trade, trade with China quintupled from 2000 to 2004, exceeding $12 billion in 2004. Brazil supplies 30 percent of China's total soybean imports and 16 percent of China's total imports of iron ore concentrates. China prefers Brazil's genetically unmodified soybeans to modified ones in the United States.[8] It has become a top destination of Brazilian oil exports, with shipments of over 50,000 barrels per day. During his 2004 visit to Brazil, President Hu announced a $10 billion energy deal with Brazil for investments in energy and transport infrastructure over the following two years. This supplemented plans for a $1.3 billion deal between China's Sinopec and Brazil's Petróbras for a 2,000 kilometer natural gas pipeline. In 2010, Sinopec bought 40 percent stake in Repsol Brazil with $7.1 billion, and in 2012, it acquired 30 percent of Petrogal Brasil for $5.2 billion.

As a developing nation that is becoming more conscious of protecting the environment and using energy efficiently, China is very interested in emulating Brazil's success in ethanol. From 2000 to 2005, China developed ethanol production capacity of a million tons per year—which it planned to double in a few years.[9]

China and Brazil formed what they call "all-weather strategic partnership" during President Hu's 2004 visit. Beyond commerce, both countries share a desire to take up a more active role in international politics. Policymakers from the two countries are pushing for a stronger say in multilateral institutions like the IMF and both governments are vocal on environmental issues, insisting that they cannot be expected to bear the same obligations as wealthier countries.

China and Brazil offer political and diplomatic support to each other. Brazil supports the "one-China" policy and backs China's bid for membership in the Inter-American Development Bank (IADB). Chinese peacekeepers in Haiti served under the command of a Brazilian general under UN auspices. Meanwhile, Brazil seeks China's support for permanent membership at the UN Security Council.

Argentina is another one of China's most important "strategic partners" in Latin America. China is particularly interested in purchasing soybeans from Argentina. It is Argentina's largest trade partner with bilateral trade surpassing $10 billion for the first time in 2008. Chinese companies have invested in coal mining in Rio Negro province and in infrastructure in the area of the trans-Andean crossing in San Juan province. China has invested $5 billion in Argentina's offshore petroleum projects.

In 1970 Chile became the first South American country to recognize the PRC (second in Latin America after Cuba). China has great interest in Chile's copper. China currently accounts for 40 percent of the global copper consumption of 19 million tons per year, most of which comes from Latin America. The metal, used in electronics and cabling, is Chile's top export and Peru's third. Trade between China, the world's

---

8   Jorge Dominguez, "China's Relations with Latin America: Shared Gains, Asymmetric Hopes," Working Paper, *Inter-American Dialogue*, June 2006, p. 27.

9   Xuecheng Liu, "China's Energy Security and Its Grand Strategy," *Policy Analysis Brief*, The Stanley Foundation, September 2006.

largest user of copper, and Chile, the world's biggest copper producer, has increased rapidly since the beginning of 2000s, making China the Andean country's biggest trading partner now. Chile was one of the first Latin American countries, along with Brazil and Argentina, to recognize China as a "market economy." Bilateral trade has grown even faster since October 2006, when their FTA took effect. It reached around $30 billion by 2012. China and Chile elevated their ties to a strategic partnership in 2012 with a target of doubling bilateral trade to $60 billion by 2015.[10]

Sino-Chilean cooperation also includes science and technology, mining and geosciences, plant quarantine, space technology, forestry, tourism, education, telecommunications, and military exchanges. China is interested in strengthening the role of Chile's deepwater ports as a platform for boosting trade between China and South America.

China and Peru inked a formal FTA during President Hu's visit to Lima, ahead of the annual APEC forum in Peru in November 2008. The FTA came into effect in March 2010. Thanks to the FTA, in 2011 bilateral trade reached over $13 billion, making China Peru's largest commercial partner. Peru is one of the world's top producers of silver, copper and zinc. The FTA will eventually eliminate tariffs on about 90 percent of goods traded between the two countries. The Chinese Development Bank and about 80 Chinese businesses agreed to pour cash into mining, infrastructure, logging, fishing, and tourism projects in Peru during President Alan Garcia's visit to China in March 2008.

China has turned to Latin America — mainly Argentina and Brazil — as a major source of its food imports. In 2003 Latin America accounted for about a third of China's agricultural imports, with Argentina representing about 15 percent and Brazil about 14 percent of China's total agricultural imports.[11] Much of this trade has been in soy-based products such as tofu.

While exports from the region to China are concentrated in food and raw materials, China's principal exports to Latin America include textiles, apparel, shoes, machinery, televisions, and plastics. Mexico is one of China's principal export markets in Latin America and China is a significant foreign direct investor in Mexico. In 2004 the stock of accumulated Chinese investment in Mexico exceeded $28 billion, with clothing manufacturing accounting for a third and plastic products nearly a fourth of the total.[12]

Amid the global financial crisis since 2008, some foreign companies have canceled their projects abroad, but that is not the case for China. China continues to purchase and invest in Latin America. There is no sign that its voracious appetite for raw materials will diminish any time soon. In May 2008 China signed a $2.2 billion deal to extract more than 7 million tons of copper ore from a single bald Peruvian peak known as Toromocho. In the same year China began negotiating to build a $3 billion steel mill in Brazil, where the Bank of China

10 "China, Chile Expected to Double Trade," *China Daily*, June 28, 2012: p.11.
11 Dominguez, "China's Relations with Latin America," p. 19.
12 Ibid, pp. 37–8.

opened a branch in 2009 with $100 million in initial lending capital. And it has also invested in oil exploration in Ecuador, Colombia and Venezuela.[13]

China considers Latin America and the Caribbean as a new market for its own products. For example, the Haier Group, China's top home appliance maker, expects its overseas sales to grow as much as 50 percent annually in the near future.[14] China's other leading electric home appliances producers, such as Lenovo and TCL, are also setting up factories in Latin America to produce television sets, DVD players, computers and mobile phones. The Chinese government encourages and supports Chinese companies to invest in manufacturing, agriculture, forestry, fishing, energy, mineral resources, infrastructure, and service sectors in Latin America and the Caribbean to promote the economic and social development of both sides. By the end of 2008, more than 400 Chinese companies had been registered to do business in Latin America.[15]

More recently China has expanded its exports to Latin America beyond the traditional consumer products. For example, Changchun Railway Vehicles Co., Ltd. exported subway trains to Argentina in April 2012, achieving a dominant position in the South American market through its presence in Argentina and a separate project in Brazil.

China has also entered the Latin American auto market. According to AT Kearney consultants, Chinese car makers exported half a million cars worldwide in 2011, and will accelerate to as many as two million by 2015 and three million by 2020. The fastest-growing destination for these exports is Latin America, where overall car unit sales in countries like Brazil, Colombia, Peru and Argentina have grown sharply in recent years. While Chinese models are scarce in North America, some 16 brands including Chery, Foton, Great Wall, Geely and Yangtze are now sold in Latin America.[16] Chinese automobiles have the price advantage. For example, one can by a brand new Chery QQ compact in Colombia for about US$9,000. Compared with the US and European markets, Latin America markets are less competitive and demanding in terms of quality and emissions standards, which offers more opportunities for Chinese-made automobiles.

Isolating Taiwan Diplomatically

For decades, the PRC and Taiwan have used dollar diplomacy to win over small Latin American and Caribbean nations. Beijing is opposed to formal diplomatic

---

13   "Slowdown Doesn't Shrink China's LatAm Ambitions," *The Associated Press*, November 17, 2008.

14   "China's Haier Says Sales Abroad to Grow 50% a Year," *Reuters*, March 19, 2008.

15   "Slowdown Doesn't Shrink China's LatAm Ambitions," *The Associated Press*, November 17, 2008.

16   "Hitting the Accelerator: China's Automakers Race to Latin America," Knowledge at Wharton (www.knowledgeatwharton.com.cn), February 1, 2012, accessed July 26, 2012.

ties between Taiwan and other governments, not to their non-governmental economic and cultural exchanges. Out of the 23 countries that recognize Taiwan as of 2013, 12 are in the Western Hemisphere and all but Paraguay are in Central America and the Caribbean.[17]

China has been courting these countries in an effort to further isolate Taiwan internationally. Beijing and Taipei frequently offer inducements to get countries to switch sides. Though Taiwan succeeded in winning over St. Lucia in April 2007 which dropped its ties with Taiwan in 1997, China quickly and quietly doubled its efforts to win Latin American and Caribbean countries away from Taiwan. China has established trade missions and/or placed official *Xinhua* news agency journalists in most of those countries that still maintain official ties with Taiwan such as Panama, the Dominican Republic and Haiti. Given Beijing's growing power and influence, it is a matter of time before some of them decide to switch recognition from Taipei to Beijing.

In June 2007 Costa Rica recognized China diplomatically after years of allying itself with Taiwan. China immediately rewarded Costa Rica by agreeing to jointly explore for oil and natural gas in Costa Rica. According to Costa Rican President Oscar Arias who paid an official visit to China in October 2007, China would build an oil refinery in Costa Rica to help the Central American nation address its energy needs.[18] China agreed to buy $300 million in Costa Rican bonds as part of the deal and donated a new 40,000 seater, $25 million sports stadium for San Jose, Costa Rica's capital.[19]

Taiwan has been seeking to solidify its existing relationships with countries like Belize, St. Kitts and Nevis, and St. Lucia with a bevy of projects, many of them agricultural, including an agreement signed with Belize in 2012 to develop the fish farming industry there. However, Taiwanese diplomats in the region concede that they can never keep up with China's largess.[20] In addition to outbidding Taiwan in financial aid and loans, China has built new stadiums, roads, schools, official buildings, power plants, ports and resorts for Caribbean countries and invested in sugar estates and cane fields.

Taiwan regularly provides generous technical and medical assistance to its allies. Starting from the mid-1990s, China has often countered with even larger assistance package. In 1997 Beijing induced the Bahamas and St. Lucia to switch recognition from Taipei to Beijing by offering a more attractive aid package. The Bahamas' move came after Hutchisom Whampoa, a Hong Kong shipping company, opened a $114 million container port in Freeport and bought three hotel resorts in Nassau. In 2004 Dominica cut relations with Taiwan upon receiving a pledge of $112 million

---

17   The 12 countries are: Belize, Dominican Republic, El Salvador, Guatemala, Haiti, Honduras, Nicaragua, Panama, Paraguay, St. Kitts-Nevis, St. Lucia, and St. Vincent-Grenadines.Also see Table 2.2.

18   "China to Build Oil Refinery in Costa Rica," *Xinhua*, October 29, 2007.

19   "Fierce Battle for Diplomatic Supremacy," *Financial Times*, September 12, 2008, p. 4.

20   Randal Archibold, "China Buys Inroads in the Caribbean, Catching U.S. Notice," *The New York Times*, April 7, 2012.

in aid over six years from Beijing when Taiwan only offered $9 million.[21] In 2005 Beijing outbid Taiwan for Grenada's allegiance and built the new national stadium in time for the 2007 Cricket World Cup. Grenadian Prime Minister Keith Mitchell reportedly encouraged a bidding war because he wanted a new stadium to host the games during the Cricket World Cup. In addition, China provided housing and agricultural support as well as a scholarship fund to Grenada.

China deployed 130 riot police to Haiti in 2004 and has since maintained a contingent of about 125 police officers as part of the UN mission to Haiti. This was the first Chinese contribution to UN missions in the Western Hemisphere. China has put pressure on the Haitian government to break with Taiwan and establish formal relations with the People's Republic. China has opened a trade office in Haiti and has regularly sent high-level diplomats to Port-au-Prince. In February 2007 the UN Security Council unanimously agreed to extend for eight months the mandate of 9,000-strong UN peacekeepers in Haiti. The agreement resulted from a compromise between the one-year extension initially suggested by Peru and a group of 25 donor countries, including the United States, Canada, Brazil, Britain and France, and the six months pushed by China, which does not have diplomatic ties with Port-au-Prince. It is thought that Haiti's recognition of Taiwan was a factor in China's position.[22] Haiti has in the past proposed bills to allow Taiwan to join the UN, which was vehemently opposed by China. With growing Chinese power at international organizations, countries that count on China's help will undoubtedly rethink their relations with Taiwan.

In Panama, perhaps Taiwan's most important diplomatic ally in the Americas, China opened a trade office in 1996. High-level diplomacy followed, including a visit in June 2004 from PRC vice foreign minister Zhou Wenzhong. Though Taiwan and Panama signed a free trade pact in 2003, Chinese–Panamanian trade boomed in 2004, exceeding $2 billion, some 15 times the volume of trade between Taiwan and Panama that year.[23] China has been sending the largest commercial delegation to the annual international trade fair Expocomer in Panama in recent years. The Bank of China has branches in Panama to facilitate trade. China is now the second largest user of the Panama Canal.

In a bid to further political relations and contribute to regional peace and prosperity, China has kicked off regular consultations with some Caribbean countries that have diplomatic ties with Taiwan. For Caribbean countries, the choice between China and Taiwan is not that difficult. Godfrey Smith, the Foreign Minister of Belize, observed that "in terms of realpolitik, it boils down to which presents the heftier cooperation package."[24] With traditional aid package from

---

21 "China Targets Caribbean Trade," *CNN World Business*, February 19, 2005.

22 "China's Position on Haiti's Peacekeeping Has Taiwan in Mind," *VOA Chinese*, February 17, 2007.

23 Dominguez, "China's Relations with Latin America," pp. 16–17.

24 Ronald Sanders, "China and Taiwan: the Caribbean Divide Revisited," *Huntington News Net* www.huntingtonnews.net, February 11, 2007.

the United States dwindling, these small Caribbean nations are most interested in how much they can receive from either China or Taiwan. Indeed, many in the region simply cannot distinguish between China and Taiwan since the official name of Taiwan is "Republic of China (ROC)." When a Chinese delegation joined Grenadian Prime Minister Keith Mitchell for the formal opening of the stadium built by Beijing in 2006, they were, embarrassingly, greeted to the tune of the ROC's national anthem. This anomaly may have been a function of incompetence in the protocol division of the Grenadian Ministry of External Affairs.

As a sign that Taiwan wanted to consolidate its diplomatic footing in the Americas, the Taiwanese government appointed Ou Hung-lien (Francisco H.L. Ou), the ROC's former ambassador to Guatemala and senior diplomat in Argentina, Chile and other countries, to be the foreign minister under the Ma Ying-jeou administration that came to power in Taipei in May 2008. Ou was the first diplomat with a Latin America background to head the foreign ministry in Taipei. He resigned in September 2009 in a reshuffling of government.

It should be noted that President Ma Ying-jeou has reversed many of his predecessor's confrontational policies towards China. As a result, cross-Taiwan Strait relations have much improved since 2008, and diplomatic competition between Taipei and Beijing in winning over allies has eased. President Ma declared a "diplomatic truce" with Beijing, meaning an end to the checkbook contest for recognition. According to Ma, El Salvador and Panama, two of Taiwan's allies, reportedly expressed interest in switching to Beijing after their new presidents were elected in 2009. Surprisingly Beijing declined the overtures from Taiwan's two allies for the sake of further improving cross-Strait relations.[25]

However, the China–Taiwan tug of war has never ended. In 2012, the Taiwanese government called in loans it made to Grenada before 2005 when Grenada switched to Beijing. After a string of bad economic setbacks, including devastating hits by hurricanes Ivan and Emily in 2004 and 2005, Grenada stopped paying back some $28 million in loans it received from Taiwan. In March 2012, a judge in New York, who has jurisdiction under terms of the loans, ruled that Grenada owes $25.9 million in outstanding principal and interest to Taiwan.

Expanding Political, Cultural and Military Influence in the Region

China's new diplomacy in Latin America and the Caribbean is part of its global efforts to enhance economic interests and expand political, cultural and military clout. Through promoting various exchanges at different levels and providing aid, China aims to win the hearts and minds of the people in the region.

China has established strategic partnerships or all-round cooperative relations with six Latin American countries: Argentina, Brazil, Chile, Mexico, Peru, and Venezuela. China has a traditional friendly relationship with Cuba. It has also

---

25   "Sorry, the Offer's Closed: Taiwan's President and China," *The Economist*, June 25, 2009.

strengthened multilateral engagements with Latin America. In addition to the observer status in the Organization of American States (OAS), China has become involved in other regional organizations such as the China-Latin America Forum, China-South American Common Market Dialogue, and China-Andean Community Consultations, among others. After acting as an observer of the IADB in 1991 and that of the Latin American Integration Association in 1993, China became an observer for the Latin American Integration Association and the UN Economic Commission for Latin America and the Caribbean (ECLAC) in 2004.

Chinese investment in Latin America has increased rapidly since 2000. In Argentina alone, Chinese investment totalled some $20 billion by 2006. China has promised an $8 billion investment in its railways, $5 billion in energy exploration, $700 million in communications and an additional $6 billion in other infrastructural projects.[26] Having lifted 500 million out of poverty, China is proud of its development; its model for growth is quite appealing to other developing countries. Investment in infrastructure and education and welcoming FDI are just some of the lessons China can offer to Latin America and the Caribbean.

During President Hu's visit to Cuba in November 2008, China agreed to send food to Cuba in the wake of three devastating hurricanes. Cuba's state-run AIN news agency reported that the two countries reached almost a dozen agreements during Hu's visit, including plans to rehabilitate the island's aging ports and earthquake detection systems. China would also provide building materials for areas affected by flooding and heavy winds in Guantánamo Province.

China is promoting tourism in the Western Hemisphere. During President Hu's visit to Latin America in November 2004, Argentina, Brazil and Chile were added to China's list of ADS. With official support, large groups of Chinese tourists can visit these countries and others in the region without restrictions. As of mid-2012, over 20 countries in the Americas had become officially approved destinations for Chinese tourists. China is already among the top ten overseas tourist markets and expected to become the world's fourth largest source of tourists by 2020. China has also signed cultural agreements with several Latin American countries to promote exchanges in film production, visual arts, musicology, library science, etcetera.

China takes every opportunity to expand its economic and political clout in Latin America. At the September 2006 Non-aligned Movement summit held in Havana, Cuba, the Chinese delegation, led by vice foreign minister and former ambassador to Washington Yang Jiechi, held bilateral meetings with a number of countries to strengthen China's ties with the region (Yang served as China's foreign minister between April 2007 and March 2013). China was invited to attend as an observer, so was the United States, but the Bush administration declined the invitation.

Interest in Latin American affairs is also on the rise in China. China has witnessed the growth of think tanks and scholars specialized in analyzing Latin

---

26   From the Chinese language source, cited in Wenran Jiang, "China's Energy Engagement with Latin America," *China Brief*, Vol. 6, No. 16 (August 2, 2006).

American affairs. The Institute of Latin American Studies of the CASS is just one such think tank. China is interested in Latin America's regional issues. It created the China-Latin America Forum and established mechanisms of dialogue with Mercosur and the Community of Andean Nations. It has also established links with other regional organizations such as the Rio Group and Caribbean Community and Common Market. China has actively expanded its contacts with regional institutions, entering into political dialogue or consultation mechanisms with the Rio Group (since 1990), Mercosur (since 1997), the Andean Community (since 2000), and the Caribbean Community (since 2002). In March 2005 China's NPC signed a cooperation agreement with the Latin American Parliament and became an observer.[27]

In March 2009 Chinese and Argentine central bank officials agreed to set up a 70 billion yuan ($10.24 billion) currency swap system, which would enable trade between the two nations to be settled in Chinese yuan. China has already signed similar deals with Malaysia, South Korea, Indonesia, Hong Kong, and Belarus. In 2012 China and Brazil agreed to set up a $29 billion local currency swap deal in their trade. Such accords will boost China's financial presence in Latin America.

According to China's 2008 policy paper on Latin America and the Caribbean, China highly values exchanges at the local government level with countries in the region. It supports the twinning of provinces/states or cities between China and Latin American and Caribbean countries, and exchanges and cooperation in business, science and technology, culture, and other fields to increase mutual understanding and friendship. Over 100 pairs of sister city relationships had been established by 2012.

China's growing ties with Latin America have a military component. China is training an increasing number of Latin American military personnel, taking advantage of a US law that has led to a sharp decline in US-run training programs for the region.[28] The commander of US forces in Latin America, General Bantz Craddock, told US Senators in March 2006 that China's military presence in the region was "widespread and growing every day" and China was sending increasing numbers of personnel for training as well as more non-lethal equipment to the region.[29] China has had exchanges of senior defence officials with Ecuador, Bolivia and Chile and provided military aid and weapons to Jamaica, Argentina and Peru. The PLA's presence in the region ranges from its participation in the UN peacekeeping operations in Haiti to its first joint military drill, the November 2010 humanitarian exercise in Peru.

---

27   Karl Buck, *China's Engagement in Latin America and the Caribbean — Expectations and Bad Dreams*. Geneva: Geneva Center for the Democratic Control of Armed Forces, 2006.

28   A 2002 US law mandates an end to military training in countries that refuse to exempt US citizens overseas from the prosecution by the International Criminal Court. 12 Latin American countries are subject to such sanctions. "China Training Latin American Military, says US General," *CNN*, March 14, 2006.

29   Luis Ramirez, "US Watching China's Growing Influence in Latin America," *VOA*, April 19, 2006.

China has helped Latin American countries to develop space programs. In October 2008, Venezuela's first satellite, *Simon Bolivar*, was launched with Chinese help from the Xichang Space Center in Sichuan Province. In March 2009, the Chinese government handed over operational control of the satellite to the Venezuelan government, which marked the first time Venezuela had acquired satellite technology. China continues to train Venezuelan space program professionals, with 30 doctoral students enrolled in Beijing's University of Aeronautics and Astronautics in 2012.[30]

As part of their "strategic partnership," Brazil and China have jointly developed a satellite program, are discussing Brazilian sales of uranium for Chinese nuclear reactors, and the Brazilian aircraft manufacturer Embraer has set up a plant in Harbin, China, which makes 50-seat regional jets and Legacy business jets, among others. In 2012 the two countries reached a new, 10-year cooperation plan to boost the strategic relationship.

Military education is becoming an increasingly important instrument of Chinese defence policy. The training of Latin American military officers in PLA academies has been on the rise. China is now training Latin American officers at all levels of command and in all services. For instance, at the PLA Navy Staff College, it is not uncommon to have Latin American junior and senior officers attending different levels of classes in the same year. This will undoubtedly enhance China's influence and prestige among Latin America's armed forces.

Perhaps more significant are the upper-echelon military officers trained at China's National Defence University (NDU) in Beijing. There the PLA conducts an intensive four-and-a-half-month course on grand strategy. The course is carried out every year and is attended by officers from all services with the minimum rank of lieutenant colonel up to major general.[31] In August 2007 the NDU hosted the Third Latin American Senior Officer Symposium and the First Symposium of Senior Defence Officers from the Caribbean and South Pacific.

The NDU opened its special "foreign course" for militaries in Latin America, Africa and the Middle East in 1985. The opportunity to study at the NDU is one that has consistently attracted the attention of Latin American military officers, especially when US ties with the region have ebbed and flowed. Officers from Venezuela, Bolivia and other states on less-than-favorable terms with Washington have attended these courses, bringing benefits to bilateral state-to-state relationships and enhancing Latin American militaries that have few educational opportunities abroad.[32]

---

30   "'Simon Bolivar' Satellite: Symbol of Technological Sovereignty," *China Daily*, June 28, 2012: p. S2.

31   Loro Horta, "China on the March in Latin America," *Asian Times Online*, June 28, 2007.

32   Cynthia Watson, "The PLA in Latin America," *China Brief*, Vol. 7, No. 20 (The Jamestown Foundation, Washington, DC), October 31, 2007.

Indeed, these professional military education (PME) courses are no longer being frequented just by officers from countries hostile to the US, such as Cuba or Venezuela. Countries with traditionally close relations with the US such as Colombia, Chile and Argentina have also sent regular participants. Colombia's participation is particularly noteworthy because US funding for "Plan Colombia" forms a crucial aspect of the Colombian government's efforts to finish off 40 year-old guerrilla groups, thus engendering tremendous loyalty on the part of the Andrés Pastrana Arango (1998–2002) and Álvaro Uribe Vélez (2002–2010) regimes. Vélez was considered a close US ally in Latin America, yet military exchanges between Bogotá and Beijing increased despite Colombia's de facto alliance with the United States.[33] In addition to training increasingly large numbers of Latin American officers, the PLA sends its own officers for training in Brazil, Chile, Argentina, Venezuela, Cuba and Mexico.

As part of the military diplomacy, nearly all the defence ministers or chiefs of defence forces from Latin America have been invited to China since the early 2000s. As of September 2009, 11 Latin American countries had maintained military attachés in Beijing. These countries were Argentina, Bolivia, Brazil, Chile, Colombia, Cuba, Ecuador, Mexico, Peru, Uruguay, and Venezuela.[34] China's November 2008 policy paper on Latin America and the Caribbean stated that "The Chinese side will, as its ability permits, continue to provide assistance for the development of the army in Latin American and Caribbean countries."[35] Obviously, the military's role constitutes an important part of China's ambition to expand influence in Latin America as a global power.

Major Chinese Strategies in Latin America

Summit Diplomacy

In international politics, contacts at the highest level between two countries are not only symbolic of the importance top leaders attach to the bilateral relations, but also very effective in getting things done. Since the early 1990s, all top Chinese leaders have visited Latin America and many Latin American leaders have visited China, often accompanied by huge trade delegations.

Three Chinese presidents have visited Argentina so far: Yang Shangkun in 1990, Jiang Zemin in 1993, 1997 and 2001, and Hu Jintao in 2004, 2005, 2008 and 2010. In 1990, partly to counter Taiwan's efforts to capitalize on the Tiananmen Square repression, President Yang visited five Latin American countries, the first

---

33   Ibid.

34   Information from the website of Beijing Military Attaché Corps, available online at http://bjmac.xtreemhost.com, accessed on September 26, 2009.

35   "China's Policy Paper on Latin America and the Caribbean," *Xinhua*, November 5, 2008.

visit to Latin America by a Chinese head of state. President Jiang's 2001 visit took him to Chile, Argentina, Uruguay, Cuba, Brazil and Venezuela, which sparked a new wave of diplomacy between China and Latin America.

President Hu Jintao traveled to Latin America in 2004 and 2005 consecutively, spending a total of 16 days there. He participated in the 12th APEC summit in Chile and made a 13-day Latin America visit to Brazil, Argentina, Chile and Cuba in the fall of 2004. During his visit, Argentina, Brazil and Chile agreed to recognize China as a market economy, a move which makes it harder to bring anti-dumping charges against China. In late 2005 President Hu traveled to Mexico as part of his North America tour.

In November 2008 President Hu returned to Latin America and attended the 16th APEC summit in Lima and paid state visits to Peru, Costa Rica and Cuba. Hu's visit to Costa Rica was the first by a Chinese president to Central America, a region where every country but Costa Rica has diplomatic relations with Taiwan. China and Costa Rica began their diplomatic relations on June 1, 2007. Costa Rica is the third Latin American country, after Chile and Peru, to have a FTA with China. China quickly became Costa Rica's second largest trading partner. President Hu's trip to Costa Rica resulted in nine cooperation agreements in various fields, such as an accord for the CNPC to take over the enlarging of the state-owned Costa Rican Petroleum Refinery, known as Recope. The two countries also signed several pacts of scientific and trade cooperation and an accord to found a Confucius Institute at the State University of Costa Rica.[36]

In April 2010, President Hu paid a state visit to Brazil and attended the second summit of the BRIC countries in Brasilia before going to Venezuela and Chile. He signed a series of agreements in the fields of culture, energy, finance, poverty alleviation, science and technology as well as product quality inspection with these countries.

"Development is the most pressing task for both China and Latin America," President Hu said in an address to Peru's Congress during his visit in November 2008. "In our cooperation we will take care of Latin America's legitimate concerns and strive to realize mutually beneficial gains for all."[37] At a speech to the Brazilian Congress in November 2004, Hu announced that China would invest $100 billion in Latin America over the next ten years.[38] Given the overall decline in net FDI flows to Latin America in recent years, many Latin American countries welcome trade with China.

Chinese Vice President Zeng Qinghong travelled to the region in 2005, covering Mexico, Peru, Venezuela, Jamaica, and Trinidad and Tobago. Zeng offered Venezuela a $700 million credit line for new housing construction to help reduce Venezuelan

---

36 "China President Hu Jintao Agrees to Trade Pact with Costa Rica and Heads to Cuba," *Latin American Herald Tribune*, www.laht.com, November 17, 2008.

37 "Hu Offers China as Cure for Latin American Woes," *Reuters*, November 20, 2008.

38 Saul Landau, "Chinese Influence on the Rise in Latin America," *Foreign Policy in Focus (FPIF)*, January 23, 2005.

poverty. Zeng also attended the opening ceremony of the first ministerial-level China-Caribbean Economic and Trade Co-operation Forum held in February 2005 in Kingston, capital of Jamaica. In February 2009 Vice President Xi Jinping visited Mexico, Jamaica, Colombia, Venezuela, and Brazil. In an unusual double-pronged diplomacy toward Latin America, Chinese Vice Premier Hui Liangyu was touring Argentina, Ecuador, Barbados and the Bahamas during Xi's Latin America trip. In June 2011, Xi returned to Latin America, with stops in Chile, Uruguay and Cuba.

In June 2012, Premier Wen Jiabao visited Brazil, Uruguay, Argentina, and Chile and proposed a free trade area pact between China and Mercosur so that China's trade with Mercosur can be doubled to $200 billion by 2016 on the basis of the 2011 level. Wen also noted that all the four countries he visited expressed hopes for more Chinese investment in infrastructure, including oil, natural gas, railways and hydropower stations.[39] In June 2013 during his second foreign trip as China's President, Xi Jinping visited Costa Rica, Trinidad and Tobago, and Mexico, pushing for further cooperation between China and Latin American countries.

NPC Chairman Wu Bangguo travelled to Brazil, Uruguay, and Chile in 2006. The NPC has strengthened friendly exchanges with parliaments of Latin American and Caribbean countries, the Latin American Parliament, the Mercosur Parliament, and the Andean Parliament. In May 2008 Vice Premier Hui Liangyu visited Venezuela, where he and President Chávez witnessed the signing of an agreement between Venezuelan state oil company PDVSA and PetroChina to build a 400,000 barrel per day refinery in China's Guangdong province.

Chinese leaders' trips to Latin America have been reciprocated by a long series of visits to China by Latin American heads of state, economic officials, and corporate leaders. In 1995 President Fernando Henrique Cardoso became the first Brazilian president to visit China. In 2004 his successor President Luiz Inácio Lula da Silva visited China, accompanied by seven cabinet ministers, four state governors, and some four hundred business executives. The year 2009 marked the 35th anniversary of the establishment of diplomatic relations between China—the largest developing nation in the world, and Brazil—the largest developing nation in the Western Hemisphere. To celebrate the occasion, President Lula da Silva paid his second official visit to China in May 2009. In April 2011 President Dilma Rousseff travelled to China shortly after taking office.

Since China and Argentina established diplomatic relations in 1972, high-level exchanges have been frequent. General Jorge Videla first visited China in 1980. President Raul Alfonsin visited in 1988. Since then, every popularly elected Argentine president has traveled to Beijing—Carlos Menem in 1990 and 1995, Fernando de la Rua in 2000, Nestor Kirchner in June 2004, and Cristina Kirchner in 2010.

China–Chile relations have received high policy attention in both countries. Since 1990 Chile has been visited by Presidents Yang Shangkun, Jiang Zemin and Hu Jintao. Every Chilean president since 1990 has visited Beijing: Aylwin in 1992, Eduardo Frei

---

39   "China-Latin America Cooperation Not To Be Impeded by Vast Ocean: Wen," *Xinhua*, June 27, 2012.

in 1995, Ricardo Lagos in 2001, Michelle Bachelet in 2008, and Sebastian Pinera in 2010. During her visit to China in April 2008, President Bachelet attended the Boao Forum for Asia (BFA)—the first time for a head of state from Latin America to attend the China-hosted forum. After her election in 2006, one of President Bachelet's first orders of business was to sign the Sino-Chilean FTA to promote exports to China. President Bachelet said the Chilean side hoped to further strengthen coordination with China in regional and international affairs, and Chile was willing to serve as a bridge between China and Latin American countries in developing their friendly relations.[40] Pinera, on his first China visit as president in November 2010, said he was always "full of passion" to enhance pragmatic cooperation with China.[41]

In 1971 Mexico became the third Latin American country after Cuba and Chile to establish diplomatic relations with China. In 1973 President Luis Echeverria became the first Latin America president to visit Beijing. Since then, every Mexican president has visited China, the longest uninterrupted record of Latin American presidential visits to Beijing.[42]

Peruvian President Alan Garcia became the first foreign head of state to meet Hu Jintao in Beijing after the latter was re-elected President of China in March 2008. During President Garcia's visit, the two sides signed nine documents intended to boost bilateral cooperation and paved way for a free trade agreement inked in November 2008, when Peru hosted the annual APEC summit. President Ollanta Humala, who took office in July 2011, already visited China twice previously and is a strong advocate of close China–Latin America relations.

China–Cuba relations greatly improved after the Cold War. President Fidel Castro visited China twice, in 1995 and 2003. President Raul Castro visited China in July 2012. He also visited China in 1997 and 2005. Chinese President Jiang Zemin visited Cuba in 2001. President Hu Jintao visited Cuba three times during his term. In January 2006, between his election and his inauguration, Bolivia's President Evo Morales visited Beijing and encouraged Chinese investment in Bolivia's energy sector.

Between February 1999 when he took office and April 2009, Venezuelan President Hugo Chávez paid six visits to China. In addition to signing energy deals with China, Chávez was also reportedly seeking political support from China to obtain a seat in the UN Security Council. "The unipolar world has collapsed. The power of the US empire has collapsed," Chávez said in Beijing after visiting Iran and Japan in April 2009. "Everyday, the new poles of world power are becoming stronger. Beijing, Tokyo, Tehran … it's moving toward the East and toward the South." "No one can be ignorant that the center of gravity of the world has moved to Beijing," Chávez told President Hu Jintao.[43] (Interestingly, this reminds one

---

40 "Senior Chinese Official Meets with Chilean President on Promotion of Cooperation," *People's Daily*, April 29, 2007.

41 "China, Chile Agree to Expand Trade," *Xinhua*, November 16, 2010.

42 Dominguez, "China's Relations with Latin America," p. 38.

43 Christopher Bodeen, "Chávez Says World 'Center of Gravity' Now Beijing," *The Associated Press*, April 8, 2009.

of what Barack Obama said during the 2008 US Presidential campaign: "We also have to look east, because increasingly the center of gravity in this world is shifting to Asia … Obviously China is rising, and it's not going away.")[44]

China has also conducted "party to party" diplomacy. For example, the relationships between the CCP and the Caribbean nations' ruling parties are getting increasingly cozy, with leading politicians regularly being invited to China for all-expenses paid "familiarization" tours.[45]

Focusing on Business and Long-term Cooperation

While Western countries have tried to impose a market economy and multiparty democracy on developing countries that are often not ready yet, the Chinese are trying to separate politics from business. China is entering the market without political expectations or demands. There are no other political conditions attached except the "one-China" policy that other countries have to follow. The Chinese government opposes embargoes, which some Western countries frequently use against disobedient developing countries. China has provided investment and development aid in Latin America and other regions where the West has been reluctant to make deals. It promotes cooperation with countries regardless of their political colors.

This practice of separating politics and business worries some people. China's willingness to deal with authoritarian leaders to overlook corruption and to ignore safety and environmental concerns may undermine democratic institutions and efforts to promote transparency and good governance. However, the PRC government was never keen on leftist activities such as those of the Shining Path guerrillas in Peru. Despite the fact that this revolutionary group defines itself as Maoist, Beijing has categorically denied any link to it and has condemned terrorist activities. In Venezuela's case, President Chávez who died in March 2013 probably presented more of an obstacle than a catalyst for better Chinese–Venezuelan relations. His rhetorical habit of repeating time and again his admiration of Mao Zedong made him a "hot potato" for China, which does not want to be seen as siding with political leaders the West frowns upon. China apparently wanted to keep some distance from Chávez. "Without him, the pace of China's business dealings and presence in Venezuela would probably be greater," commented Carlos Malamud, senior analyst for Latin America at Elcano Royal Institute.[46]

Traditionally China has purchased commodities such as iron, copper, soy and fishmeal that do not require complex transactions or an extensive local presence. More recently China has cautiously established an investment presence in key

---

44   Transcript, "The Democrats' First 2008 Presidential Debate," *The New York Times*, April 27, 2007.

45   Steven W. Mosher, "Red China on the March," *National Review* www.nationalreview.com, February 14, 2006.

46   Carlos Malamud, "Outside Players in Latin America: China," Working Paper 50/2007, Real Instituto Elcano, April 12, 2007.

commodity sectors. In Venezuela, it moved from modest oilfield operations in the Lake Maracaibo area to a more important and potentially riskier presence as a minority partner in developing the massive heavy oil reserves in the Orinoco river basin. In Peru, China Aluminum Corporation committed to investing up to $2.2 billion over the next 30 years for the rights to operate a mine at Toromocho. In February 2009 during an official visit to Brazil, then Vice President Xi Jinping signed a preliminary accord for a $10 billion loan to the Brazilian national oil company Petrobras, providing it with capital for developing new deepwater oil reserves, which could ultimately be exported to China.[47]

As China deepens structural reform in its own manufacturing industry, it has expanded exports to Latin America both quantitatively and qualitatively. It has complemented its offerings of labor-intensive goods such as toys, clothing, and footwear with a broad selection of more advanced products such as motorcycles, cars, heavy machinery, appliances, and consumer electronics. China is also taking advantage of the regional FTAs to pry access into third-country markets. For example, Chinese auto companies Dong Feng, Geeley, and FAW have announced plans to create assembly plants in the Mexican *maquiladora* sector, in order to achieve duty-free access to the US auto market under provisions of the North American Free Trade Agreement.[48]

During Premier Wen's visit to Latin America in June 2012, China offered $10 billion in credit for infrastructure projects. China is also considering negotiating agreements for local currency swap with more Latin American countries. Wen called for cooperation from regional leaders on food security and invited Latin American and Caribbean agriculture ministers to a food security meeting in China in 2013.[49] Wen also proposed to establish between China and the region an emergency food reserve mechanism of 500,000 tons, which will be used for natural disasters and humanitarian aid. During the same trip, Wen and Chilean President Sebastian Pinera signed accords to strengthen legal safeguards for investors from either country. Apparently China is not just interested in Latin America's resources; it aims to establish a long-term strategic relationship. "That's very good news for the region," remarked Alicia Barcena, head of the UN ECLAC.[50]

Meanwhile, China continues to increase its investment in Latin America. According to the UN data, China was the number three international investor in the region (9 percent) after the United States (17 percent) and the Netherlands (13 percent) in 2011. China's investment was about $22.7 billion, up sharply from $15 billion in 2010.[51] Most of Chinese investment went into mining and other extractive industries. Chinese banks have lent over $75 billion to Latin

47   Evan Ellis, "China's Maturing Relationship with Latin America," *China Brief*, Vol. 9, No. 6 (March 19, 2009), p. 5.
48   "Chinese Cars Coming to Mexico," *Business Week*, November 23, 2007.
49   "China's Wen Offers $10 Billion Latin America Credit Line," *Reuters*, June 27, 2012.
50   Ibid.
51   "China, Latin America Trade 'On Solid Footing,'" *AFP*, November 23, 2011.

America since 2005, and in 2010 gave more than the World Bank, Inter-American Development Bank and US Ex-Im Bank combined.[52]

Avoiding Direct Confrontation with the United States

Chinese trade with Latin America may be expanding rapidly, but the region still trades more with the United States. Despite growing Chinese activities in Latin America, many analysts doubt that any of China's initiatives will provoke a confrontation with the United States in the Western Hemisphere. China is fully aware that the United States is watching closely at its new multidirectional diplomacy. It has tried to avoid direct confrontation with the United States in international and regional affairs. It is not seeking to replace the United States as the global power. Most importantly, China realizes that there is nothing in Latin America which would justify jeopardizing US–China relations.

China has been careful in its dealings with leftist governments in Latin America. The Chinese government never openly endorsed President Chávez's negative comments on the United States. On the contrary, China has appeared keen to play down any implications that China's developing relationship with Venezuela might have for the United States. China does not want to become embroiled in any US–Venezuelan disputes. For China, a stable US–China relationship is far more important than oil from Venezuela or any sort of alliance with it. President Chávez seemed interested in establishing a multipolar, anti-American axis through words and deeds, but China never embraced Chávez's idea. President Chávez threatened to reduce his country's oil export to the United States and increase exports to China; meanwhile he intended to purchase weapons from China as well as Russia. But China was lukewarm to his overture, especially with regard to weapons sale.

While China's military contacts with Latin America have increased substantially, its military influence in the region remains minimal. The United States remains by far the single largest provider of military equipment and aid to the region. The relevance of China's growing military relations with the region lies in the fact that it grew rather rapidly from almost nothing. This rising military influence is a natural development of China's rising economic presence in the Western Hemisphere. Some regimes have urged further military cooperation and arms sales, but China has so far adopted a very cautious approach. China is rather reluctant to increase its Latin American military ties for fear of antagonizing the United States.

Cuba is another country which the United States is watching attentively as Chinese influence is expanding. But Sino-Cuban relations may not be as close as many think. As a WTO member and a major trading nation now, China wants to be recognized as a market economy to protect it from anti-dumping measures. Yet, during President Hu Jintao's visit in 2004, Cuba did not recognize China as a "market economy"—the only Latin American country he visited then that failed

---

52   "Chinese Lending to Latin America Tops $75bn," *Financial Times*, February 16, 2012.

to reach that conclusion. From its own national interest, Cuba has emphasized that China is "socialist," not market-oriented.[53] China characterizes its relations with Cuba as "friendly cooperative relations," lower than the "strategic partnership" that it has established with Argentina, Brazil, Chile, Mexico, Peru and Venezuela. Also, China generally supports calls for ending US sanctions on Cuba, but it has never committed itself to taking concrete actions or making it an issue with the US government. China is simply not interested in a political alliance with any country to balance US power in the region.

Promoting Soft Power

China has learned to win the hearts and minds of the governments and people in Latin America and the Caribbean by enhancing its soft power. The Confucius Institute has become an important symbol of China's soft power. The first Confucius Institute in Latin America was established in Mexico City on February 15, 2006. According to *Hanban*, by mid-2012 33 Confucius Institutes had been established in 11 Latin American countries—eight in Chile, five in Mexico, five in Brazil, four in Peru, three in Colombia, two in Argentina, and one in Cuba, Costa Rica, Jamaica, Ecuador, Bolivia, and Bahamas each.

In February 2009, during his visit to Jamaica, Vice President Xi Jinping attended the opening ceremony of the Confucius Institute on the Mona Campus of Jamaica's prestigious University of the West Indies, in Kingston, the first Confucius Institute established in the English-speaking Caribbean region. The Chinese government has encouraged the opening of Chinese culture centers in Latin America and will offer 5,000 scholarships to Latin American students over the next few years.[54]

The China fever can be felt in many countries. In Sao Paulo, Chinese language classes are packed. Not only are students taught how to speak Mandarin, but they are also guided in cultural habits such as attending banquets and singing Chinese folk songs. "Thanks to the cultural links, many Peruvians now will say 'Chifan,' the Chinese term for 'have a meal,' instead of Spanish in local Chinese restaurants," said Peruvian Ambassador to China Luis Chang.[55]

The Chinese government has discussed with relevant Latin American countries ways to relieve their debts as China's ability permits. It has continued to call upon the international community to take more concrete steps to reduce and cancel debts owed by Latin American and Caribbean countries. According to China's 2008 policy paper on Latin America and the Caribbean, the Chinese side will promote wider application of Chinese technologies on energy conservation, digital medical treatment, small hydropower and other results of scientific

---

53   Dominguez, "China's Relations with Latin America," p. 45.

54   "Wen Urges Enhanced Cooperation," *China Daily*, June 28, 2012: p. 11.

55   "China, Latin America Forge Closer Links for Win-Win End," *Xinhua*, October 6, 2006.

research and advanced applied techniques in Latin America and the Caribbean. China will also provide Latin American countries with technical training, services and demonstration, and step up cooperation and exchanges on the educational front with them.

Argentine and Brazilian soccer stars such as Maradona and Ronaldo are household names in China. But the ordinary Chinese know little about these stars' homelands. Most Latin Americans do not know much about China either. The Chinese government has facilitated people-to-people contact by making it easier for Chinese to travel to Latin America. After the Beijing Olympics, China has kept the momentum of exchanges with the sports authorities and national Olympic committees of Latin American countries, and encouraged direct contacts between sports associations.

The hot Chinese market has lured investors from Latin America. For example, the Latin American food and drink industry is trying to take a bite in the huge Chinese market. From Brazilian Barbecue to bread and cakes branded "Bimbo," many Beijing residents now have chances to taste Latin American delicacies. Latin culture remains exotic and appealing to many Chinese. Exhibitions of Latin American cultures from countries like Peru and Mexico at the National Museum in Beijing have attracted many curious Chinese in recent years.

China has established an embassy in each of the Caribbean nations that recognize Beijing. These embassies hold regular meetings and informal dinners with leading political figures, and to monitor local political and economic development on a daily basis. By contrast, the United States does not maintain a single diplomat in the Eastern Caribbean. Instead, the US ambassador to Barbados is jointly accredited to the other island nations in the Eastern Caribbean and is a complete stranger to most Eastern Caribbean figures in the public and private sectors.[56]

In January 2009 China became a formal member of IADB, the Inter-American Investment Corporation and the Multilateral Investment Fund of the group, and contributed $350 million as it expands its influence in Latin America and the Caribbean. China funded a number of initiatives to help Latin American countries cope with the global financial crisis, including $125 million for the IADB's Special Operations Fund that lends to the poorest countries. It became the 48th member of the development bank, and is the third from East Asia, following Japan and South Korea. China is quickly emerging to be the second biggest trading partner of Latin America and the Caribbean.[57] In January 2010 when a devastating earthquake hit Haiti, the Chinese government immediately offered

56   Steven W. Mosher, "Red China on the March," *National Review* www.nationalreview. com, February 14, 2006.

57   "China Joins IDB, Gives $350 million To Help LatAm," *EasyBourse.com* (France), January 13, 2009. Also, "China Becomes Formal Member of Inter-American Development Bank Group," *Xinhua*, January 13, 2009.

aid and sent a 60-member rescue team despite the fact that Haiti recognizes Taiwan instead of China.

Assessment

China shares much common ground with Latin American countries. They have all experienced and fought against imperialism and colonialism and struggled for independence in the past century. Both belong to the developing South and both are seeking cooperation in the increasingly competitive international political economy. Their cooperation generally contributes to development and peace in the region.

China's Influence in Latin America is Still Limited but Quickly Growing

Because of the differences in size, China is economically much more significant for Latin America than the region is for China. The region as a whole accounted for only 3 percent of China's exports and supplied 3.8 percent of its imports in the mid-2000s.[58]

The United States, due to its preoccupation with Iraq and Afghanistan since the early 2000s, has paid little attention to Latin America, which provides opportunities for other powers like China and India to make their inroads into the backyard of the United States. The US economic slowdown in the late 2000s has hit Latin American exports as well as remittances from Latino migrants. "The reality is that to some degree the fate of Latin America has been decoupled from the US," remarked Daniel Erickson, of the think tank Inter-American Dialogue. "Or at least it's not as tightly entwined as it used to be."[59]

While US exports in dollar amounts have increased in the Americas, its share of the market has declined since 2000. China is quickly rising as the top trade partner of major economies in Latin America. Nevertheless, China's global influence is overwhelmed by America's stronger ties with key players in every region. Latin America's relations with China will not eclipse its relations with the United States because of proximity, long-standing ties, and far deeper economic and societal links. In the mid-2000s the United States still accounted for about half of all Latin American trade.[60]

What is most impressive is the speed China–Latin America trade is growing. Latin American exports to China increased by 20 times from 1990 to 2005,

---

58   Rhys Jenkins, Enrique Dussel Peters, Mauricio Mesquita Moreira, "The Impact of China on Latin America and the Caribbean," *World Development*, Vol. 36, No. 2 (2008), p. 237.

59   Rory Carroll, "President's Latin America Tour Cements Beijing's Trade Clout," *The Guardian*, November 19, 2008.

60   Dan Erikson and Adam Minson, "China's Ties to Latin America: US Policy Implications," *Inter-American Dialogue*, January 2006.

Chinese exports to the region exploded by 30 times during the same period. In 2008 China–Latin America trade exceeded $140 billion, compared to US–Latin America trade of $560 billion and EU–Latin America trade of $280 billion.[61] In 2012 China accounted for 10 percent of Latin America's exports and was the leading export destination for Brazil and Chile. Even so, the United States and Europe remain Latin America's most important trading partners, accounting for 40 percent and 14 percent of its exports, respectively. The United States is, moreover, a key provider of remittances to Latin America—accounting for 75 percent of the $60 billion the region received in 2008—and, thus, a critical source of foreign exchange for many countries in the region.[62]

Many Latin American countries have become dependent on Chinese economy now. Commodities make up more than 60 percent of exports in all major Latin American economies, except Mexico, and slowing Chinese growth can potentially hurt these countries. China's economy began to slow down in 2012, although not to a level that endangers its Latin American partners. However, Latin American countries have become concerned. Luis Miguel Castilla, Peru's finance minister, reportedly said that "the truth is I light a candle every day and pray that China's growth does not fail."[63]

China's direct investments abroad amounted to $90.63 billion by the end of 2006, according to figures released by the Commerce Ministry of China. China poured 25 percent of its total overseas investments into Latin America in 2006 (about $22 billion), according to a Chinese trade official, who also said that Chinese enterprises were engaged in 30,000 projects in Latin America at the time.[64] But China's total investment was less than one tenth of US investment in the region at the same time, which was about $300 billion.

China–Latin America trade relationship is a fairly lopsided one. China is the leading trade partner of major Latin American economies, but none of them makes China's top 10 commercial partners. There is also a clearly defined pattern of trade in which natural resources move eastwards from Latin America, and manufactured and industrial goods pass in the other direction. There is obviously a huge potential for Chinese investments in Latin America. According to the Brazil-China Business Council, by the end of 2011 only 57 Brazilian firms had Chinese investments, which constituted less than one percent of Brazil's total FDI.[65]

In June 2013, just after President Xi Jinping's visit to Latin America and the Xi-Obama summit in California, the Congress of Nicaragua, which still maintains

---

61   "China-Latin America Trade: New Record," *Latin Business Chronicle*, November 23, 2009.

62   Uri Dadush and Shimelse Ali, "China's Rise and Latin America: A Global, Long-Term Perspective," Carnegie Endowment for International Peace, March 8, 2012.

63   "Best Friends Forever," *Week in China* (Hong Kong), June 29, 2012.

64   "25% of China's Investments Abroad Received by L. America," *Xinhua*, April 16, 2008.

65   "Best Friends Forever," *Week in China* (Hong Kong), June 29, 2012.

diplomatic relations with Taiwan, granted a 50-year concession to a Hong Kong-based Chinese company to develop and build a new canal across Nicaragua.

It's also worth pointing out that Latin America is not just looking to China but also to other Asian countries for trade and investment, such as Japan, South Korea, India, Indonesia, and Singapore. And China is not alone in seeking out opportunities in Latin America. South Korean President Lee Myung-Bak, who attended the APEC summit in Lima in November 2008, added a Brazil leg to his South America trip to speak with President Lula da Silva about bilateral trade and investment in natural resources and agriculture. Japan's Prime Minister Taro Aso met Lula in Washington, DC on the sidelines of the G-20 summit before the 2008 APEC meeting to discuss similar issues. Indonesian President Susilo Bambang Yudhoyono, meanwhile, dropped in on Mexican counterpart Felipe Calderon to discuss cooperation between their two state oil companies. Since the mid-2000s, India has launched nearly two dozen cooperative oil exploration projects in Latin America, especially in Brazil and Colombia.

According to UN data, 17 percent of Latin America's exports went to Asian–Pacific countries in 2010, more than tripling from 5 percent in 2000. Over the same span, the share of the region's total exports that went to the United States dropped from 60 percent to 40 percent. Some economists predict that Asia is poised to overtake the United States and the EU as Latin America's top trading partner within a decade.

Latin American Countries Generally Welcome Chinese Presence but are also Concerned about Economic Competition from China

For many Latin American countries, China is no longer a distant Asian power but an indispensable partner, a big investor, a mighty rival, as well as a potential great power friend and counterweight to the United States. Some Americans' concern about China's growing influence does not seem to bother Latin Americans. As Chile's ambassador to the United States Mariano Fernandez put it, the competition between the United States and China is an American discussion, not a Latin American issue.[66]

The economies of China and Latin America are in some ways complementary. With galloping economic growth and a scarcity of arable land, China's appetite for natural resources and farm products seems insatiable, and Latin America fortunately has both. Producers and exporters of raw materials such as Argentina, Brazil, Chile, and Venezuela and sectors such as agriculture and agro-industry are considered "winners" in trade with China. On the other hand, little attention has been paid to the long-term ecological, social, and economic sustainability of exports of these countries. Given the shared interest of China and Latin America in promoting economic growth, their cooperation is mutually beneficial.

66 Stephanie Ho. "China Raises Profile, Concerns in Latin America," *Voice of America*, November 1, 2006.

For some Latin American countries, China is not just a partner, but also a competitor. The China–Latin America trade is still unbalanced. For example, China provides 15 percent of Mexico's imports, but only 2 percent of Mexico's exports go to China while about 80 percent go to the US. A wide variety of industrial and agricultural sectors in Latin American countries are worried about the massive entry of low-cost Chinese goods in their domestic markets. Sharp criticism of Chinese imports has become quite common in countries such as Mexico and Argentina.[67] Mexico and the Central American countries that specialize in commodity chains such as yarn-textile-garments, and in electronics, automobiles, and auto parts seem to have faced the toughest competition from China. Investment that focuses heavily on extracting raw materials can be frustrating for host governments that want to boost skills and employment, and to add value locally. Brazil could be compromised by Chinese competition in sectors such as cars. Some countries fear that their textile and shoe exports to the United States will lose out to China's. Such concerns also explained why the Mercosur countries were reluctant to accept a FTA offer from Premier Wen Jiabao during his June 2012 tour of the region.

China has received "market economy status" from more than half of Latin American countries, making it possible for Chinese goods to enter the Latin markets without duties. Several countries such as Mexico and Argentina are particularly hard hit by China's flood of low-end manufacture exports. China's cheap labor has lured away *maquila* investors. As a result, anti-China sentiments are rising in the region, which have triggered some protectionist calls for action. The resentment also emerged as a result of China not fulfilling all promises in investments. Shoddy and pirated goods from China are another source of complaint. According to one account, two thirds of pirated products discovered in Brazil were produced in China.[68]

Textile and apparel production have become an important niche industry in the Hemisphere, providing critical jobs and income. Major changes in these industries will have a significant economic and social impact on the region — primarily in Mexico, Central America, and the Caribbean. The Chinese have been outselling Brazilians in shoes. By one estimate done by the Brazil-China Business Council, Chinese competition is responsible for Brazil losing more than 90 percent of its shoe sector in the US market.[69] Mexico has also suffered and in 2007 it ran a $28 billion trade deficit with China.

The boom in trade and investment between China and Latin America has not had an equal impact throughout the region. As Matthew Ferchen pointed out, exports to China have been largely concentrated in a small number of raw materials (copper,

---

67   Carlos Malamud, "Outside Players in Latin America: China," Working Paper 50/2007, Real Instituto Elcano, April 12, 2007.

68   Karl Buck, *China's Engagement in Latin America and the Caribbean—Expectations and Bad Dreams*. Geneva: Geneva Center for the Democratic Control of Armed Forces, 2006.

69   Julie McCarthy, "Growing Trade Ties China to Latin America," *National Public Radio*, All Things Considered, April 1, 2008.

iron ore, soy and oil) from a core group of South American countries (Argentina, Brazil, Chile and Peru). Other countries throughout the region, with Mexico as a primary example, have a more competitive relationship with China's export sector. Even in those countries like Brazil, whose iron ore and soybean producers have benefited greatly from China's growing appetite, domestic manufacturers have come under heavy pressure from Chinese competition.[70]

Local resentment is sometimes vented out against visiting Chinese dignitaries. During a visit to Peru in November 2008, Jack Ma, a Chinese web entrepreneur sometimes called China's "Bill Gates," was jeered by angry Peruvian textile workers who saw him as the negative personification of China–Peru FTA. As more Chinese companies invest in Latin America, more and more Chinese workers live in the region now. The safety of these Chinese has become a new issue in China–Latin America relations. For example, 4 Chinese oil workers were held by the Revolutionary Armed Forces of Colombia, or FARC, for 17 months before they were released in November 2012.

Latin American exports to China are concentrated on a very narrow range of products. Over 75 percent of China's imports from Argentina and Chile are of soya and copper, respectively. Two thirds of imports from Brazil are soya and iron and steel, while a similar proportion of imports from Peru are of copper and fishmeal.[71] Thus far major Latin American exporters to China have been unable to diversify their products beyond a few primary commodities. Trade with China has not brought about "*bom futuro*" (good future) to everyone. Mexico has perhaps been hit the hardest by China's booming trade and its challenges.

Competition from China also lies in the flow of FDI. The attraction of China as a host for foreign investors has reduced FDI flows to Latin America and the Caribbean over the past two decades. To protect their own businesses, some Latin American countries have applied new tariffs and set minimum thresholds for local content in key industries. For example, in September 2011, after a surge in imports of Chinese cars, tariffs were increased by 30 percent for vehicles sold in Brazil with less than 65 percent local content. Similar regulations have been introduced in oil and mining sectors.[72]

The Brazilian real appreciated 41 percent against the yuan between 2008 and 2012. President Rousseff, unlike her predecessor Lula, publicly raised the issue of the yuan's exchange rate. Shortly after taking office in January 2011, her trade minister, Fernando Pimentel, said Brazil would make China's currency policy a "priority" in bilateral talks.[73] To diversify exports to China and help domestic

---

70   Matthew Ferchen, "China-Latin American Relations: the end of honeymoon"? *China Brief*, January 16, 2012.

71   Rhys Jenkins, Enrique Dussel Peters, Mauricio Mesquita Moreira, "The Impact of China on Latin America and the Caribbean," *World Development*, Vol. 36, No. 2 (2008), pp. 237–8.

72   "Best Friends Forever," *Week in China* (Hong Kong), June 29, 2012.

73   "Rousseff Wants China Buying More Than Soybeans, Vale's Iron Ore," *Bloomberg*, April 11, 2011.

industries, President Rouseff wants to sell more airplanes, processed food, and other value-added goods.

China's "no political conditions attached" (except for the one-China policy) approach to its commercial relations with countries in Latin America may also frustrate these countries' efforts to develop and consolidate their democracies, especially in building a transparent and clean government. China's turning a blind eye to the problems in the region, based on its traditional "non-interference" policy, may also run counter to its pledged role of a responsible stakeholder in the international system.

Impact on the United States

Since US President James Monroe declared in 1823 that European powers should refrain from interfering with affairs on the Western Hemisphere, the United States has considered Latin America and the Caribbean as its own exclusive sphere of influence. Never has the US government ever envisioned a day when another major power will make inroads into this backyard of the United States and expand its political, economic, and cultural influence there.

China is primarily interested in oil and other resources in Latin America and does not seem to have a grand design for the region. However, some in the United States have become concerned, as indicated by a January/February 2006 *Foreign Affairs* article titled "Is Washington Losing Latin America"? The United States has watched Chinese expansion of influence in the region with caution, but it is not overly alarmed. After all, in terms of economic, political, diplomatic, and cultural linkages with the region, the United States remains predominant.

There is no clear consensus on how China's presence in Latin America is likely to affect US interests in the region. Essentially there are two opposing views: those who hold that China–Latin America ties constitute a threat to US interest and those who argue that China–Latin America ties are not a strategic challenge. Most observers do not see Latin America as a base "for (China's) projecting military and security interests, but rather for trade and investment," remarked Anthony Harrington, former US ambassador to Brazil. He added that Washington should not view China's presence in Latin America as a threat.[74] Some American politicians disagree. "It's extremely important that we don't let a potential enemy of the US become a dominant force in this part of the world," Congressman Dan Burton (R-IN) remarked, "we should always look at Latin America in relation to the Monroe Doctrine."[75]

The United States is perhaps most concerned about Chinese military and intelligence activities in Latin America, especially out of Cuba. China's interest in developing good relations with Brazil and Suriname, both of which have facilities for launching satellites and spacecraft into orbit, also creates some apprehension in the United States, especially in the Department of Defense. When China showed interest in the operation and ownership of the Panama Canal, it sparked concern

74   Ho, "China Raises Profile, Concerns in Latin America."
75   "Chinese Influence in Brazil Worries US," *BBC News*, April 3, 2006.

that China's interest is a danger to the United States. However, others point out that China's interest in the Canal is a natural extension of the fact that China is the second largest user of the Canal.[76] Despite some concerns and suspicions, neither China nor the United States wants to enter a strategic competition over Latin America. The United States has fundamental interests in promoting democracy, stability and economic prosperity in Latin America. According to former Chinese ambassador to the US Zhou Wenzhong, US concern over China's activities in Latin America is unnecessary, because China's trade and investment have promoted growth in Latin America and do not challenge US interests.[77]

Chinese military contacts with Latin America and peacekeeping activity may be growing, but it started from a relatively low baseline. Moreover, these contacts are occurring at a time of unprecedented cooperation between the United States and the countries of the Western Hemisphere on security matters. In 2005 the United States provided more than $112 million in Foreign Military Financing (FMF) to the region, making it the third consecutive year that FMF assistance had exceeded $100 million.[78]

The United States and China have launched bilateral dialogue on Latin America to enhance understanding of each other's policies and to ensure that they do not get their "wires crossed."[79] In April 2006 Thomas Shannon, US assistant secretary of state for Western Hemisphere affairs, visited Beijing ahead of President Hu Jintao's visit to Latin America and consulted with China on Latin America for the first time. The two sides agreed to meet annually to discuss Latin America. Such consultations are helpful to dispel misunderstanding and enhance mutual trust. On many occasions, the Chinese government has stated that the development of China–Latin America relations is not aimed at any third party.

In public the US government does not seem to worry too much about China's activities in Latin America. At a press conference at the November 2004 APEC summit in Santiago, Chile, then US Secretary of State Colin Powell was asked whether he was worried about China's role in Latin America, at a time of simultaneous visits to the region by the Presidents of China and the United States. Secretary Powell responded, "I'm pleased that President Hu Jintao is having good visits here in the hemisphere."[80] Shannon, the assistant secretary of state, dismissed concerns that

---

76 Erikson and Minson, "China's Ties to Latin America: US Policy Implications."

77 "China Does Not Compete with the US over Latin America," *BBC Chinese*, May 4, 2006.

78 Testimony of Roger F. Noriega, Assistant Secretary of State for Western Hemisphere Affairs before the House Subcommittee on the Western Hemisphere, "China's Influence in the Western Hemisphere," US Congress, Washington, DC, April 6, 2005.

79 "US and China to Launch Latin America Dialogue," *The Washington Post*, March 21, 2006.

80 US Department of State, "Joint Press Conference with Foreign Minister Ignacio Walker of Chile," Santiago, Chile, November 20, 2004.

China is seeking to foster closer military relations with countries in Latin America. "China's military engagement in the region is pretty light, by our standards," he said at a news conference, "China is not selling major military weapons systems in the hemisphere."[81] During his Beijing visit, Chinese officials assured him that China's engagement in the region was focused primarily on economic and trade issues and was not interested in exporting any kind of political model.

Privately, however, many US diplomats are increasingly worried about the Chinese presence "less than 190 miles from the United States" and are speculating on its purposes. According to a 2003 US diplomatic cable released through WikiLeaks, one theory suggested that China was lining up allies "as a strategic move" for the eventual end of the Castro era in Cuba.[82]

US businesses, on the other hand, seem more concerned about competition from China. They complain that the US is paying too much attention to Asia now at the cost of Latin America. They have pushed the US government to focus more on Latin America. Partially in response to such calls, President Barack Obama attended the 5th Summit of the Americas in April 2009 in Port of Spain, Trinidad and Tobago after visiting Mexico. He reached out to Cuba and Venezuela, expressing his willingness to improve US' strained relations with the two countries. Obama took his second trip to Latin America in March 2011, stopping off in Brazil, Chile, and El Salvador. In October 2011, the US approved long-awaited free trade deals with Panama and Colombia. Obama also attended the 6th Summit of Americas held in Colombia in April 2012. He noted that US–Latin America ties are strong and the US exports three times more to Latin America than to China.

Meanwhile, some businesses have taken advantage of the "China fever" in Latin America. For example, in 2012 Citigroup Inc. launched Renminbi (RMB) Letters of Credits (LC) for Importers and Exporters to offer a trade services solution suite available in RMB. This new means would enable clients in Latin America to issue, receive and settle RMB denominated LCs with their Chinese trading partners whilst also giving clients new options for trade financing, trade processing and risk mitigation.

China is a relatively new player in the Western Hemisphere. Its interests in Latin America and the Caribbean are substantial, but not vital. The region's importance to China lies primarily in three areas. First is its ability to provide China increasingly easy access to much needed resources. Second is China's quest to isolate Taiwan by enticing Latin American nations to shift diplomatic recognition from Taipei to Beijing. Third is China's interest in promoting its soft power in the region as it has been doing elsewhere. China's diplomatic activities in Latin America are consistent with its global efforts to project it as a responsible economic, political and cultural power.

---

81   Tim Johnson, "China Assures US it Won't Export Political Model to Latin America," *Knight Ridder Newspapers*, April 14, 2006.

82   Randal Archibold, "China Buys Inroads in the Caribbean, Catching U.S. Notice," *The New York Times*, April 7, 2012.

China's influence in Latin America is not going to supersede that of the United States any time soon. US trade and investment in Latin America not only dwarfs that of China, but its economic engagement is also qualitatively different from that of China—as a provider of high-tech and knowledge-based goods and services. The power asymmetry between China and the United States and Beijing's domestic priorities ensure that China will continue to steer clear of confrontation with the US.

Concluding Remarks

In November 2008 before President Hu Jintao's third visit to Latin America, the Chinese government released its first policy paper on Latin America and the Caribbean, seeking to deepen relations with the region. The white paper identified political, economic, cultural/social, and security/judicial cooperation as the four major cornerstones of China's efforts to bolster relations with Latin America and the Caribbean. This first Chinese white paper on Latin America and the Caribbean marks a milestone in Sino-Latin American relations and demonstrates the significant progress made in the rapid development of Sino-Latin American relations in recent years. Previously, China only issued policy papers on the European Union in 2003 and on Africa in 2006.

"The move toward multi-polarity is irreversible," stated China's white paper. Latin America and Caribbean countries are an important part of the developing world and a major force in the international arena, and China is "ready to carry out friendly cooperation with all countries on the basis of the Five Principles of Peaceful Coexistence and build a harmonious world of durable peace and common prosperity."[83] As in other developing regions, China's growing profile in Latin America and the Caribbean reflects its broader emergence as a global political and economic power. China does not seek to replace the United States as the dominant power in international affairs, but it does promote a multipolar world in which China can play an increasingly important role and China's development interests are served.

While the United States may still regard Latin America as its backyard, its dominance is no longer unquestioned. China has displaced the United States as the leading market for several countries in the region. China and Latin America face the common challenge of achieving further growth. There is no fundamental conflict of interests between them except some economic rivalry. China has been quite successful in translating its economic power into greater influence around the world, including in Latin America. China's close commercial ties with Latin America are a potent example of "South-South" cooperation in international political economy. The growing ties and cooperation across the Pacific are mutually beneficial for China and most Latin American countries.

---

83   "China's Policy Paper on Latin America and the Caribbean," *Xinhua*, November 5, 2008.

China can learn from Latin American countries in terms of development models. For example, China has focused on investment (at nearly 50 percent of its GDP in 2011) while Brazil opted to spend on social welfare (at about 40 percent of its GDP in 2010). As a result, even if China's economy has grown faster than Brazil's, Brazil outperforms China on criteria such as per capita income, health care, and social security. Obviously, as the income gap widens in China, Brazil's more distributive economic model offers a helpful lesson.

China's diplomacy in the Western Hemisphere presents both opportunities and challenges. After 9/11 China has infiltrated into the region through growing trade, investment, military assistance, and other exchanges. Some Latin American countries have said *basta* to the "Washington Consensus" and are likely to seek a new partnership with Beijing. The Chinese development model of government-managed, export-oriented market economy provides an alternative for some Latin American countries.

There is no evidence suggesting that China intends to replace the United States as the dominant power in the Western Hemisphere. The US concern over China's expanding activities in Latin America notwithstanding, it needs to assess China's diplomacy objectively and ensure that China's fundamental interests such as energy needs are satisfied. China, on the other hand, must be cautious to avoid challenging the United States in its traditional sphere of influence. For Latin American countries, they must try to strike a balance between forging closer ties with China and maintaining the ever-important relationship with the United States.

Questions for Discussion

1. Why is China interested in Latin America? What are the geopolitical and geoeconomic values of Latin America to China?
2. How has China promoted relations with Latin American countries since the early 1990s?
3. How many "strategic partnerships" has China established with Latin American countries? How many FTAs has China signed with Latin American countries?
4. How does China's active diplomacy in Latin America affect US–China relations? Is there a competition for resources and influence between China and the United States in Latin America?
5. How does China's new diplomacy affect Latin American political economy?
6. What opportunities does China's growth bring to Latin American countries? What are some problems and challenges in China–Latin America relations?

Chapter 5
China and Central Asia

Since the 1980s Chinese leaders have made a deliberate effort to formulate an integrated periphery policy (*zhoubian zhengce* 周边政策) known as good neighbor diplomacy (*mulin waijiao* 睦邻外交), aimed at exploring the common ground with neighboring countries in both economic and security arenas and conveying the image of a responsible power willing to contribute to stability and cooperation in China's neighborhood. Russia and Central Asian nations are part of China's *zhoubian guojia* (periphery countries 周边国家). Additionally, Russia is a key partner in China's great power diplomacy (*daguo waijiao* 大国外交), which also covers China's relations with the United States, Japan, and major EU countries. Russo-Chinese relations are complex that warrant lengthy discussions in a separate book. This book and this chapter only discuss Russia as far as China's new energy and security diplomacy is concerned.

Central Asia used to be a sphere of influence of the former Soviet Union. After the Soviet Union disintegrated in 1991, Russia's grip over the region has been tenuous, which paved the way for outside powers to step in. The disintegration of the Soviet Union allowed Central Asia to open its doors once again to the outside world. Trade with and investment from Europe, Japan, South Korea, the United States, China, and India have flourished. The September 11, 2001 terrorist attacks on the US soil offered an opportunity for the United States to send troops to Central Asia and establish military bases there. Great powers have either entered or returned to Central Asia now.

The five predominantly Muslim countries that won independence after the Soviet Union collapsed—Kazakhstan, Kyrgyzstan, Tajikistan, Turkmenistan and Uzbekistan—are attractive to various players largely because of their rich resources and strategic locations. Interest in Central Asian resources is not a contemporary phenomenon. During the 19th and early 20th centuries, the jostling for resources by European powers and Russia was infamous as the Caspian basin became carved into spheres of influence. While the era of what became known as "The Great Game" has long ended, China's quest for energy has now driven it to search for energy supplies in Central Asia, making it increasingly active in the region.[1]

Sharing a long border, China and Central Asia have had a complex relationship. China established close relations with Central Asia as early as 2,000 years ago, largely through their interactions along the ancient Silk Road. In more recent history,

---

1   Stephen Blank, "China's Emerging Energy Nexus with Central Asia," *China Brief*, Vol. 6, No. 15 (July 19, 2006).

China turned its back on Central Asia while Central Asia became isolated during the late 19th and much of the 20th centuries. In 1954 the Chinese government published a map showing parts of Kazakhstan, Kyrgyzstan and Tajikistan as Chinese territory and claimed that Tsarist Russia had annexed these territories in the 1880s. China and the Soviet Union did not start the dialogue on border dispute until 1987 after Mikhail Gorbachev's July 1986 Vladivostok speech in which he offered to hold talks with Chinese leaders on the Sino-Soviet border issue.[2]

After the collapse of the Soviet Union, the Chinese government was very apprehensive about its western border. In the early 1990s, maintaining stability in Xinjiang and resolving the border dispute with Russia and the Central Asian republics were at the top of Chinese agenda. China sought to demarcate, demilitarize, and stabilize borders with Russia, Kazakhstan, Kyrgyzstan, and Tajikistan. Subsequently, energy issues, threats from the so-called "three evils" of terrorism, separatism, and extremism, and drug trafficking became important factors in China's policy calculus toward Central Asia. Just about a decade ago, China essentially played no role in Central Asian politics. By the early 2010s, Central Asia had become a major venue for the new wave of Chinese diplomacy. Though Russia continues to enjoy decisive historical, cultural and economic advantages in Central Asia, China's relations with Central Asian states have matured into a multidimensional interactions involving political, economic, energy, strategic and cultural cooperation.

Central Asia is often thought of as the "second Middle East" for its rich oil and gas resources. An energy-hungry China has moved to lock Central Asian oil and gas into its orbit. As Western countries poured billions of dollars into bank bailouts to address the financial crisis that had hit virtually everywhere by 2008, China quietly announced in September 2008 to invest $100 billion building roads and railways to open up Central Asia to the rest of the world in the next decade. More than 20,000 kilometers of rail track will be built in the coming decade to bring Chinese goods into Central Asia and carry back oil and metals to China. The new railways and roads will, as one commentator remarked, create a contemporary equivalent of the ancient Silk Road.[3] China shares a long border with three Central Asian states—Kazakhstan, Kyrgyzstan, and Tajikistan. In addition to trade with these three immediate neighbors, China also has energy projects in other Central Asian states including Turkmenistan and Uzbekistan.

The vast expanse of the Chinese region of Xinjiang, which is inhabited by the Uyghur Muslim minority, poses a security predicament for China. Since the Uyghurs have strong religious and ethnic links traditionally with the Middle East and Central Asian republics, China is very keen that the militant fundamentalist ideology such as the Taliban be prevented from spilling over into Xinjiang. The

---

2   Ramakant Dwivedi, "China's Central Asia Policy in Recent Times," *China and Eurasia Forum Quarterly*, Vol. 4, No. 4 (2006), pp. 139–40.

3   Isabel Gorst, "Oil-rich, Remote and Difficult," Special Report on Investing in Central Asia, *The Financial Times*, October 30, 2008, p. 1.

July 2009 ethnic clash in Xinjiang and the alleged link between Uyghur extremists and al-Qaeda demonstrate the complexity of the security challenge for China.

There reportedly are over one million ethnic Kazakhs in China, with most residing in Xinjiang. Several tens of thousands have moved to Kazakhstan in recent years. These ethnic Kazakhs bring Chinese language skills and cultural awareness that have facilitated Kazakhstan–China ties, particularly in trade. However, some ethnic Kazakh migrants also bring critical memories of perceived prejudices against Muslims in Xinjiang, which may negatively influence the views of other Kazakhs and conceivably affect Kazakhstan–China relations.[4] Additionally, the presence of sizeable Western military forces in Central Asia and Afghanistan is also a source of key security concern for China.

The Shanghai Cooperation Organization (SCO) has been a major multilateral forum for China to conduct its new diplomacy towards Russia and Central Asian countries since the late 1990s. The six member states of the SCO include China, Kazakhstan, Kyrgyzstan, Russia, Tajikistan, and Uzbekistan. Mongolia, India, Iran, Pakistan and Afghanistan had the observer status in the SCO as of 2013.

Motivations Behind China's New Diplomacy in Central Asia

Since the early 1990s, Chinese interests in Central Asia have widened from maintaining stability at the borders to encompassing trade and investment, energy security, geopolitics, and combating the "three evils" of separatism, terrorism and extremism.

Energy and Economic Benefits

To secure energy to satisfy its domestic economic growth is obviously a major driving force behind China's current policy towards Central Asia and other oil-rich regions. For this purpose, China has set up trade missions in every Central Asian country. China has granted several Central Asian countries including Kyrgyzstan, Tajikistan and Kazakhstan loans in *renminbi* to buy Chinese goods. The Chinese Ministry of Commerce has established commercial centers in several cities in Central Asia with the specific purpose of increasing trade between China and the Central Asian states.[5] Economic ties between China and Central Asian nations are on the upswing. The volume of commodity turnover between China and Central Asian republics had grown from $400 million in 1992 to $10 billion in 2006, that

---

4   Thomas Lum, et al. "Comparing Global Influence: China's and US Diplomacy, Foreign Aid, Trade, and Investment in the Developing World," Congressional Research Service, Washington, DC, August 15, 2008, p. 91.

5   Niklas Swanstrom, "China Conquers Central Asia Through Trade," *The Analyst*, Central Asia Caucasus, April 11, 2001, accessed from www.cornellcaspian.com on September 17, 2007.

is 25 times bigger.[6] In 2010, China-Central Asia trade volume topped $30 billion. (See Table 5.1). The EU had long been Central Asia's largest trading partner; in 2010 it was overtaken by China.[7] Trade between China and Central Asia had been favored by both sides in history. The only change today is that the traders have replaced jade, tea, silk, and rhubarb with oil, gas, weapons, and more modern consumer products.

Sino-Kazakh trade is the largest, constituting over 80 percent of total China-Central Asia trade. China and Kazakhstan signed two joint communiqués in August 2007 and April 2008 respectively, which were aimed to enhance Sino-Kazakh cooperation in non-resources fields, including machine-making, transportation infrastructure, power plant construction, petrochemical industry, and medicine. The two sides had hoped that bilateral trade would reach $15 billion by 2015, but by the end of 2008, Sino-Kazakh trade had already surpassed $17 billion.[8] In 2011 it reached $25 billion and is expected to hit $40 billion in 2015.

The Middle East remains China's top supplier of oil. The US invasion of Iraq in 2003 wiped out China's earlier oil deals with the Saddam government. To a great extent, the Iraq war was a turning point in China's new energy strategy. China realized that it was too risky to rely on a single region for its critical energy import, especially a region with chronic instability. Since then China has sought to strike oil deals with countries in different parts of the world including Central Asia. 20 percent of Kazakhstan's oil exports went to China as of 2012.

Russia remains China's largest and most important trading partner in the region. Russia currently supplies about 15 percent of China's oil imports. Russia and China have been in talks for years to transport Russian oil and natural gas to China via new pipelines, but Russia has been slow to move ahead with concrete projects. During President Hu Jintao's March 2007 visit, the two sides signed contracts worth more than $2 billion, including a deal to increase imports of

Table 5.1   China–Central Asia trade volume: selected years (in billions of US dollars)

Year	1992	2000	2003	2006	2007	2008	2009	2010
Volume	0.4	1	3.3	10	17	25	26	30

Source: Ministry of Commerce, the People's Republic of China (http://english.mofcom.gov.cn), various years.

Note: The volume does not include China–Russia trade.

---

6   "China Will Outrun the US and Become the World's Second Exporter," *Kazinform (Kazakhstan)* www.inform.kz, September 17, 2007.

7   According to the European Council on Foreign Relations (ECFR), China's trade with the five Central Asian states in 2010 was €23 billion, compared to Europe's €21 billion. See "The New Great Game in Central Asia," ECFR, September 2, 2011.

8   "China-Kazakhstan Economic and Trade Cooperation," *Ministry of Commerce of the PRC*, November 12, 2009.

crude oil by rail from Russia. China is Russia's second largest trade partner though less than 10 percent of Russian trade is conducted with China, compared with more than half with the EU.[9] Currently oil and oil products account for over 50 percent of Russia's trade with China; in 2006, nearly 6 million tons of oil were exported to China, a 25 percent increase over 2005 exports. 15 million tons of crude oil are expected to be transported from Russia to China annually between 2010 and 2030. China is also Russia's second largest arms export market, only exceeded by India.[10] In June 2003 China hailed a $150 billion agreement with Russia to tap fields in Siberia and send the oil through a new pipeline to China. The project was to supply as much as one third of China's needed imports by 2030.[11] Unfortunately, the deal fell through a year later when Yukos Oil Co., the Russian signatory, slipped into trouble after its chief founder was jailed on tax-evasion charges. Yukos was later dismantled and sold at auction, mostly to state-run OAO Rosneft. Rosneft had been in talks with China since 2010 for the construction and operation of a refining and petrochemical complex in Tianjin. The detailed terms were discussed during Chinese Vice Premier Wang Qishan's visit to Russia in December 2012.

China is very interested in the Central Asian gas market. CNPC is one of the most important investors in Central Asia. In 2006 CNPC signed an initial gas pipeline construction agreement with the Kazakh authorities. In July 2008 CNPC and KazMunayGas signed a second agreement for construction and operation of the Kazakh section of the natural gas pipeline. Beginning on the right bank of the Amu-Daria, it will cover only 180 kilometers on Turkmen soil before crossing the Turkmenistan–Uzbekistan border, and will run for more than 500 kilometers across Uzbekistan and for nearly 1,300 kilometers across Kazakhstan before reaching Xinjiang via Shymkent and Khorgos.

Chinese business presence is largest in Kazakhstan and Kyrgyzstan among the Central Asian republics. Small and medium sized investors from China are now dominating a number of economic sectors in Kyrgyzstan, especially in the north, and the Chinese represent virtually the only group eager to invest in this small and poor Central Asian country.[12] Likewise, China is a major investor in Kazakhstan's oil industry, as a way to insure increased access to Caspian oil and gas reserves. Within years, significant quantities of natural gas will move via pipelines from Central Asia through Xinjiang to China's industrial centers on the east coast.

---

9   Henry Meyer, "Hu in Moscow Seeking Oil, Gas for China," *Bloomberg*, March 27, 2007.

10   John C.K. Daly, "Premier Wen's Eurasia Tour: Beijing and Moscow's Divergent Views on Central Asia," *China Brief*, Vol. 7, No. 21 (November 14, 2007), The Jamestown Foundation, Washington, DC.

11   "Big Shift in China's Oil Policy," *The Washington Post*, July 13, 2005, p. D01.

12   Martha Brill Olcott, "Is China A Reliable Stakeholder in Central Asia"? Testimony before the US–China Economic and Security Review Commission, Washington, DC, August 4, 2006.

The Kazakh section of the pipeline was inaugurated in December 2009 during President Hu Jintao's visit to Kazakhstan. The second gas line was completed in 2010. The third line designed to deliver gas from Turkmenistan, Uzbekistan and Kazakhstan to China began construction in 2012. The gas supply is expected to reach the designed capacity of 65 billion cubic meters (bcm) by December 2015, which will significantly help China in meeting its energy demands.

In the past, Turkmenistan's natural gas has mainly been routed to Europe through Russia. To avoid overdependence on Russia, Turkmenistan has accelerated its cooperation with China more recently. According to CNPC, introducing natural gas from Turkmenistan would not only help meet China's burgeoning energy demand, but also improve its energy consumption structure. It is estimated that with the pipeline in use, the percentage of natural gas in China's total energy consumption will increase by nearly 2 percent, meaning China will be able to significantly reduce its emission of carbon dioxide, sulfur dioxide, smoke and dust, and nitrogen oxides.[13]

In addition to gas and oil, China has invested in the telecommunications market in Uzbekistan. Internet and cell phone uses are on the rise in Uzbekistan, and China is quickly seeking to establish a regional and global presence in this sector. The two responsible ministries in each country concluded an agreement on telecom cooperation during President Islam Karimov's visit to China in May 2005. Uzbekistan has long sought a buyer for the state-owned Uzbektelecom, and it now seems that Chinese giants China Mobile Communications Corporation (CMCC) and Alcatel Shanghai Bell are ready to strike a deal on purchasing some of the shares of the state company. Other major Chinese telecom groups such as Huawei Technologies and ZTE have also signed business deals with Uzbek companies.[14]

China enjoys some trade advantages in Central Asia. Chinese goods tend to be of better quality than Russian goods, and they are cheaper than American or Japanese products. Xinjiang and Sichuan are the main trading partners with Central Asian states. Some 600,000 Central Asians visit Urumqi, capital city of Xinjiang, to conduct trade, and according to official statistics, the number of Chinese visiting Central Asia is about the same every year.[15] The real number of visitors is probably much higher, since there are large black markets on both sides.

In 2011 the Chinese government upgraded the 19-year-old Urumqi Foreign Economic Relations and Trade Fair into the China-Eurasia Expo in order to make Xinjiang a gateway for further cooperation between China and other Eurasian countries. Vice Premier Li Keqiang attended the first China-Eurasia Expo and Premier Wen Jiabao opened the second China-Eurasia Expo in 2012.

---

13   "Central Asia Pipeline to Secure Gas for China," www.chinastakes.com, July 2, 2008.

14   Alisher Ilkhamov, "Profit, Not Patronage: Chinese Interests in Uzbekistan," *China Brief*, Vol. 5, No. 20 (September 27, 2005).

15   Niklas Swanstrom, "China and Central Asia: A New Great Game or Traditional Vassal Relations"? *Journal of Contemporary China*, Vol. 14, No. 45 (November, 2005), p. 580.

Strategic Considerations

China's policy toward Central Asia and Russia is driven by an overriding priority of building a peaceful environment abroad and achieving growth at home. Improving relations with Russia and Central Asia serves this purpose well. China views Central Asian states in the context of Eurasian political economy. Central Asia has been called a bridge between East and West. It links Asia, Europe, and the Middle East not only in a geographical sense but also in political and cultural dimensions. China is intensely interested in the stability and prosperity of Central Asia because turbulence there will directly affect the future of political and economic cooperation of the whole Eurasian continent. A primary strategic concern for China is that Central Asia must be stable. Because of the long and porous borders, if Central Asia runs into military conflicts or ethnic riots, they are likely to spread over to Xinjiang. So it is no exaggeration to say that stability in Central Asia means stability for China. For Beijing, the "strategic partnership" with Moscow also provided a model for Chinese efforts to ensure stable relations with neighbors and major world powers.[16]

The quest for natural resources shapes China's policies in Central Asia, but it is not the whole picture, commented Niklas Swanstrom, executive director of the program for contemporary Silk Road studies at Sweden's Uppsala University. China wishes to project itself as a major power in the region. It might even directly challenge the supremacy of the United States and Russia in the future. But before that happens, Chinese leaders are trying to create a zone of friendly and stable countries around China's borders that will give them political support, as well as economic leverage in the future, suggested Swanstrom.[17] China has improved relations with Russia. In 1996, after 22 rounds of talks, two important agreements were signed to settle the border issue between China and Russia: Deepening Military Trust in Border Regions, and Reduction of Military Forces in the Border Areas. Resolution of the border dispute paved the way for strategic and economic cooperation between China and Russia.

China has been heavily dependent on Middle Eastern oil, but oil from the Middle East has to be transported to China by sea. China is deeply uncomfortable that major global shipping lanes are policed by the US Navy. China has focused on securing new oil sources in neighboring countries such as Kazakhstan and Russia, to diversify energy sources and limit dependence on shipping lanes. It wants a steady supply that would be blockade-proof in case of a conflict over Taiwan or other problems along the long sea route. Central Asian energy supplies, unlike Middle Eastern, Southeast Asian, African or Latin American supplies—do not require maritime security. Oil and gas from Central Asia are transported to China via pipelines and freight trains and are thus not vulnerable to disruptions on the sea. China even reportedly overpaid when purchasing PetroKazakhstan in 2006,

---

16   Robert G. Sutter, *Chinese Foreign Relations: Power and Policy Since the Cold War* (Lanham: Rowman & Littlefield, 2008), p. 326.

17   Jeremy Bransten, "Central Asia: China's Mounting Influence," *EurasiaNet* (www. eurasianet.org), September 17, 2007.

but for China, "price is less important than reliability and building good will" in Kazakhstan, commented a Free University of Brussels scholar on China-Central Asia relations.[18] Geographical proximity of Central Asian countries has made them attractive candidates as suppliers of both oil and gas to China. Furthermore, the pipelines can also be used to transport Middle Eastern oil to China in the future.

To pursue both Russian and Central Asian energy sources is also part of China's "Go West" development strategy enacted in the early 2000s. As a result of uneven development in the past three decades, regional gaps in China have widened. The "Western Development" strategy was designed by the Chinese government to help inland areas, mostly located in China's West and Northwest, to catch up. Trade with Central Asia countries and Russia is a convenient way to promote growth in China's vast hinterland.

A century of Russification left Russian as the language of business and the elite in Central Asia, and the entirety of Soviet-era infrastructure is geared toward linking the region's economy to Russia. Roads, railways and pipelines almost exclusively connect to Russia. Central Asian states have tried to loosen the Russian hold, but for the most part, the region remains Russia's backyard. This is changing. In addition to building oil and gas pipelines, China is also in the midst of an aggressive effort to harness the region's rail network. Pipelines are certainly important in orienting a country's geopolitics, but rail lines allow for two-way trade and deep economic penetration that involves the entire populace. Energy transactions only involve a very few people. Rails, far more than pipes, are truly the ties that bind. In 2007 China broke ground on two projects to link itself to Central Asia via railways. One will link Kazakhstan's Almaty region to China's rail network via the border town of Korgas. The other will link the Chinese city of Kashi—at the terminus of China's own system—to the Ferghana Valley and on to the Uzbek capital, Tashkent. Both routes also lay the groundwork for later road and pipe connections.[19]

China's involvement in Central Asia has fundamentally changed the strategic picture of the region. For Central Asian states, China is a crucial actor locally and could be a long-term counterbalance against the United States and Russia. They are aware that the Americans will probably leave and the Chinese will always be present due to geographical proximity and economic interdependence.

China and Kazakhstan signed Good-Neighborly Treaty of Friendship and Cooperation in 2002, which serves as a cornerstone of their strategic partnership in the early 21st century. According to President Nazarbayev, China had provided security guarantee to Kazakhstan after the latter gave up developing nuclear weapons.[20] The two countries have satisfactorily resolved the boundary issue, and turned their border region into a land of friendship and trade. As a fellow

---

18   "China Sees Kazakhstan as Safe Source of Oil," *The International Herald Tribune*, March 17, 2006.

19   "China: Railroading Central Asia," *Stratfor.com*, January 31, 2008.

20   "Nazarbayev Calls for Closer Ties between China, Kazakhstan," The Chinese Government's official website (http://www.gov.cn), April 14, 2009.

SCO member, Kazakhstan firmly supports China's combat against the "three evil forces" of separatism, terrorism, and extremism.

Though Kazakhstan has extensive military cooperation with Russia, the Sino-Kazakh strategic partnership makes provision for the development of military cooperation between the two countries. Military contacts between China and Kazakhstan are still in their infancy. Collaboration between the Chinese and Kazakh armies takes place principally during the multilateral operations organized by the SCO, such as the Peace Mission undertaken in Cheliabinsk in summer 2007. The Kazakh military has since 1997 received more than 50 million yuan of Chinese aid in communications technology and jeeps, and hopes to obtain free transfers of decommissioned military assets from China.[21]

Counter the "Three Evils"—Separatism, Terrorism and Extremism

Another major concern in China-Central Asia relations is the separatist movement in China's northwest. Separatist movement in Xinjiang has long troubled the Chinese government. After a series of "Color Revolutions"—the "Rose Revolution" in Georgia in 2003, the "Orange Revolution" in Ukraine in 2004, and the "Tulip Revolution" in the Kyrgyz Republic in 2005—China became concerned that Uyghur extremists may become emboldened and externally exploited.

When China opened up the borders for trade in the 1980s, many people from Central Asia came over. As a result of increased cross-border interaction among the Uyghurs and Central Asians, pan-Turkic nationalism was on the rise. Some Uyghurs in Xinjiang desire political freedom and even independence from China. Some have used violence in an attempt to establish a separate state called East Turkestan. China's primary security concern is the East Turkestan terrorist group, which was alleged to be closely linked to terrorist groups in the Middle East and Central Asia. Evidence reveals that Osama bin Laden told the East Turkestan terrorists: "I support your jihad in Xinjiang."[22]

About 10 million Uyghurs live in China, mostly in Xinjiang. The estimated 350,000 Uyghurs in Kazakhstan and Kyrgyzstan create, for China and the Central Asian governments, a disturbing base for political mobilization in Central Asia. It is clear that the separatists in Xinjiang have received an increased amount of military resources and support from their ethnic and/or religious brothers in Central Asia since 1991.[23] In the early 1990s, Kazakhstan tolerated advocacy by its resident ethnic Uyghurs for greater respect for human rights and autonomy for their cohorts in Xinjiang. In the late 1990s, however, Kazakhstan cracked down on such activism at China's behest. Nonetheless, Kazakhstan allegedly

---

21   Peyrouse, "Sino-Kazakh Relations," p. 12.

22   Guang Pan. "China and Central Asia: Charting a New Course for Regional Cooperation," *China Brief*, Vol. 7, No. 3 (February 7, 2007), p. 5.

23   Swanstrom, "China and Central Asia: A New Great Game or Traditional Vassal Relations?," p. 575.

has remained a base for clandestine Uyghur groups advocating independence for "East Turkestan."[24] Dozens of Uyghur separatists had been trained abroad and then transported to China through Central Asian states. It is important for China to count on the support of its Central Asian neighbors in its campaign against the Uyghur extremists. Similarly, Central Asian countries also receive support from China in combating their own terrorist and extremist groups, such as the Islamic Movement of Uzbekistan and Hizb-ut-Tahrir (the Islamic Party of Liberation).[25]

Uyghur communities in Central Asia provide an impetus to separatist movements in Xinjiang in two important ways. First, they gave significant moral support to the Uyghur cause in Xinjiang. Second, they provide important regional and international coverage of the Uyghur cause, lobbying international organizations and governments to press Chinese leaders for greater Uyghur autonomy in Xinjiang.[26] Central Asian nations' dependence on Chinese investments would enable China to influence these states' policy toward Uyghur rebels in Xinjiang.

Fighting "the three evils" has become a common interest of all nations in the region. In 2004 the SCO established the Regional Anti-Terrorist Structure. In August 2007 approximately 6,500 soldiers from all six members of the SCO conducted the largest joint military exercises held by the group. Named "Peace Mission 2007," the exercises were held in two areas, first at the Russian Army's 34th Motorized Rifle Division facility in the Volga-Urals Military District. The exercises were later shifted to Urumqi in Xinjiang. China has also successfully solicited support from other SCO members in adding the fight against "the three evils" clause in the jointly issued statement of the SCO.

In April 2009, China, Russia, Kazakhstan, Tajikistan and Kyrgyzstan took part in a new round of war game in the first such exercise since the Kyrgyz government announced in February 2009 it would shut the last US air base in Central Asia. The Manas base has played an important role in supplying US-led troops fighting in Afghanistan and its closure will pose a challenge to plans by President Barack Obama to send additional troops there to fight the growing Taliban insurgency. The plot of the war game featured al-Qaeda members who had crossed over the border from Afghanistan and captured a chemical factory, taking its workers hostage. The soldiers freed the hostages with the help of planes and parachutes. About 1,000 soldiers took part in the 2009 exercises. A few months later, at a military training base in Shenyang of northeast China, China and Russia held their Peace Mission 2009 joint military exercises designed to defend against terrorism. The biennial military exercises were also conducted in 2005 and 2007.

Indeed, winning support from Central Asian states and Russia is critical in China's war against "the three evils." Shortly after the July 5, 2009 ethnic riots

---

24   Lum, et al. "Comparing Global Influence," p. 91.

25   Pan, "China and Central Asia: Charting a New Course for Regional Cooperation," p. 5.

26   Kevin Sheives, "China Turns West: Beijing's Contemporary Strategy Towards Central Asia," *Pacific Affairs*, Vol. 79, No. 2 (Summer, 2006), p. 209.

in Xinjiang, the SCO's Secretary General issued a statement, saying that the member states regard Xinjiang as an inalienable part of the PRC and the situation in Xinjiang was purely China's internal affairs. The statement added that the SCO believed that measures the Chinese government was taking in accordance with the country's laws could restore peace and order in the region. The statement also vowed that the organization would enhance cooperation among member states in fighting "the three evils" as well as transnational organized crimes to maintain peace and stability of the SCO area.[27] This was a rare public support the Chinese government received in the aftermath of the government crackdown on the riots, highlighting the diplomatic, political, and strategic values of the SCO to China.

Security cooperation is also an important dimension of China's relations with individual Central Asian states. For example, Sino-Kazakh strategic cooperation has increased to cover cross-border security. Since 2008 the two countries have undertaken joint operations to counter drug traffickers, who cross the border clandestinely, especially at Usharalsk in the Almaty region. It is reported that the Kazakhstan National Security Service has stepped up the monitoring of Uyghur militants based in Kazakhstan and has increased intelligence exchanges with China on this issue.

Chinese Strategies in Central Asia and Russia

China has pursued both bilateral ties with each Central Asian state and Russia as well as multilateral ties through the SCO. China has concluded friendship and cooperation treaties with Kazakhstan, Kyrgyzstan, Tajikistan, and Uzbekistan. China and Kazakhstan proclaimed a "strategic partnership" in 2005. At the August 2007 SCO summit in Bishkek, Kyrgyzstan, a multilateral friendship and cooperation treaty was signed. The Bishkek Declaration stated that "Central Asia's security and stability first relies on the efforts of various countries in this region." Major Chinese strategies in Central Asia and Russia include:

Top-level Involvement

Involvement of top leaders is testimony of the attention both sides pay to the relationship. Exchange of visits at the highest level is particularly helpful to warming bilateral relations. At this high level, relations are clearly moving in a positive direction between China and Central Asia. Top leaders of China and Russia and Central Asia have met on a regular basis since the early 2000s. In January 1992, only one month after the founding of the new Central Asian countries, a Chinese delegation led by then Minister of Foreign Trade and Economic Cooperation Li Lanqing visited five Central Asian countries and signed a series of agreements

---

27   "SCO Expresses Condolence to Families of Victims in Xinjiang Riot," *Xinhua*, July 11, 2009.

to establish diplomatic relations with all of them. Since then all Central Asian top leaders have visited Beijing and their counterparts in China have traveled to Central Asia multiple times.

In June 2003, on his first overseas trip as the Chinese head of state, President Hu Jintao paid official visits to Russia, Kazakhstan, and Mongolia after attending the informal South-North Leaders dialogue in Evian, France. During President Hu's second visit to Russia in July 2005, China and Russia signed a joint declaration on the international order in the 21st century, cooperative agreements between specified Russian and Chinese financial institutions, and long-term cooperation agreements between Russia's Unified Energy Systems power monopoly and the China State Grid Corp., as well as between Russian state oil firm Rosneft and CNPC. President Hu also remarked that the two countries would strengthen support for one another with respect to Chechnya and Taiwan.

In March 2007 President Hu made his third state visit to Russia since he took office in 2003, underscoring China's intense interest in Russia's energy resources and strategic values. Russia is Europe's main energy supplier, but is keen to use energy as a weapon and to find new markets in Asia. China and Russia are also natural allies as they each have grievances against the West. In June 2009 President Hu attended the ninth annual summit of the SCO and the first BRIC summit in Yekaterinburg, Russia, and paid a state visit to Russia again. In June 2012 President Putin attended the SCO summit in Beijing, and in September 2012 President Hu attended the APEC summit in Russia's far eastern port city Vladivostok and met with President Putin and other Asia–Pacific leaders.

President Hu visited Kazakhstan four times between 2003 and 2009. In June 2003 President Hu included Kazakhstan in his first official trip abroad. In July 2005 he traveled to Kazakhstan again to attend the SCO summit in Astana, capital of Kazakhstan. The two countries already signed the Treaty of Good-Neighborliness and Friendly Cooperation earlier. During Hu's visit, the two countries reached important consensus on further strengthening China–Kazakhstan friendly cooperation and decided to uplift the bilateral relations to the level of strategic partnership. They also affirmed their intention to build an oil pipeline from western Kazakhstan to China (Atasu-Alashankou). In August 2007, after attending the 7th Session of the Council of Heads of States of the SCO in Bishkek and observing the SCO joint anti-terrorism military exercise in Russia, President Hu paid another state visit to Kazakhstan. During this visit, China and Kazakhstan signed a joint communiqué on relations and trade promotion as well as international issues of common concern. The two countries pledged to strike a balance between import and export and make concerted efforts to help the annual bilateral trade volume reach $15 billion by 2015.[28]

President Hu journeyed to Turkmenistan and Tajikistan in August 2008. Hu's visit to Turkmenistan coincided with the one-year anniversary of the launching of

---

28　"China, Kazakhstan Sign Joint Communiqué on Promoting Relations, Trade," *Xinhua*, August 18, 2007.

the grand Turkmenistan–China gas pipeline project in Samandepe, on the right bank of the Amu Darya River in eastern Turkmenistan. The two sides signed a new agreement on increasing the volume of gas to be pumped to China and opened up new areas of cooperation such as in textile and chemical industries. President Hu met with Uzbekistan's President Islam Karimov at the sidelines of the SCO summit held in the Russian city of Yekaterinburg in June 2009. The two also met during the 2008 Summer Olympic Games in Beijing. In Decmber 2009 President Hu visited Turkmenistan and Kazakhstan and officially opened the Turkmenistan–Uzbekistan–Kazakhstan–China gas pipeline.

Other senior Chinese leaders have visited the region. Premier Wen Jiabao visited Uzbekistan and Turkmenistan in November 2007. He traveled to Russia and Kazakhstan in October 2008. During the October 2008 travel, he also attended the 13th regular meeting between Chinese and Russian prime ministers in Moscow and the 7th prime ministers' meeting of SCO member countries in Astana. Vice Premier Li Keqiang visited Uzbekistan and Turkmenistan in June 2009.

In January 2006 Vice President Zeng Qinghong went to Kazakhstan to attend the inauguration ceremony of Kazakhstan's re-elected president on behalf of President Hu. Zeng and Kazakh President Nursultan Nazarbayev discussed the construction of a natural gas transportation system following an oil pipeline linking the two countries was built in December 2005. In July 2005 Vice Premier Wu Yi led a large delegation of 80 businesspeople to Uzbekistan and signed a framework agreement with Uzbekistan on investments worth $1.5 billion. Foreign Minister Yang Jiechi visited Kyrgyzstan, Kazakhstan and Kyrgyzstan in July and August 2007. Finance Minister Jin Renqing visited Uzbekistan in July 2007. Cao Gangchuan, Vice Chairman of China's Central Military Commission, State Councilor and Defense Minister, visited Kyrgyzstan in June 2007. In December 2012 Vice Premier Wang Qishan visited Russia and Kazakhstan in his first foreign trip after becoming a new CCP Politburo Standing Committee member at the 18th CCP national congress less than a month earlier. In December 2012, Premier Wen Jiabao attended the SCO prime ministers' meeting in Bishkek, capital of Kyrgyzstan.

In return, leaders from Russia and Central Asian republics have frequently traveled to China. In March 2006 Russian President Vladimir Putin visited China. President of the southern Russian republic of Chechnya Alu Alkhanov, who accompanied Russian President Vladimir Putin during his visit to China, revealed that the Chechen government, Russia's Vneshekonombank, and the State Development Bank of China had signed an agreement on investment cooperation in Beijing. After two wars, the economy and infrastructure of Chechnya had been seriously damaged. China was the first foreign country that pledged to invest in Chechnya's post-war reconstruction. China planned to invest a total of $300 million in Chechnya's agriculture, infrastructure, and other areas.[29]

Beijing's over $3 trillion in foreign exchange reserves give it unusual leverage to strike deals at a time when the global financial crisis has left other governments

---

29   "China Plans to Aid Chechnya's Reconstruction," *VOA Chinese*, October 19, 2006.

scrambling for cash. It has struck deals with Russia, Venezuela and Brazil since mid-February 2009 to trade loans or investment for long-term oil supplies. Kazakh President Nursultan Nazarbayev visited Beijing in April 2009 in the midst of the global financial crisis. This was Nazarbayev's second state visit to China after he was re-elected in 2005. During his visit, China announced a $5 billion loans-for-oil deal with Kazakhstan. According to the deal, state-owned CNPC will lend $5 billion to Kazakhstan's KazMunaiGaz EP for the joint purchase of MangistauMunaiGaz, which owns oil and gas fields.[30] The deal could help Kazakhstan diversify its export routes. It already has an oil pipeline to China but most production goes across Russia to Western buyers. China imported 42 million barrels of Kazakh oil through the pipeline in 2008. President Nazarbayev visited Beijing again in June 2012.

In May 2005 Uzbek President Karimov and President Hu signed a treaty on friendly and cooperative partnership during President Karimov's visit in Beijing, signaling new determination on both sides to further consolidate their traditional friendship and cooperation. President Karimov visited China again in June 2012, sealing more deals in energy and economic cooperation.

Expanding Trade and Increasing Investment

Like elsewhere, a major strategy China has taken is to promote trade with and increase investment in Central Asia. The Chinese strategy for the purchase of oilfields is influenced by Beijing's late arrival to the Central Asian market — China can only acquire sites of relatively marginal importance. In spite of this disadvantage, China has invested in fields in the Aktobe region and near the Caspian Sea in order to establish some presence in the energy sector of Central Asia. China is also involved in more isolated fields along the route of the Sino-Kazakh pipeline. The general Chinese strategy is to connect all acquired fields along the Sino-Kazakh pipeline, which will connect the shores of the Caspian to the Dostyk/Alashankou border post. The first section, which links the Kenkiyak field to Atyrau, became operational in 2003; and the second section, connecting the pumping station and railway terminal in Atasu to the Dostyke/Alashankou station was opened in May 2006. China managed to buy a key Kazakh oil company in 2007 and in 2005 a 1,000-mile pipeline began carrying Kazakh crude oil to China. China extended the pipeline westward in 2011 to funnel Caspian oil eastward. This third and last section of the pipeline, which runs through central Kazakhstan, will increase the pipeline's global export capacity to 20 million tons per year, and will secure about five percent of the total volume of Chinese oil imports.[31]

China plans to build 12 highways to link its remote northwest to Central Asia, targeting a key source for energy and commodities to fuel its rapid economic growth.

---

30   Joe McDonald, "China, Kazakhstan Sign $5 billion Loans-for-Oil Deal," *Business Week*, April 17, 2009.

31   Peyrouse, "Sino-Kazakh Relations," p. 12.

The longest will stretch 1,680 kilometers (1.045 miles) from Urumqi to Istanbul. The planned highways would connect China with Russia, Kazakhstan, Tajikistan and Pakistan.[32] In 2005 China allocated $3.75 million to repair the 16 miles of roadway between the Kyrgyz capital of Bishkek and the Manas airport. In September 2006 China provided a loan for Kyrgyzstan's purchase of automobiles worth $1.8 million. In January 2007 Chinese and Tajik firms signed an agreement in Beijing for the provision of a $200 million loan (for 25 years with an annual interest rate of one percent) to build a 150-megawatt hydroelectric power station on the River Zarafshon in northern Tajikistan. In 2006 China extended a $24.5 million low-interest loan to finance construction or revamping of fiber optic and cellular telephone networks throughout Turkmenistan. In 2007 China provided a $24 million loan for the purchase of Chinese drilling equipment and field camps for geological work and a $36 million loan to purchase Chinese railway passenger cars.[33]

Trade patterns across the borders have changed over the years. In the 1960s China and the Soviet Union fought bloody skirmishes along the Amur River that divides the two countries. When relations began to thaw in the 1980s, many Chinese flocked across the border to buy Soviet cars, farm machinery, kitchen utensils—anything they could get their hands on. Now trade moves in the opposite direction. In the city of Blagoveshchensk, which sits on the Amur River, the Chinese are sustaining the local economy. The Chinese presence is strikingly obvious. A Chinese company constructed the Asia Hotel—the tallest building by far in Blagoveshchensk with the city's only world-class accommodations.

Reactions to Chinese trade are mixed. Increased trade has created real and potential tensions between China and Central Asian nations and Russia. Racist hate crimes are on the rise in Russia, and nationalists speak of a Chinese menace growing on Russia's border. But Blagoveshchensk residents tend to be less suspicious of the Chinese than they were a few years ago. On the city's main street, clothes designer Tatyana Sorokina said she felt closer to China than Moscow, which is thousands of miles away. "That's just a fact of life … after all, China's just across the river. We depend on the Chinese for so many things. Any development here is good for us," she remarked.[34]

The 2008–2009 global financial crisis hit every corner of the world. The Chinese government's 4 trillion yuan ($585 billion) stimulus package put its economy in a relatively better shape. In a 2009 regional report, the International Monetary Fund (IMF) projected a stark economic forecast for Central Asia. The IMF predicted that the economic growth rate which stood at 12 percent in 2007 and 6 percent in 2008 would slow down to less than 2 percent in 2009 as a "great recession" took hold. A senior IMF official said, "Until recently, the region had been awash with commodity-export receipts, capital inflows and remittances. This

---

32 "China Plans 12 Highways to Central Asia," *CNN*, April 5, 2007.

33 Lum, et al. "Comparing Global Influence," pp. 112–13.

34 Gregory Feifer, "Russia, China's Fortunes Reversed in Frontier City," *National Public Radio* www.npr.org, All Things Considered, April 5, 2008.

had led to significant economic gains in recent years with real per capita GDP growing impressively." However, the conditions are deteriorating. Oil and gas exporters are heavily affected by the decline in global demand and the sharp fall in their prices. Central Asian countries have difficulty in obtaining foreign capital now. The good news is that trade with China and continued Chinese investment have greatly helped these Central Asian countries in dealing with the economic crisis.

In an unprecedented "oil-for-loans" agreement signed with Russia on February 17, 2009, the China Development Bank promised to lend $25 billion at 6 percent annual interest to Russia's state-owned oil company Rosneft and oil pipeline monopoly Transneft. In return, China will receive roughly 20 million tons of oil annually from Russia starting from 2011 for a 20-year period. The total volume of the Russian oil supplies within this framework is the equivalent of about four percent of China's current consumption of oil and about 8 percent of China's present imports. Rosneft will receive $15 billion out of the Chinese loan. Transneft will receive the remaining $10 billion towards the cost of building a spur from the East Siberia-Pacific Ocean (ESPO) pipeline originating from Skovorodino in eastern Siberia to China's Daqing petrochemical hub.[35] The Chinese loan came as a great relief to the two cash-strapped Russian energy companies to realize their refinancing loans as well as to continue with their capital expenditures. The loan also to some extent made up for the flight of Western capital from Russia. Through trade and investment, China has projected a strong presence in Central Asia and Russia.

Promoting Cultural and Societal Exchanges

As part of its global efforts to consolidate societal links and expand soft power, China has promoted cultural, educational, sports, and other social exchanges with Central Asian nations. The first Confucius Institute in Kazakhstan opened its doors at Gumilyov Eurasian National University on December 5, 2007. The University already admitted over 300 students who studied Chinese at the Institute.[36] During the visit of President Hu to Uzbekistan in June 2004, the two governments signed an agreement to set up a Confucius Institute in Tashkent, which was officially established in May 2005. This Institute is located in the center of Tashkent. It has modern linguistics classrooms, a library and an activity center. The Confucius Institute in Tashkent has been named one of the "Confucius Institutes of the Year" several times. In addition, as of 2012, Kazakhstan hosted two Confucius Institutes, Kyrgyzstan had two, and Tajikistan had one too.

China has played a pivotal role in catalyzing cultural cooperation. President Hu remarked at the 2005 SCO summit, "We shall, by effective measures, conduct and

---

35   M.K. Bhadrakumar, "Cash-rich China Courts the Caspian," *Asia Times Online*, April 18, 2009.

36   "Kazakhstan's Confucius Institute Unveiled," *Xinhua*, December 5, 2007.

deepen our cooperation in culture, disaster relief, education, tourism, journalism, etcetera. Human resources capacity building should be another area of cooperation, and China will set aside a special fund to train 1,500 management and professional talents in different fields from other member states within three years."[37] This project which was geared at training young professionals from Central Asia had been progressing well. At the August 2007 SCO summit, President Hu called for bolstering scientific, cultural, educational, sports, and healthcare exchanges and cooperation, and announced that China would offer 20 college scholarships per year to SCO members. He also called on SCO members to start short-term student exchanges and announced that China would invite 50 college and high school students from SCO member states to visit China each year. President Hu announced in December 2009 in Kazakhstan the doubling of the number of scholarships for Kazakh students to study in China from 2010.

To attract athletes and tourists from Central Asia, China built a mosque ahead of the 2010 Asian Games in Guangzhou. Academic exchanges are also growing. In March 2006 China sent a large delegation to the conference "Kazakhstan and China: Strategic Partnership for Development," held in Almaty. Chinese academic institutions and think tanks are conducting exchanges with their Central Asian counterparts. For example, the Institute of Russia, Middle Asia and Eastern Europe under the CASS has co-hosted conferences or conducted exchange programs with the Center for Strategic Research at Kainar University in Kazakhstan, the Kazakh Institute of Strategic Research, the World Economy and Policy Institute, and the Orientalism Institute of Kazakhstan.

Interest in each other's culture remains strong and cultural cooperation has huge potentials between China and Central Asia. The SCO has held several Cultural and Art Festivals in member states. Culture-oriented tourism along the ancient Silk Road has become attractive to China's growing middle class. Many more Chinese than Americans travel to Central Asian countries now. In 2008 the Kyrgyz Interior Ministry reported that over 49,000 foreigners from 110 countries had visited Kyrgyzstan in 2007, over 12 percent of whom were from China. The State Statistics Agency of Kazakhstan reported in 2005 that the United States was among the top seven countries of origin for inbound tourists (over 19,500), while Russia remained first with 1.7 million inbound tourists, followed by China with over 76,800. Russia was the top destination for citizens of Kazakhstan traveling abroad (with 1.65 million visitors), followed by China (nearly 85,000). The United States was not even among the top eight destinations.[38] Other exchanges between China and Central Asia include regular inter-parliamentary dialogues between China's NPC and its counterparts in Kazakhstan, Kyrgyzstan, Turkmenistan and Uzbekistan.

---

37   Hu Jintao, "Strengthening Solidarity and Cooperation to Promote Stability and Development," A speech at the Shanghai Cooperation Organization's Astana summit meeting, July 5, 2005.

38   Lum, et al. "Comparing Global Influence," p. 95.

Working Through the SCO

Economic, political, security and cultural cooperation between China and Central Asia and Russia has become institutionalized through the formation and development of the SCO, which is a major instrument for China to carry out its new diplomacy in Central Asia. Covering an area of over 30 million square kilometers, with a population of some 1.55 billion, the SCO is an intergovernmental security and economic cooperation organization between China, Central Asia and Russia. In July 2001 Russia and China, the organization's two leading nations, signed the Treaty of Good-Neighborliness and Friendly Cooperation. In June 2002 the heads of the SCO member states signed the SCO Charter in St. Petersburg, expounding on the organization's purposes, principles, structures and form of operation, and establishing it officially from the point of view of international law. Since then the SCO has been playing an active role in promoting economic and security cooperation among its members.

Major activities of the SCO include economic cooperation, security cooperation, and cultural and other exchanges. The SCO is not a mutual defense pact, but its members have conducted joint military exercises since 2003. Different from Russia which has primarily been concerned about security, China was more interested in the SCO developing into a nascent trade organization loosely based on the EU model.[39] China hopes that the SCO can help it achieve its primary economic and trade objectives. More recently China is also using the SCO as a platform to achieve its political and security objectives.

The SCO is not without any problems. Attempts to expand SCO's mandate, particularly in the economic domain, have produced disagreements, often with China on one side and Russia on the other. In 2002 Beijing proposed that the SCO be made into a free trade zone. Russia contended that free trade zones could only work when the countries involved had the same economic levels. Given the discrepancy among the members, it is unlikely a free trade zone will be established in the near future. Central Asian countries such as Kazakhstan fear that they could be transformed into a Chinese economic protectorate.[40] The members have not reached consensus on the enlargement of the bloc either, especially with regards to Iran's full membership.

Has the SCO emerged as a powerful anti-US bulwark in Central Asia? Some may consider SCO as a counterweight to the North Atlantic Treaty Organization (NATO) and US hegemony, but SCO members have expressed their support for US and NATO efforts to stabilize Afghanistan. Many believe that because of inherent and historical frictions between its two main members, Russia and China, the SCO is unlikely to form a serious united front and pose a real threat to US

---

39   John C.K. Daly, "Premier Wen's Eurasia Tour: Beijing and Moscow's Divergent Views on Central Asia," *China Brief*, Vol. 7, No. 21 (November 14, 2007), The Jamestown Foundation, Washington, DC.

40   Peyrouse, "Sino-Kazakh Relations," p. 14.

interests. Nevertheless, what happened in July 2005 created much concern in the United States. On July 5, 2005, the SCO issued a declaration implicitly calling for the United States to withdraw its military forces from Uzbekistan. Uzbekistan and the United States already had a frayed relationship over the Uzbek authorities' crackdown on a May 2005 uprising in Andijan and the Uzbek government's suspicion of US involvement in pro-democracy revolutions in Georgia, Ukraine, and Kyrgyzstan, but the SCO declaration accelerated the withdrawal of US forces. Furthermore, in 2005 the United States sought but was denied observer status in the SCO. No wonder the United States has viewed the SCO with caution and concern.

Recent Developments in China's Relations with Central Asia and Russia

Kazakhstan

China–Kazakhstan trade represents more than two thirds of all trade between China and Central Asia. In less than a decade, Chinese companies have successfully established a solid footing in the Kazakh energy market, and by 2006 China had been managing approximately 24 percent of Kazakh oil production, mainly by accepting the Kazakh authorities' requirement that the state firm KazMunayGas be associated with all activities.[41] In January 2012, Kazakh President Nazarbayev set the end of the year as the target date for joining the WTO. Kazakhstan's entry into the WTO is likely to further boost bilateral trade in the years ahead.

CNPC inaugurated an oil pipeline running from Kazakhstan to northwest China. Initially, half the oil pumped through the new 200,000 barrels per day pipeline was expected to come from Russia because of insufficient output from nearby Kazakh fields. In October 2005 CNPC bought PetroKazakhstan, a Canadian-run company that had been the largest independent oil company in the former Soviet Union, for $4.18 billion, and spent another $700 million on a pipeline that will take the oil to the Chinese border.[42] At the time, the PetroKazakhstan deal was the largest foreign purchase ever by a Chinese company. Following up on a $25 billion loan to Russia that it dished out in February 2009, China agreed to lend $10 billion to Kazakhstan to cope with the financial crisis. It expects Kazakhstan to reciprocate by bolstering its energy supplies to China. During his December 2009 visit, President Hu and his Kazakh counterpart agreed to speed up implementation of the $10 billion loan.

Kazakhstan was the first stop for the Beijing Olympic flame on its 130-day global tour which started on April 2, 2008, and President Nazarbayev participated in the torch relay. "The fact that the city of Almaty became the first point of the Olympic flame's run proves China's good attitude to Kazakhstan, and President Hu Jintao's

---

41   Peyrouse, "Sino-Kazakh Relations," p. 11.

42   "China Sees Kazakhstan As Safe Source of Oil," *The International Herald Tribune*, March 17, 2006.

good attitude to me personally," said President Nazarbayev before his short symbolic torch run.[43] Performers in national costumes, symbolizing the multiethnic population of Kazakhstan, participated in a lavish ceremony to welcome the Olympic torch to Kazakhstan. This was in sharp contrast to what happened to the torch relay in London, Paris, and San Francisco, where anti-China protestors disrupted the relay. In Paris pro-Tibetan independence protestors even attempted to seize the torch and extinguish the flame. The Paris city hall displayed the banner "Paris defends human rights all over the world" during the chaotic Paris-portion of the torch relay. President Nazarbayev later attended the opening ceremony of the Beijing Olympics in August 2008.

Kazakh Prime Minister Karim Masimov visited China in April 2008 and attended the BFA in Hainan. In Beijing he signed a series of agreements with Premier Wen Jiabao. Reflecting expanding relations between the two sides, these agreements covered cooperation in non-resource economy, finance, agriculture, electricity and hydropower. Wen proposed to further strengthen coordination to ensure the smooth construction of the China–Kazakhstan crude oil pipeline and natural gas pipeline projects, earnestly implement the agreement on non-resource economy and encourage bilateral investment, increase customs clearance capacity, quicken road construction, and step up exchanges and cooperation in culture, education, science, technology and sport.[44] Masimov said Kazakhstan was ready to cooperate with China in law enforcement and security, fight "the three evils" and push forward the development of SCO. As of 2012 the China–Kazakhstan oil and gas pipelines had started operation, and the second cross-border railway between China and Kazakhstan had been successfully linked up. A new natural gas pipeline linking the two countries is being built by the Chinese and is to be completed in 2014.

Turkmenistan

During a summit meeting in Beijing in April 2006, Chinese President Hu Jintao and Turkmen President Saparmurat Niyazov signed a major agreement on the construction of a gas pipeline directly linking their countries and facilitating the flow of Turkmen gas to China. China planned to move up to 30 billion cubic meters (bcm) of Turkmen gas annually in 2009, through a pipeline which goes through Kazakhstan, to China. By the end of 2008, after extensive dialogue, Turkmenistan agreed to increase the annual volume of gas to China from 30 bcm to 40 bcm for the 30 years starting from the fourth quarter of 2009. Some analysts suggested that this would immensely challenge Russia's monopoly over the transportation and export of Turkmen gas. For Turkmenistan, however, reaching out to new markets is a means of diversifying the trade routes, and the authorities have promised to continue to take on all of the obligations regarding the bilateral agreements with

---

43   Anton Dosibiyev, "Olympic Torch Passes through Kazakhstan," *The Associated Press*, April 2, 2008.
44   "China, Kazakhstan Vow to Further Enhance Co-op," *Xinhua*, April 10, 2008.

Russia.[45] By 2008 China had signed 49 agreements with Turkmenistan worth a total of $1.3 billion. Over the period of a projected 30 years ahead, CNPC is planning to invest $30 billion into Turkmenistan' production of oil, gas, silk, minerals, fertilizers and cotton processing.[46]

After President Niyazov suddenly died of a heart attack in December 2006, President Hu sent a message of condolences to Turkmenistan's acting President Gurbanguly Berdymukhamedov. Hu's message expressed "deep-felt" condolences and "sincere" sympathies to the government and people of Turkmenistan and the president's family. He said in the message that President Niyazov was an "intimate" friend of the Chinese people and had made an "outstanding" contribution to the friendly and cooperative relations between China and Turkmenistan. Hu stressed that China was willing to work with Turkmenistan to continue developing the friendly and cooperative relations between the two countries.[47] On February 14, 2007, President Hu's special envoy and Vice Chairman of the NPC Ismail Amat attended the inauguration ceremony of Turkmenistan's newly elected president Gurbanguly Berdymukhamedov.

Military exchanges between China and Turkmenistan have been expanded. Lieutenant General Serdar Chariyarov, first deputy-defense minister and chief of general staff of the Turkmenistan armed forces, visited China in July 2002. Defense Minister Agagelgy Mametgeldiyev of Turkmenistan visited China in November 2007, during which he and his Chinese counterpart Cao Gangchuan agreed that the two armed forces were ready to develop the friendly and cooperative ties in various fields and at multiple levels.[48] After Defense Minister Mametgeldiyev's visit to Beijing, China agreed to provide weapons, equipment, and training to the Turkmen military. According to Mametgeldiyev, China will also provide a $3 million preferential loan to Turkmen military to help it modernize. This is a significant amount of money, given that Turkmenistan's total military budget is only between $70 million and $80 million a year.[49] China is clearly using its trade and aid to increase its influence in Turkmenistan and other Central Asian countries.

In September 2012, Zhou Yongkang, a member of the Standing Committee of the CCP's Politburo, visited Turkmenistan and met with Turkmen President Berdimuhamedow. The two leaders vowed to promote cooperation in energy, communication, health care, security, and cultural exchanges.

---

45   Chemen Durdiyeva, "Hu Jintao's Visit to Turkmenistan Intensifies Chinese-Turkmen Partnership," *Central Asia-Caucasus Institute Analyst* http://www.cacianalyst. org, September 17, 2008.

46   Ibid.

47   "Chinese President Offers Condolences over Death of Turkmenistan's President," *Xinhua*, December 21, 2006.

48   "China, Turkmenistan Agree to Promote Military Ties," *Xinhua*, November 6, 2007.

49   Bai Hua, "China and Turkmenistan Strengthening Military Cooperation," *VOA Chinese*, November 29, 2007.

Kyrgyzstan

Kyrgyzstan is strategically located. The United States has been using the military base at Manas since 2001 to send troops and cargo to Afghanistan in the war against terror. Kyrgyz President Kurmanbek Bakiyev announced in early February 2009 that the base would be closed in six months. Kyrgyz and Russian officials denied that the announcement was related to a $2.15 billion Russian aid package announced the same day, though most analysts believed the Russian aid prompted the Kyrgyz decision.[50] Meanwhile, Kyrgyz Parliament decided to delay a vote on expelling American troops from the air base until it receives a $450 million down payment in aid and loans promised by Russia. The delay allowed the United States time to make a counteroffer.[51] The United States set up Manas and a base in neighboring Uzbekistan to back operations in Afghanistan. Uzbekistan expelled US troops from the base on its territory in 2005, leaving Manas as the only US military facility in Central Asia.

In early June 2009 President Bakiyev said he would consider new ways of expanding ties with the United States upon receiving a personal letter from President Barack Obama. After intensive negotiations, the Kyrgyz government decided in late June 2009 to allow the United States to continue to use the Manas air base. Under the one-year lease approved by President Bakiyev, the air base would be designated as a transit center and the rent increased to $60 million a year, from $17 million. William Burns, the US undersecretary of state for political affairs who was sent to Bishkek to seal the deal, said that the new agreement would help to ensure stability across Central Asia.[52] The United States has continued to use the Manas facility which is called a transit center instead of an "air base" now. In 2012, the China–Kyrgyzstan–Uzbekistan highway was launched. A multidimensional new "silk road" consisting of roads, railways, air flights, communications and oil and gas pipelines is taking shape.

Uzbekistan

Uzbekistan has the second largest energy resource endowment behind Kazakhstan in Central Asia. China and Uzbekistan have agreed to hasten construction of transit roads through Kyrgyzstan. The deal was confirmed during Premier Wen Jiabao's visit to Uzbekistan, Turkmenistan, Belarus and Russia in November 2007. China

---

50   According to a US State Department cable of February 2009 released by WikiLeaks, American officials suspected China of offering Kyrgyzstan $3 billion to shut down the American air base there. See "China Quietly Extends Footprints into Central Asia," *The New York Times*, January 2, 2011.

51   "Kyrgyzstan: Vote to Close US Base is Delayed," *The New York Times*, February 10, 2009, p. A11.

52   "US says Kyrgyzstan Base Deal Will Boost Security," *The Associated Press*, July 12, 2009.

and Uzbekistan planned to build highways and railroads to link the two countries through Kyrgyzstan.

China appreciates the support of Uzbekistan on Taiwan and Tibet issues, as well as its cracking down on "East Turkistan" terrorist forces. In October 2008, CNPC signed a cooperation deal with the Uzbekistan State Holding Oil and Gas Company, Uzbekndftegaz, on the joint exploration of the Mingulak oilfield in Uzbekistan. In December 2009, the new Turkmenistan–China gas pipeline that passes through Uzbekistan and Kazakhstan became operational.

In June 2012 President Islam Karimov attended the SCO summit in Beijing and signed a joint declaration on the establishment of "strategic partnership relations" with President Hu Jintao. Prior to President Karimov's visit, General Chen Bingde, chief of the general staff of the PLA visited Uzbekistan to deepen security cooperation. During President Karimov's visit, China and Uzbekistan signed an agreement to sell an annual 10 bcm of Uzbek natural gas to China. Uzbekistan started regular gas exports to China in August 2012.

The Uzbekistan–China pipeline, part of the Central Asia–China gas pipeline, is used to export the gas to China. Construction of the 7,000-km Central Asia–China pipeline to take natural gas from Turkmenistan, Kazakhstan and Uzbekistan to China began in 2008. The first line was completed in December 2009 and the second was finished in 2010. The two lines have combined capacity to carry 30 bcm of gas per year. Uzbekistan and China began building the third line of the Uzbek section of the Central Asia–China gas pipeline in December 2011. The $2.2 billion project was financed with loans from China Development Bank and direct investment from CNPC. Gas is expected to be pumped along the third line in 2014.

Tajikistan

Bordering China, Tajikistan was seriously affected by the riots in Xinjiang in early July 2009. According to Yormahmad Faqirov, the deputy customs chief for Tajikistan's eastern Badakhshan Province, border traffic between China and Tajikistan had nearly stopped in the immediate aftermath of the violence in Xinjiang. Before the deadly riots broke out, some 25 vehicles loaded with goods crossed the border every day; since the riots began in Urumqi, just three or four each day.[53] Traffic picked up in recent years. In 2012 Chinese labourers continued to build new roads to connect Tajikistan and China.

Russia remains Tajikistan's closest ally. In October 2012, President Vladimir Putin flew to Dushanbe for an official visit and wrapped up the deal to prolong the lease for the Russian military base in Tajikistan for another 30 years, until 2042.

China–Tajik trade increased by 14 times between 2007 and 2012. Tajikistan has leased out 600 hectares of agricultural land in its south to a Chinese company.

---

53 "Violence in Western China Harms Trade With Tajikistan," *Radio Free Europe/ Radio Liberty*, July 17, 2009.

Since 2005, China has disbursed $900 million to help Tajikistan build new roads, tunnels and electricity lines. In 2012, the two sides signed new agreements for Beijing to lend Dushanbe another $1 billion for infrastructure and development.[54]

In 2010 China held border negotiations and signed a draft agreement with Tajikistan and Afghanistan. In 2012 the foreign ministers from the three countries signed the agreement in Beijing. The agreement, which is of significance to maintain peace and security along the border areas, was ratified by China's NPC in October 2012. In June 2012, the SCO held joint military exercises in Tajikistan, dubbed "Peace Mission 2012," with about 2,000 troops from Russia, China, Kazakhstan, Kyrgyzstan and Tajikistan participating in the drills.

Russia

Russia and China began to hold joint military exercises in 2005. They held another round of joint military exercises in July 2009 to protect their core security interests against terrorists, separatists and extremists. About 1,300 army and air force personnel from each side participated in the exercise, codenamed Peace Mission 2009. This was particularly significant since it took place shortly after the ethnic riots in Xinjiang on July 5. The two countries held a naval exercise in the Yellow Sea in 2012. Russia and China share a common stated desire to curb US global influence and establish what they call a "multipolar world." The two countries also routinely cooperate on the UN Security Council to thwart the Western initiatives on issues ranging from Kosovo's independence to sanctions against North Korea and Iran.

Russia–China bilateral trade reached $83 billion in 2011 and is projected to top $100 billion in 2015, with expanded cooperation in space technology, oil and gas, and nuclear energy. China and Russia also coordinated their positions on Syria and opposed Western nations' efforts to oust President Bashar al-Assad as Syria's civil war deepened in 2012.

Assessment: Implications and Challenges

Trade with China is largely beneficial to Russia and Central Asia. For Russia's Far East, dependence on China is hardly new. Residents say they wouldn't have weathered Russia's steep economic decline in the 1990s without affordable Chinese products. Since the mid-1990s, Chinese traders have crossed the China–Central Asia and China–Russia borders to set up stalls in local marketplaces. There are hundreds of Chinese markets across Central Asia. Its quick bounce from the 2008–2009 global financial crisis gives China a crucial role to lead the world economy as a whole and the Central Asian region in particular.

---

54   Olivia Kroth, "Russia, China and Iran Close Ranks in Tajikistan," *Pravda* (Russia), October 30, 2012.

While Chinese business people offer much-demanded products from household appliances and clothes to consumer electronics, not everyone in Central Asia is happy about China's expansion into the region. For example, Kazakhstan, though a vast country, only has a population of some 14 million. Murat Auezov, a former Kazakh ambassador to China, suggested that China may have territorial intentions. "As a historian, I'm telling you that 19th century China, 20th century China and 21st century China are three different Chinas. But what unites them is a desire to expand their territories."[55] However, Auezov did not support his argument with evidence.

The rapid entrance of Chinese companies into the Turkmen market has created a mixed reaction among the local population. The majority of the population in rural areas is happy to be employed since they no longer have to leave for countries like Turkey or Russia to earn a living for their families. On the other hand, a small part of the population feels apprehensive about the sudden influx of a big number of Chinese into Turkmen society, especially in rural areas. Since elements of nationalism have been deeply imbedded in the people's mind, rural society is still hesitant toward fully accepting what is considered as foreign. That said, most of the Turkmen population seems to have an optimistic outlook. Many expect that today's small rural towns will soon become quite modernized and relatively developed cities with the help of Chinese investments.[56]

Despite tremendous growth in trade and expansion of relations in other aspects, China's influence in Central Asia is still limited. Many in Central Asia remain suspicious of China's intentions. According to a 2006 survey conducted by the Institute for World Economics and Politics in Almaty, only 20 percent of surveyed experts were convinced that Beijing would become a major player in Central Asian security. This was compared to the 44 percent who believed that Beijing would not be able to achieve anything, at least in the short term. Meanwhile, most Kazakh experts considered that the only partner that would be really willing to accept the political and financial burden of a military intervention and that would also have the material means to do so is Russia.[57]

The question of cross-border water resources is a potential problem in Sino-Kazakh relations. Kazakh authorities have criticized China's low regard towards their ecological and industrial concerns and China's refusal to fast track the collective management of water. For authoritarian states like Uzbekistan, closer ties with China present a great advantage. China, unlike the United States, does not attach political conditions to its trade relations with other countries; in particular, it does not pressure its allies to democratize or liberalize its markets. In

---

55   Jeremy Bransten, "Central Asia: China's Mounting Influence," *EurasiaNet* www.eurasianet.org, September 17, 2007.

56   Chemen Durdiyeva, "Hu Jintao's Visit to Turkmenistan Intensifies Chinese-Turkmen Partnership," *Central Asia-Caucasus Institute Analyst* http://www.cacianalyst.org, September 17, 2008.

57   Peyrouse, "Sino-Kazakh Relations," p. 13.

fact, the so-called "Beijing Consensus," which promotes economic development while maintaining tight political control, seems to be very appealing to many a developing nation. Chinese businesses also demonstrate their capacity to use local corruption schemes and internal Central Asian weaknesses in their own interests: smuggling with China, especially the export of metals and the import of consumer goods, has proved to be a very profitable venture for Central Asian high-level officials.[58] In the long term, the Chinese practices may backfire since China is not interested in promoting human rights and good governance in the region. People looking up to China for leadership as a global power will be disappointed when realizing that China puts its economic interests first.

The investment environment in Central Asia also creates challenges for Chinese businesses. In Uzbekistan, for example, corruption and nepotism are rampant, and institutional instability is a serious hurdle for investors. Chinese companies often can only count on the personal guarantees from President Karimov, who has been in office since 1991. The discrepancy in rules and laws between China and Central Asian countries creates problems for further cooperation. For China to expand its influence in Central Asia, language and cultural barriers are hard to surmount. Suspicions about China run deep in some Central Asian countries, even among the younger generation. A 30-year-old construction worker in Almaty cited a popular proverb to explain why Kazakhstan should favor Russia over China as an ally: "If the 'black' Chinese [hordes] come, the 'white' Russian will seem like your own father."[59]

While locals feel they have much to gain from the Chinese, analysts warn that Russia may face a long-term threat from China. China is buying Russian arms for its major military buildup and pressuring Moscow to speed the building of oil and gas pipelines to feed China's growing need for energy, even as Russia faces problems meeting its own energy demands. Sociologist German Zheliabovskii has suggested that Moscow does not realize that, sooner or later, Russia will have to share land with China. "Our military alone won't be able to hold the Far East," Zheliabovskii says. "There have to be Russian people living here." He points out that Russia only took Blagoveshchensk from the Chinese in 1856 — and that China may soon control the city once again.[60]

Both China and Russia view a long-term US presence in Central Asia as detrimental to their own interests. However, China and Russia remain suspicious of each other and they do not always share one another's views on issues related to Central Asia. Russia is concerned about China's recent moves into the Central Asian market, where Russia has long dominated. Russia still accounts for the

---

58 Sadykzhan Ibraimov, "China-Central Asia Trade Relations: Economic and Social Patterns," *China and Eurasia Forum Quarterly*, Vol. 7, No. 1 (2009), pp. 47–59.

59 Jeremy Bransten, "Central Asia: China Brings Electronics, But Not Democracy," *Radio Free Europe/Radio Liberty*, October 25, 2005.

60 Gregory Feifer, "Russia, China's Fortunes Reversed in Frontier City," *National Public Radio*, All Things Considered, April 5, 2008.

largest share of Kazakhstan's and Uzbekistan's imports, but China is right behind it and closing the gap quickly.

China imports a large amount of its energy from Russia, but has become increasingly interested in buying directly from Central Asian suppliers. To avoid having the majority of Turkmen gas flowing to China, Russia has taken steps to ensure that it controls the distribution of Turkmen gas via its network of pipelines. "I wouldn't say it is a conflict; that is too strong a word," says Fyodor Lukyanov, editor in chief of the Moscow-based journal *Russia in Global Affairs*. "We will see a soft competition that could heat up as China becomes more successful. Russia doesn't want to be China's junior partner in this region."[61] How China and Russia manage the competition for resources in the region will fundamentally affect the future of Central Asia.

Illegal migrants from China pose another problem for Central Asian states. The Kyrgyz State Committee on Migration and Employment reported in 2008 that there were about 8,000 Chinese illegal immigrants in Kyrgyzstan. Fears of annexation and mass Chinese immigration have grown in some countries. In Kazakhstan, President Nazarbayev raised concerns in 2006 that Chinese energy companies operating in the country were employing illegal Chinese workers, and Kazakh legislators alleged that these illegal immigrants numbered about 100,000 by late 2007.[62] Some Central Asian analysts and diplomats fear a "creeping Chinese expansion" in the region especially in Kazakhstan, Kyrgyzstan and Uzbekistan. Others have voiced concerns over China's plans to extract water from the Ili and Irtysh rivers for oilfield development in Xinjiang.[63] This is an extremely important question for Astana as water has become a strategic issue in the Central Asian region. Both rivers rise in China: the Ili passes through Kazakhstan before terminating in Lake Balkhash and the Irtysh travels through Kazakhstan before joining up with the Russian Ob River.

Concluding Remarks

China considers Central Asia as a critical frontier for its energy security, trade expansion, ethnic stability and military defense. But China is not the only external player with strong interests in the region. For example, Uzbekistan's most prominent East Asian investment partner is South Korea. President Karimov enjoys close personal ties with a succession of South Korean presidents. As of 2012, South Korea had over $10 billion in total direct investment in Uzbekistan,

---

61 Brian Whitmore, "Central Asia: Behind the Hype, Russia And China Vie For Region's Energy Resources," *Radio Free Europe/Radio Liberty*, March 22, 2008.

62 Lum, et al. "Comparing Global Influence," p. 92.

63 Ramakant Dwivedi, "China's Central Asia Policy in Recent Times," *China and Eurasia Forum Quarterly*, Vol. 4, No. 4 (2006), pp. 155–6.

as opposed to just over $5 billion from China.[64] South Korea has built a sprawling special economic zone in southern Uzbekistan with new factories and office buildings and a cargo airport. Japan is another major East Asian power to have a strong interest in Central Asia. After China decreased rare earth export to Japan following the 2010 incident involving the Japanese coast guard and a Chinese fishing vessel, Japan pledged to spend $700 million in Central Asia to help the resource-rich region promote trade, energy saving and regional cooperation and opened a rare earth joint venture with Kazakhstan in November 2012.

Russia is still very active in Central Asia, has considered the region as its sphere of influence, and has historic links with all Central Asian countries. On the other hand, China is obviously pulling a huge amount of influence in the region. China seems to have more to offer in terms of trade and investment, which may trigger Russia-China rivalry in the region. To avoid potential conflict, China must be aware of Russia's continuing influence in Central Asia and refrain from confronting Russia. For historical, linguistic, and cultural reasons, Russia remains the most dominant power in Central Asia. After 9/11, the United States has also attempted to establish a military stronghold in the region, competing for influence with Russia. But neither China nor the United States can exclusively dominate the region. European powers, Iran, India, Pakistan, and Turkey are some other actors of importance that attempt to influence the region.

China and Central Asia have a long history of interactions. The recent wave of warming relations is built upon common interests of promoting economic growth. Though Chinese firms encounter the same difficulties getting profits out of Central Asia as other foreign firms, investment from China is expected to grow in the years ahead. China's involvement in Central Asia has been largely beneficial to all parties concerned. China's economic and security policies towards Central Asia and Russia are part of its global diplomacy to seek energy and expand soft power. Chinese policies towards Central Asia are primarily driven by concerns of energy security, regional stability, and its global stature.

In Central Asia, China and Russia have cooperated on a wide range of issues where they have common interests such as countering "the three evils" and guarding against a unipolar world system dominated by the United States. Though there is no evidence suggesting that China and Russia are engaged in strategic rivalry in Central Asia, the two countries' competition for resources and allegiance of Central Asian nations may become a contentious issue in the future. Despite cooperation between China and Russia on many international and regional issues, the prospects for an anti-Western Sino-Russian alliance are less promising than official statements may suggest. Sino-Central Asian relations face many challenges due to a lack of continued historical ties between the two regions and the enduring predominance of Russia in its traditional backyard. It will take a long time before China can firmly establish itself as a major power in Central Asia.

---

64   Uzbekistan's Balancing Act with China: A View from the Ground," *China Brief*, July 20, 2012.

Questions for Discussion

1. Why is Central Asia a key player in the chessboard of global political economy and security?
2. What are China's main strategies in securing relations with Central Asian countries?
3. What potential challenges does China face in its relations with Central Asia?
4. How do regional countries respond to China's growing trade, investment, and influence?
5. Do Russia and the United States view China's expanding reach into Central Asia differently? Why?
6. What are the challenges in China–Russia relations?

Chapter 6

China and the South Pacific

The South Pacific region includes Australia, New Zealand, and all the neighboring small island nations in the southern part of the Pacific Ocean. Australasia and Oceania are sometimes used to refer to this region. China has maintained strong relations with Australia and New Zealand since it established diplomatic relations with the two largest South Pacific states in 1972.

Modern relations between China and the South Pacific date back to Chinese labor migrations of the late 19th century. Among all small South Pacific nations, only Tuvalu, Tokelau, and Niue have no recorded history of Chinese settlement.[1] Although China has maintained an official presence in the region since the mid-1970s, when it first established diplomatic ties with Fiji, Western Samoa, and Papua New Guinea (PNG), these small South Pacific nations did not loom large on China's foreign-policy radar screen.

The 14 small independent states in this area (excluding Australia and New Zealand) have a population of about 8 million. Although small in total population and relatively less developed economically, the Pacific island region is located strategically at the gateway of the Pacific Ocean from east to west and south to north.

The Pacific used to be an "American lake."[2] The United States downgraded its involvement in Oceania after the Cold War, paving way for other powers to move to the region. Japan became the region's largest donor. South Korea and Taiwan were not too far behind. But it is China that has become the most significant new player in South Pacific at the beginning of the new century.

Since the mid-1990s new economic and strategic elements have emerged in the Sino-South Pacific relationship and tens of thousands of Chinese have moved to the South Pacific islands, running grocery stores, restaurants and other small businesses. The numbers may not seem significant in a global context, but the new wave of Chinese migration into these lightly populated Pacific states has upset traditional ethnic, social and economic patterns. For example, in the Tongan capital of Nuku'alofa there was not a single Chinese-owned grocery store 20 years ago. In 2007, more than 70 percent of them were reportedly owned by newly-arrived Chinese immigrants.[3]

---

1   Terence Wesley-Smith, *China in Oceania: New Forces in Pacific Politics* (Honolulu, HI: The East-West Center, 2007), p. 9.

2   Peter Hayes, Lyuba Zarsky and Walden Bello, *American Lake: Nuclear Peril in the Pacific* (Penguin, 1987).

3   Bertil Lintner, "The Sinicizing of the South Pacific," *Asia Times Online*, April 18, 2007.

The shops and restaurants are the most visible signs of a growing Chinese presence in the South Pacific. Chinese restaurants have sprung up all over the region, some of them big and grand, most little more than shacks with corrugated-iron roofs. Often they are next door to Chinese-run grocery stores, where shopkeepers hunker down behind iron-bar grilles and sell everything from candles to corned beef. South Pacific may have a reputation as an earthly paradise of coral reefs and coconut groves, but it is fast becoming a stage on which China flexes its political, economic, and diplomatic muscles. While the region is unlikely to become the center of superpower competition, it may well become an important arena for China to establish footholds of influence, recruit new allies and to test its growing strength and ability to command allegiance in a region hitherto dominated by Western powers, commented two scholars from Australia and New Zealand.[4] Most of these countries are focused on China's continued growth, anticipating the economic benefits in trade and investment it will bring them. China's insatiable appetite for energy and other natural resources is feeding an economic boom in Australia and, like other countries in the Asia–Pacific region, Australia wants China's growth to continue without disruption by conflicts over Taiwan, commented Singapore's senior statesman Lee Kuan Yew.[5] This chapter will focus on China's relations with Australia, New Zealand, and small South Pacific island nations as part of its global diplomacy. It will examine China's motivations and strategies in the South Pacific and discuss their significance.

Motivations Behind China's New Diplomacy in Australia and New Zealand

Economic Priority

Today Australia and New Zealand like to consider themselves as part of Asia, as opposed to being a separate continent. Both consider China's rapid economic growth as an opportunity and have enjoyed dynamic interactions with China. Indeed, China has maintained very close relationships with Australia and New Zealand since the mid-1990s. China has dynamic and expanding trading relations with both countries. It surpassed the United States as Australia's biggest source of imports in 2006 and has been Australia's largest trading partner since 2007 after eclipsing Japan, Australia's traditional top trading partner. In 2010 Australia was China's seventh largest trade partner and its sixth largest import supplier.[6] The growing trade between Australia and China is due to Australia's voracious demand for Chinese manufactured imports and China's equally huge demand for Australia's mineral and other exports. Australia is the world's biggest wool

---

    4   John Henderson and Benjamin Reilly, "Dragon in Paradise: China's rising star in Oceania," *The National Interest* (Summer, 2003), p. 94.
    5   Lee Kuan Yew, "China's Soft Power Success," *Forbes*, June 18, 2007.
    6   US-China Business Council (https://www.uschina.org/statistics/tradetable.html).

exporter and China its biggest customer, buying $1.3 billion worth, or more than 60 percent of Australia's total clip each year.[7] Australia boasts nearly 40 percent of the global reserves of uranium, another major import for China. The bilateral agreement that allows China to import uranium from Australia is demonstration of how close the relationship has become since enriched uranium can be used, among other things, in nuclear weapons industry.

Two-way trade, which excludes Hong Kong's trade with Australia, reached $60 billion in 2008. By 2011 it had hit $118 billion. Leading Australian exports to China include iron ore, coal, crude petroleum, wool, lead, zinc and manganese ores, copper, and uranium. Main exports from China include clothing, computers, telecommunications equipment, toys, games and sporting goods, and furniture. Australia has been negotiating a FTA with China since 2005. In September 2007 the two countries signed a $35 billion agreement for Woodside Petroleum to export liquefied natural gas (LNG) to China.[8] In the 12 months to March 2009, wine exports to China, Australia's largest Asian wine market, totaled A$81.2 million. China is Australia's eighth largest wine export market by volume and fifth largest by value.[9]

In April 2008 New Zealand became the first developed country to sign a comprehensive trade agreement with China. The agreement provided for free trade in goods and services, and included protections for bilateral investment flows. The deal also included provisions on both education and labor supply, among other issues. This was the largest FTA for New Zealand since it signed the Closer Economic Relations agreement with Australia in 1982. New Zealand Trade Minister Phil Goff predicted that the FTA deal "will boost New Zealand's exports of goods and services to China by up to 400 million New Zealand dollars ($326 million) a year."[10] Unlike China's previous FTAs, in which trade of goods served as the starting point and other fields later become areas for expansion, the agreement with New Zealand covered trade in goods and services, and investment from the moment it took effect.

According to New Zealand's Ministry of Foreign Affairs and Trade, securing preferential access to China's economy has the potential to deliver significant gains to New Zealand's exporters. China's middle class is now estimated to be more than 100 million people and growing—which will fuel the demand for New Zealand's agricultural products. There should also be gains to New Zealand's manufacturers and services operators under the FTA with China.

By 2011, China had become New Zealand's second largest market for both exports and imports, with bilateral trade totalling at $11 billion. Former New Zealand Prime Minister John Key predicted China would eventually surpass Australia to

7   "Shear Delight? China's Hu Visits Aussie Sheep Farm," *Reuters India*, September 5, 2007.

8   "Aust, China Sign $36b Gas Deal," *ABC News* (Australia), September 6, 2007.

9   "Australia Signs Wine Trading Contract with China," *Xinhua*, April 17, 2009.

10   "NZ, China Free Trade Deal in April," *The Associated Press*, February 26, 2008.

become his country's biggest market for exports. Major New Zealand exports to China include dairy products, wood, wool, and sea food; major imports from China include machinery, knit apparel, furniture, and iron and steel. China is also the largest source of international students for New Zealand, with 21,258 students studying at New Zealand colleges in 2010.[11] Both Australia and New Zealand will benefit from the impressive purchasing powers of Chinese tourists in the years ahead.

In addition to imports and exports between China and Australia and New Zealand, China has started to invest in the economies of the two countries. In March 2009 the Australian government approved Hunan Valin Iron and Steel of China's purchase of up to 17.55 percent stake in Fortescue Metals, Australia's third largest iron ore exporter. Andrew Forrest, Fortescue chief executive, welcomed the "passive investment" to be made by Valin, which included about A\$1.2 billion for new and existing shares. Valin was restricted from increasing its holding beyond 17.55 percent, but its chairman had the right to join Fortescue's board.[12] In early 2009 Chinalco, a state-owned Chinese aluminum producer, planned a \$19.5 billion investment in Rio Tinto, the world's third largest mining company with headquarters in Melbourne and London. For political and strategic reasons, Rio Tinto turned down Chinalco's investment in June 2009 in favor of a tie-up with rival giant BHP Billiton, to the disappointment of many in China.[13] Since then Rio Tinto has continued to ship iron ore to China, the world's largest buyer. In early 2012 Chinese property developer Shanghai Pengxin Group Co. won approval to buy 16 dairy farms in New Zealand.

Despite political tensions between Beijing and Canberra over the Rio Tinto case and the visit to Australia by Rebiya Kadeer, an exiled Uyghur businesswoman that Beijing believed to have instigated the July 2009 ethnic riots in Xinjiang, the two governments continued to pursue economic and energy cooperation. In August 2009 Australia and China struck a deal for PetroChina to purchase a 20-year supply of LNG from a massive project off Australia's west coast. The deal, valued at about A\$50 billion (\$41.1 billion), was the largest ever between the two countries. The LNG would come from Exxon Mobil's 25 percent interest in Australia's Gorgon gas development. Under terms of the agreement, Exxon would supply 2.25 million metric tons per year of LNG to PetroChina.[14]

---

11   New Zealand Ministry of Foreign Affairs & Trade website (http://www.mfat.govt. nz), October 1, 2012.

12   Peter Smith, "Australia Clears China's Fortescue Deal," *Financial Times*, March 31, 2009.

13   In July 2009, four employees of Rio Tinto including Australian national Stern Hu were detained and later formally arrested by Chinese security forces on charges of commercial espionage and bribery, creating a diplomatic tension between Beijing and Canberra. Many suspect the arrests were retribution for Rio Tinto abandoning a \$19.5 billion investment from Chinalco a month earlier.

14   "PetroChina Signs LNG Deal With Exxon," *The Wall Street Journal*, August 19, 2009.

Australia's Potential Bridging Role Between the United States and China

The fact that Australia is a key US ally and China is Australia's largest trading partner gives Canberra some unique roles to play in bridging the two great powers. In March 2006 the United States launched a political forum for dialogue with Australia and Japan in a bid to checkmate China in the Asia–Pacific region. Barely a month later, on April 3, 2006, Australian Prime Minister John Howard and his visiting Chinese counterpart Wen Jiabao oversaw the signing of a bilateral nuclear energy deal. Revealing was not only the triumph of China's diplomacy but also Australia's autonomy and independence as regards the United States. Unlike Japan or the United States, Australia holds a more benign view of China's rise. In September 2007 Prime Minister Howard announced that Australia would begin security talks with China the following year, a move regarded as an effort to ease concerns in Beijing about the trilateral security talks among the US, Japan and Australia.[15]

Geopolitically, Australia increasingly considers itself part of Asia, though it has traditionally maintained close ties with Great Britain, the United States, and other Western powers. When meeting with Premier Wen in April 2006, Prime Minister Howard said that the relationship with China was one of Australia's most important foreign relationships. Australia very much welcomes China's development and appreciates its positive role in international and regional affairs. China's rapid development is beneficial for the world at large and it is no good to contain China, remarked Howard.[16] After the United States decided to "pivot" toward Asia in 2010 and President Obama's 2011 announcement to station troops in Darwin, Australia, the Australian government made it clear that its strong alliance with the United States was not aimed at China.

Like South Korea which is another major ally of the United States, Australia has expressed interest in serving as a bridge or balancer between the United States and China to help manage relations between the two big powers.[17] Such a move is certainly welcomed by China as it will consider these countries to be friendly or at least neutral and not so uncritically siding with the United States if a crisis, especially over Taiwan, were to arise in the future.

---

15   "China Puts Bush in Summit Shade," *Financial Times*, September 7, 2007.

16   "Premier Wen Jiabao Holds Talks with His Australian Counterpart Howard," Ministry of Foreign Affairs of the People's Republic of China, April 4, 2006.

17   In a series of speeches in 2005, former President Roh Moo-hyun of South Korea unveiled a new foreign-policy doctrine by declaring that Korea must play the role of a balancer so that tensions do not revive and escalate in Northeast Asia. Roh stated that South Korea could serve as an honest broker between China and Japan and between the United States and China. Prime Minister John Howard articulated similar goodwill intentions for Australia to serve as a balancer between the United States and China.

China's Strategies in Australia and New Zealand

It takes two to tango. Australia's and New Zealand's strong desire to maintain good ties with China and China's increasingly sophisticated diplomacy make it possible for China to enjoy a relatively favorable image in both countries. Chinese strategies include, among others:

Summit Diplomacy

High-level exchanges have been frequent between Chinese leaders and their counterparts in Australia and New Zealand. President Hu Jintao paid a state visit to Australia in October 2003 and became the first Chinese leader to have been given the honor of addressing the joint sitting of the Australian parliament. He visited Australia again in September 2007 and attended the 15th APEC Leaders' Informal Meeting, which was held in Sydney. President Hu and Prime Minister Howard jointly declared the establishment of China–Australia strategic dialogue mechanism. The two countries issued a joint statement on climate change and energy and signed a number of contracts and agreements covering economy, trade, energy, culture and other fields, which upgraded the relationship to a new level. During the Informal Meeting, President Hu took the opportunity to meet with other leaders including New Zealand Prime Minister Helen Clark.

Premier Wen Jiabao visited Australia in April 2006. During the visit, Wen and Prime Minister Howard agreed to establish the mechanism of regular exchanges of visits and meetings between the leaders of both countries and exchange views in time on major issues in bilateral relations.[18] Less than three months later, Prime Minister Howard traveled to China. On June 28, 2006, Wen and Howard jointly attended the ceremony in Shenzhen on the operation of the first-phase Guangdong LNG project which was the first natural gas cooperation project between China and Australia.

Both President Hu and Premier Wen made public speeches during their visits to Australia in efforts to reach out to the Australian public. They talked about how both countries could benefit from a cooperative relationship and how China was committed to peaceful development. These words and deeds helped create an open, friendly and peaceful image of China in the South Pacific region and beyond.

Other Chinese leaders have traveled to Australia too. For example, NPC Standing Committee Chair Wu Bangguo paid a visit to Australia in May 2005. In March 2009 Li Changchun, a member of the Standing Committee of CCP's politburo visited Australia, discussing with Prime Minister Kevin Rudd ways to cooperate in dealing with the financial crisis and to promote cultural exchanges. Li welcomed Australia's participation in the 2010 Shanghai Expo.

China has hosted leaders from Australia and New Zealand. In April 2008, New Zealand's Prime Minister Helen Clark and Australia's new Prime Minister Kevin

---

18   "Premier Wen Jiabao Holds Talks with His Australian Counterpart Howard," Ministry of Foreign Affairs of the People's Republic of China, April 4, 2006.

Rudd both visited China. The first FTA between China and a developed nation was signed during Prime Minster Clark's visit in Beijing. The New Zealand-China FTA entered into force on October 1, 2008. Rudd, a former Australian diplomat in Beijing and a fluent Mandarin speaker, also attended the BFA in Hainan during his China trip. A few months later, Mr. Rudd went to China again, attending the Beijing Olympics opening ceremony in August 2008. New Zealand Prime Minister John Key visited China in 2010 and set the objective of doubling bilateral trade from $10 billion to $20 billion by 2015. As of 2013, New Zealand remained the first and only Western country that has signed a FTA with China.

Chinese and Australian leaders also meet frequently on the sidelines of international and regional conferences. For example, in April 2009, at the G-20 summit in London, Prime Minister Rudd and President Hu met to discuss cooperation in the global financial crisis. At the summit in London, Rudd advocated a bigger role for China in the International Monetary Fund in the midst of the global economic downturn.

During her first visit to Beijing as Australian Prime Minister in April 2011, Julia Gillard assured Premier Wen Jiabao that Australia wanted to deepen its engagement with China as it continued to increase its global influence, and flatly rejected any notion the US and its allies should seek to contain the rising superpower. The Prime Minister also guaranteed Australia would remain a long term and reliable supplier of energy resources including coal and liquefied natural gas to China.

Promoting Societal Exchanges

China and Australia and New Zealand are setting an example in bilateral relations for countries of different social and political systems and cultural backgrounds. Cultural exchanges form a major dimension in China's relations with Australia and New Zealand. On May 20, 2005, the Confucius Academy, the first Confucius school in Australia, was officially launched at the University of Western Australia (UWA) in Perth. Present at the ceremony was a high-level Chinese delegation led by Redi, Vice Chairman of the NPC. The selection of UWA as the site of the Confucius Institute was significant, since the last six Australian Ambassadors to China have all come from Western Australia with five graduating from UWA.[19] The establishment of the Institute helps promote a greater awareness and understanding of China and Chinese language and culture in the broader West Australian community—particularly in government, business, education and industry sectors, stated a media release by UWA.[20] By the end of 2012, 35 Confucius Institutes and Confucius Classrooms had been established in Oceania.

People-to-people exchanges have become more frequent now. The number of Chinese tourists visiting Australia is growing the fastest and reached one million

---

19   "The First Confucius Academy in Australia Established in Western Australian University," The Office of Chinese Language Council International (*hanban*), May 27, 2005.

20   "Australia's First Confucius Institute in UWA," UWA Media Release, May 20, 2005.

in 2013. The Chinese–Australian population is growing, with 690,000 Australians (3.4 percent of the resident population) claiming Chinese ancestry, and people born in China forming the third biggest immigrant group in Australia, after Britain and New Zealand.[21] Overseas students are now a key source of revenue for Australian universities and China is Australia's largest source of international students, providing a quarter of all enrollments. As popular destinations after North America and Europe, Australia and New Zealand are likely to continue to attract more Chinese students in the years ahead. In addition, both Australia and New Zealand encourage investment immigration. Many rich Chinese have become permanent residents of these two countries through this channel.

In New Zealand, the first Confucius Institute was officially opened on February 16, 2007 at the University of Auckland as a joint program between the University and Fudan University in Shanghai. While launching the Institute, Prime Minister Clark said that New Zealand could be both a contributor to and a beneficiary of China's growth and development. "Over the years, China and New Zealand have built a strong relationship based on building on our common interests and discussing differences openly and freely, marked by a spirit of dialogue, forward-looking co-operation and a commitment to find ways in which we can bring benefit to each other," she remarked.[22]

By 2012 China had surged ahead of the United States and was on the verge of becoming New Zealand's second biggest tourist market, according to the latest International Visitor Survey. China had already overtaken Germany and the United States and will soon overtake the United Kingdom to be New Zealand's second largest visitor market.[23] Warming relations at the societal level help bilateral relations in political, economic and other areas.

Reaching Out to the Public

During his September 2007 visit to Australia, President Hu Jintao demonstrated his personable side by talking to the Australian public. In addition to meeting with Australian officials, he went to Western Australia to hear presentations by executives of Australian enterprises and research institutes, watched a three-dimensional show of geological modeling on mining and exploration, and visited two laboratories.[24] President Hu also visited a sheep farm outside Canberra and drank tea with farmer Ian Cusack and his family, who, according to a *Reuters* report, were "very impressed by Hu's charm."[25]

---

21   Tom Hyland, "Hard Power, Soft Targets," *The Age*, November 11, 2007.
22   "Prime Minister Launches Confucius Institute in New Zealand," University of Auckland news release, February 16, 2007.
23   "Surge in Chinese Tourists to NZ," *The New Zealand Herald*, August 7, 2012.
24   "President Hu Visits Australia, Attends APEC Meeting," *Xinhua*, September 4, 2007.
25   "Shear Delight? China's Hu Visits Aussie Sheep Farm," *Reuters India*, September 5, 2007.

Chinese leaders also seem to understand the importance of cultivating good relations with opposition parties and future leaders. During the same September 2007 visit, President Hu met with Kevin Rudd, then the opposition Labor Party head, who became Australia's Prime Minister in December 2007. At the meeting, President Hu invited Rudd and his family to attend the 2008 Beijing Olympics, which Rudd gladly accepted.[26] Rudd was stationed in Beijing as a young diplomat in the 1980s. At the December 2007 federal elections, the Labor Party defeated the Conservative Party, and Kevin Rudd became the prime minister (2007–2010). China lost no time to cultivate good relations with this first Mandarin-speaking Western leader. Wen Jiabao was one of the first foreign leaders to send congratulatory messages to Rudd. Following his election, Rudd spoke by phone to the leaders of Australia's traditional allies—George W. Bush in Washington and Gordon Brown in London. But Wen Jiabao was the first foreign leader Mr. Rudd had conducted phone discussions with since being sworn in as prime minister.[27] Rudd has maintained a cordial relationship with the Beijing leadership since. He later served as Australia's foreign minister (2010–2012) under Prime Minister Julia Gillard. Interestingly, his Mandarin skills can become a target of attack by his opponents. When the Rio Tinto case broke out in July 2009, in which four Rio Tinto employees including Australian national Stern Hu were detained by China on espionage charges, opposition politicians asked Rudd why he did not pick up the phone and talk to President Hu directly to seek the release of Rio Tinto employees held by the Chinese security on espionage charges.

As another example of how China is demonstrating its soft power and reaching out to the Australian public, Beijing announced ahead of the 2007 APEC summit that it would lend two giant pandas to the Adelaide Zoo for ten years.[28] The two giant pandas arrived at the Zoo in November 2009. The panda diplomacy remains a powerful tool in China's foreign relations.

Assessment: Challenges in China's Relations with Australia and New Zealand

Amid the 2008–2009 global economic slowdown, China's economy grew by an impressive 8.7 percent in 2009, in a startling turnaround fuelled by a huge stimulus package. The stimulus package helped boost car sales 8.4 percent in June 2009 from a year earlier and also helped push property sales in the first half of 2009 from a year earlier. In 2012 China's growth rate dropped to below 8 percent but remained the highest among major economies. Meanwhile, in Australia unemployment hit 9.2 percent in Canterbury and Bankstown, 6.5 percent in inner Sydney, and

---

26   "Hu Invites Rudd Family to Beijing Olympics," *The Sydney Morning Herald*, September 7, 2007.

27   "Australia to be 'Climate Bridge,'" *BBC News*, December 6, 2007.

28   "China Puts Bush in Summit Shade," *Financial Times*, September 7, 2007.

4.7 percent in St George and Sutherland.[29] As Australia's largest trading partner increases production, there are hopes that Australia's unemployment rate may decline. Strong economic growth in China is a positive sign for the Australian economy, Federal Treasurer of Australia Wayne Swan remarked during a visit to New Zealand in July 2009. China's demand for commodities undoubtedly contributed to Australia's economic recovery.

Commercial ties are mutually beneficial to China and Australia and New Zealand. However, their relations are not without problems. The July 2009 Rio Tinto case highlights the risks of foreign investment in China as well as the complexity of Sino-Australian relations. Although China's influence has been growing in Australia and New Zealand, the two sides have huge differences over certain issues, which may from time to time disrupt normal relations. Major sources of potential conflict include:

Human Rights

Close economic, political and cultural links between the two countries notwithstanding, Australia does not kowtow to China on human rights issues. For example, despite repeated warnings from China, both Prime Minister John Howard and then the opposition Labor Party leader Kevin Rudd met with the Dalai Lama in June 2007. The Australian side emphasized that these meetings were "private" and would not hurt bilateral relations. In July 2009 China attempted to stop the Melbourne International Film Festival from showing a documentary about exiled Uyghur businesswoman and former political prisoner Rebiya Kadeer and bar her from appearing at the film festival. The organizer of the film festival rejected the Chinese request. The Australian government issued a visa to Rebiya, who attended the film festival in August 2009 and met with journalists while in Australia. The Chinese government considers Rebiya as the mastermind behind the ethnic riots in Xinjiang in early July which left 200 dead.

Since the Chinese government routinely considers foreign officials' meetings with the Dalai Lama and events promoting Rebiya as interference in its internal affairs, Australia's continued interest in Tibet and the Dalai Lama, Xinjiang and Rebiya Kadeer, and human rights in general may present an obstacle in China–Australia relations. At the core of the issue are their different views on human rights.

Even human rights violations in China's neighbors or countries friendly to China may create some tensions between China and Australia. For example, during the September 2007 protests and democracy movement in Myanmar, Prime Minister Howard said his government would press Beijing to urge the junta to end its violent repression. China refused to condemn Myanmar's military rulers for the crackdown of the protests, and together with Russia, it contended at the UN that situation in Myanmar was an internal affair and did not threaten international

---

29   "Chinese Growth Leaving Australia Behind," *The Age*, July 17, 2009.

peace and security. China may face increasing pressure from the international community including Australia and New Zealand to intervene in places where human rights are grossly violated such as Sudan, Syria, and Zimbabwe.

Security Concerns

Since the mid-2000s, at the suggestion of the Japanese government and then US Vice President Dick Cheney, Australia strengthened security talks with Japan and the United States. Many consider this as America's and Japan's efforts to counterbalance China's rise. To avoid possibly offending China, Australia is the only one among the three that has explicitly stated that the talks are not aimed at containing China.[30] It appears that the Australian government is a little less concerned about China's rising military strength than Japan or the United States. Nevertheless, many in Australia have questions about how China is going to use its growing power.

A 2008 poll by the Lowy Institute for International Policy, a leading strategic think tank in Australia, is quite telling of many Australians' mixed feelings about China. While an overwhelming majority of the surveyed (62 percent) agreed that China's growth has been good for Australia, a slim majority of them (52 percent) believed that Australia should join with other countries to limit China's influence, and only about a third thought that Australia's interests would not be harmed if China gained more power and influence.[31] In early September 2007, Australia, though extremely worried about upsetting Beijing, participated in a joint naval exercise with the United States, Japan, India and Singapore in the Bay of Bengal. Participants stressed that the exercise in no way would threaten a certain growing Asian power to the north, but there was little doubt that such military exercises pointed toward the future geopolitical arrangement in the Asia–Pacific region. As Brahma Chellaney, Professor of Strategic Studies at the Delhi-based Center for Policy Research, commented, some of the countries involved didn't want to promote this too much to avoid affronting China, but at the same time it was a very important reminder to China.[32]

Apparently to maintain a delicate balance between China and the United States, shortly after the joint exercise in the Bay of Bengal, the Australian government invited two Chinese warships to visit Australia at the end of September 2007 for a joint naval exercise involving the Chinese, Australian, and New Zealand navies in early October. According to Australian Defense Minister Brendan Nelson, more military exercises and cooperation are planned between his country and China.[33]

---

30   "Australia Says Not Trying to 'Contain' China," *Reuters India*, June 5, 2007.

31   Fergus Hanson, "Australia and the World: Public Opinion and Foreign Policy," *The Lowy Institute Poll 2008*, Sydney, Australia.

32   "A Gunboat Message to China," *Time*, September 5, 2007.

33   "Chinese Warships in Sydney for First Sino-Australian Exercises," *AFP*, September 27, 2007.

These balancing efforts notwithstanding, Australia does have security concerns over China's rapid military modernization. Australia's 2007 defense strategy report, for example, pointed to the destabilizing effect of China's growing military strength. "The pace and scope of its military modernization, particularly the development of new and disruptive capabilities such as the anti-satellite missile, could create misunderstandings and instability in the region," stated the paper which was released in early July 2007, coincident with the visit to Sydney of the USS Kitty Hawk.[34] Australia's defense reports in following years voiced similar concerns. Australia's participation in a four-nation security dialogue that also included the United States, Japan and India, was perceived by some analysts as "encirclement" of China.

In April 2009 the Lowy Institute for International Policy released a report that said Australia should dramatically increase its defense spending to meet the strategic challenges presented by the rise of China. While the report did not mention China as a direct threat to Australia, it viewed the rise of China as creating uncertainty and a higher risk of regional conflict. The report advocated a progressive increase in defense spending from the current level of about 2 percent of GDP to 2.5 percent. This would allow Australia's submarine fleet to be enlarged and the current order of F-35 Joint Strike Fighters to be increased, as well as an expansion of the Australian Army; in short, a big boost for each of the Australian services.[35] As an indication that this might be the view held by some in the government, the Lowy report was authored by Hugh White, a former Deputy Secretary of the Department of Defense and now head of the Strategic and Defense Studies Centre at the Australian National University (ANU). In maintaining its vibrant commercial, political, and cultural relations with Australia and New Zealand, China must be conscious of these security concerns of its partners.

US deployment of troops in Darwin, Australia beginning in 2011 added a new dimension in China–Australia relations. Despite Australia's repeated assertion that it is not interested in containing China, its closer security relations with the United States may become a source of concern for China.

Disrupting the Status Quo

Australia's traditional sphere of influence covers many small South Pacific islands, especially Melanesia (PNG, Solomon Islands, Fiji, Vanuatu). China is moving into the region at a time when many Pacific Island countries, particularly PNG and Fiji, have been critical of the Australian government's heavy-handed tactics in the region.

Australia is by far the biggest aid donor in the region with the annual Australian Overseas Development Assistance budget to the Pacific standing at $720 million.

---

34   "US, Australians Wary of China's Military Buildup," *Taipei Times*, July 6, 2007, p. 1.

35   Sam Bateman, "The Great Australian Defense Debate: Is China a Threat"? RSIS Commentaries 40/2009, Nanyang Technological University, Singapore, April 24, 2009.

However, the aid comes with conditions. A major part of the donation, in recent years, has been earmarked for "strengthening governance and reducing corruption" in recipient countries. Under these aid schemes, Australia has stationed bureaucrats, police officers and financial advisors in strategic departments and law enforcement agencies in the region. In PNG and Fiji this has been greatly resented and seen as an attempt to undermine their sovereignty. In May 2005 a Supreme Court decision in PNG sent packing 800 Australian police officers deployed in the country under the aid program.[36]

On the other hand, China has expanded trade and other relations with small Pacific nations. Much like China's diplomacy elsewhere, Chinese trade and loans come with few political conditions attached other than an affirmation to the "one-China" policy and the insistence that Chinese enterprises should be selected as contractors for soft loan investments. This is in sharp contrast to Australia's emphasis on good governance, economic reform, anti-corruption, and environmental protection policies. The PRC and Taiwan have been accused of engaging in "checkbook diplomacy" to gain favor with Pacific leaders, which distorts the political process in those countries. China's and Australia's different approaches to development and governance issues may create frictions between the two countries in the future.

Indeed, though Australia and New Zealand generally welcome China's contribution to regional development, they are concerned about how Chinese aid can benefit small island countries. As New Zealand Prime Minister John Key put it, "From New Zealand's point of view, we don't seek to try and stop countries giving aid to other countries, but where we have a particular level of expertise—like the Pacific—what New Zealand's been trying to do is work alongside those partners so that the aid that is given is beneficial." On the other hand, even if New Zealand didn't like China's growing footprint, "it's not about to stop," Mr. Key said. "What we'd rather do is focus our energy to making sure that the aid is constructively delivered."[37]

Chinese Motivations in Small South Pacific Island Nations

Diplomatic Values

The South Pacific's strategic and diplomatic values lie mainly in the region's importance for China in its effort to isolate Taiwan diplomatically. Beijing has competed with Taipei for diplomatic recognition as well as access to natural resources such as vast reserves of fish, minerals and timber. Loans and other

---

36   "South Pacific: Chinese Relief From Domineering Australia," *Inter Press Service*, April 17, 2006.

37   Quoted in "Clinton's Pacific Visit In Step with China," *The Sydney Morning Herald*, August 29, 2012.

investments as well as the construction of roads and sporting facilities are used by both sides to foster loyalty. The main driver of Chinese aid to the region remains halting and reversing diplomatic recognition of Taiwan. As of 2013, six of the 23 countries recognizing Taiwan—Kiribati, the Marshall Islands, Palau, Nauru, Tuvalu and the Solomon Islands—were in the South Pacific. If China wishes to completely suffocate Taiwan internationally, it still has much to do in this area to check and reverse Taiwan's diplomatic inroads. Pacific nations may be miniscule and little known, but they are vitally important in the diplomatic game between Beijing and Taipei. Taipei maintains one of the very few diplomatic missions on Nauru, a country so small it can be driven around in half an hour.

The Taiwan factor may decline as a key Chinese motivation after Taipei and Beijing reached a tacit understanding in 2008 that neither would try to poach the other's allies. This temporary "diplomatic truce" was confirmed by officials from both China and Taiwan who attended the Pacific Islands Forum (PIF) summit in Cairns, Australia in August 2009.[38]

Over the years, Beijing has gained the upper hand and has more friends in the neighborhood. China has strong diplomatic relationships with both Australia and New Zealand. It has formal ties with eight of the 14 members of PIF, including the largest island nations, Fiji and PNG. Other members that recognize China are Vanuatu, the Federated States of Micronesia, Tonga, the Cook Islands, Niue, Samoa, and Tahiti. China maintained a care-taking group in Kiribati after it switched diplomatic ties to Taipei in 2003.[39] China is reported to have more diplomats posted in the region than any other country.[40] In international organizations where "one country-one vote" is the rule, regional blocs can be important. The 14 island states constitute a significant voting bloc in international forums, particularly the UN. Seeking the support from these nations and other developing nations is naturally one of China's diplomatic priorities.

China has a growing business presence in the Pacific and Taiwan does not want to be left behind. There were more than 3,000 Chinese state-owned and private enterprises, from mining ventures to restaurants in 2005, and an economic development and cooperation framework between China and the Pacific Island countries was signed in April 2006 during Premier Wen Jiabao's first ever visit to Fiji, marking a milestone in China–Pacific ties.[41] Shortly after the China–South Pacific summit was held during Wen's visit to Fiji, the first Taiwan-Pacific Allies Summit was held in Palau in September 2006. Delegates identified nine areas for economic, technical and cultural cooperation and agreed to hold a second summit in the Marshall Islands in September 2007. Solomon Islands hosted the 2009

---

38   "China and Taiwan End War over Pacific Aid," *The Australian*, August 10, 2009.

39   Tamara Renee Shie, "China Woos the South Pacific," PacNet No. 10A, *Pacific Forum CSIS*, Honolulu, Hawaii, March 17, 2006.

40   Robert Sutter, *Chinese Foreign Relations: Power and Policy Since the Cold War* (Rowman & Littlefield, 2008), p. 288.

41   "Aid Package Announced for South Pacific States," *China Daily*, April 6, 2006.

summit. Such escalating rivalry for influence in the South Pacific has attracted much critical attention from observers.

There were claims that Taiwanese money was used to bribe politicians during an election in the Solomon Islands in 2006. Riots broke out in the capital Honiara when Snyder Rini was appointed Prime Minister. He later resigned amid allegations he used money from local Chinese businessmen and Taiwan to buy support. Mr. Rini denied the allegations, and the Taiwanese government vehemently rejected accusations that it had tried to influence the political process.[42] In the future it will become increasingly difficult for Taiwan to maintain its aid-based efforts in the face of the PRC's superior resources and more active diplomacy.

China is a major donor to the PIF and the highest paying subscriber to the South Pacific Tourism Organization (SPTO). China has had a hand in promoting or delaying votes on UN membership for Kiribati, Nauru, Tonga, and Tuvalu. In October 2005 Beijing lobbied against Taiwan's inclusion in the SPTO, saying this would "sabotage" China's own relations with the region. After China pledged an additional $500,000 in organizational support, the organization vetoed Taiwan's admission a week later.[43] It was revealed in April 2008 that Taiwan lost $29.8 million in a failed 2006 attempt to establish ties with PNG. The money was intended as economic aid for PNG, provided it switched recognition from China. It was given to two middlemen in 2006 on the assumption they could induce the impoverished Pacific nation to abandon Beijing. The attempt was aborted after only several months, when Taiwanese authorities concluded that they could not convince PNG to cross over into the Taiwanese diplomatic column. One of the middlemen, Ching Chi-ju, has since disappeared, along with the money. Three senior Taiwanese officials, Foreign Minister James Huang, Deputy Premier Chiou I-jen and Vice Defense Minister Ko Cheng-heng, resigned over the scandal in May 2008.[44] The diplomatic bungle underscored the struggle between Taipei and Beijing to curry favor among potential foreign allies.

Over the long term the South Pacific may prove an even more important strategic asset to China. In 1997 China established a satellite-tracking station on South Tarawa Atoll in Kiribati. The station was the only one of its type outside Chinese territory and was run by the Chinese military. Ostensibly built to assist with China's space program, there was speculation that the station may have also been used to spy on the US missile range in the nearby Marshall Islands. The station was dismantled after Kiribati's diplomatic defection to Taiwan in November 2003, but Beijing was reportedly looking for another place in the region to set up shop.[45] As it is expanding interests and influence from land to sea, China will pay more attention to the South Pacific island nations due to their

---

42   "Chinese Rivals Grapple for Pacific," *BBC News*, April 4, 2007.

43   Shie, "China Woos the South Pacific."

44   "3 Senior Taiwanese Officials Resign over Papua New Guinea Diplomatic Bungle," *International Herald Tribune*, May 6, 2008.

45   Shie, "China Woos the South Pacific."

critical locations. Observatories could be set up in the Pacific for China's space and military purposes.

Indeed, China's most significant strategic interest in the South Pacific is military access, the most important aspect of which is signals intelligence monitoring. The Chinese fishing fleet operating out of Fiji is said to provide cover for signals intelligence monitoring, particularly of US bases in Micronesia. China is also seeking naval access to the region's ports and exclusive economic zones, engages in military assistance programs, and is negotiating access to facilities for maintenance and resupply purpose.[46]

Economic Benefits

Resources are a growing interest of China in the South Pacific island nations. Copper, zinc and nickel from PNG, timber from the Solomon Islands, manganese and cobalt from the seabed are all vital to feed China's extraordinary pace of development. China's trade with the 14 island states that make up the PIF (excluding Australia and New Zealand) increased from $121 million in 1995 to $1.2 billion in 2006. *Xinhua* predicted China–South Pacific trade would reach $3 billion in 2010.[47] PNG is the largest trading partner and investment destination for China in South Pacific. Bilateral trade amounted to $1.265 billion in 2011, which is almost 10 times of the trade volume between the two countries in 2001.[48]

China imports significant quantity of timber and fish from Pacific countries, including Solomon Islands and PNG. Melanesia contains extensive mineral and forestry resources. China has the world's largest fish production and consumption and has funded several fish processing plants and the construction of the Tuna Management Commission headquarters in the Federated States of Micronesia. A number of Chinese fishing fleets are already operating in the region.

China has shown a keen interest in PNG's resources in particular and invested $651 million in the Ramu nickel/cobalt mine in 2006.[49] Over 3,000 Chinese state and private entities have established themselves in South Pacific, with investment worth some $800 million. China has also agreed to fund the establishment of a Pacific Trade Office in Beijing to promote trade and investment between China and Pacific Island nations, with proposals for another trade post in Hong Kong.[50] As in other regions, economic benefits will remain a key motivation behind China's new diplomacy in the South Pacific.

---

46   Joanne Wallis, "China's South Pacific Diplomacy," *The Diplomat*, August 30, 2012.

47   "China to Step up Trade with Pacific Island Countries," *Xinhua*, September 7, 2008.

48   Remarks by Chinese ambassador to PNG, Qiu Bohua, at the reception marking the 63rd anniversary of the founding of the PRC, September 27, 2012, Port Moresby, PNG.

49   Hanson, *The Dragon in the Pacific: More Opportunity than Threat.*

50   Henderson and Reilly, "Dragon in Paradise: China's rising star in Oceania," p. 103.

Beyond timber, fish and seabed minerals, South Pacific is also a great destination for tourists. As the middle-class Chinese begin to travel around the world, South Pacific, due to its exotic scenery, gentle weather, and relative inexpensive cost, has the potential to become a new spot for Chinese tourists.

Desire to Expand Soft Power

With trade and aid, China has been slowly building its soft power in the South Pacific. This is consistent with China's global efforts to promote its influence. China has presented a self-claimed image as a responsible power in the South Pacific, helping the small island nations to develop economically. China attempts to treat all states, big or small, equally in its diplomacy. In 1980 China's ballistic missile tests in the Central Pacific provoked strong protests from Pacific island governments, prompting a Chinese apology and reassurance of benign intentions. In 1985 CCP General Secretary Hu Yaobang visited the region and stressed that China fully respected the sovereign rights of the Pacific island countries and their existing relationships with outside states. China also moved quickly in 1987 to sign the protocols of the 1985 South Pacific Nuclear Free Zone Treaty, and has played a cautious hand in regional disputes.

China has been careful not to be perceived as a bully in the region. It has sometimes been reluctant to move beyond rhetoric in countering Taiwanese overtures to Pacific Island states. For example, it used its position on the UN Security Council to delay, but not veto, Nauru's and Tuvalu's applications to join the United Nations in 1999 and 2000 respectively, despite both countries having formal diplomatic ties with Taipei. Aside from the Taiwan issue, China is likely to continue to project its image as a benign and responsible global power in the region. In addition to its familiar pattern of building high-profile government buildings, sports stadiums and other public infrastructure in island capitals, China has expanded both its diplomatic network and its aid disbursements to friendly island governments, hoping to win hearts and minds of the locals.

Chinese Strategies in Small South Pacific Nations

High-level Involvement

In April 2006 Premier Wen Jiabao, after visiting Australia, went on to Fiji for the first summit between China and Pacific Island states. The China-Pacific Island Countries Economic Development and Cooperation Forum held during Wen's visit underscored China's heightened interest in the South Pacific. Fiji was the first Pacific island country to establish diplomatic relations with China in 1975. This was also the first visit by a Chinese premier to South Pacific small islands. During Wen's visit, China announced a wide-ranging package of aid to South Pacific island countries as part of efforts to strengthen relations. Besides 3 billion yuan ($375 million) in preferential loans over the next three years, Beijing granted zero-tariff treatment to goods from the islands, canceled their debt that matured at the end of 2005 and made all island states with diplomatic ties approved tourist destinations. China also would train 2,000 Pacific government officials and provide free anti-malaria medicines for the next three years.[51]

Vice President Xi Jinping made a transit visit to Fiji on his way to Latin America in February 2009 and met with Fiji leaders, with both sides expressing wishes to strengthen the cooperative partnership between the two countries. In December 2005, CCP Politburo member Luo Gan and his delegation made a two-day stopover in Tahiti while en route to South America. The visit came a day after the official announcement that China would open a consulate general and cultural center in Tahiti's capital Papeete in 2006 as well as the Chinese government's conferment of ADS for Chinese tourists to visit French Polynesia.[52] These moves were symbolic of China's efforts to increase its presence in the South Pacific. Vice Premier Zeng Peiyan took a trip to the South Pacific in April 2007.

While attending the 16th Leaders' Meeting of the APEC forum held in Lima, Peru in November 2008, President Hu Jintao met with PNG's Prime Minister Michael Somare on the sidelines of the summit and affirmed China's policy of continuing high-level exchanges with PNG and deepening mutual political trust and steadily broadening cooperation in such fields as trade, agriculture, culture, education and health care.[53] Prime Minister Somare appreciated China's support and aid to his country in investment, infrastructure construction, medical service and health care. He welcomed Chinese companies' investments and cooperation in energy and resources, adding that China's economic and technological support to South Pacific countries is very important for the region's development.

In September 2012, China's NPC Standing Committee Chairman Wu Bangguo visited Fiji to promote cooperation in infrastructure, tourism and agriculture. Wu emphasized that China would treat countries, big or small, equally. For his part, Fijian Prime Minister Voreqe Bainimarama reiterated that Fiji firmly supports the one-China principle and hopes China could achieve peaceful reunification with Taiwan.

Leaders from the region have traveled to China. China has hosted the leaders of PNG, Fiji, Vanuatu, Samoa, the Federated States of Micronesia, Tonga, Kiribati, and other countries in recent years. Nowadays many South Pacific leaders tend to make their first overseas trips to China. Between March 2004 and July 2005, for example, eight heads of state of South Pacific countries paid official visits to China at the invitation (and most likely with financial support) of the Chinese government. An 80-person entourage accompanied PNG Prime Minister Somare on his February 2004 visit. In August 2010, Fijian Prime Minister Bainimarama visited Beijing and Shanghai and secured vital aid from the rising superpower.

---

51   "Aid Package Announced for South Pacific States," *China Daily*, April 6, 2006.
52   Shie, "China Woos the South Pacific," PacNet No. 10A.
53   "Chinese President Meets Papua New Guinea's PM," *Xinhua*, November 23, 2008.

"[The Chinese] think outside the box," he told reporters, "they are visionary in what they do."[54] "It is now accepted routine that the first official overseas visit by a new head of government from the region is made to Beijing, not to Canberra, Washington or Wellington," commented two scholars from New Zealand and Australia.[55]

Since 2011, the Chinese People's Political Consultative Conference (CPPCC) has hosted several groups of South Pacific Island politicians, with members from Fiji, Micronesia, Samoa, Tonga and Vanuatu, to promote bilateral exchanges and advance practical cooperation.

Expanding Economic Aid and Cooperation

China is interested in obtaining minerals, timber and fish from the South Pacific while providing much needed investment in infrastructure and industries in the region. Over 3,000 Chinese state-owned and private enterprises have been registered in the Pacific region with investments of about A$800 million.[56] The influx of Chinese diplomats and business people has been matched by the arrival of a new diaspora.

China is quickly becoming a significant player in the South Pacific. According to the China-Pacific Island Countries Economic Development and Cooperation Guiding Framework which was concluded in 2006, China had pledged $375 million in development assistance and low-interest loans without any political strings attached.[57] It gives aid to the eight developing PIF countries that recognize it: the Cook Islands, the Federated States of Micronesia, Fiji, Niue, PNG, Samoa, Tonga and Vanuatu. The total value of its pledged aid projects to these countries over the period 2005–2007 suggests a large and rapidly growing program: $33 million in 2005, $78 million in 2006 and $293 million in 2007, making China the third largest donor to the region after Australia and the United States.[58] In 2009 China pledged over $200 million in grants and soft loans to the region. China has become the region's second largest trading partner after Australia.

China has promised to provide enterprises of the Pacific island countries with more favorable loans and aid programs in the years ahead. It gave zero-tariff

---

54   "China Broadens Its Strategy in the South Pacific," *Time*, September 7, 2010.

55   Henderson and Reilly, "Dragon in Paradise: China's Rising Star in Oceania," p. 95.

56   Graeme Dobell, "China and Taiwan in the South Pacific: Diplomatic Chess Versus Pacific Political Rugby," *Policy Brief*, January 2007, Lowy Institute for International Policy, Sydney, Australia.

57   Zhang Guihong, "China's Pacific Strategy Unfurled," *Asia Times Online*, April 10, 2008.

58   Hanson, *The Dragon in the Pacific: More Opportunity than Threat*. Hanson later suggested that the 2007 figure was somewhat distorted by two large soft loans to Fiji and Tonga. He put the total Chinese grants and loans for 2008 at $206 million. See Fergus Hanson, "China: Stumbling through the Pacific," Lowy Institute for International Policy, Sydney, Australia, July 2009.

treatment to the majority of exports to China from the least developed countries in the region. It also expressed interest in a FTA with Pacific Island countries. Furthermore, as a dialogue partner of PIF, it has set up the China-PIF Cooperation Fund to help finance the Pacific Plan designed to promote regional cooperation.

Much of the assistance from China to date has been used for highly visible projects, including the construction of a new parliamentary complex in Vanuatu, a multi-storey government office in Samoa, the new foreign ministry headquarters in PNG, as well as hotel developments in Tonga and the provision of a ferry for Kiribati. China also built the sports stadium in Fiji for the 2003 South Pacific games, and has made a practice of donating a fleet of VIP cars to the island state hosting the annual Forum meeting.[59]

China has invested in PNG's mining, forestry and fishing sectors. Chinese aid to PNG is now second only to Australia's $300 million per year. It had already invested in the development of the $1 billion Ramu nickel mine in the remote Mandang province. According to official estimates, there are currently about 10,000 Chinese citizens in PNG, which is now the largest recipient of Chinese aid of any Pacific island nation.[60]

China has a particular interest in PNG's vast energy and mineral resources. Officials of China's biggest oil company, CNPC, have discussed the possibility of building a plant to produce LNG in PNG, a prospect that may have improved since early 2007 when Exxon Mobil finally scrapped its plans to pipe huge quantities of natural gas to Australia. In addition, the PNG government signed an agreement in 2006 to allow China Exploration and Engineering Bureau to explore further opportunities to develop gold, copper, chromites, magnesium, or other mineral resources.[61]

Beijing helped pay for the construction of the venue of the 2003 South Pacific Games in Suva, Fiji. Following the December 5, 2006 military coup, Fiji's two largest neighbors Australia and New Zealand stopped all military ties and placed a travel ban on officials in the interim administration. The interim government of Fiji adopted the "Look North" policy, which provided an opportunity for China to expand its trade and influence in Fiji. Indeed, officials from the China Development Bank went to Fiji at least three times in 2007 to look at the possibility of setting up a bank there. Interim Prime Minister Voreqe Bainimarama said that he would send an official party to four Asian countries including China in a bid to seek financial support and to compensate what Fiji had lost from Australia's and New Zealand's sanctions. A Fiji trade and investment mission to China returned in September 2007 and reported "positive outcomes."[62] In February 2008 China donated $200,000 to Fiji to assist in rural recovery efforts after Cyclone Gene

---

59   Henderson and Reilly, "Dragon in Paradise: China's Rising Star in Oceania," p. 102.
60   Ibid.
61   Wesley-Smith, *China in Oceania: New Forces in Pacific*, pp. 10–11.
62   "Chinese Government Seeks to Open Bank in Fiji," *Fijilive* http://www.fijilive. com, September 17, 2007.

caused severe damage across the country. China provided $240 million to Fiji for rural development, a key area the interim Government targeted in 2009. It will also assist the interim Government with funds and expertise to build low-cost housing projects, according to Bainimarama.[63] Shunned by Western donors, Fiji's interim government has received a huge increase in grant support from China, with no hectoring about democracy and human rights. Australia restored full diplomatic relations with Fiji in 2012 and eased sanctions it imposed on the military regime.

China has been a strong supporter for the PIF. It has continued to assist the region in its implementation of the Pacific Plan since it was endorsed by Forum leaders in 2005. In November 2007 China presented $650,000 as a grant to the PIF Secretariat for the funding of several regional projects, including the Forum's import management project, the Forum Aviation Action Plan, Integrated Port Development Project, and the Rural and Remote Information Communication Technology Access.[64]

The Pacific Island states are struggling to make headway toward reaching the UN Millennium Development Goals. China is well positioned to provide much needed infrastructure and is already driving substantial increases in trade flows.

Promoting Cultural, Educational, and Other Societal Exchanges

In addition to trade and investment, China is engaging the South Pacific in other ways, which include broadcasting Chinese television programming, expanding student exchanges, and paving the way for an increase of Chinese tourists with the granting of ADS to all Pacific island nations that have diplomatic relations with China. China joined SPTO in April 2004, becoming the organization's first member from outside the region. The SPTO, established in 1986 and based in Suva, Fiji, is a regional inter-governmental organization for the joint promotion of the region as a tourist destination. China's participation helps boost the regional tourism and enhance the understanding between China and the island countries. To attract Chinese tourists, Air Pacific launched a direct service from Fiji's Nadi International Airport to Hong Kong and opened an office in Shanghai in December 2009. To promote educational exchanges, China has helped build a law school at the regional University of the South Pacific. In August 2012, China and New Zealand agreed to work together to deliver an improved water mains system in Rarotonga, the Cook Islands.

The Chinese who settled in the island nations in earlier eras had fled the chaos and poverty of their homeland. The new Chinese arrivals can look to the motherland in ways not available to previous generations: a prospering economy and a supportive government at home. A good example of this change occurred in 2006, when Chinese diplomats called up planes to evacuate 300 Chinese nationals from Honiara after the April riots in Solomon Islands. China's growing activities

---

63   "Fiji-China's South Pacific 'Client State,'" *New Zeal*, September 12, 2008.
64   "China Presents Grant to South Pacific Projects," *Xinhua*, November 21, 2007.

have occurred in the context of an increasingly distracted and disengaged United States and other powers. In the 1990s the United States closed US Information Agency offices, its USAID Regional Development Office, and ended the Fulbright exchange program in the region. The number of US Peace Corps missions in the South Pacific has been halved since 1995. Additionally, the United Kingdom recently closed three diplomatic posts in the region and withdrew from the Pacific Community, the regional development body.[65]

China has also expanded its military links in the region, inking military cooperation agreements with Fiji, Vanuatu, Tonga and PNG—the Pacific states that maintain standing armies—and announcing future plans to train their senior military officers in Beijing. According to ANU senior lecturer Benjamin Reilly, China's military assistance to these states has consisted of training and logistical support rather than weaponry, but military assistance has increased sharply recently.[66] Following the coup in Fiji, China quickly volunteered to fill the gap left by the suspension of military assistance from Australia and New Zealand.

Assessment

China's influence has penetrated into the South Pacific region since the mid-1990s. It's obviously elbowing for room in waters long kept calm by the US and its allies. Just a few years ago, China did not weigh much in the South Pacific region. Today, it has been so deeply involved that any significant diplomatic discussion in the South Pacific must factor in China's wishes. Economic problems, political instability, and neglect by other powers, most notably the United States, have led these small nations to "look north," and China has encouraged this process through the extensive use of its economic and diplomatic power.

China has quietly extended its influence among poor island nations dotted across the South Pacific, a region with rich fishing grounds and potential resources. Some small island nations here have become dependent on financial aid from China. For example, China accounted for about 62 percent of Tonga's total external debt at the end of 2011.[67] And Toga's government asked Beijing for more money to build schools, health centers and community halls. As a result, less money from Beijing could make life tough for many Tongans and force more to leave in search of work in Australia and New Zealand.

Most Pacific island states have viewed China's growing role in Oceania "with favor rather than fear," according to two scholars from the region.[68] "China's

---

65   Shie, "China Woos the South Pacific."

66   Benjamin Reilly, "Japan's Return to Guadalcanal," *The Wall Street Journal*, August 1, 2008. Also Bertil Lintner, "The Sinicizing of the South Pacific," *Asia Times Online*, April 18, 2007.

67   "China Seeks to Star in South Pacific," *The Wall Street Journal*, April 27, 2012.

68   Henderson and Reilly, "Dragon in Paradise: China's Rising Star in Oceania," p. 95.

rising status as an economic and military power is becoming an important pillar for developing countries like PNG," said Tarcy Eri, a high-ranking PNG foreign ministry official. China's voice at the UN, he said, was "one for the developing world."[69] Unlike the West, China's investment comes with no political conditions. "China is not rich. Still, we are ready to provide assistance without any political strings attached," Premier Wen Jiabao said in a keynote speech during his visit to Fiji in April 2006.[70] China's rise offers Pacific Island states opportunities not available under established structures of power and influence, argued Terence Wesley-Smith, professor and graduate chair in the Center for Pacific Islands Studies at the University of Hawaii at Manoa.[71] For many developing nations including those in the South Pacific, China's rapid growth since the late 1970s is something they admire and want to learn from.

Despite China's expanded ties with the South Pacific, its trade with the region is still small. The South Pacific's total worldwide trade was less than $13 billion in 2006 with China's share only $743 million.[72] And China's trade with the South Pacific is a tiny fraction of China's total trade globally. The South Pacific is not essential to China's economic security strategy since none of the island states lies close to the sea lanes that service the bulk of China's trade in energy and raw materials. In capital investment, China is a long way from supplanting the West. China's investment in PNG's nickel sector, for example, pales in comparison to the ExxonMobil-led LNG project in the same country that is set to add an extra 15 to 20 percent to its GDP each year.[73]

China's involvement in South Pacific economies has grown rapidly. From 2005 to 2009, China's grants and loans to Pacific islands swelled to $600 million from $23.2 million, according to the Lowy Institute in Australia.[74] The United States began to pay more attention to the region now. US financial support for the region was up around a third in 2010 from five years before, to around $200 million.

China's presence has created new challenges for these developing nations. Ideological differences exist between China and the South Pacific nations, which have a strong Christian tradition. The term "Communist China" still appears in local newspapers today. New Chinese immigrants are sometimes resented by locals for competing for jobs and for corrupting local officials and politicians. Riots targeting at Chinese businesses broke out in the Solomon Islands and Tonga in April and November 2006 respectively. Deadly anti-Chinese riots also took place in PNG in May 2009, which highlighted the need for the Chinese government to protect its business people and workers abroad.

---

69   Lintner, "The Sinicizing of the South Pacific," April 18, 2007.

70   "Aid Package Announced for South Pacific States," *China Daily*, April 6, 2006.

71   Wesley-Smith, *China in Oceania: New Forces in Pacific Politics*, p. 1.

72   Hanson, *The Dragon in the Pacific: More Opportunity than Threat*.

73   Fergus Hanson, "China and the South Pacific: No Cause for Panic Yet," PacNet #15, Pacific Forum, CSIS, March 4, 2011.

74   "China Seeks to Star in South Pacific," *The Wall Street Journal*, April 27, 2012.

The two internal major powers—Australia and New Zealand—and two external major powers—the United States and France—have their respective traditional spheres of influence and provide security and stability for the Pacific Islanders. So far China's limited but growing influence in the region has been mainly diplomatic and economic. Natural resources, trade and economic cooperation, and diplomatic victory over Taiwan are China's basic interests and primary objectives in the Pacific, and therefore the most important motives of China's active engagement in the region. It does not intend to disrupt the existing power structure in the Pacific. It is not here to garner influence to replace the United States or Australia as the regional hegemon. But to avoid potential confrontation with others, China's engagement in the region has to consider the interests and concerns of both the small island countries and major external powers.

There has been some speculation that China has military objectives in the Pacific. A Lowy Institute research suggests that Chinese assistance to regional forces is small, tending to be limited to more benign assistance such as upgrading a military hospital in PNG or the supply of non-lethal equipment like uniforms and cars for the Vanuatu Mobile Force. So China's defense aspirations in the South Pacific are likely to remain limited.[75] China does not appear to be setting itself up to challenge the status quo in global politics or to assume a leadership role in the South Pacific. As University of Hawaii's Terence Wesley-Smith has argued, there is little evidence to support the notion that China has gained influence by exploiting regional vulnerabilities, or that its activities have encouraged corruption and instability in the Pacific. In fact, China's heightened profile in the region has been generally welcomed by local leaders.[76]

The economies of China and the Pacific island countries are complementary. China has funding, technical expertise, and most importantly development experience. The island countries are rich in natural resources. They are all developing economies. Their cooperation is another good example of "South-South" cooperation in promoting common development and prosperity. China's aid to Pacific island nations is not conditional on them improving standards of governance or human rights, which is perhaps fine with China and many of these countries right now. In the long term, whether China's policy is sustainable and in the best interest of these countries is questionable.

China's presence in the South Pacific has already created challenges and potential problems. Chinese dominance of the Tongan economy, for example, was the main reason why violent riots erupted in the Tongan capital in November 2006. Ostensibly demonstrating for democratic reforms, the mobs looted and burned at least 30 Chinese-owned stores before Australian and New Zealand peacekeepers arrived. The Tonga riots followed widespread rioting in the Solomon Islands, where angry mobs also attacked and ransacked Chinese-owned stores, prompting Beijing to send an airplane to evacuate more than 300 of its nationals. Recent

---

75   Ibid.
76   Wesley-Smith, *China in Oceania: New Forces in Pacific Politics*, p. 2.

Chinese immigrants are resented by many locals for allegedly taking away jobs and perpetuating corruption. Passport scams and smuggling of people and drugs are believed to be major crimes committed by some new Chinese immigrants. In April 2006, Honiara's Chinatown was looted and burned by Solomon Islanders, who believed that Asian, especially Chinese, businessmen bribed members of parliament and bought the prime ministership for Snyder Rini.

China's rising political and economic influence has helped it persuade more countries to recognize Beijing instead of Taipei. Both the PRC and Taiwanese governments have allegedly been involved in local politics. Litokwa Tomeing was elected by lawmakers as president of the Marshall Islands on January 7, 2008, a move that could end the South Pacific nation's diplomatic recognition of Taiwan. With a population of about 62,000 people today, the Marshall Islands became independent in 1986 after being administered by the United States. Tomeing had vowed to end the Marshalls' diplomatic recognition of Taiwan and adhere to the "one-China" policy that identifies Taiwan as Chinese territory. Taiwanese officials have accused China of interfering in the Marshall Islands' elections by funneling money through local businessmen to opposition candidates.[77] Yet Taiwan itself reportedly gave $14 million in aid to the Marshall Islands annually.[78] The competition between China and Taiwan for diplomatic recognition has destabilized island states in the South Pacific, making Pacific politics more corrupt and violent, according to one analysis released by Lowy Institute.[79] Checkbook diplomacy is believed to have fostered and furthered corruption in domestic politics in the South Pacific. Australia has warned both China and Taiwan not to interfere in the politics of its regional neighbors. "We don't want to see checkbook diplomacy entering the Pacific," said foreign minister Alexander Downer in 2007.[80] The Taiwan factor as a major motive in China's diplomacy has somewhat receded into the background after the 2008 power transfer in Taipei. However, the checkbook diplomatic competition has never ended, as evidenced by the resignation of the Solomon Islands' Prime Minister Danny Philip in November 2011 on allegations of misappropriation of aid from Taiwan.

Since the end of the Cold War, Western aid programs have often attached political conditions such as good governance, policy transparency, government accountability, and human rights. In contrast, China, except for its insistence on the "one-China" principle, has practiced the policy of "no conditions attached" based on its "non interference" tradition, without lecturing these governments or getting involved in local politics. The two different approaches may lead to conflict in the South Pacific.

---

77 "Marshall Islands Elects Tomeing As President, May End Taiwan Recognition," *International Herald Tribune*, January 7, 2008.

78 "Taiwan Positive Marshall Islands Won't Switch Its Loyalty to China," *Radio New Zealand International*, December 18, 2007.

79 Dobell, "China and Taiwan in the South Pacific."

80 "Chinese Rivals Grapple for Pacific," *BBC News*, April 4, 2007.

China's growing influence in the South Pacific has triggered competition from its rivals. For example, both Japan and the United States have strengthened their ties with the region to curb China's increasing presence in the region. Japan has hosted the triennial summit between Japan and the Pacific Islands Forum since 1997. Japan counts on South Pacific nations' support as it pursues a permanent seat at the UN Security Council. In the 2012 summit held in Okinawa, Japan promised to provide up to $500 million in aid to Pacific island nations over the next three years and sought energy, fishery and defence cooperation with these nations.[81] Most notably, the United States took part for the first time in the 2012 summit, which may reflect Washington's shift of focus to the Asia–Pacific amid China's rising clout. The maritime issue was also taken up as an agenda item for the first time in the 2012 summit, apparently amid the ongoing territorial disputes between Beijing and other Asian nations, notably the Philippines and Vietnam, in the South China Sea.

It's no secret the United States and China are jockeying to be better friends to Pacific nations in terms of aid and development. In August 2012, US Secretary of State Hilary Clinton attended the Pacific Forum in the Cook Islands. She was the highest ranking US official to have ever attended the forum. Her visit was believed to be aimed at curbing China's growing influence in the region. China has sent senior officials to the forum since the early 1990s. Vice Foreign Minister Cui Tiankai, as the representative of the Chinese government, attended the 2012 Pacific Forum and laid out a 10-point specific action plan to help promote economic and social development of island nations, including further exempting the-least developed island countries from debts and granting zero-tariff treatment to 95 percent of the tariff items of exports to China from these countries, building commercial centers, upgrading roads, building and repairing passenger-cargo ships, building community colleges, etcetera. In competition, the US government opened an USAID office in Port Moresby in October 2011.

China's presence in the South Pacific is a fact of life now. As Australian Foreign Minister Bob Carr put it, "Australia and New Zealand have got to live with the fact that China will want to deliver aid in this part of the world (and) there is nothing we can do to stop it."[82] Competition for resources and influence between China and other powers will be inevitable as Chinese presence deepens.

Concluding Remarks

China's deepening involvement in South Pacific coincides with the relatively waning influence of the United States and other Western powers. The foreign affairs, defense, and trade division of the Congressional Research Service (CRS) drafted a 30-page

---

81   "Japan, Pacific Islands Agree on Maritime, Disaster Cooperation," *The Mainichi*, May 26, 2012. Also, "Checkbook Diplomacy Aimed at Reining China," *China Daily*, May 28, 2012.
82   Quoted in "Clinton Visit Raises Concerns," *China Daily*, August 29, 2012.

report, "The Southwest Pacific: US Interests and China's Growing Influence," to US Congress in July 2007. The report noted increasing opposition to Australian government interventions in the region and warned that the regional hegemony established by the US and its allies in the aftermath of World War II was being undermined by China.[83] Nevertheless, China's engagement in the South Pacific does not represent an end to the West's dominant influence in the region or a first-order threat to the United States and its allies, remarked Lowy Institute scholar Fergus Hanson.[84]

Aimed at reasserting its influence in the strategically important region, the US State Department designated 2007 as the "Year of the Pacific" and pledged to reverse what it characterized as US "neglect" of the region since the end of the Cold War. Secretary of State Condoleezza Rice hosted a meeting of Pacific governments in Washington in May 2007 and announced a number of new diplomatic initiatives, including pledging more aid to the region and opening a new regional office of the State Department's public diplomacy bureau in Fiji. The May 2007 Washington meeting was the eighth Pacific Island Conference of Leaders (PICL). The triennial PICL is normally held in Hawaii and sparks little international interest except from various donor countries' aid officials. The 2007 conference was held for the first time in Washington DC under the auspices of US State Department. In her opening address, Secretary of State Rice explained that the phrase Year of the Pacific "encapsulates our efforts to expand our engagement with your countries and to reaffirm America's historic role in the Pacific. Maintaining security and stability in the Pacific region is crucial to the interest of every country and every territory represented at the conference, including the United States."[85] Clearly the United States has felt the need to maintain its hold on the region.

The compact between the United States and the Free Associated States (FAS) of the Republic of Marshall Islands, the Federated States of Micronesia, and Palau gives the United States control over defense issues in return for generous economic assistance. Such economic largesse gives the United States a veto over the compact states' foreign policies. The United States maintains a firm control over the northern part of the "second island chain," particularly Guam and the Northern Mariana Islands where the US military could stage and maneuver in the events of any conflict with China over Taiwan. The FAS, together with Guam and the Northern Mariana Islands, form a security perimeter of the United States.[86]

China's new diplomacy in the South Pacific mirrors its diplomatic approaches in other developing regions. It is primarily driven by its economic interests,

83   Patrick O'Connor, "US Congress Receives Warning of China's Growing Influence in South Pacific," *World Socialist Web Site* (www.wsws.org), August 29, 2007.

84   Fergus Hanson, "China and the South Pacific: No Cause for Panic Yet," PacNet #15, Pacific Forum CSIS, March 4, 2011.

85   Patrick O'Connor, "Bush Administration Hosts Meeting of Pacific Island Governments," *World Socialist Web Site* (www.wsws.org), May 18, 2007.

86   Jian Yang, "China in the South Pacific: A Strategic Threat"? a paper to *Asia: NZ* www.asianz.org.nz, 2008, accessed on August 1, 2009.

diplomatic competition with Taiwan, and efforts to project soft power. It is part of Beijing's strategy to diversify energy and commodity resources; it is also part of its global efforts to expand its political, diplomatic, economic, and cultural influence. China asks little beyond recognition of the "one-China" policy. It does not seem to have vital interests in small island nations in the South Pacific. China's involvement has generally promoted economic growth of countries in the Pacific, and Chinese aid can be good development opportunities for these countries.

The Rio Tinto and Rebiya Kadeer cases and sporadic attacks against Chinese interests in several countries demonstrate the limitations of Chinese diplomacy in the South Pacific. Long-term relations between China and Pacific island nations depend on how China can help South Pacific island countries from being marginalized in an era of globalization and how China can work with them to deal with challenges such as environmental degradation, growing corruption, and the rise of sea level. Australia, New Zealand, the United States and France have their respective spheres of influence and provide security and stability for the Pacific islanders. China's engagement in the region has to consider the interests and concerns of these traditional players. As a nation that abhors foreign interference in its internal affairs, China must also be careful in not getting entangled in domestic affairs of small South Pacific nations.

Some people may continue to debate over whether China's increased activity in Oceania constitutes a zero-sum game for the island nations as well as the United States, Australia, New Zealand and others. But China is in the South Pacific to stay, and it will continue to attach greater importance to its relations with Australia, New Zealand and the small island nations. There is no clear evidence that China's deepening involvement in the South Pacific is calculated to compete with Australia, New Zealand, the United States, and other powers in the region. China's economic success has broadened the menu of options for the island states as they seek development. The Western powers have little choice but to accept this changed conditions. What they can do is to urge China to become a more responsible player and shoulder more responsibility by promoting both development and good governance in the region.

Questions for Discussion

1. What is the status of China–Australia and China–New Zealand relations?
2. Why is China interested in small South Pacific island nations?
3. To what extent is China disrupting the status quo in the South Pacific?
4. How do Australia and New Zealand view China's rise?
5. How do Pacific island nations view China's expanding trade, investment and influence in the region?
6. Are China and the United States engaged in a strategic competition in the South Pacific?

Chapter 7

China and Southeast Asia

Chinese–Southeast Asian relations have experienced ups and downs since 1949. During most of the Cold War, China was seen by many Southeast Asian nations as an exporter of communism. In the eyes of many people in the region, communist China was a country to be feared and avoided. Diplomatic relations were strained as Southeast Asian governments suppressed communist insurgents, many of whom were ethnic Chinese. In fact, ASEAN was first established in 1967 as an anti-communist political group.[1] Normal political and economic relations between China and most Southeast Asian nations were almost non-existent. Given such a shaky foundation, it is truly amazing that China–ASEAN relations have developed so tremendously since the end of the Cold War.

For China, Southeast Asia is a close neighbor which is strategically important for its national security. China and ASEAN established official links in 1991. In the early 1990s, the relationship was still tentative at best. To a large extent, the 1997 Asian financial crisis, which offered an opportunity for China to upgrade its relations with the region, was a turning point and fundamentally changed Chinese–Southeast Asian relations. While the United States was critical of Southeast Asia's development model and slow in its response when the crisis hit the region, China quickly responded to ASEAN's acute need, with an immediate promise not to devalue its currency, the *Renminbi*, and further destabilize the region. After the crisis, ASEAN Secretary General Rodolfo Severino announced, "China is really emerging from this smelling good."[2] By November 1997, the lukewarm relationship had evolved to the level of annual ASEAN plus China summits. Since the 1997 Asian financial crisis, it has become increasingly difficult for ASEAN states to resist China's ever-growing influence in economic assistance and soft power.[3]

The fact that China has become an engine for economic growth for Southeast Asian nations and that the United States diverted its attention from the region in the war against terror provides China with a great opportunity to expand its influence in Southeast Asia. Since the late 1990s China has advanced its relations with ASEAN

---

1   ASEAN was established on August 8, 1967 in Bangkok by the five original members: Indonesia, Malaysia, the Philippines, Singapore, and Thailand. Brunei Darussalam joined in 1984, Vietnam in 1995, Laos and Myanmar in 1997, and Cambodia in 1999.

2   Quoted in Joshua Kurlantzick, "China's Charm: Implications of Chinese Soft Power," *Policy Brief No. 47* (June 2006), Carnegie Endowment for International Peace.

3   Sheng Lijun, "Is Southeast Asia Becoming China's Playpen"? *YaleGlobal Online*, January 11, 2007.

states in fields of foreign aid, trade, finance, infrastructure, labor, environment, tourism, education, etcetera. To achieve continued economic growth at home, the Chinese leadership is intent on securing smooth relations with the rest of the world. It is only natural for China to exercise its new and friendly diplomacy in Southeast Asia. For China, strong ties with ASEAN are particularly significant in its relations with the rest of the world. They are a crucial part of China's good neighbor diplomacy (*mulin waijiao* 睦邻外交). If relations with ASEAN nations are smooth, China can claim that it is a peaceful power and is trusted in its own neighborhood.

The United States has been the dominant power in the region since WWII. Though not a member of ASEAN, it has taken part in ASEAN's economic and security discussions through strong bilateral relations and multilateral platforms such as ARF and APEC. ASEAN members are particularly cautious not to get caught between an increasingly assertive China and a historically hegemonic United States. China's influence in the region has grown to a level at which America's reliance on support from Southeast Asian nations in case of a US–China conflict is no longer guaranteed.

Realizing its relative neglect of the region since 9/11, the United States began to introduce a policy called "pivot" or strategic rebalancing towards Asia in 2009.[4] In a speech to the Australian parliament in November 2011, visiting US president Barack Obama declared that "the United States is a Pacific power, and we are here to stay." Defence Secretary Leon Panetta announced in June 2012 that the US would move 60 percent of its naval fleet to the Asia–Pacific region by 2020. Due to strategic, economic and geographic importance of the region, there will be increased competition for influence in Southeast Asia among major powers including China, the United States, Japan, and India.

Sino-ASEAN trade grew from $8 billion in 1991 to over $200 billion in 2007 and $230 billion in 2008. When the ASEAN-China FTA was implemented in January 2010, the world's largest free trade zone was created with 1.7 billion people, a total GDP of $2 trillion, and total trade volume exceeding $1.2 trillion.[5] (See Table 7.1a and Table 7.1b.) In 2011 ASEAN overtook Japan to become China's third largest trading partner, with the trade volume surpassing $362 billion—up 24 percent from a year earlier. In the same year, China had $446.6 billion in trade with the US and $567.2 billion with the EU. According to the China Association of International Trade, ASEAN will become China's largest trading partner by 2015.[6]

---

4   Secretary of State Hillary Clinton first officially announced the US strategic shift to Asia in 2009. "The United States is back," she declared upon arriving in Bangkok for the ASEAN summit on July 21, 2009. Clinton also penned an article in the November 2011 issue of *Foreign Policy*, titled "America's Pacific Century," in which she argued that the future of international politics will be decided in Asia and the United States will be right at the center of the action.

5   Evelyn Goh, "China and Southeast Asia," *Foreign Policy In Focus*, December 12, 2006.

6   "ASEAN To Be Top Trade Partner," *China Daily Asia Weekly*, April 27-May 3, 2012: p. 20.

Table 7.1a   China–Southeast Asia Trade Volume: Selected Years (in billions of US dollars)

Year	1991	2000	2001	2002	2003	2007	2008	2011
Volume	8	39.5	41.6	42.8	55.2	200	230	362

Table 7.1b   China's Growing Trade with Selected Southeast Asian Countries (in US dollars)

Year Country	2004	2006	2007	2008	2010	2011
East Timor	1.2 million	2 million		9.4 million	43 million	
Malaysia			33 billion		50 billion	90 billion
Philippines	6.1 billion	8.3 billion		30 billion		32 billion
Singapore		41 billion	47 billion	62 billion		83 billion
Vietnam	4.9 billion		16 billion		25 billion	40 billion

Sources: 1) Association of Southeast Asian Nations (ASEAN) (http://www.aseansec.org); 2) Singapore Chinese Chamber of Commerce & Industry (http://english.sccci.org.sg); and 3) China Customs, various years.

Southeast Asia, home of majority of the Chinese overseas, is also a major investor in China's economic and social projects. By the end of 2005, Southeast Asian nations and businesses had invested in nearly 30,000 projects in China, totaling about $40 billion.[7]

Motivations of China's New Diplomacy in Southeast Asia

Strategic Importance

Southeast Asian nations are considered China's "periphery countries" (*zhoubian guojia* 周边国家) that China pays particular attention to during the reform era. China needs a peaceful environment for its continued economic growth. China's relations with Southeast Asia serve as a barometer of how China will develop its relations with other regions.

Southeast Asia contains all the shipping routes for China's energy imports and transportation from the Middle East, Africa and Latin America. China is heavily dependent on at least four sea lane routes in Southeast Asia: first, from the Middle East/Africa through the Malacca Strait, then the South China Sea to China for

---

7   Wen Jiabao, "Creating a Beautiful Future of China-ASEAN Relations," A speech made at the conference commemorating the 15th anniversary of China–ASEAN dialogue, Nanning, China, October 30, 2006.

tankers under 100,000 tons; second, from the Middle East/Africa through the Sunda Strait, then the Gaspar Strait and the South China Sea to China for very large crude carriers (VLCC) over 100,000 tons; third, from Latin America/South Pacific through the Philippine Sea, then the South China Sea to China; and fourth, the alternative route, the Middle East/Africa through the Lombok Strait to the Makassar Strait or Maluku Strait, then the Philippine Sea to the West Pacific then China.[8] These sea lanes and narrow straits are like choke points in China's energy transportation. Roughly 80 percent of China's energy imports transit through the Malacca Strait, so it is extremely important to maintain friendly relations with littoral states of the Strait. China is expected to import more energy and other resources through these sea routes, especially the Malacca Strait, yet it is extremely vulnerable to any disruptions at these choke points. China wishes to reduce its dependence on energy supplies through the Malacca Strait but has few alternatives now. This predicament has been dubbed China's "Malacca Dilemma" by Chinese scholars and media. China's efforts to expand oil and gas imports via land from Central Asia may lessen its heavy dependence on these sea lanes in the future.

In October 2006 Liang Guanglie, then Chief of the General Staff of the PLA, visited Cambodia, Laos and Myanmar to promote military exchanges with these countries. China is one of Myanmar's closest allies and has helped with the construction of naval bases in the Bay of Bengal and the Adaman Sea. In June 2009 CNPC announced a plan to construct an oil pipeline connecting Myanmar with China. The 1,100 kilometer crude oil line starts from the port of Kyaukryu in Myanmar and end in Kunming, the capital of China's Yunnan province. The oil pipeline, when completed, will be used to transport oil to China from the Middle East and Africa as well as Myanmar itself.

Southeast Asia itself is rich in resources. To diversify sources of energy import, China has considered Southeast Asia as an important supplier of energy. For example, in 2006, both Indonesia and Malaysia signed agreements with China to provide LNG to China. To reduce tensions in the region, especially the South China Sea area, China and ASEAN have held security dialogues since 1991. Significantly, ASEAN members and China signed a declaration on the conduct of parties in the South China Sea in November 2002, in which all parties concerned undertook to resolve their territorial and jurisdictional disputes by peaceful means, without resorting to the threat or use of force, through friendly consultations and negotiations by sovereign states directly concerned.[9] This followed China's armed conflicts in the South China Sea with Vietnam and the Philippines, and the code of conduct has guided China's relations with other claimants of the South China Sea since.

Southeast Asia also serves other strategic purposes of China. After the Cold War and during much of the 1990s, there was a heated debate in the United States

8   Xuegang Zhang "China's Energy Corridors in Southeast Asia," *China Brief*, Vol. 8, No. 3 (January 31, 2008), The Jamestown Foundation, Washington, DC.

9   The full text of the declaration can be found on ASEAN's website at http://www.aseansec.org/13163.htm.

regarding its policy toward China: engagement or containment. Since the mid-1990s, China has supported ASEAN as a collective body in order to balance the strategic pressure of the United States. Many Chinese efforts to promote relations with ASEAN were intended to forestall a possible US containment strategy.

Reaping Benefits from Trade and Investment

Southeast Asia is fast emerging as an important supplier of China's industrial commodities and energy, and the region as a whole runs a trade surplus with China. China displaced the United States as ASEAN's top trading partner in 2008 and trade further expanded as the Sino-ASEAN FTA came into force in 2010. As planned, trade in goods became liberalized in January 2010 for China and the six older ASEAN members, and will be in 2015 for China and the four newer members: Cambodia, Laos, Myanmar, and Vietnam.

Poorer countries in Southeast Asia benefit most from China's investment with added infrastructure—roads, ports, bridges, hospitals, schools, etcetera. The infrastructure projects funded by China seem clearly aimed at helping to assure China's access to natural resources and to enhance its soft power. Economic cooperation remains the focus of China's relations with Southeast Asian nations. China and Singapore enjoy strong economic ties. Trade volume between the two sides has grown by more than 20 percent annually since the early 2000s. Singapore is China's largest overseas labor market, and China is Singapore's second largest trading partner and biggest investment destination. As of the end of 2006, Singapore had invested $30 billion in more than 15,000 projects across China. China and Singapore signed a FTA in October 2008. Chinese Premier Wen Jiabao and Singaporean Prime Minister Lee Hsien Loong witnessed the signing ceremony in Beijing, with Singapore hailing the deal as an economic boon for the tiny Southeast Asian city-state.[10] Under the agreement, Singapore would abolish tariffs on all products imported from China from the beginning of 2009. In return, China would reduce the tariff to zero on 97.1 percent of goods imported from Singapore by January 1, 2012.

During Premier Wen Jiabao's previous visit to Singapore in November 2007, he and Prime Minister Lee signed several cooperation agreements including the deal for the eco-city in Tianjin near Beijing. The eco-city will adopt high environmental technologies to create an attractive quality living environment. The Sino-Singapore Tianjin Eco-city will be developed by a joint venture company formed by consortia from both sides, with Singapore's Keppel Corporation playing a lead role.[11] Singapore was a leading investor in a multi-billion dollar industrial park in Suzhou near Shanghai during the 1990s.

Relations between China and ASEAN are at their best in decades. China is interested in energy and natural resources in Southeast Asia and has promoted

10 "China, Singapore Sign Free-Trade Pact: Officials," *AFP*, October 23, 2008.
11 "China, Singapore Sign Eco-City Deal," *AFP*, November 18, 2007.

economic cooperation with all countries in the region. Two-way trade between China and Malaysia is expanding by 20–25 percent per year.Malaysia also looks set to cash in on China's growing appetite for natural gas. In November 2006, Malaysia's state-owned energy company, Petronas, won a 25-year contract to supply Shanghai with three million tons of LNG per year in a deal worth $25 billion—by far the largest single trade deal between the two countries.

Until a few years ago, China was considered an almost hostile power in Indonesia, and the Chinese government was upset by what it considered the Indonesian government's discriminatory policies toward the ethnic Chinese in its population. Now China is forging close diplomatic and political links with Indonesia, which has deep reserves of oil as well as LNG. Sino-Vietnamese trade has also jumped from the modest $30 million in 1991 and $4.9 billion in 2004 to a record $40 billion in 2011. This makes China Vietnam's biggest trading partner. Cambodia is believed to have granted China the rights to one of its five offshore oilfields that could yield as much as $700 million to $1 billion a year.[12]

Burma, renamed Myanmar by the military junta in 1989, was the first non-communist country to recognize the PRC in 1949. Northern Myanmar has a large ethnic Chinese population, creating cultural ties that facilitate trade, both legitimate and illicit, between the countries. With proven natural gas reserves of about 2.48 trillion cubic meters, representing 1.4 percent of the world supply, and little capital or infrastructure to exploit it, Myanmar is increasingly at the center of a growing competition between China and India to develop and transport offshore natural gas to their respective home markets.[13] China has built dams and roads connecting the interior of Myanmar to China's southern flank, and is reported to be working on a deepwater port on Myanmar's west coast. In March 2009 China and Myanmar signed an agreement for the construction of fuel pipelines that will transport Middle East and African crude oil from Myanmar's Arakan coast to China's Yunnan province. Under the agreement, a gas pipeline will tap into Myanmar's reserves at the Shwe gas fields, and an oil pipeline will carry Middle East and African crude that is currently transported in tankers through the Malacca Strait to China.

Construction of the $1.5 billion oil pipeline and the $1 billion gas pipeline was completed in 2013. CNPC, China's largest oil and gas company, holds 50.9 percent stake in the project, with the rest owned by the Myanmar Oil and Gas Enterprise (MOGE). The entire cost of constructing the pipelines will be borne by China.[14] The roughly 2,000 kilometers of pipeline will cut through the heart of Myanmar, beginning on the Arakan coast and ending at Kunming in Yunnan province. China's influence is clearly growing in Myanmar, so much so that the United State sees

---

12   Jane Perlez, "China Competes with West in Aid to its Neighbors," *The New York Times*, September 18, 2006.

13   Drew Thompson, "US Turns to China to Influence Myanmar," *Asia Times Online*, September 21, 2007.

14   Sudha Ramachandran, "China Secures Myanmar Energy Route," *Asia Times Online*, April 3, 2009.

China as a logical instrument with leverage to drive political change in Myanmar. In June 2007, China brokered an unusual direct meeting in Beijing between a senior US State Department official and Myanmar's minister of foreign affairs.[15]

The new Asian regionalism stimulated by the China–ASEAN Free Trade Agreement (CAFTA) would dominate the future economic landscape of Asia. With CAFTA taking effect for China and six ASEAN countries in 2010 and expanding to all ASEAN countries by 2015, China is now laying the foundation for multiple economic corridors in the Greater Mekong Subregion (GMS), particularly the North-South Economic Corridor. This effort will involve water transport along the Upper Lancang/ Mekong River covering China, Laos, Myanmar, Thailand, and Vietnam; and rail and road links that will stretch down from Yunnan Province of China to Chiang Rai of Thailand and eventually connect to ASEAN's Singapore-Kunming Rail Project.[16]

In Cambodia, Prime Minister Hun Sen boasted of China's offer of $600 million in "no strings attached" loans, which was made during a visit from Chinese Premier Wen Jiabao in Spring 2006. The money helped pay for two major bridges near the capital, Phnom Penh, which link to a network of roads; a hydropower plant; and a fiber-optic network that connects Cambodia's telecommunications with that of Vietnam and Thailand.[17] According to Hun Sen, the traditional lenders, such as the World Bank, the Asian Development Bank (ADB), the United States and Japan, together pledged just $1 million more than China, and the money came laden with conditions, including World Bank anti-corruption clauses. Previously, the World Bank had suspended several programs in Cambodia after its investigators found corruption among Cambodian officials in the procurement process. In 2003 media in Phnom Penh reported that during the visit of the PLA Chief of General Staff, China provided $3 million annually to Cambodia for military training.[18] The PLA also offered training to other Asian nations including militaries of Pakistan, Vietnam, Indonesia, Singapore, Bangladesh, Mongolia, and the Philippines.

In the Philippines, China was offering in 2006 an extraordinary package of $2 billion in loans each year for three years from its Export-Import Bank. That made the $200 million offered separately by the World Bank and the Asian Development Bank "look puny," and easily outstripped a $1 billion loan under negotiation with Japan.[19] To compete with America's influence in the region, China has pledged an initial $6.6 million grant to the Philippine Army during Defense Minister Cao Gangchuan's visit to Manila in September 2007. China had offered provisionally to provide as much as $1.2 billion in financial facilities

---

15   Thompson, "US Turns to China to Influence Myanmar," September 21, 2007.

16   Fu-kuo Liu, "Beijing's Regional Strategy and China-ASEAN Economic Integration," *China Brief*, Vol. 8, No. 10 (May 13, 2008).

17   Perlez, "China Competes With West in Aid to Its Neighbors," September 18, 2006.

18   Thomas Lum, et al. "Comparing Global Influence: China's and US Diplomacy, Foreign Aid, Trade, and Investment in the Developing World," Congressional Research Service, Washington, DC, August 15, 2008, p. 39.

19   Perlez, "China Competes with West in Aid to its Neighbors," September 18, 2006.

for the Philippine military. It has also supplied weapons to the Philippine military such as Harbin Z-9 utility helicopters.[20]

China is appreciated as a lender by many poor countries because it is willing to take on complicated projects in distant areas that others are not, and it does not attach any political conditions to the aid program except the "one-China" principle. During the October 2006 ASEAN-China summit held in Nanning, China, Premier Wen Jiabao urged pressing ahead with plans for the construction of a Kunming-Singapore Railway and an Asia highway system linking China more closely with the region. China also pledged to train 8,000 ASEAN professionals in the next five years and invited 1,000 young people from the region to visit China. The Chinese model of development which liberalizes the economy slowly while retaining control of the political system has become a viable option for some developing nations, including those in Southeast Asia.

Seeking ASEAN's Support Against Taiwanese Independence

Beijing's "one-China" principle forbids other nations from recognizing "two Chinas" or "one-China, one Taiwan" in their formal relations with China. Specifically, the PRC government does not allow any country that recognizes the Beijing government to have official ties with Taiwan. The PRC does not tolerate Taiwan's move toward *de jure* independence.

Due to historical reasons, Taiwan, especially the KMT (the Nationalist Party), enjoys a considerable support base in Southeast Asia. With China's growing power and influence in the region, most Southeast Asian nations have demonstrated deference to China over the Taiwan issue. They seem to appreciate China's policy of maintaining the *status quo* across the Taiwan Strait and opposed Taiwan's destabilizing policies during the Chen Shui-bian administration (2000–2008). Rodolfo C. Severino, a former ASEAN secretary general, remarked that being an inter-governmental organization, ASEAN does not find it proper to deal officially with Taiwan in the same way that it conducts relations with sovereign states. He said for the sake of regional prosperity and stability, ASEAN would love to see Taiwan avoiding any moves toward *de jure* independence.[21]

The Singapore government has repeatedly expressed its concern about Taiwan's movement toward formal independence and explicitly voiced its opposition to Taiwanese independence. For example, Prime Minister Lee Hsien Loong made clear Singapore's position on the Taiwan issue while holding talks with visiting Chinese Premier Wen Jiabao on November 18, 2007. "We have discussed the cross-Taiwan Strait situation," Lee told a press briefing after the talks. "Singapore

---

20   Noel Tarrazona, "US, China Vie for Philippine Military Influence," *Asia Times Online*, September 20, 2007.

21   Rodolfo C. Severino, "Taiwan: the View from Southeast Asia," *PacNet Newsletter* No. 36, CSIS, September 20, 2007.

supports the one-China policy and opposes 'Taiwan Independence.'"[22] Singapore has occasionally played the role as an intermediary between the PRC and Taiwan. Singapore's Minister Mentor and founding father Lee Kuan Yew helped both sides communicate in the 1970s and 1980s, and in 1993 Singapore hosted the historic talks between envoys from the two sides of the Taiwan Strait.[23]

Deferring to China's wishes, most governments in Southeast Asia have banned minister-level officials from visiting Taiwan. As an indication of the PRC's victory over Taiwan in the diplomatic competition, Taiwan does not have formal diplomatic relations with any of the ASEAN members. However, Taiwan maintains a huge substantial presence in Southeast Asia through the official "economic and cultural representative offices" across the region. Likewise, most Southeast Asian nations also maintain semi-official trade and cultural offices in Taipei. Except for the "one-China" principle, China barely attaches any other political conditions in its commercial relations with other countries.

China's Strategies in Southeast Asia

China has pursued a combination of both bilateral and multilateral strategies in its relations with ASEAN. Its approach has mostly been non-threatening and pragmatic, without attaching political, environmental, human rights and other conditions to its trade with and aid to Southeast Asian countries.

Promoting Trade and Investment

Flush with over $3 trillion in foreign currency reserves, China is making big loans and making huge investments abroad, including Southeast Asia. The Chinese loans are often more attractive than the complicated, conditions-attached loans from the

---

22   "Prime Minister: Singapore Supports One-China Policy," *Xinhua*, November 18, 2007. Singapore's Minister Mentor, Lee Kuan Yew, visited Beijing between November 14 and 17, 2007 and met with several members of China's top leadership. Before concluding his China visit, Lee was interviewed by Singaporean journalists and reiterated his opposition to Taiwan independence. He warned Taipei leaders that they should listen carefully to what Beijing leaders have been saying. He also believed it would be naive to think that Beijing would tolerate Taiwan independence for the sake of holding the 2008 Olympics smoothly. Apparently Beijing puts national security interests above the Olympics. Lee is respected by both sides of the Taiwan Strait, and his words carry much weight. "As a friend of Taiwan," he advised Taipei against moving rashly towards independence. See "Lee Kuan Yew: Worried about Taiwan, China Will Not Care about Olympics," *The China Times (Taipei)*, November 19, 2007.

23   In April 1993, the two sides of the Taiwan Strait held the first high-level semi-official talks after 1949 in Singapore. Koo Chen-fu, Chairman of Taiwan's Straits Exchange Foundation (SEF) and Wang Daohan, President of the Association for Relations Across the Taiwan Straits (ARATS) in Beijing, made history as they shook hands in Singapore.

West. China has provided generous aid packages to Southeast Asian nations. In April 2005 Chinese President Hu Jintao signed a Strategic Partnership agreement with President Susilo Bambang Yudhoyono of Indonesia, extending credit and loans for $300 million worth of infrastructural projects and more than $10 billion of private sector investment to Indonesia. In September 2006 China announced a large aid package comprising $2 billion of loans a year for the next three years for the Philippines, outshining offers of $200 million from the World Bank and ADB, and negotiations for $1 billion from Japan.[24] In Cambodia and Laos, hundreds of Chinese engineers and workers are helping knit together a 1,200-mile route from the Chinese city of Kunming through Laos to the Cambodian port of Sihanoukville on the Gulf of Thailand.[25]

Throughout the 1990s, Sino-Philippine relations had centered on the contentious issue of ownership of the Spratly Islands, resulting in tense physical and diplomatic stand-offs between the two countries. After President Gloria Macapagal Arroyo assumed power in 2001, Sino-Philippine relations experienced something of a renaissance. Relations between China and the Philippines grew so fast that President Arroyo reportedly appointed at least four special envoys to manage the two countries' growing economic, political, and strategic ties.[26] During one of Arroyo's visits to Beijing, she signed a confidential protocol with China related to the exploration of South China Sea oil resources. The agreement would allow China to explore for oil resources within the Philippines' exclusive economic zone (EEZ), including within areas the two sides have historically disputed. The value of two-way trade rose from $1.77 billion in 2001 to $5.3 billion in 2003, and hit $8.29 billion in 2006. Unlike some of its ASEAN partners, the Philippines has enjoyed a healthy trade surplus with China since 2002. Pleased with the status of Sino-Philippine relations, in 2007 President Arroyo declared China to be "a very good big brother."[27] The two sides set an annual target of $30 billion in bilateral trade by 2010. The target was achieved in 2008. Sino-Philippine relations experienced some difficulties after 2010 due to renewed dispute in the South China Sea.

China has provided billions of US dollars worth of Official Development Assistance (ODA) to Southeast Asian nations. Some politicians in the region praised China for the fast approval of concessional loans—contrasting it with Japan's cumbersome process or the "strings" in the form of accountability guidelines and exhortations to improve governance which usually accompany Western aid. In a short time span, the PRC has become a major player in ODA to the Philippines: according to one report, in 2006 it ranked fifth, behind Japan, the

---

24   Goh, "China and Southeast Asia," December 12, 2006.

25   Perlez, "China Competes with West in Aid to its Neighbors," September 18, 2006.

26   Noel Tarrazona, "US, China Vie for Philippine Military Influence," *Asia Times Online*, September 20, 2007.

27   Ian Storey, "Trouble and Strife in the South China Sea Part II: The Philippines and China," *China Brief*, Vol. 8, No. 9, The Jamestown Foundation, (April 28, 2008).

ADB, World Bank and United Kingdom, providing 5 percent, or $460 million, of $9.5 billion in total ODA.[28]

A fast-growing Chinese presence is one of the most striking features in Laos these days. Since 2000 China has been pouring billions of dollars in development aid and investment into the land-locked country. Chinese companies are involved in almost all areas of the country's economy, from hydropower to mining, agriculture and hospitality. Thousands of Chinese laborers were brought in by the China Yunnan Construction Engineering Group Corporation to build an $80 million stadium in Xaythany district in Vientiane's outskirts. The new stadium, built for the Southeast Asia Games in 2009, was financed by the China Development Bank. According to official statistics, at least 30,000 Chinese live in Laos, but in reality the figure could be ten times greater.[29] Not only is the Chinese presence highly visible in the northern border areas, but in the capital as well. As of May 2008, China had unilaterally given 83 trading items for zero tariffs to Cambodia, 91 items to Laos, and 87 items to Burma.[30]

In October 2008 China held the 5th China-ASEAN Expo and China-ASEAN Business & Investment Summit, successfully inviting 1,154 ASEAN-based companies to participate in the exhibition, signing 1,372 investment agreements, and attracting a turnover of $1.6 billion.[31] The annual China-ASEAN Expo promotes various business links between Chinese businesses and the Southeast Asian business community, highlights China as a window of commercial opportunities and expands Beijing's sphere of economic influence in the ASEAN markets. China is Cambodia's largest investor and largest aid donor.

In 2006 China's Guangxi Autonomous Region government made a proposal to build a Pan-Beibu Gulf (Tonkin Gulf) Economic Zone. In the meantime, local leaders and experts in Guangxi outlined a grand scheme of regional cooperation between China and ASEAN. This scheme has been described as an M-shaped "One Axis, Two Wings" strategy for economic integration between China and ASEAN. Those proposals have received strong support from the central government in Beijing. The new vision includes the Pan-Beibu Gulf Economic Zone and Greater Mekong Subregion (GMS) as the two wings and the Nanning-Singapore Economic Corridor as the axis. The envisioned N-S Economic Corridor attempts to encompass South China and Indochina. In all, it will cover China, Vietnam, Laos, Cambodia, Thailand, Malaysia and Singapore while Myanmar and some ASEAN archipelagic countries such as Indonesia can be drawn in by extension. If properly constructed and managed, the North-South corridor could become the backbone of China–ASEAN economic cooperation. It could become a corridor for

---

28 Quoted in Storey, "Trouble and Strife in the South China Sea Part II."

29 Nga Phan, "China Moves Into Laid-back Laos," *BBC News*, April 8, 2008.

30 Fu-kuo Liu, "Beijing's Regional Strategy and China-ASEAN Economic Integration," *China Brief*, Vol. 8, No. 10 (May 13, 2008).

31 H.H. Michael Hsiao and Alan Yang, "Transformations in China's Soft Power toward ASEAN," *China Brief*, Vol. 8, No. 22 (November 24, 2008), p. 12.

the flow of human resources, commodities, information, and capital. It will make multilateral cooperation possible in many fields such as trade, investment, tourism, ports, and economic cooperation along the borders.[32]

China was the first country to establish diplomatic relations with East Timor when the latter gained independence on May 20, 2002. Though China's aid and investment in East Timor is dwarfed by that from major donors such as the EU and Australia, China has focused its investment on key public projects. In early 2008 China finished the Ministry of Foreign Affairs building, a large office complex built at a cost of $7 million. Several miles away, the construction of the new presidential palace, paid for with $6 million in Chinese aid, was completed in 2010. China handed over to the East Timor Armed Forces a military neighbourhood with 100 houses in August 2011. China has also provided military aid and sold military equipment to East Timor.

China helped improve East Timor's human resources. Since 2002, over 400 East Timorese civil servants and technical personnel have undertaken training in the PRC, including in public administration, economic planning, tourism, health, construction, and technology. The Chinese government has made available a number of university scholarships for East Timorese. Since 2004, China has dispatched resident medical teams of more than 20 doctors to the country. Chinese experts have also helped East Timorese farmers to increase rice output by launching a hybrid rice plantation project.[33]

In 2001 China agreed to pump ODA into several large infrastructure projects in the Philippines. The most high-profile of these projects were railways and the provision of network technologies for establishing an e-government. In 2003 China agreed to fund the North Luzon Railway (NorthRail), the rehabilitation of a 20-mile line from Metro Manila to the Clark Economic Zone (the former US air base vacated in 1991) at Pampanga in the Central Luzon Region. Another major project was the National Broadband Network (NBN), a $329.5 million initiative designed to link 2,295 national offices and 23,549 village and municipal offices and give the government an online presence throughout the archipelago. The deal, signed by President Arroyo on the sidelines of the BFA on Hainan Island, China in April 2007, was covered by a 20-year loan of 3 percent interest per annum. The loan was conditional, however, on Chinese company Zhongxing Telecommunication Equipment Company Limited (ZTE) being appointed exclusive supplier and provider. By early 2008, all of these deals had come under heavy criticism from opposition groups, the business community, and civil society groups in the Philippines for their lack of transparency, overpricing and claims of kick-backs.[34]

---

32   Xiaosong Gu and Mingjiang Li, "Nanning-Singapore Corridor: A New Vision in China-ASEAN Cooperation," RSIS Commentaries, 114/2008, Nanyang Technological University, Singapore, October 24, 2008.

33   Ian Storey, "China's Inroads into East Timor," *China Brief*, Vol. 9, No. 6 (March 19, 2009), pp. 7–10.

34   Storey, "Trouble and Strife in the South China Sea Part II."

China–ASEAN cooperation now covers agriculture, information industry, human resources development, transportation, energy, culture, tourism, development of the Mekong River, and public health. Like elsewhere, China's preference for dealing only with the government or the ruling party in its trade and investment often creates tensions between China and various NGOs in its trading partners. As China refines its new diplomacy, it must do a better job in reaching out to different key players of other countries.

Exercising Soft Power

China seems to understand that its huge size alone may look threatening to some small nations. It has employed strategies to emphasize the softer side of its power and intentions. China's approach to Southeast Asia since the mid-1990s has been characterized by a conscious dampening of outstanding regional disputes, a willingness to engage in multilateral dialogue and institutions, and rhetoric of good neighborliness and mutual benefits.[35] China has made efforts to accommodate its smaller neighbors, many of which have long had tense relations with Beijing. It has tried to present an image of a friendly, peaceful, caring, and responsible neighbor. It has also participated assiduously in the ASEAN-led regional institutions such as the ARF and APT dialogues, promoting regional security.

Providing financial assistance to its neighbors is a major form of projecting soft power for China. Between 2002 and 2007, China pledged $12.6 billion in economic assistance to Southeast Asian nations.[36] Most significantly, the assistance came without any political conditions. In 2006 China announced it would donate $1 million to ASEAN Development Fund and provide another $1 million to support programs of the ASEAN community. In addition, China would train 8,000 people for ASEAN in the next five years, and invite 1,000 to visit China.[37] It also announced it would sign a treaty establishing a "nuclear weapons free" zone in Southeast Asia, a largely symbolic move that signals its increasing willingness to forge closer ties with regional nations. In December 2006 China agreed to provide Myanmar with satellite images to help monitor opium fields in the Kachin and Shan States, both bordering China's Yunnan Province.

China negotiated a Declaration on the Code of Conduct for the South China Sea and formally acceded to the Treaty of Amity and Cooperation of ASEAN in 2003 as the first external signatory. Its willingness to negotiate multilaterally with rival Southeast Asian claimants the territorial disputes in South China Sea reassures them that China is sensitive to the concerns of its neighbors.

China's assistance often comes when most needed. In the wake of the 1997–1998 Asian financial crisis, China offered $1 billion in financial assistance to regional countries. In 2004 China was quick to send $60 million worth of aid

---

35   Goh, "China and Southeast Asia," December 12, 2006.
36   Lum, et al. "Comparing Global Influence," p. 84.
37   Wen, "Creating a Beautiful Future of China-ASEAN Relations," October 30, 2006.

and supplies to regional countries affected by the tsunami.[38] The sum of Chinese foreign aid in Southeast Asia has surpassed the amount provided by the United States. For example, in 2002 China's aid to Indonesia was double that of the United States. In 2006 China's aid to the Philippines was four times that of the United States, while the amount to Laos was three times US aid.[39]

China's financial assistance contributes to local infrastructure and capacity-building programs. In December 2006 China announced it would provide $200,000 in aid to the typhoon-ravaged Philippines. Typhoon Durian caused widespread damage, including 1,000 people dead or missing in the north-central province of Albay. China also agreed to provide an interest-free loan of $12.5 million to Cambodia in the next five years to implement the projects agreed upon by both sides.[40] The 2008–2009 global financial crisis resulted in economic and market turmoil in many Southeast Asian countries. Leaders from ASEAN states such as Cambodia, Laos, and the Philippines called upon China to invest more in ASEAN so as to stabilize the economic growth of the region.

China has used public diplomacy to reinforce the concept of peaceful development, such as through museum exhibits in Malaysia to celebrate the 600th anniversary of the voyage of Zheng He, a Ming Dynasty admiral who sailed across the world, encountering but never conquering other nations. These efforts have paid off. In Thailand, polls show that more than 70 percent of Thais now consider China Thailand's most important external influence, though Thailand had long been a US ally.[41] The difficulty of gaining US visas immediately after 9/11 propelled many Thais and other Southeast Asians to travel to China as students and tourists. Studying in China has become an easy sell to young Asians eager to reap economic benefits from today's interdependent world.

To promote Chinese language and culture, the Chinese government has opened Confucius Institutes throughout Southeast Asia. As of early 2013, at least 30 Confucius Institutes had been established in the region, including Jakarta Confucius Institute in Indonesia which was opened on September 28, 2007, two in the Philippines—at Ateneo de Manila University and La Consolacion College Manila, one at Nanyang Technological University in Singapore, and 13 in Thailand such as the institutes hosted by Mae Fah Luang University and Prince of Songkla University, and one at Chiang Mai University, which was opened in 2006 with support from Yunnan Normal University and *hanban* in Beijing.

---

38   David Fullbrook, "China's Strategic Southeast Asian Embrace," *Asia Times Online*, February 21, 2007.

39   Kurlantzick, "China's Charm: Implications of Chinese Soft Power," p. 3.

40   Robert Sutter and Chin-Hao Huang, "China-Southeast Asia Relations: Summitry at Home and Abroad," *Comparative Connections: A Quarterly E-Journal on East Asian Bilateral Relations*, CSIS, December 2006.

41   Kurlantzick, "China's Charm: Implications of Chinese Soft Power," p. 4.

Status-conscious Asian families used to send their children to study in the United States or Europe. Now a berth in a top Chinese university is seen as increasingly attractive. In Malaysia, students of non-Chinese background are flocking to primary schools where Chinese is taught, a reversal of a more than three-decade trend, said N.C. Siew, the editor of the country's major Chinese language newspaper, Sin Chew Daily.[42] In Singapore, the government still sends a handful of students on scholarships to the top universities in the United States and Great Britain, but it has introduced a parallel program to send equal numbers of its best students to China and India. In the past, experience in the United States was important; now experience in China is just as good.[43]

Clearly, China's soft power is rising in Southeast Asia. "They are very clever," Vanchai Sirichana, President of Mae Fah Luang University in northern Thailand, commented on China's soft approach to the region. "They understand the way of life here and they understand the people, so the way they do is softer than what Americans did, using friendship as a spearhead to do the business. ... And it's working. In terms of Thai students, you know that five to ten years ago, most of them [wanted] to go to study in the States. And now, the idea has changed ... to China."[44] Cultural exchange is a two-way street. Chinese students number in the thousands in colleges and vocational schools in several Southeast Asian nations. In 2003 11,000 PRC nationals were enrolled in Malaysian schools, representing a quarter of all foreign students and the largest single group of students in Malaysia.[45]

Observers of China–South Asia relations have to be amazed at the speed China is gaining popularity in this part of the world. Not too long ago, most Southeast Asian nations had a rocky and tense relationship with the communist government in Beijing. A 1965 coup attempt allegedly by Indonesia's Communist Party helped convince the Indonesian military of China's expansionist impulses. The militaries in Southeast Asia had been concerned about the "yellow fever"—the threat from the north. Indonesia's military leader at the time, Suharto, saw the country's ethnic Chinese minority as a potential fifth column. As a result, public displays of Chinese culture and heritage were banned. Ethnic Chinese lived as second-class citizens in their own country. Ten years after the fall of Suharto in 1998, dragon dances were no longer forbidden and the Chinese New Year has become an official holiday. Indonesia's ethnic Chinese have their own newspapers, and Chinese firms are now competing with US and European companies for Indonesia's vast reserves of oil, minerals and gas. In addition, Confucianism is recognized as one of the country's official religions.

---

42   Jane Perlez, "Chinese Move to Eclipse US Appeal in South Asia," *The New York Times*, November 18, 2004.

43   Ibid.

44   Michael Sullivan, "Neighbors Feel China's Expanding Power," *National Public Radio* www.npr.org, All Things Considered, April 3, 2008.

45   Ian Storey, "Malaysia's Hedging Strategy with China," *China Brief*, Vol. 7, No. 14 (July 11, 2007), p. 10.

Soft power of a different kind can be seen in the Philippines, where a new rail line links metro Manila to central Luzon—a $500 million project funded by a low-interest loan from the PRC. "They obviously have been one of the fastest-growing economies in the world. They've had a very successful development experience, and so they have a lot to offer in terms of both knowledge as well as financing," says Larry Greenwood, vice president of the ADB in Manila. "Certainly our experience with China has been very positive in the sense that they are very good at helping design and execute projects which have had very good impacts and outcomes in terms of development effectiveness."[46] China's development trajectory since 1979 serves as an inspirational model for many developing countries.

China has actively promoted tourism in Southeast Asia. China's rapid economic growth has resulted in more than 15 million arrivals per year in ASEAN region (especially Thailand, Singapore and Malaysia) during the early 2000s. Over the last decade, this figure has experienced an annual growth of 30 percent. The number of Chinese visitors to Vietnam alone reached 778,000 in 2004.[47] In 2007 3.4 million Chinese tourists visited the ASEAN region, a number that, for the first time, surpassed the amount of Japanese tourists.[48] Over 7.3 million Chinese travelled to the region in 2011.[49] The ASEAN-China Center for trade, investment and tourism promotion will be established in the near future to upgrade the quality and collaboration of tourism. China is also promoting cooperation with ASEAN in eco-tourism in the Mekong River basin.

The Singapore–Malaysia–Thailand route is very popular among the Chinese middle class. These nations have relaxed visa restrictions for Chinese nationals, resulting in increasing numbers of tourist arrivals. Chinese tourists, less fearful than Americans of the threat of being targets of terrorism after 9/11, are becoming the dominant tourist group in the region, outnumbering Americans and the ubiquitous Japanese. The Chinese tourists carry with them not just cash but a new image of China—richer, more confident, more civilized, and more Westernized. "Among some countries, China fever seems to be replacing China fear," said Wang Gungwu, Chairman of the East Asian Institute at the National University of Singapore.[50] All ten ASEAN countries are approved tourist destinations for Chinese now. Massive tourist developments in Singapore, including integrated resort-casinos, are not so subtly aimed at cashing in on Chinese tourists.

There are also military exchanges between China and Southeast Asian nations. A number of Malaysian military officers have attended military academies in China, and vice versa. China has offered to sell weapon systems, including naval ships, to

---

46   Sullivan, "Neighbors Feel China's Expanding Power," April 3, 2008.

47   Do Thi Thuy, "China and Vietnam: From 'Friendly Neighbors' to 'Comprehensive Partners,'" RSIS Commentary, July 9, 2008, Nanyang Technological University, Singapore.

48   H.H. Michael Hsiao and Alan Yang, "Transformations in China's Soft Power toward ASEAN," *China Brief*, Vol. 8, No. 22 (November 24, 2008), p. 12.

49   "ASEAN Targets Chinese Tourists," *Hotel Management Asia*, November 14, 2012.

50   Perlez, "Chinese Move to Eclipse US Appeal in South Asia," November 18, 2004.

Malaysia.[51] In August 2009 China launched the communications satellite Palapa D for Indonesia from the Xichang Satellite Launch Center in southwest China, using a Chinese-made Long March 3B rocket. The Palapa D satellite, owned by Indonesian satellite communications company Indosat, will provide satellite links and broadcasting services for Indonesia and other Southeast Asian nations. China also brings young politicians and diplomats from Southeast Asia to study trips in China, hoping to foster a longer-term relationship with future leaders of the region.

To mark the 20th anniversary of diplomatic ties, two giant pandas, Kai Kai and Jia Jia, arrived in Singapore from China in September 2012 on a ten-year loan as a symbol of close ties between the two nations. The Chinese government continues to use the cuddly and furry animals to smooth relations with key diplomatic allies.

Highest-level Involvement

Southeast Asia has been a key destination for Chinese leaders' journeys abroad since the early 2000s. High-level delegations from China today far surpass those of the United States or any other outside power. These visits, coupled with generous aid programs, promote relations between China and Southeast Asia. In November 2000 Chinese President Jiang Zemin made his first visit to Cambodia and Laos as the head of state. In an attempt to raise the bilateral relations to a new height between "good neighbors, good friends, good comrades and good partners," Chinese and Vietnamese leaders have exchanged many visits. In November 2006 President Hu Jintao visited Vietnam and attended the 14th APEC summit in Hanoi. He went on to visit Laos and met Laotian President Choummaly Sayasone. The two leaders agreed to expand bilateral trade and deepen cooperation. China also offered Laos $45 million in economic assistance and debt forgiveness, jointly develop Laos' infrastructure and communications system, and broaden commercial ties through China's Yunnan Province and northern Laos.

Premier Wen Jiabao visited Singapore in November 2007 and attended the 11th APT Summit and the 3rd East Asia Summit held there. Premier Wen also officiated at the launch of the Singapore-China Foundation which provides scholarship and exchange programs for government officials.[52] In November 2009 President Hu Jintao attended the 17th APEC summit in Singapore.

Then Vice Premier Li Keqiang paid an official visit to Indonesia in December 2008. Li said upon arrival that China highly valued the strategic partnership with Indonesia and hoped that his visit would boost bilateral relations to a higher level.[53] During Li's visit, the two countries signed energy and trade deals worth more than $4 billion. The two countries had also signed a memorandum of understanding for a $1 billion loan from the China Export Bank to allow

---

51   Storey, "Malaysia's Hedging Strategy with China," p. 11.

52   Le Tian, "Eco-City Pact Inked with Singapore," *China Daily*, November 19, 2007.

53   "Li Keqiang Begins Indonesia Visit," *Xinhua*, December 20, 2008.

Indonesia to buy Chinese goods including machinery and steel.[54] China and Indonesia signed an agreement on strategic cooperation in 2005, which has helped strengthen the bilateral ties since. Then Vice President Xi Jinping visited Myanmar and Cambodia in December 2009 as part of his Asia tour which also took him to Japan and South Korea. While in Cambodia, he unveiled the first Confucius Institute in the country.

Leaders from Southeast Asia have travelled to China often. Vietnamese Communist Party leader Nong Duc Manh visited China twice in 2007 and 2008. To further this growing tradition, Manh and President Hu announced the establishment of a high-level hotline for consultations on major issues — the first of its kind between a Vietnamese leader and a foreign counterpart.[55] Apart from annual leadership visits, the two neighbors have numerous exchanges between governmental and non-governmental officials on an almost daily basis. In October 2008 Vietnam's Prime Minister Nguyen Tan Dung journeyed to China and attended the Asia–Europe summit in Beijing. A joint statement issued at the end of his visit said that "the two sides shared the view that to expand and deepen the China–Vietnam comprehensive strategic partnership of cooperation in the context of the complex and changing international political and economic situation is in the fundamental interests of the two parties, two countries and two peoples and conducive to peace, stability and development of the region and the world."[56] Most significantly, the two sides reiterated during Dung's visit that they would continue to work closely to earnestly implement the Beibu Bay (Gulf of Tonkin) Demarcation Agreement and the Beibu Bay Fishery Cooperation Agreement, to carry out joint inspection of common fishing areas in the Beibu Bay, joint survey on fishery resources and joint patrol of navies, to make substantive progress in cooperation in cross-border gas and oil exploration, and to steadily advance the negotiations on demarcation of the sea area beyond the mouth of the Beibu Bay. After relations soured between 2010 and 2012, China and Vietnam began to improve ties in 2013, with Vietnamese President Truong Tan Sang and Chinese President Xi Jinping declaring in Beijing in June 2013 that the South China Sea dispute should not prevent the two neighbors from strengthening friendly cooperation.

Since Singapore and China established diplomatic relations in 1990, bilateral relations have been developing rapidly. Minister Mentor Lee Kuan Yew maintains close personal relations with several generations of the PRC leaders and is a frequent traveler to Beijing and other places in China. Singapore sometimes

---

54   "Indonesia, China Sign US$4b in Energy and Trade Deals," *Channel NewsAsia* (Singapore), December 22, 2008. http://www.channelnewsasia.com/stories/afp_asiapacific_ business/view/398003/1/.html.

55   Do Thi Thuy, "China and Vietnam: From 'Friendly Neighbors' to 'Comprehensive Partners,'" RSIS Commentary, July 9, 2008, Nanyang Technological University, Singapore.

56   "China-Viet Nam Joint Statement," Ministry of Foreign Affairs, Beijing, October 25, 2008.

serves as "a spokesman for China in the Asian region," said Guan Anping, a Beijing-based trade lawyer and former Chinese trade official. "Sometimes when it's not convenient for China to say certain things, it passes the message through Singapore." China also helps Singapore balance a sometimes contentious relationship with Malaysia. Singapore, which buys most of its water from Malaysia, counts on China to weigh in on disputes when they occur across the Singapore Strait, according to Guan.[57]

High-level exchanges between the Philippines and China have been frequent, especially during President Gloria Arroyo's term (2001–2010). President Arroyo visited China several times while President Hu Jintao paid a state visit to the Philippines in April 2005. In addition, the annual PRC-Philippines defense talks were inaugurated in 2005. In October 2006 Chinese Defense Minister Cao Gangchuan met in Beijing with visiting Philippine Undersecretary of the Department of National Defense Antonio Santos and agreed to foster closer strategic relations between the two countries, including closer exchanges between the two militaries.

Thai Prime Minister Samak Sundaravej visited China in July 2008, his first since taking office in January 2008. Samak, who was concurrently defense minister, also met with new Chinese Defense Minister Liang Guanglie during the visit and the two sides agreed to strengthen bilateral military ties. Thai Prime Minister Yingluck Shinawatra paid an official visit to China in April 2012 after taking office a few months earlier. In October 2006 Indonesian President Susilo Bambang Yudhoyono visited China and met with Chinese Vice Premier Huang Ju for the second Sino-Indonesian Energy Forum in Shanghai. The two countries signed a memorandum of understanding on energy cooperation and agreed that beginning in 2009, Indonesia's Tangguh gas field will provide 2.6 million tons of liquefied natural gas annually to China's Fujian Province for 25 years.[58] Chinese Premier Wen Jiabao hosted a gathering of ASEAN leaders in the southern city of Nanning in October 2006 to celebrate 15 years of Chinese dialogue with ASEAN.

On December 30, 2008, the Chinese government announced the appointment of a senior woman diplomat as the first envoy to ASEAN, signaling China's growing attention to the region. The envoy, Xue Hanqin, is an expert on international law who served as ambassador to the Netherlands and permanent representative to the Organization on the Prohibition of Chemical Weapons. She also worked as director general of Chinese foreign ministry's department of treaty and law. The appointment came after the United States and Japan had sent envoys to the bloc earlier and showed China's willingness to strengthen ties with ASEAN. It is interesting to note that Xue's two successors, Tong Xiaoling and Yang Xiuping,

---

57   Allen T. Cheng, "Singapore-China Ties to be Boosted by Wen's Visit," *Bloomberg News*, November 18, 2007.

58   Robert Sutter and Chin-Hao Huang, "China-Southeast Asia Relations: Summitry at Home and Abroad," *Comparative Connections: A Quarterly E-Journal on East Asian Bilateral Relations*, CSIS, December 2006.

are both senior female diplomats too, and Yang became China's first resident ambassador to ASEAN in July 2012. In February 2012 Ma keqing, another senior female diplomat, became China's ambassador to the Philippines. At a time when China has rocky relations with several ASEAN members over the South China Sea sovereignty dispute, such appointments are quite significant (See Table 7.2.).

Table 7.2   China's Special Envoys on Regional Affairs

Envoy's Name	Responsible region	Appointment date
Wang Shijie	The Middle East	September 2002
Sun Bigan	The Middle East	April 2006
Wu Sike	The Middle East	March 2009
Liu Guijin	Africa/Sudan	May 2007
Zhong Jianhua	Africa	February 2012
Xue Hanqin	Southeast Asia	December 2008
Tong Xiaoling	Southeast Asia	October 2010
Yang Xiuping	Southeast Asia	July 2012

Source: Ministry of Foreign Affairs of the PRC.

Wooing Overseas Chinese

Southeast Asian nations have the largest concentration of Overseas Chinese. Approximately 30 to 40 million people of Chinese ancestry, or over 6 percent of the region's population, live in Southeast Asia. Their presence has brought about a local familiarity with Chinese culture. Since the beginning of Beijing's open door and reform policies in the late 1970s, Overseas Chinese living in Southeast Asia as well as those in Taiwan, Hong Kong and Macao have been a major source of FDI into the Chinese mainland. The Chinese economy has depended heavily on such investment, which makes cultivating good relations with Overseas Chinese a policy priority for the Chinese government.

There are roughly 6 million ethnic Chinese in Indonesia. Although their numbers are small, Chinese Indonesians control a huge amount of wealth—one half to three quarters of private wealth in Indonesia by most estimates, and more than three-quarters of Indonesia's 20 wealthiest people are ethnically Chinese.[59] According to one study, at least 90 percent of Sino-Indonesian trade involves Chinese Indonesians. Buttressed by reduced cultural barriers to doing business and a ready-made, national distribution network due to Chinese Indonesian ownerships of small businesses, they are simply the natural trading partners for

---

59   Brian Harding, "The Role of the Chinese Diaspora in Sino-Indonesian Relations," *China Brief*, Vol. 8. No. 16 (August 1, 2008), The Jamestown Foundation, Washington, DC.

Chinese manufacturers. Indonesian investment in China has also been driven by Chinese Indonesians. With almost all of Indonesia's largest corporations and financial houses controlled by Chinese Indonesians, they are natural players in the China market.[60] These ethnic Chinese are citizens of their resident countries, but many of them maintain strong family and economic ties with their ancestral homeland.

In Cambodia, China Radio International (CRI) and Cambodia's national radio station jointly launched an international radio service in December 2008, with 18 hours of broadcasting in Cambodian, Chinese, English, and Chaozhou (Southern Min) dialect. The programs cover current news, economy, culture, sports, and entertainment. Popular Chinese music is also introduced in the program. This new radio service was reportedly developed to counter the influence of VOA and Radio Free Asia in Southeast Asia and to cater to the needs of the Overseas Chinese in the region.[61] In addition, three Chinese language newspapers are published daily in Cambodia. The local Chinese communities in Southeast Asia serve as a strong linkage between these countries and China.

Assessment

China Enjoys Close Relations with Nearly All ASEAN Nations, But Its Influence Is Still Limited

Southeast Asian leaders and the public generally view China's development favorably. The changing perception of China has been fed by a number of developments since the financial crisis hit the region in 1997. These include China's pledge not to devalue the *yuan* during the economic crisis, its offer of a FTA to ASEAN, a joint declaration on a code of conduct in the South China Sea, cooperation with ASEAN to combat the SARS outbreak in 2003, and China's decision to accede to the Treaty of Amity and Cooperation.

Singapore's Minister Mentor Lee Kuan Yew has visited China at least once a year since 1976. While some Western politicians and activists were considering boycotting the opening ceremony of the 2008 Beijing Olympics in protest of China's crackdown on Tibetan protesters and its human rights record, Lee said he and other Asian leaders would attend the ceremony since "there is no reason for us to offend the Chinese."[62] Eventually over 80 heads of government or state including President George W. Bush attended the opening ceremony of the Beijing Olympics, a new record in Olympic history.

---

60   Ibid.

61   "War between CRI and VOA," *Duowei News* dwnews.com, March 9, 2009.

62   Grant Clark and Haslinda Amin, "Beijing Olympics Air Quality to Meet World Standards, Lee Says," *Bloomberg News*, May 5, 2008.

In May 2008 China garnered the support of ASEAN on the Tibet issue during an APT meeting in Singapore among senior foreign ministry officials from ASEAN, China, Japan and South Korea. Peter Ho, permanent secretary in the Singapore foreign ministry, who chaired the meeting, said that ASEAN "welcomed the restoration of normalcy and the latest move of the Chinese government to have contact and consultation with the private representative of the Dalai Lama. This will help restore stability."[63]

The "China heat" is unmistakably perceptible. Chinese language programs attract many young students across Southeast Asia. These students who once would have headed to the United States or Europe are now looking to universities in Shanghai and Beijing. Aileen Baviera, Dean of the Asian Center at the University of the Philippines, remarked that China has "learned how to speak the language of the region, of Southeast Asian diplomacy—multilateralism, (and) confidence building—much more than the United States has."[64] In November 2000 when President Jiang Zemin visited Cambodia, his Cambodian host had thousands of children line the streets of Phnom Penh, waving tiny Chinese flags or small photographs of Jiang. The scene resembled that of a papal visit to a devoutly Catholic nation, commented Josh Kurlantzick, author of *Charm Offensive: How China's Soft Power is Transforming the World.*[65] When Premier Wen Jiabao visited Indonesia in 2003, he was toasted with frequent ovations. In contrast, when President George W. Bush visited the same year, many Indonesian cultural and political leaders would not even meet with him.

However, there are lingering suspicions about China in some parts of Southeast Asia. Demonstrators in Hanoi protested in early 2008 against what they saw as Chinese aggression in the Spratly Islands. Such protests were rare in Vietnam but were tolerated by the government, in part because they tapped into a deep well of nationalism with roots in Vietnam's long and often bitter experience with its giant neighbor to the north. More than a thousand years of domination by China have left many Vietnamese deeply suspicious of China, although China has become Vietnam's largest trading partner now.

China's territorial disputes and historical conflicts with Vietnam, including a bloody border war in 1979, have placed some limits on deepening relations between the two communist neighbors. Chinese companies' efforts to expand trade and investment in the region are not always welcomed especially when they fail to generate local jobs. For instance, the Vietnamese government approved a project in late 2007 to exploit reserves of bauxite—the key mineral in making aluminum—with an investment of $15 billion by 2025. The state-owned Chinese mining group Chinalco had already put workers and equipment to work in the remote Central Highlands as of early 2009. More than 2,000 Chinese workers were expected to be imported to work in the project, which led to an outcry from many

---

63   "ASEAN Backs China on Tibet Issue," *Kyodo News International*, May 7, 2008.

64   Sullivan, "Neighbors Feel China's Expanding Power," April 3, 2008.

65   Josh Kurlantzick, "Chinese Soft Power in Southeast Asia," *The Globalist online* www.theglobalist.com, July 2, 2007.

unemployed Vietnamese suffering from the global economic downturn. The project was also opposed by leading figures such as Vietnam's great war hero General Vo Nguyen Giap, a comrade of the country's founding father, Ho Chi Minh. General Giap and others said the Chinese-run project would be ruinous to the environment, displace ethnic minority populations and threaten national security with an influx of Chinese workers and economic leverage.[66] Opponents of the project used the Internet to express dissent while bloggers and commentators challenged the government's decision to allow the project to proceed. Similar complaints about Chinese investment have been heard in other Southeast Asian countries, where Chinese workers have been brought in to work on China-invested projects. Frictions in Sino-ASEAN relations concerning Chinese investment underscore the limits of Beijing's charm offensive in Southeast Asia.

In East Timor, China has established itself as an important player in the country's economic affairs after its independence in 2002. However, China's role is still limited when compared to Australia, Portugal, Indonesia, and the UN. Its efforts to access East Timor's oil and gas reserves have made little headway. After the 2004 Indian Ocean tsunami that hit several Southeast Asian nations, the United States pledged $305 million to affected countries compared to China's $63 million and Taiwan's $50 million. The US emergency response helped to improve the image of the United States in the region, particularly in Indonesia, somewhat reversing a dramatic rise in negative public perceptions of the United States after its invasion of Iraq in 2003.[67] China's growing ties with ASEAN notwithstanding, other powers especially the United States, Japan, Australia, and India maintain considerable influence and have a strong presence in the region.

Contentious Issues

Contentious issues exist between China and Southeast Asia, one of the most salient of which concerns human rights, particularly of Myanmar, the largest country by geographical area in mainland Southeast Asia. Myanmar's political system was under the tight control of the State Peace and Development Council, the military government after 1992. Under heavy international pressure, Myanmar began to move towards democratization in 2011.

On August 8, 1988, the Myanmar military opened fire on demonstrators in what is known as 8888 Uprising and imposed martial law. The 1988 protests paved way for the 1990 People's Assembly elections. However, the election results were subsequently annulled by Senior General Saw Maung's government. The National League for Democracy, led by Aung San Suu Kyi, won over 60 percent of the vote and over 80 percent of parliamentary seats in the 1990 election, the first held in 30 years. The military-backed National Unity Party won less than 2 percent of the seats.

---

66   Seth Mydans, "War Hero in Vietnam Forces Government to Listen," *The New York Times*, June 28, 2009.

67   Lum, et al. "Comparing Global Influence," pp. 79–80.

Aung San Suu Kyi has earned international recognition as an activist for the return of democratic rule, winning the Nobel Peace Prize in 1991. The ruling regime repeatedly placed her under house arrest. Despite a direct appeal by former UN Secretary General Kofi Annan and pressure by ASEAN, the military junta extended Aung San Suu Kyi's house arrest for another year in May 2006 and again in August 2009. Myanmar's situation was referred to the UN Security Council for the first time in December 2005 for an informal consultation. In September 2006 ten of the UN Security Council's 15 members voted to place Myanmar on the council's formal agenda. On January 8, 2007, UN Secretary General Ban Ki-moon urged the national government to free all political prisoners, including Aung San Suu Kyi. In late 2007 Myanmar's military government violently put down another pro-democracy protest movement led by Buddhist monks, drawing international condemnation, and tighter US sanctions. Ban Ki-moon made a similar appeal in July 2009 and encouraged a dialogue between Myanmar's government and the opposition. Aung San Suu Kyi was finally set free in 2011 and has been able to travel outside of Myanmar since. However, China has not publically praised her fight for freedom and democracy in Myanmar.

China is one of Myanmar's major trading partners and investors, including $1.4 billion to $2 billion in weaponry to the ruling junta since 1988 and pledges of nearly $5 billion in loans, plants and equipment, investment in mineral exploration, hydro power, oil and gas production, and agricultural projects.[68] A Myanmar opposition group, the 88 Generation Students organization, urged the boycott of Beijing Olympics in protest against what it called China's "bankrolling" of the Myanmar military government. Like on the Sudan issue, though China is not the cause of problems in Myanmar, as a responsible power China needs to do more to prevent massive human rights violations in those faltering countries.

After Myanmar's transition to democracy began in earnest in 2011, China has tried to maintain the strong relationship with its southern neighbour. China remains the largest investor in Myanmar, with its investment topping $20 billion in 2011. To promote the Sino-Myanmar comprehensive strategic partnership, President Thein Sein and China's NPC Chairman Wu Bangguo exchanged visits in September 2012. However, some projects with Chinese involvement have encountered problems. Myanmar suspended work on a $3.6 billion Chinese-led dam in Myitsone in September 2011, Myanmar's largest hydropower project, citing complaints from local residents and opposition parties. The future of the project remains unsettled as of this writing.

Perhaps the most controversial issue between China and Southeast Asian nations is the overlapping claims of sovereignty over the South China Sea. The South China Sea is considered to have great gas and oil potentials. Most of the hydrocarbon fields explored in the area contain gas. Estimates by the US Geological Survey indicate that between 60 and 70 percent of the region's hydrocarbon resources are gas. In addition, a significant proportion of the more

---

68   Ibid, p. 85.

than six million barrels of oil per day produced by China and Southeast Asian countries comes from the South China Sea region.[69] The situation in the Spratlys worsened in 1995 when China built controversial structures on Mischief Reef.

Demonstrations by Vietnamese youths broke out outside Chinese diplomatic missions in Hanoi, Ho Chi Minh City, Paris, and London in late 2007 following reports about China's intention to establish Sansha city to govern the Paracels and Spratlys over which Hanoi claims sovereignty. In April 2009, Vietnam appointed an official to be the chairman of Hoang Sa District (Paracel Islands), which was denounced as illegal by China. In 2012, China officially established the city of Sansha and approved the routine military patrol of the region despite Vietnamese protests.

In 2011–12, the South China Sea dispute erupted again, with the Chinese and Philippine navies standing off for two months near the Huangyan Island (Scarborough Shoal). Anti-Chinese demonstrations took place in the Philippines and Vietnam. China's issuance in 2012 of a new passport including a map of China that covers the whole South China Sea angered several of China's neighbors. The United States, though not taking a position regarding the sovereignty of the South China Sea, has strengthened security ties with the Philippines and Vietnam as part of its new "pivot" or "strategic rebalancing" toward Asia. While these smaller countries welcome America's presence in the region and are looking for a multilateral solution to the problem, China generally opposes what it calls "internationalization" of the dispute and prefers to deal with each of the other claimant nations bilaterally.

These controversial issues remain potential flashpoints between China and Southeast Asia. Living with a giant neighbor, Southeast Asian nations are very sensitive to China's attitude towards them. A China that is perceived arrogant and uncompromising is not welcome by these countries. China needs to do a better job in treating these smaller neighbors as equals not just in trade but also in political and territorial issues. There is an emerging consensus in China on the need to safeguard and expand its maritime interests in East Asia and Southeast Asia.Meanwhile, China has given priority to improving relations with neighboring countries. As Li Mingjiang remarked, these two sets of policy objectives may not be mutually reconcilable and it is difficult to maintain a balance between the two.[70]

Competition for Influence in Southeast Asia?

Though US economic, political, and security interests in Southeast Asia are very broad, it was perceived after 9/11 as being consumed by its own agenda that

---

69   Michael Richardson, "A Southward Thrust for China's Energy Diplomacy in the South China Sea," *China Brief* (The Jamestown Foundation), Vol. 8, No. 21 (November 7, 2008), p. 7.

70   Li Mingjiang, "China's Rising Maritime Aspirations: Impact on Beijing's Good-Neighbor Policy," RSIS, Nanyang Technological University, March 28, 2012.

emphasized the campaign against terror and problems in the Middle East. "I have never seen a time when the United States is so distracted from the region," said Ernest Z. Bower, the president of the US-ASEAN Business Council that represents big American corporations in Southeast Asia. In contrast, he said, "China is focused on the region like a laser beam."[71] China has made some gains relative to the United States in the areas of cultural and political soft power. A 2007 Pew Research poll found that only 29 percent of Indonesians and 27 percent of Malaysians had a favorable view of the United States as opposed to 83 percent of Malaysians and 65 percent of Indonesians who had favorable views of China.[72] Other polls suggest that the United States is still viewed as the predominant soft power influence in Asia. According to a Chicago Council on Global Affairs survey in 2008, despite China's growing influence, the United States remains the undisputed leader in soft power in Asia.[73] While many in Asia consider China to be the future leader of Asia, China faired much worse than expected in soft power—its political system, legal system, respect for human rights and normative appeal all scored very low in the eyes of Beijing's neighbors. The American culture, from Hollywood movies to MTV, remains vastly more popular and accessible, and the United States is still holding the dominant military power in the region. However, the trend is clear: the Chinese are quickly catching up.

China has made deep inroads into Southeast Asia since the mid-1990s. When leaders of China and the United States visited countries in Southeast Asia, they seemed to have brought with them two different sets of agendas. According to an article in Singapore's *Straits Times*, Chinese President Hu Jintao spent his time "touring a market place" while US President George W. Bush was "surveying the battlefield."[74] The United States, especially under President George W. Bush, did not seem to understand that economic imperative, not war against terror, is an issue of top concern in Southeast Asia and Southeast Asian nations want to be respected and treated as economic partners by major powers. US-ASEAN relations had sagged under the Bush administration. Former Secretary of State Condoleezza Rice missed two ASEAN regional forums that have traditionally been obligatory events for US chief diplomats.

China has been actively expanding public diplomacy in Southeast Asia while the United States was cutting it back. CRI, with upbeat news and features, broadcasts in English 24 hours a day, while VOA broadcasts 19 hours and will soon be cut back to 14 hours, said Paul Blackburn, a former public affairs officer of the United States Information Service who served at four US embassies in Asia in the 1980s and 1990s.

---

71   Jane Perlez, "The Charm from Beijing," *The New York Times*, October 9, 2003.

72   Lum, et al. "Comparing Global Influence," pp. 89–90.

73   The findings and summary of the survey were reported in June 2008 and the final report, which was released in April 2009, can be found on the Chicago Council on Global Affairs' website at www.thechicagocouncil.org/softpowerindex.

74   Evelyn Goh, "A Chinese Lesson for the US: How to Charm South-east Asia," *The Straits Times*, October 31, 2003

CCTV-9, China's premier state-owned English television channel, which features suave news anchors and cultural and entertainment shows, is broadcast worldwide. America may have CNN International, but in the realm of public policy, the United States has "nothing comparable," remarked Mr. Blackburn.[75] Across Southeast Asia, American centers run by the former US Information Agency, which once offered English-language training and library services, were closed and staff was slashed as part of the worldwide cutbacks in the 1990s.

On the other hand, China had established over 30 Confucius Institutes and cultural centers throughout Southeast Asia by early 2013. When Vanchai Sirchana, the president of Thailand's Mae Fah Luang University which hosts a Chinese cultural center, proposed a balancing act to the American ambassador to Thailand, Darryl Johnson, by offering collaboration between the American government and universities in this area, the ambassador could only laugh since there was no money coming from Washington.[76]

The Barack Obama administration that came to office in January 2009 paid more attention to Southeast Asia. President Obama flew to Singapore in November 2009 to attend the APEC summit. Six months into her new role as secretary of state, Hillary Clinton already visited Southeast Asia twice. While attending the ASEAN forum in July 2009, Clinton declared that "the United States is back in Southeast Asia." She signed ASEAN's Treaty on Amity and Cooperation and said the United States would name a permanent ambassador to the ASEAN secretariat in Jakarta and seek a "comprehensive partnership" with host country Indonesia. Within days of his re-election in November 2012, President Obama attended the East Asia Summit in Cambodia and visited Thailand and Myanmar, highlighting his "pivot" to Asia policy.

China's recent gains are not necessarily at America's expense. There is little chance of Southeast Asia being subjected to a Chinese Monroe Doctrine, even if China had such an intention of denying the region to outside powers like the United States. The United States has more power, more instruments, and provides more common security goods for the region than China does. Southeast Asians generally appreciate US involvement in the region. Specifically, countries like Singapore, Thailand, the Philippines, and Vietnam are buying a strategic insurance policy from the United States by facilitating US forward military deployment in the region to deter potential Chinese aggressiveness.

As a result of deep-seated distrust of China in some parts of the region, some Southeast Asian nations are adopting a strategy of "hedging" in dealing with great powers. While engaging China, these countries are also developing robust and close ties with the United States and other powers to balance China. As a scholar in Southeast Asia commented, Asian countries do not have much trust for one another, and the United States is perceived as the least distrusted of all major

75   Perlez, "Chinese Move to Eclipse US Appeal in South Asia," November 18, 2004.
76   Ibid.

powers.[77] Most countries in Southeast Asia are welcoming continued US presence in the region. US naval ships regularly visit Singaporean and Malaysian ports, and the US navy holds annual joint exercises with their counterparts in the region. The Philippines and Thailand now enjoy major ally status with the United States. In coping with the most pressing security challenge, terrorism, ASEAN remains dependent on America's help. In addition, ASEAN has also deepened its relations with other powers such as India and Japan.

It would be a mistake to view China's new diplomacy in Southeast Asia as necessarily malignant or adversarial to US interests. In fact, what ASEAN needs most are stability and development, the twin goals which both the United States and China can help to achieve. China's continuous advance into the region through both bilateral and multilateral cooperation does not necessarily mean that the United States' substantial role will be replaced. The United States and China can cooperate on many issues in the region, such as securing energy supply, cracking down on narcotics and human trafficking, and promoting stability.

Other powers such as Japan, India, and South Korea have become more involved in regional affairs too. For example, as relations between the US and Myanmar improved and Western sanctions began to be lifted in 2012, Japan quickly wrote off the 300 billion yen (or $3.7 billion) debts Myanmar owed to Tokyo and resumed full-fledged development aid for the first time in 25 years. Japan also pledged $7.4 billion in aid to help five Mekong states—Cambodia, Laos, Myanmar, Thailand, and Vietnam—develop infrastructure projects along the Mekong River.[78] South Korean President Lee Myung-bak made a landmark visit to Myanmar in May 2012, the first by a ROK president since 1983, and promised more financial assistance to Myanmar.

Since Japanese Prime Minister Fukuda Takeo visited ASEAN in 1977 and announced the Fukuda Doctrine to promote relations with ASEAN countries on an equal footing, Japan has maintained its strong presence in Southeast Asia including Myanmar despite decades of isolation of the Southeast Asian nation. In 2012 three Japanese companies including Mitsubishi signed an agreement with the Myanmar government to develop a 2,400-hectare site east of Yangon for housing, commercial buildings and an industrial park.

The unfolding US–China rivalry creates challenges for India as well. As the *Times of India* commented, India is uneasy about China's enlarging power and influence and wants unhindered access to and through the South China Sea. Yet, it does not want to be seen as being part of any American grand design to contain China.[79] India wants to further step up its defence cooperation with the US on a bilateral basis but does not want additional naval forces in an already-militarized

---

77   Sheng, "Is Southeast Asia Becoming China's Playpen"?
78   "Japan to Support Mekong Project," *China Daily Asia Weekly*, April 27-May 3, 2012: p. 2.
79   "US, China Woo India for Control over Asia–pacific," *The Times of India*, June 7, 2012.

Indian Ocean region and surrounding areas. In another indication of India not being supportive of US actively jumping into the fray in the South China Sea, Indian defence minister AK Antony said it was "desirable" that the "parties concerned themselves should settle contentious matters in accordance with international laws."[80] India won a contract in 2006 to jointly explore oil and natural gas with PetroVietnam in the Phu Khanh basin. ONGC Videsh, the state-owned Oil and Natural Gas Corp's overseas arm, has 45 percent stake in one gas field off Vietnam's south coast. During his visit to Southeast Asia in March 2012, Indian Commerce and Industry Minister Anand Sharma pushed for increased collaboration with Vietnam and other countries in energy, mining and infrastructure sectors.

The US has traditionally provided security but China is the largest trading partner of almost every country in the region now. Countries in Southeast Asia are trying to maintain good relations with both great powers. The last thing regional countries want to do is to be forced to take sides in the potential US–China conflict. Meanwhile Southeast Asian nations continue to benefit from the engagement of external powers.

Concluding Remarks

The speed of transformation of China–Southeast Asia relations since the mid-1990s has been stunning given that not long ago many countries in Southeast Asia were firmly anti-communist, and countries like Indonesia were mortal enemies of the PRC. Today, China has a powerful presence in the region and is generally considered a good neighbor by most Southeast Asian nations. The success of Chinese diplomacy in Southeast Asia is due to a combination of bilateral and multilateral economic, political, and cultural strategies.

China's sophisticated diplomacy, geographic proximity, economic complementarity, and a large presence of overseas Chinese willing to promote relations between their countries of residence and their ancestral homeland all contributed to China's rising popularity in Southeast Asia. Southeast Asian nations generally view China's development as an opportunity for their economic growth. Interest in China has greatly increased. Many in Southeast Asia tend to have a more benign view of China's rise to a great power status than those in Japan or the United States. China's responsible behavior during the 1997–1998 Asian financial crisis and the 2008–2009 global economic downturn has been highly praised by many governments and the public in the region. Though suspicions and disagreements still exist, Sino-ASEAN relations as a whole are very strong and close. The deterioration of relations between China and the Philippines and Vietnam in 2011–12 was a brief departure from the generally positive trend. With Xi Jinping in power and with America's implementation of its "pivot to Asia"

---

80   Ibid.

strategy, China is likely to pay more diplomatic attention to Southeast Asia and improve its relations with all ASEAN countries in the years ahead.

For Southeast Asian nations, while the United States can be a distant ally with other priorities, China is right next door and is going to stay. Realizing the sensitivities of the region, China has been careful not to appear threatening as its power continues to grow. China is not engaged in a political or strategic competition with the United States. It does not seem to have a grand strategy aimed at driving the United States out of Asia. Southeast Asian nations wish to maintain good relations with both the United States and China, and they do not want to be forced to choose side if a conflict occurs between the two big powers. Most ASEAN states have been assuaged by Beijing's assertion of peaceful development and its willingness to deepen relations. Despite some long-standing issues between China and several Southeast Asian nations such as the South China Sea sovereignty and drug trafficking between China and the Golden Triangle — Myanmar, Laos and Thailand, it is fair to say that Beijing's new diplomacy has successfully created a win-win situation for China and ASEAN states to foster close ties and achieve common objective of development.

Questions for Discussion

1. What are the Five Principles of Peaceful Coexistence? How significant are they in China's foreign relations?

2. What is the "Malacca Dilemma"? Why is Southeast Asia important to China strategically, politically, and economically?

3. Is China engaged in a competition with other powers such as India, Japan, and the United States for resources and influence? How do Southeast Asian nations respond to growing involvement of these powers?

4. What are major disagreements or difficulties in China's relations with Southeast Asian nations?

5. How would you evaluate China's new diplomacy in Southeast Asia? What can China do to improve its relations with ASEAN countries?

6. Is the US "pivot" to Asia aimed at countering China's expanding influence in the region? How will it affect US–China relations?

Chapter 8
International Responses

Mixed Responses

Chinese diplomacy has exhibited several major transformations since the early 1990s. The developing world, once considered either too far or too poor for any significant economic and strategic investments, has become a newfound location to implement key objectives of China's multidimensional diplomacy. China's new diplomacy after the Cold War has much to do with the changed international environment. The fierce reactions of Western countries to the 1989 Tiananmen Square incident compelled Beijing to seek closer ties with non-Western countries, starting with its neighbors in Northeast and Southeast Asia before expanding to other developing regions. China's own development throughout the 1990s led to its multilayered diplomacy in different parts of the world. This book has emphasized China's needs to secure energy, to expand trade, investment and export markets, to compete with Taiwan for diplomatic recognition, and to enhance its image as a peaceful and responsible great power.

In the mid-1990s, China imported 70 percent of its oil from just three countries—Yemen, Oman, and Indonesia.[1] Since then it has significantly diversified oil sources, importing large quantities from Saudi Arabia, Angola, Iran, Sudan, and Russia. Other potential major sources of suppliers include Central Asia and Venezuela. China has quickly grown to become the world's second largest consumer and importer of oil. It has ramped up investment across the developing world in return for access to oil, natural gas, metals and other raw materials to fuel its rapidly expanding economy. China's trade and investment that have grown extraordinarily in many parts of the world have been welcomed by most developing countries. Investment and aid from China have helped many African, Latin American, Southeast Asian, Central Asian, and South Pacific countries to develop and to weather the 2008–2010 global financial crisis. China's model of rapid growth, especially its success in significantly reducing poverty, has much to offer to the developing world.

One can see two major trends in China's engagement around the world: increased trade and investment to fuel domestic growth needs; and efforts to match growing economic activities with political, cultural and military influence. The PRC already inked free trade agreements with ASEAN, Hong Kong, Macao, Singapore, New Zealand, Chile, Peru, and Costa Rica. It is negotiating or having discussions with about two dozen other economies including Australia, South

---

1   "Galloping Demand Raises Big Questions," *Financial Times*, October 20, 2006, p. 4.

Korea, Pakistan, Iceland, Switzerland, the Gulf countries, and the Southern Africa Customs Union.In 2010, the PRC and Taiwan signed a special FTA, the historic ECFA, further boosting cross-Taiwan Strait trade and exchanges. By the end of 2006, more than 5,000 Chinese companies had already established nearly 10,000 overseas direct invested enterprises in 172 countries or territories around the world, according to PRC government figures.[2] Continued domestic growth and a huge foreign exchange reserves ensure that China will keep on promoting trade and investment in the years ahead.

Chinese banks have stepped up overseas push too. ICBC, China's largest bank by assets, already had branches and operations in 37 countries by the end of 2012 and plans to spread its presence to 50 countries and regions within two years. China's other top banks—Bank of China, China Construction Bank, and Agricultural Bank of China—have also adopted the "go global" strategy aimed at stabilizing overall profits and diversifying the country's mammoth foreign exchange reserves especially in emerging markets.[3] Meanwhile, a new wave of Chinese tourists and immigrants has hit different parts of the world, increasing cultural and societal exchanges between China and the rest of the world.

The Chinese enter the market of the developing world without Western-style political expectations or demands except its much-cherished "one-China" principle in the diplomatic tussle with Taiwan and its insistence to give preference to Chinese companies for projects supported by soft loans from China. China's long-standing "non-interference" policy has been characterized as sensitive to local conditions rather than imposing political demands. Many developing countries seem to appreciate the Chinese business style while developed nations tend to fault China with its inattention to human rights or environmental concerns. Chinese practice around the world is seen by some analysts as undermining efforts to encourage good governance, improve human rights, and protect the environment. China's "no Western-style political strings attached" approach, its neglect of the environment and workers' safety, its focus on fostering strong ties with the elites without paying much attention to NGOs and the general populace have sparked resentment in some developing nations. This largely mercantilist approach may exacerbate political and economic problems and harm sustainable growth in some of the developing countries.

In addition to trade and investment, China is actively participating in international affairs. The PLA first participated in a UN peacekeeping mission by sending military observers to the Middle East in 1990. According to China's Defense White Paper of 2006, between 1990 and 2006 China sent a total of 5,915 military personnel to join 16 UN peacekeeping operations.[4] In 2008, China ranked 12th in the number of military and police personnel participating in UN

---

2 Ministry of Commerce, the PRC, "2006 Statistical Bulletin of China's Outward Foreign Investment," c. 2007, p. 51.

3 "Chinese Banks Go Global," *The Wall Street Journal*, November 13, 2012, p. C3.

4 "China's National Defense in 2006," The PRC State Council, December 29, 2006.

peacekeeping operations, with 1,981 personnel in 12 UN missions. In comparison, the United States ranked 43rd, contributing only 300 personnel.[5] China is also one of the top ten contributors of funding for UN peacekeeping missions.[6] As of the end of 2012, over 2,000 Chinese peacekeeping personnel were carrying out UN missions around the world. China has the largest number of peacekeeping forces abroad among the permanent members of the UN Security Council.[7]

Taiwan remains a top priority for China, but it can hardly explain the full scale of Chinese diplomacy today. As cross-Strait relations improve, competition for diplomatic recognition with Taiwan is likely to take a back seat in China's foreign policy. Likewise, the need for energy and resources in order to maintain continued economic development at home cannot fully explain what and why China has been doing since the mid-1990s such as its generous aid to resource-poor countries. China's new diplomacy in Africa, the Middle East, Latin America, the South Pacific, Central Asia, Southeast Asia and other regions share some common strategies, including frequent high-level visits, aid packages with no requirement for political reforms, investments in industries and critical infrastructure, and expanding cultural and societal exchanges. China's diplomatic philosophy seems to be "live and let live," a rather non-confrontational approach in international affairs. Chinese diplomats are becoming more sophisticated and starting to use effective public relations campaigns to win hearts and minds of other peoples.

China's activities in the global regions surveyed in the previous chapters are all parts of China's new diplomacy as an emerging global power. Chinese diplomacy has received different responses from the international community. For some countries, China's staggering economic development with its insatiable purchasing power is a panacea or bonanza for their own problems; others see China as a rival or even a threat since they cannot compete with China and fear losing jobs and foreign investment. A small group of countries such as Cuba, Venezuela, Zimbabwe, Sudan, North Korea and Iran even consider China as an ideological or political ally, often to the embarrassment of China. As argued throughout the book, China's lack of effective anti-bribery or anti-money laundering laws and its negligence of the environment or human rights will have a negative impact on developing countries in their efforts to fight corruption and improve governance. China may even push some of these countries further into "extraction economies," which rely heavily on exports of raw materials and have little value added, generate few new jobs, and benefit only a few big companies and elites. In other

---

5 United Nations, "Ranking of Military and Police Contributions to UN Operations," April 2008. The top ten contributing nations to UN peacekeeping operations were: Pakistan, Bangladesh, India, Nigeria, Nepal, Ghana, Jordan, Rwanda, Italy, and Uruguay.

6 United Nations, "United Nations Peacekeeping Fact Sheet," February 2008. The top contributors of funding were: the United States, Japan, Germany, United Kingdom, France, Italy, China, Canada, Spain, and South Korea.

7 "A Decade of Rapid Growth in Sino-US Relations," Chinese ambassador to the US Zhang Yeshui's interview with Xinhua News Agency, October 20, 2012.

words, China may be blamed for non-development of some countries and the marginalization of some groups in global trade.

China's expanding influence and growing military expenditure have elicited considerable concerns among countries that perceive China as a competitor or potential threat. While some countries have questioned the rationale for China's military modernization and budget increase, many have considered China's involvement in the anti-piracy campaign by sending warships to the coast off Somali in December 2008 as a positive development. In the anti-piracy case, China was deemed to be using its greater military might for constructive purposes, rather than challenging the current international order. In a Pew poll of 2007, the PRC's image was regarded as "decidedly favorable" in 27 of 47 nations surveyed. The responses reflect a view of China's economic influence as largely positive, especially among developing countries that do not compete directly with China. Yet concerns about China's military strength are evident in much of Europe, Japan, and South Korea.[8] While developing countries generally view China's growth in a more positive light, some Western countries have become increasingly critical of China's role in world affairs. In a 2008 Harris poll, among major European countries, China overtook the United States as the "biggest threat to global stability."[9] Clearly, while promoting relations with the developing world, China must strengthen its traditional relations with developed countries.

The Developing World

China pays particular attention to the developing world in its new diplomacy. As economic engagement deepens, China also attempts to play a bigger political role. To facilitate China's increasing involvement in troubled areas such as the Middle East and Sudan and help find solutions to the conflicts, China has appointed special envoys to these regions.

Rome was not built in one day. In Africa, China's current diplomacy is built upon its friendly policy towards almost every country on the continent in the previous 60 years. Africa's deep reservoir of good feelings towards China makes it relatively easy for China to expand its influence there and Beijing continues to consolidate its firm footing on the continent. Since the early 1990s, China's Foreign Minister has always made Africa the first stop in his annual overseas trips. No other major powers have ever done so or perhaps even thought about this diplomatic strategy. While the international community has come to realize the success of China's diplomacy in Africa in recent years, it tends to ignore China's long-term investment and painstaking efforts in Africa in the past few decades. China formed a firm solidarity with African countries in their struggle

---

8   The Pew Global Attitudes Project, "Global Unease with Major Powers," June 27, 2007.

9   Ben Hall and Geoff Dyer, "China Seen as Bigger Threat to Security," *Financial Times*, April 15, 2008.

for independence in the 1950s and 1960s. Now they are engaged in South-South cooperation for common economic development. Rapidly expanding China–Africa trade and economic cooperation and the apparent relevance to Africa of China's fast economic development have led many Africans to view China as an alternative model to Western democracies. Though China has never officially promoted the "Beijing Consensus" in Africa or elsewhere, it seems obvious that the Chinese growth model has gained popularity in the developing world. The Chinese style of market economy under a strong central government is particularly appealing to many developing countries.

China is not the only player in Africa as far as energy is concerned. For example, in the mid-2000s Korea National Oil Corporation obtained 65 percent oil and gas production rights in two Nigerian offshore blocks, and India's Oil and National Gas Corporation (ONGC) Videsh Limited obtained a 25 percent stake. The big oil companies of developed countries are still playing a dominant role in the African oil market.[10] In the 2008–2009 global financial crisis, China stood firmly with developing countries. During his Africa tour in January 2009, Foreign Minister Yang Jiechi vowed that China would continue to invest in Africa and help Africans even though China itself was reeling from the effects of the financial crisis. "China will keep its promise of continuing to make good investments in Africa, will continue its aid program, and will continue to carry out what we have promised," said Yang.[11]

While visiting Malawi, which cut diplomatic relations with Taiwan just a year earlier in favor of the PRC, Minister Yang said, "We have agreed to increase our co-operation in political, trade and economic areas" after signing two agreements, including a concessionary loan of $90 million to construct a five-star hotel and conference center. China is also building a Parliament house and a highway linking northern Malawi to Zambia. Yang's Malawian counterpart Joyce Banda said that ties with China would benefit the impoverished southern African state more than ties with Taiwan. In the rivalry with Taipei, Beijing has gained an upper hand in the developing world. Countries like Malawi and Senegal made their own choices to develop official relations with Beijing rather than Taipei. Taiwan will face an increasingly difficult job of keeping its 23 diplomatic allies since some of them such as Panama, Nicaragua and Haiti may wish to profit from China's rapid growth and expanding power and adjust their foreign relations.

With its economic might, China has invested in many parts of the world to the cheers of many and the resentment of others. African governments generally welcome China's aid and investment. They laud China for giving aid without the political strings Western governments attach, and are counting on China standing by them in tough economic times. Critics, on the other hand, say that China's

---

10   Xuecheng Liu, "China's Energy Security and Its Grand Strategy," *The Stanley Foundation Policy Analysis Brief*, September 2006, p. 11.

11   "China Vows to Keep up Africa Investment, Aid Despite Financial Crisis," *The Wall Street Journal*, January 16, 2009.

aid and investment are meant only to secure access to the continent's natural resources. They accuse China of being willing to do business with dictators to get what it wants. The fact that China buys over half of Sudan's petroleum exports puts China in an awkward position to pressure the Sudanese government to end the civil conflict. In March 2009 China backed calls by African and Arab countries to have the International Criminal Court drop its warrant for the arrest of Sudanese President Omar al-Bashir on charges of war crimes and crimes against humanity in Darfur. In July 2008 China and Russia vetoed a US-sponsored UN Security Council resolution that proposed worldwide sanctions against Zimbabwean President Robert Mugabe, accusing him of trampling Zimbabwean's democratic rights and ruining the once prosperous nation's economy.[12] China may be acting out of its own national interests, but its perceived support for dictatorships has deeply hurt China's international prestige. China must do a better job in balancing its national interests and international responsibility as a great power.

Chris Burke, a research associate with the Center for Chinese Studies based in Uganda, says China's presence in the country—as elsewhere on the continent—has grown rapidly in recent years. But levels of Chinese assistance are still low compared to the amount received from Western donors, and Chinese trade with African countries remains limited. According to Burke, the criticism of China's presence in Africa in Western media, particularly the claim that low-wage Chinese workers are displacing local Africans, is often overblown. "One of the biggest complaints we hear across the continent is the massive use of Chinese labor," notes Burke. "My colleagues and I have been to a couple dozen of African countries over the last three to four years and we've found absolutely no evidence of this."[13] Whether this observation is valid or not, in the worsening employment conditions following the global economic crisis, China should become more sensitive to local residents and allow greater use of local labor in its projects.

On August 3, 2009, a clash occurred when a parking dispute escalated between a young Chinese and a young Algerian in the Bab Ezzouar district in the eastern suburbs of Algiers, an area frequented by many Chinese vendors. Friends and relatives of both sides later joined the fight, causing injuries to some Algerians and Chinese. Several Chinese stores were looted. Resentment against the Chinese presence reportedly resulted from some "bad" Chinese behaviors such as drinking beer and wearing shorts in front of local residents. In the aftermath of the conflict, some Chinese merchants in Algeria released an open letter to the Algerian people in which they expressed grief over the brawl between some local Algerians and some Chinese in Algiers, stressing that China and Algeria have shared a long history of friendship and hoping that the incident will not affect friendly relations between Chinese and Algerians.[14] Meanwhile, Chinese ambassador in Algeria Liu

---

12   "Glance at China-Africa Relations," *The Associated Press*, March 23, 2009.

13   "China's Foreign Minister Wrapping up Africa Tour," *VOA*, January 16, 2009.

14   "Chinese Merchants in Algeria Write Open Letter to Algerians after Clash," *Xinhua*, August 9, 2009.

Yuhe called upon the Chinese entrepreneurs to take part in a program of building Chinese citizens' image abroad and respecting local customs. The Chinese government and Chinese businesses seem to have learned the lesson and have become more receptive to local criticisms.

In March 2009 the South African government refused to issue a visa to the Dalai Lama for his attendance at a peace conference in Johannesburg. This is a reminder of how deeply China has been involved in African affairs. Even though China had not openly pressured South African government on this issue, South Africa's decision revealed how influential China has become in South African politics. The Tibetan spiritual leader and Nobel Laureate did not receive a visa because it was not in South Africa's interest for him to attend the conference, said Thabo Masebe, a South African presidential spokesman. South Africa's reasoning was that, if the Dalai Lama attended the conference, the focus would shift away from the 2010 World Cup—the global soccer championship South Africa hosted in 2010. "We cannot allow focus to shift to China and Tibet," Masebe said, adding that South Africa has gained much from its trading relationship with China.[15]

Indeed, China's role in Africa is broadly welcomed across the continent. The evidence does not support the claim that Africans feel exploited by the Chinese. A 2007 Pew Research Center survey of 10 sub-Saharan African countries found that Africans overwhelmingly viewed Chinese economic growth as beneficial. In virtually all countries surveyed, China's involvement was viewed in a much more positive light than America's; in Senegal, 86 percent said China's role in their country helped make things better, compared with 56 percent who felt that way about America's role. In Kenya, 91 percent of respondents said they believed China's influence was positive, versus only 74 percent for the United States. And the charge that Chinese companies prefer to ship Chinese employees (and even prisoners) to work in Africa rather than hire local African workers flies in the face of employment data. In countries like Zambia, the ratio of African to Chinese workers has exceeded 13:1, and there is no evidence of Chinese prisoners working there.[16]

The non-interference policy is often used by China to defend its practices. The reality is that China has, either directly or indirectly, been involved in African politics. People around the world have high expectations for China as a rising global power. It is a tall order for China to assume moral leadership in international affairs when China itself has serious corruption, human rights and environmental problems, but even symbolic gestures, such as putting more public pressure on authoritarian regimes, will help improve China's image. China must also reach out to opinion leaders, local communities, and other non-state actors to make sure that more ordinary people, not just political elites, will benefit from trade and investment.

---

15   "Dalai Lama Denied Visa for South Africa Peace Conference," *CNN*, March 23, 2009.

16   Dambisa Moyo. "Beijing, A Boon for Africa," *New York Times*, June 27, 2012.

The Chinese government has successfully wooed the governments of Southeast Asia, where the majority of the overseas Chinese live. Leaders in the region are talking about great opportunities associated with China's growth. Singapore's founding father Lee Kuan Yew, among others, has repeatedly defended China's policy of peaceful development. China's influence is undeniably on the rise in Southeast Asia. In January 2007, at the second East Asia Summit of 16 Asian nations held in the Philippines, the country's president, Gloria Macapagal Arroyo, declared: "We are happy to have China as our big brother."[17] Despite lingering disputes over the Spratly Islands, China and other claimants have attempted to downplay the issue and focused on economic cooperation. Significantly, the Philippines also welcomed China's move to deploy its navy to the seas off Somalia to back international anti-piracy efforts. As long as China continues to be a good neighbor, its navy could help stabilize the region, Vice Admiral Ferdinand Golez, Philippine Navy chief, told *Reuters* in an interview. "I don't think that's a cause of worry for us... because they are our good neighbors," said Golez after China's historic deployment of naval ships in Africa.[18] In this broad context, the deterioration of Sino-Philippine relations in 2012 was really an unfortunate departure from what both countries desired for.

Despite the generally positive trends, Southeast Asia–China relations are still shadowed by deep-seated suspicions and concerns about China's long-term intentions. While welcoming China's rise and the opportunities it brings about, some are worried that China may become an economic challenge and security threat. China must address these genuine concerns and explain its long-term intentions to others. It must also avoid focusing its efforts only on the governments and ethnic Chinese in the region. Overseas Chinese in Southeast Asia have contributed much to China's economic growth and to promoting relations between China and Southeast Asia, but they are the minority in the region. Southeast Asia is diverse in culture, religion, language, politics and history. China needs to consider tapping the potential goodwill among all ethnic groups in Southeast Asia. With regard to the South China Sea dispute, what is China going to do after it becomes militarily more powerful? People in and outside Southeast Asia are closely and anxiously watching China's every move.

In Latin America, China has taken advantage of the post-9/11 US preoccupation with the Middle East to advance its interests. To find alternatives to trading with the United States, several Latin American nations have been strengthening their economic relations with Asia, particularly with China. In May 2004 Brazilian President Lula visited China with 18 ministers and some 500 representatives from all sectors of Brazilian business and industry. Shortly afterwards, Argentine President Kirchner flew to China with a team of ministers and 270 business people.

---

17 "Smile Diplomacy: Working magic along China's periphery," *The Economist*, April 4, 2007.

18 Manny Mogato, "Manila Says Not Worried over Strong China Navy," *Reuters India*, December 26, 2008.

Venezuelan President Chavez was a frequent traveler to China, garnering dozens of trade and investment agreements. These agreements involve joint ventures in oil, agriculture and technology, and include extensive Chinese investments in oil and gas exploration in Venezuela. The US government may become concerned about the domino effect of Latin American countries' increasing tendency toward independent trade policies and their trade with China. Largely because of its exports of oil, natural gas, agricultural products and minerals, Latin America enjoys a trade surplus with China.

In Central Asia, through the mechanism of the SCO, China has tasted the fruits of multilateralism. China has also strengthened bilateral economic cooperation with each Central Asian nation and Russia. For Central Asian states, the Chinese energy market provides "not only an opportunity to break the Russian stranglehold but also a long-term access to a region where continued oil and gas demand is assured."[19] The development of energy linkages between Russia and China provides a critical economic basis to the warming relationship which would otherwise be different. By enhancing economic cooperation, Russia and China can hopefully change the relationship that has been politically hot and economically cold for a long time.

In the Middle East, China enjoys close relations with both Israel and Arab nations, making it potentially the most trusted external power in helping resolve the Israeli–Arab conflict. In the South Pacific, China has quickly replaced the United States and Australia to become the top trading partner of many nations.

Communities in these regions have mixed reactions towards China's new diplomacy. The general response has been quite positive, but there are concerns about and even resentment toward Chinese policies. Competition from China is real. China must be careful in not dividing these societies and creating further social and economic discrepancies. China's gains in these regions are not necessarily losses of the United States. To assuage America's and other countries' anxiety about potential negative impact of Chinese activities in these regions, China can take the initiative to cooperate with the United States and countries in these regions on a wide range of issues, from reducing poverty and promoting development to fighting piracy and protecting the environment. China must also learn to work with non-governmental players and the civil society in these developing nations. A cooperative, helpful and caring China is less likely to be perceived as a threat by others.

US Allies: Japan, South Korea, Australia, and Britain

Japan, South Korea, and Australia are key US allies in Asia. Their reactions to China's active diplomacy around the world are reflective of how they will handle their respective relations with the two big powers. Japan welcomes a prosperous

---

19   Roland Dannreuther, "Asian Security and China's Energy Needs," *International Relations of the Asia-Pacific*, Vol. 3 (2003), p. 209.

China that can contribute to Japan's economic recovery and international development. "There is no sense of competition or anything at all against China," Japanese special envoy for Japan–Africa cooperation Nobutake Odano said at the press briefing after the closure of the first regional preparatory meeting of the fourth Tokyo International Conference on African Development (TICAD) held in Lusaka in October 2007, "Rather than that, we are glad to welcome China's positive engagement in Africa."[20] Mr. Odano said the two Asian powers have established platforms for dialogue and cooperation on a variety of issues. "China has developed quite rapidly, and there must be some secret behind it," the ambassador said, adding that China, which has reaped astonishing achievements in eradicating poverty with a huge population burden, can show "good practice and advice" to Africa.[21] Indeed, as a fellow developing nation, China's development experience has more relevance to developing countries in Africa and elsewhere.

High-level contacts between China and Japan resumed in 2006 after Prime Minister Junichiro Koizumi left office. Koizumi infuriated China and Korea by visiting the controversial Yasukuni Shrine annually. All Koizumi's successors worked hard to improve Japan's relations with its neighbors. Prime Minister Taro Aso paid an official visit to Beijing at the end of April 2009. He called for Tokyo and Beijing to unite in facing the world's environmental and economic challenges, while playing down concerns over China's military power. In a wide-ranging speech in Beijing, Aso floated the prospect of a bilateral free trade deal and joint peacekeeping operations, and said that closer ties between the historic rivals were the only way forward. "Cooperation between Japan and China is a pre-condition for taking advantage of Asia's potential as the growth centre for the 21st century," Aso told a gathering of business leaders from both nations.[22] Due to domestic pressure, Aso's successors Yukio Hatoyama, Naoto Kan, Yoshihiko Noda and Shinzo Abe took a harsher approach to China. China's high-handedness in dealing with the Diaoyu/Senkaku dispute also contributed to worsening of relations after 2010. Despite growing tensions between the two countries in 2011–13, Sino-Japanese economic ties remain strong.

However, Japan's unease about China's rise is an open secret. Japan has felt strong rivalry from China. In the context of China's increasing investment in Africa, Japan announced in 2005 that it would double its financial aid to Africa, in an attempt to win back the lead in the run for popularity among African countries. In the South Pacific, the Japanese government announced a substantial increase in aid in May 2006 as an apparent move to counter Beijing's growing sway in the region.[23] Japan has also strengthened its alliance with the United States to jointly deal with China's rise and the delicate situation on the Korean Peninsula. Some

---

20 "Japan Welcomes China's Positive Engagement in Africa," *China Daily*, November 1, 2007.

21 Ibid.

22 "Aso Calls for Japan, China to Unite," *AFP*, April 3, 2009.

23 "Japan Lavishes Aid on Pacific Islands," *The Associated Press*, May 28, 2006.

in China worry that Japan will use China's rise as an excuse to transform the Self-Defence Forces into a regular military and may even revive its militarism. Japan welcomed the US "pivot" to Asia after 2010 in response to China's continued economic development and military modernization.

South Korea generally welcomes China's development. China's rise presents an economic opportunity rather than a threat, according to Il SaKong, a former South Korean Finance Minister and presidential economic adviser.[24] China has replaced the United States as South Korea's largest trading partner and is the number one destination for Korean investment abroad. Some observers notice that South Korea has moved much closer to China economically, culturally, and even politically after the 1997 Asian financial crisis. However, South Korea remains unhappy with China's tacit support of North Korea, especially in the aftermath of North Korea's alleged sinking of South Korean warship *Cheonan* and shelling of South Korean island of Yeonpyeong in 2010. After Kim Jong-il's death in December 2011, his youngest son Kim Jong-un took control of North Korea. A defiant North Korea launched a long-range rocket in December 2012 and conducted a nuclear test in February 2013. How to deal with a nuclear-capable North Korea will continue to be a major challenge in China–South Korea relations.

Australia enjoys a dynamic and strong relationship with China. China's growing influence in Australia was reflected by the fact that during the APEC summit in Australia in September 2007, the Australian government hosted only one formal state dinner to officially welcome just one delegation—the Chinese delegation. New South Wales Premier Morris Iemma, who hosted the state dinner that was attended by three former Australian prime ministers and other distinguished guests, remarked that "Australia views China's achievements with admiration and satisfaction, not simply because we rejoice in the prosperity of a friend."[25] China has become Australia's largest trading partner and the two countries have been negotiating a FTA since 2005. China is "vital to Australia's future economic prosperity," declares Australia's Department of Foreign Affairs and Trade.[26]

While visiting the United States in March 2009, Australian Prime Minister Kevin Rudd suggested that China was not an enemy but represented "a huge opportunity for us all in the 21st century." Rudd was asked on the PBS television program "The News Hour with Jim Lehrer" whether Americans should view China as an ally, an enemy, or some other way. "When you look at China in the future, I don't think anything is to be served by simply assuming it's all going to go bad," Rudd replied, noting China has a big part to play as "the center of global economic gravity" shifts toward the Asia–Pacific region.Rudd also pushed for China to have a more central role in the IMF at a meeting of leaders from the world's 20 major economies held in London in April 2009. Rudd argued that China should be

---

24   "For South Korea, China's Rise Is An Economic Opportunity Not a Threat," *East-West Wire*, East-West Center, August 15, 2005.

25   "Ewe Beaut Day for Hu As He Praises Labor PMs," *The Age*, September 6, 2007.

26   See the Department's website at http://www.dfat.gov.au/fta/acfta/.

elevated within the IMF in an overhaul of the world economic order. "Let's just get up with reality of the 21st century," he said before attending the London summit, adding the IMF's current voting rights reflect the balance of power in the wake of World War II.Under Australia's plan, China's voting stake would be increased in return for its providing financing to fill part of an around $500 billion financing shortfall in the developing world. Under the current IMF structure, China has only a 3.7 percent voting stake, the United States has 17 percent, Germany's 6 percent, and France and Britain with 4.9 percent each.

The Julia Gillard government since 2010 has maintained strong economic ties with China through agreements to explore clean energy and to make sure Australia remains a long-standing and reliable supplier of energy and natural resources. Prime Minister Gillard has stated that Australia will continue positive and constructive engagement with China but will maintain security ties with the United States based on shared values. However, the Gillard government's action to station US troops in Australia as part of America's "pivot" to Asia was viewed with suspicion by China.

In October 2012 the Australian government released a White Paper titled "Australia in the Asian Century," which claimed that Australia's alliance with the United States and a strong American presence in Asia would support regional stability, as would China's full participation in regional developments. The paper accepted that China's military growth was a natural and legitimate outcome of its growing economy and broadening interests. The paper steered a middle course in addressing the problem Australia faces in managing its relations with the United States and China. It stated the need to deepen Australia's already close relationship with China at every level, including enhancing defence cooperation, while at the same time continuing to support US engagement in the region and its strategic rebalancing in the Asia–Pacific.

Both Australia and South Korea have in the past offered to serve as a balancer between the United States and China. China–South Korea relations and China–Australia relations are good examples of countries with different political systems to live in amity and to embark on mutually beneficial cooperation. Distinct differences with South Korea and Australia have not posed obstacles to developing close bilateral relations between China and these two US allies. South Korea and Australia have their own sets of priorities. At times they may disagree with the United States and adopt policies that seemingly tilt towards China. But China is unlikely to replace the United States in these countries' foreign relations. For one thing, China cannot provide the security guarantees that the United States has offered to most of the countries in the Asia–Pacific. For both South Korea and Australia, the United States remains the most important ally and partner in their foreign relations, but China has become an increasingly critical partner in today's political economy. For their own national interests, South Korea and Australia will have to maintain good relations with both great powers. South Korea and Australia's closer relations with China do not mean that they will be runaway allies from the United States. In the foreseeable future, South Korea and Australia will remain in the US-led security structure and, at the same time, will further expand their burgeoning ties with China.

Japan, South Korea and Australia enjoy productive relationships with China, although their relationships are not without problems. China must ensure that the good momentum in these relationships is maintained so that China's primary focus on economic development is not distracted by disputes with these important nations.

In Europe, Great Britain's attitude toward Chinese new diplomacy has been very positive. According to Britain's Department for International Development (DFID), China's relatively open trade regime, her highly competitive construction industry, low-cost trade and investment financing, and development experience offer a major opportunity for African development.[27] China's trade, investment and aid to Africa are very constructive and improve the prospects for achieving the Millennium Development Goals in Africa. DFID has created a dedicated team in Beijing to work closely with Chinese government and businesses. Senior officials from China and Britain now meet every six months do discuss a wide range of international development issues including Africa.

On January 22, 2009, a week before Premier Wen Jiabao's visit to London, the British government issued its first policy document to spell out a new strategy for dealing with China. According to the 20-page document, building a strong relationship with China was now a "major priority" for Britain as it could help the rest of the world tackle the fallout from the financial crunch. China's increasing power made it a "vital" partner for Britain in restoring world economic stability as countries try to drag themselves out of the global financial downturn. Prime Minister Gordon Brown said in the foreword: "The emergence of China as a global economic and political force is one of the most significant developments of our time. "We must work together if we are to deal with the major challenges we face. I am convinced that Britain, Europe and the rest of the world can benefit from China's rise—provided we get our response right."[28]

Brown also noted that over the next decade, China will present more opportunities for British businesses "than any other country." There is extensive mention in the document of China's growing role in the world, its potential contribution to easing global warming, and making it a responsible stakeholder in international society. "Cooperation with China is vital to reduce poverty, to resolve conflict, and to develop an effective framework to address climate change. To achieve all of this we need China and China needs the rest of the world."[29]

Brown's successor David Cameron continued to promote cooperation between the UK and China though he was critical of China's human rights and policy toward Syria. Prime Minister Cameron said during his 2012 trade mission to China: "I am passionate about growing the links between Britain and China and growing the trade between Britain and China." In December 2012, Cameron decided to relax

---

27 "Achieving the Millennium Development Goals in Africa: Working with China," *DFID*, UK, November 2007.

28 "Government Makes China 'Major Priority' in Global Strategy," *AFP*, January 22, 2009.

29 Jonathan Marcus, "Britain and China 'to Co-operate,'" *BBC*, January 22, 2009.

visa rules to encourage more Chinese tourists to visit Britain despite concerns that the move could fuel organized crime.[30]

Issues concerning the Dalai Lama, trade, and lifting of sanctions on weapons sales to China are some of the potential obstacles in furthering relations between China and the EU. The EU as a bloc is China's largest trading partner. Obviously China must maintain good, productive relations with Britain and other major powers in the EU while expanding its diplomacy in the developing world.

A US–China Competition?

China's new diplomacy often leads to discussions about US–China relations. It also raises an interesting political economy question about whether the Chinese model is applicable to other developing countries. Neither coined nor sanctioned by the Chinese government, the term "Beijing Consensus" has gained popularity since 2004.[31] It was used by Joshua Cooper Ramo, a journalist–editor, to summarize the developmental model based on economic liberalization under tight political control. Does the Chinese model challenge the "Washington Consensus" which suggests that the best way to achieve economic growth is through the adoption of a series of liberal, free-market economic and political policies?[32] Whether China's development model

---

30   "David Cameron overrules Theresa May to relax Chinese visa rules," *The Telegraph*, December 4, 2012.

31   The term "Beijing Consensus" was believed to have existed since the 1990s. Joshua Cooper Ramo popularized it in 2004 when the United Kingdom's Foreign Policy Center published a paper by Ramo titled *The Beijing Consensus*. Ramo laid out in the paper some broad guidelines for economic development based on China's policies as an alternative economic development model to the "Washington Consensus," which was a US-subscribed liberal plan for reforming and developing the economies of poor, third-world countries. Ramo was a former editor of *Time* magazine and later a partner at Kissinger Associates, the consulting firm of former US Secretary of State Henry Kissinger.

"Beijing Consensus" and "China model" are not the same but are sometimes used interchangeably. For scholarly discussions of the "China model," see, for example, Zheng Yongnian, *The China Model and Its Future* (World Scientific Publishing, 2011); Arif Dirlik, "The Idea of a 'Chinese model': A critical discussion," in *International Critical Thought*, Vol. 1, No. 2 (June 2011): pp. 129–137; and Christopher A. McNally, "Sino-Capitalism: China's Reemergence and the International Political Economy," in *World Politics*, Vol. 64, Issue 4 (October 2012): pp. 741–776.

32   The term "Washington Consensus" was initially coined in 1989 by John Williamson of the Peterson Institute for International Economics to describe a set of ten specific economic policy prescriptions that he considered should constitute the "standard" reform package promoted for crisis-ridden developing countries by Washington, DC-based institutions such as the International Monetary Fund (IMF), World Bank and the US Treasury Department. In a broader sense, the term has become associated with neoliberal policies and has led to the debate among politicians and economists over the expanding role of the free market, constraints upon the state, and US influence on other countries' national sovereignty.

offers an alternative path to growth for developing countries remains debatable, but China has certainly become a major economic partner of many countries today.

When Deng Xiaoping initiated China's reforms in the late 1970s, he believed it was important to maintain the CCP's dominance, which was crucial for creating a stable social and political environment for economic development. Deng clearly indicated that the goal of China's reform was to "eliminate poverty and backwardness, move toward prosperity and modernization, and build socialism with Chinese characteristics."[33] Deng is sometimes compared with Mikhail Gorbachev as both were creative leaders who tried to reform the communist system. Gorbachev introduced *glasnost* (political openness) and *perestroika* (economic restructuring) simultaneously, reform policies that unleashed forces leading to the demise of the Soviet Union. By choosing to start with economic reform and doing so very cautiously, the CCP had a greater capacity to manage the change, and China's economy prospered without fundamentally changing the political structure. For many developing nations, China's economic success is impressive and its development model is inspirational.

In foreign policy, Beijing has focused on its own economic and security interests and largely ignored other issues such as human rights, governance and environment. The question is: is such a strategy or the so-called China model sustainable?

Whether the "Beijing Consensus" challenges the "Washington Consensus" or not remains a policy debate, but already some developing countries in Africa and Latin America seem very interested in the Chinese development path. Much of the "Washington Consensus" was right, especially the points that focused on sound macroeconomic policies such as fiscal discipline and public expenditure on health care, education, and infrastructure. Indeed, China itself has followed some of these macroeconomic policies. Clearly one should not look at China's experience from the dichotomy of "Beijing Consensus" versus "Washington Consensus." China's development is more complicated than what a single model can describe.

For China, its bilateral relationship with the United States supersedes its relations with any other country. China is fully aware that its national interests are best served by maintaining a policy of cooperation with the United States. Beijing realizes that the United States is the primary force for stability in the world today. After 9/11, the United States lost interest in much of the developing world, which provided an opportunity for China to move in with trade and investment. However, China has worked carefully not to confront US interests. As China scholar Bates Gill suggested, by and large China has increasingly carried out its diplomacy convergent with international norms, regional expectations, and US interests and aimed at improving its images and position in world affairs.[34]

---

33   Deng Xiaoping, *Deng Xiaoping Wenxuan (Selected Works of Deng Xiaoping)*, Vol. 3 (Beijing: Renmin Chubanshe [People's Publishing House], 1993), p. 122.

34   Bates Gill, *Rising Star: China's New Security Diplomacy* (Washington, DC: The Brookings Institution Press, 2007), p. 137.

President George W. Bush said during his February 2008 visit to Africa that the United States and China could both pursue opportunities in Africa without stoking rivalry. "I don't view Africa as zero-sum for China and the United States. I think we can pursue agendas without creating a great sense of competition," Bush said, "Do I view China as a fierce competitor on the continent of Africa? No I don't."[35] In general, the United States welcomes China's trade and investment in Africa, Latin America, Southeast Asia and elsewhere. On the other hand, the United States is apprehensive about China's close ties with countries with poor human rights record such as Sudan, Iran, Cuba, North Korea, and Myanmar.

More recently, the United States has become anxious about China's expanding influence in the developing world. The United States has taken a two-pronged approach in response to China's continued rise: The Obama administration began strategic rebalancing toward Asia in 2010; it pursued Trans-Pacific Partnership (TPP) to expand American exports to the Asia–Pacific. The US government seemed determined to "return" to Asia.

Hillary Clinton, the US secretary of state (2009–2013), took an 11-day tour of Africa in August 2012 by contrasting America's commitment to democracy and human rights with rival powers' focus on exploiting resources. In Senegal, Clinton told a university audience that the US was committed to "a model of sustainable partnership that adds value, rather than extracts it" from Africa. Unlike other countries, "America will stand up for democracy and universal human rights even when it might be easier to look the other way and keep the resources flowing."[36] Although Clinton did not mention any country by name, her remarks were widely interpreted as a swipe at China. In response, the Chinese state media slammed Clinton to be either ignorant of the facts about China's investment in Africa or ignoring them.

Secretary of State Clinton also visited the South Pacific in August 2012 to pledge renewed American commitment to the security of the Asia–Pacific. In the Cook Islands, she said "Here in the Pacific, we want to see China act in a fair and transparent way." "We want them to play a positive role in navigation and maritime security issues. We want to see them contribute to sustainable development for the people of the Pacific, to protect the precious environment, including the ocean and to pursue economic activity that will benefit the people."[37] Though both countries deny that they are engaged in a strategic competition, the rivalry for influence and resources in the developing world is real.

As China deepens its economic and diplomatic engagement with Africa, the United States has been steadily increasing its military presence in the region, supplying arms, training troops and opening new bases for US personnel. Efforts such as the Trans-Saharan Counterterrorism Initiative have brought US

---

35   "Bush Says No Plans for New U.S. Bases in Africa," *Reuters*, February 20, 2008.

36   "Hillary Clinton Launched African Tour with Veiled Attack on China," *The Guardian*, August 1, 2012.

37   "Clinton in South Pacific with China in Focus," *The Associated Press*, August 31, 2012.

forces into many African countries for the first time as part of the global war against terror. The creation in February 2007 of United States African Command (USAFRICOM), a new US regional combatant command for Africa, reflected Washington's renewed interest in the area. Some analysts suggest that despite the anti-terrorism rhetoric, it appears that the main function of USAFRICOM will be to secure energy supplies in a region that is expected to provide a growing share of the United States' future energy needs.[38] Both President Obama and Secretary of State Clinton travelled to Africa in the first few months of the Obama presidency to reassert America's interest in the continent. President Obama visited Africa again in June 2013. Apparently the United States does not want to be left behind by a rising power and a potential challenger in Africa. American leaders' "don't worry" public statement notwithstanding, competition for resources and influence between the two powers may intensify in Africa, Latin America and elsewhere.

The United States is most concerned about China's long-term intentions, or how China is going to use its increasing power in the future. As Admiral Gary Roughead, US chief of naval operations, commented in April 2009 while in China to mark the 60th anniversary of the PLA Navy, "The advancement and the growth of the navy is consistent with China's economic advancement and its role in a globalized world. I think it is important, however, that ... there should be clear communications with regard to what the intentions of that capability are."[39] Issuing defense white papers and inviting foreign militaries to visit Chinese military facilities are some of the useful steps China has taken to dispel anxiety.

The United States has helped China to integrate into the international political and economic systems. The United States and other powers welcome a peacefully rising, responsible and cooperative China in world affairs. China still considers itself as a developing nation and appears unwilling to lead in international affairs or challenge US hegemony around the world.

The United States has mixed feelings towards China's growing activities globally. US–China relations are marked by cooperation and competition. On one hand, the two powers have common interests in promoting cooperation in trade, regional and international security, climate change, energy safety, green technology, etcetera. A recent example of cooperation is the Joint China-US Training Program for Afghan Diplomats held in both China and the United States in 2012.On the other hand, the United States is wary of China's intentions. Since 2010 it has adopted a series of policies to reassert its global dominance, which include dispatching the Secretary of State to Africa, Central Asia, South Pacific, Southeast Asia and other regions where China's influence has been growing. Such visits and America's renewed efforts to enhance economic and security ties with its allies and friends in Asia are widely considered to be countering China's growing

---

38 Andrew McGregor, "China's Oil Offensive Strikes: Horn of Africa and Beyond," *China Brief*, Vol. 7, No. 16, The Jamestown Foundation, Washington, DC (August 8, 2007).

39 "News Digest: US Seeks Clarity on Chinese Navy," *The Financial Times*, April 20, 2009, p. 2.

power. Most notably, the Obama administration decided to "pivot" toward Asia with strategic rebalancing in the region. Ostensibly the policy adjustment is not aimed at China, but what the United States has been doing such as stationing troops in Australia, beefing up alliances with Japan and South Korea, enhancing military and security cooperation with the Philippines and Vietnam, and expanding ties with Myanmar and Mongolia, smack of a policy of encircling China. As the two powers compete for influence especially in Asia, they need to build more trust between themselves to avoid misunderstanding of their intentions.

China and Neocolonialism

One assumption that many people hold about China's diplomacy is that Beijing is purely motivated by its search for resources and is exploiting developing countries like former colonizers. A closer look at China's activities around the world suggests otherwise. China is not one-dimensional in its goals or interests as some people believe and as realist theories might suggest. It is not only trading with and investing in resource-rich countries but also expanding aid programs to resource-poor nations, especially in Africa. Furthermore, the majority of the developing world benefits from China's growing engagement and welcomes China's presence. China's more active approach to the developing world is something desired by both sides. China does not have territorial intentions in these countries. It is not imposing any ideology or growth model on other countries. In this new diplomacy, China emphasizes cooperation and mutual benefits. Even the Confucius Institutes are jointly operated by a Chinese institution of higher learning and a foreign counterpart.

For many African countries that are developing their own industries, competition from China is a serious challenge. The low safety and environmental standards of many Chinese firms in Africa have been criticized by some African politicians and NGOs. However, most African leaders do not consider China's investment and influence on the continent as a form of neocolonialism. For Africa, China has been a partner in its struggle for independence and post-colonial development. African leaders do not mind that China reaps benefits from its diplomacy in Africa, so long as African countries themselves benefit from it.[40] Ghana's President John Kufuor, while meeting with President George W. Bush who was visiting Africa in February 2008, remarked that China "is coming not as a colonial power, as far as we can see. It's coming ... as a guest and I believe on our terms, on the terms of the African nations."[41]

China is clearly sensitive to the charge that it's a neocolonialist power and is trying hard to refute it. China has emphasized that it is helping build Africa's

---

40   Li Ya, "How Do Africa Experts View China's Influence," *VOA Chinese*, September 13, 2007.

41   "Bush Says No Plans for New US Bases in Africa," *Reuters*, February 20, 2008.

productive capacity by improving its infrastructure and boosting the manufacturing sector, rather than involving the so-called resource-grabbing practice. President Hu Jintao called China–Africa cooperation "a new type of strategic partnership" at the 2012 China–Africa Forum in Beijing, when China offered a $20 billion new loan to African countries over the next three years. African leaders tend to agree. As South African President Jacob Zuma put it, "Africa's past economic experience with Europe dictates a need to be cautious when entering into partnerships with other economies. We are particularly pleased that in our relationship with China we are equals and that agreements entered into are for mutual gain."[42]

Chris Alden, a China–Africa relations expert at the London School of Economics, remarked that the hallmarks of colonialism—the ideology of a "civilizing mission," the accompanying territorial imperative and forging of exclusionary trade relations—were distinctly lacking in China's Africa policy.[43] He is right, and the Chinese government has adamantly denied that its policies and approaches to the developing world are practices of neocolonialism. Chinese foreign-policy doctrine of the Four No's as proclaimed in April 2004 by President Hu—no hegemonism, no power politics, no arms races and no military alliances—has gained much support in the developing world.

China's contribution to African development is unmistakable. As of 2007 there were over 900 development projects in Africa that were being implemented by China. China's trade with Africa is indeed growing fast and a big slice of China's imports are resources, but for all the hype surrounding China's grab for African oil, in 2007 just 9 percent of Africa's oil went to China: the EU and the US took 36 percent and 33 percent respectively.[44]

China is not colonizing any part of the world; instead, it is interested in promoting mutual growth and development. An export-oriented economy, China has exported to and invested in many developing countries. At the same time, China is also the largest recipient of FDI, including investment from developing nations. For example, in 2006 alone, South Africa invested some $700 million in China's breweries, hotels, energy and other sectors. Multinational media giant MIH, huge brewer SAB Miller, and energy tycoons Sasol and Anglo-America are all striving to expand their already strong presence in China.[45] For many developing countries, China's new diplomacy presents unprecedented opportunities and challenges. On one hand, the Chinese development model provides an attractive alternative to other models. Extraordinarily high demands from China for minerals and energy have created a mining and resource boom in many countries. The growth in Chinese investment and China's more flexible investment policy potentially allow

42   "China Offers $20 bn of Loans to African Nations," *The Guardian*, July 19, 2012.

43   Chris Alden, *China in Africa* (London and New York: Zed Books, 2007), p. 127.

44   "Achieving the Millennium Development Goals in Africa: Working with China," Department for International Development (DFID), United Kingdom, November 2007.

45   Hu Yuanyuan, "S. Africa to Invest More in China," *China Daily*, March 20, 2008, p. 13.

recipient nations to enhance their bargaining power with foreign entities as the Chinese compete with major resource investors such as the United States, Canada, Australia, Japan and others. For many countries of the "global South," China's peaceful rise is favorable for mutual benefits and international cooperation, as well as preventing Cold War-like international conflicts and confrontations.

On the other hand, Chinese economic activities also bring about many challenges to developing countries. Chinese businesses are crowding out local competitors. For example, food and fodder exports to China such as soy products have led to booms in rural areas of Argentina, Brazil, Paraguay and other Latin American nations, creating a pattern of economic recovery and expansion that is highly dependent on external forces. In the view of some observers, China's new role as a massive importer has caused prices of basic food products to rise and conditions of scarcity to occur for some commodities, giving rise to what has been termed the "global food crisis." The more advanced manufacturing products from China are also causing electronics firms to abandon production or outsource their manufacturing. This effect took a new form and became more acute as Chinese-made autos debuted in Mexico and other nations in 2008.

China has its own interests and its policies have been consistent. First of all, China's diplomatic approach to the developing world has shifted from an ideology-oriented one in the past to a rational one today with a high priority on economic development and security interests. China's trade and investment are based on mutual gains. Secondly, China's foreign-policy principles have been consistent in the past 60 years. It has always emphasized the importance of national sovereignty and non-interference in other countries' internal affairs. Why didn't the West have any problems with China's practices in the previous 50 years and only found problems in the past ten years? One can argue that the real reason behind some Western countries' dissatisfaction with China's policy is their perceived challenge or threat from the rising Chinese power to their economic and political interests in the developing world.

The debate over whether China is practicing neocolonialism is likely to continue. From its own perspective, China is a victim of Western colonialism in the past and therefore is not going to practice any colonial policies toward the developing world. To avoid criticism of its practices, China will have to do more to distinguish it from Western colonialists by taking such steps as strengthening labor and environmental standards in Africa, joining NGOs and the public in their efforts to enhance governance, and pressuring dictatorial regimes to end human rights abuses.

To defend its policy toward Africa and other developing regions, China has launched a public relations campaign of its own style. On the delicate issue of Darfur, for example, China has been accused of not doing enough to end the violence and killings. However, according to China's special envoy to Africa, Liu Guijin, China had provided over $10 million in humanitarian aid to the Darfur region by early 2007. Chinese companies completed the water-supply project in Darfur, which would be useful for UN peacekeeping forces. As the UN planned to deploy peacekeeping forces to Darfur to join AU forces in October 2007, China already had over 400 peacekeeping personnel in southern Sudan as part of the UN mission and later sent 315 engineers to Darfur to prepare for the deployment of the UN-AU joint peacekeeping forces.[46] China also supported the Annan Plan, put forward by former UN Secretary General Kofi Annan, which committed the UN to provide aid to AU troops stationed in Darfur.

These activities, which were barely mentioned in the Western media, directly refute those charges that China has not been promoting peace and helping the reconstruction of Darfur. China cares about its international image. As one leading Chinese expert on Africa commented, China played "a critical role" in influencing the Sudanese government's decision on August 1, 2007 to accept the UN resolution approving a joint AU-UN peacekeeping force in Darfur.[47] When some influential individuals and human rights groups tried to link the Beijing Olympics to the Darfur issue, Beijing became very puzzled and concerned, but it quickly took actions. China has demonstrated more flexibility in its dealing with the Sudanese government and cooperated with other powers on the Darfur issue at the UN since 2007. China's often behind-the-scene diplomacy in Darfur reveals its attempt to strike a balance between the traditional principle of "non-interference in other's internal affairs" and the needs and wishes of the international community.

Concluding Remarks

Though seeking energy is at the core of China's new diplomacy, the study of China's activities in different parts of the world reveals that the new diplomacy has been driven by several motives, which include promoting continued domestic growth, projecting soft power, presenting an image of a responsible and caring global power, and competing for diplomatic allies with Taiwan. Since the early 1990s, China has adopted an increasingly active, integrated, and pragmatic approach around the world that emphasizes complementary economic interests, mutual benefits in cooperation, and peaceful intentions of China. It has used various soft power tools such as public diplomacy, good neighbor diplomacy, foreign aid, global investment, and promotion of Confucian culture.

While promoting its own economic interests and helping developing countries to grow, China has paid little attention to these nations' internal problems so far. It has largely turned a blind eye to governmental abuses of human rights, environmental degradation, and lack of good governance. In other words, China has not contributed much to the sustainable development of many of these

---

46   "Chinese Official Defends China's Activity in Darfur," *VOA Chinese*, September 12, 2007. Also "China Will Dispatch the First Troops for the Joint UN Peace-Keeping Mission," *China News Service*, September 12, 2007.

47   He Wenping, "The Balancing Act of China's Africa Policy," *China Security* Vol. 3, No. 3 (Summer 2007), p. 35.

countries. Though China often uses its policy of "non-interference" to defend its practices, it has come under fire for not behaving like a responsible world power. It will be a great challenge for China to achieve a balance between protecting its own national interests and shouldering global responsibility.

For many developing countries, China is a model, a market, a partner, and a competitor. China's development trajectory and its experience in raising living standards offer helpful lessons for countries that are struggling to lift their populations out of poverty. At the same time, China also presents formidable competition, especially for traditional industries in these developing countries such as shoe-making and textiles. China is not exporting any ideology, but the "Beijing Consensus" does provide an alternative path to development. In fact, there is no single model for development, and all roads lead to Rome. Other developing nations have to find out the best development model based on their own history, culture, political system, economic structure, and social conditions. China is an inspiration, but may not necessarily be a shining example. In fact, the many problems associated with China's growth, especially environmental degradation and widening income gap, have raised questions about China's sustainable development.

For the United States, China's rise is both an opportunity and a challenge. The two powers share many common interests today such as controlling the global financial crisis, combating terrorism, curbing piracy, and dealing with climate change. They both share the responsibility to eliminate poverty around the world and promote peace in unstable regions. Without cooperation between the two great powers, not much can be achieved in solving today's global problems. The United States still enjoys a commanding dominance in global affairs. Both its hard power and soft power are overwhelming. China is just beginning to reach out to different parts of the world. Due to China's non-democratic political system, some in the West have found it hard to accept that China is going to be an increasingly important player in the world. And some have interpreted the US strategic rebalancing toward the Asia-Pacific region since 2010 as US efforts to counter and even contain China's growing influence.

China's re-emergence as a great power will be one of the most significant events in the 21st century. China has attempted to depart from the historical pattern in which a rising power will challenge the dominant power violently. It has professed a peaceful development strategy. It has become more sophisticated in promoting soft power abroad. Obviously, China wants to be perceived as a friendly and constructive power. It is learning to be a more mature and responsible player in international affairs by becoming one of the rule-makers. The United States and other powers should encourage China's positive participation in international affairs. Working together, China, the United States, and other powers can create a better future for all.

Questions for Discussion

1. Is there a difference between developing countries and developed countries in their reactions to China's growing influence around the world?
2. Is China practicing neocolonialism in Africa? To what extent are such charges true or false?
3. What is the "China model" of growth? To what extent is it sustainable or not?
4. What does China's development model mean to the developing world?
5. How does China's new diplomacy enhance South-South cooperation?
6. Is mistrust growing between the United States and China as China continues to expand its global reach? Why?

Chapter 9

China and the World in the 21st Century

Confucius, giant pandas, and pirates in Somali, what do they have in common? They all have something to do with China's new diplomacy. To expand its soft power, China has established hundreds of Confucius Institutes globally since early 2000s; to demonstrate its peaceful and friendly intentions, China has resorted to panda diplomacy, good neighbor diplomacy and other public relations charm offensives; and China has taken more global responsibilities such as hosting the Six-Party Talks and sending naval warships to fight piracy off the Somali coast. In the 21st century, China's role in international affairs has been changed from being a bystander to an active participant and rule-maker. The leaps-and-bounds developments in China's relations with different parts of the world are truly phenomenal. What is the rationale behind China's new diplomacy? What are China's strategies to implement its new diplomacy? What are the implications for international political economy? The previous chapters have attempted to answer these questions by examining China's diplomatic activities in different parts of the developing world. This final chapter summarizes major findings and arguments and discusses key challenges China faces in its foreign relations in the years ahead.

China's activities in different parts of the world are part and parcel of its twin policy objectives of satisfying domestic growth needs and expanding its global clout. The previous chapters have examined China's new diplomacy in Africa, the Middle East, Latin America, Central Asia, the South Pacific, and Southeast Asia as well as international responses. A striking feature of China's new diplomacy is that it has become more active, nuanced, sophisticated, and flexible. The scale and scope of the new diplomacy notwithstanding, China is still learning to be a global power and to reconcile its own interests with those of the international community. China is creating a new identity of a peaceful, responsible, cooperative, and helpful great power as it continues to grow.

The primary rationale of Chinese new diplomacy is economic and strategic rather than ideological. A key engine that has driven global economic growth, China has contributed positively to economic development of many developing countries. China deeply cares about its international image; it wants to be perceived as a benign power. It has begun to take on more international responsibilities. China's investment, trade and other economic activities abroad, together with its efforts to promote cultural and societal exchanges and to enhance soft power globally are integral parts of its strategy to present China as a friendly and constructive great power in the international political economy of the 21st century.

Explaining China's New Diplomacy

It is clear from previous chapters that China's diplomacy has undergone great transformations since the early 1990s. Major changes in China's diplomacy include:

- From being "passive" to being "active"
- From "bringing in" (*yin jin lai* 引进来) to "going out" (*zou chu qu* 走出去)
- From focusing on hard power to expanding soft power
- Emphasizing the doctrine of "peaceful development" (*heping fazhan* 和平发展) as a new guiding principle in China's foreign policy.

Throughout the 1980s and 1990s, China had followed Deng Xiaoping's admonition to "keep a low profile and hide brightness" so as to concentrate on domestic economic development. Today China has become much more active in international affairs. Before the mid-1990s, China's predominant political, economic, and diplomatic strategies had been to bring foreign investment and technology into China to help China's growth. Since the mid-1990s China has been reaching out for energy and for enhancing China's global influence. It has invested heavily in energy sectors of many countries and has started to purchase foreign assets. It has also learned to project its smart power. The concept of "peaceful rise" or "peaceful development" has become a fundamental guiding principle of China's new diplomacy in the 21st century.

At the beginning of the 21st century, much of China's growing power comes from its ever-expanding economy, which is entering a new "going out" phase. After years of functioning as a foreign investment-driven export platform, China is moving up the value chain. Its companies are searching for new markets and technologies. They are using the foreign currency earned from trade to snap up foreign properties, from companies and securities to energy supplies. Many of the resources it is acquiring are in developing countries, where instability and bad governance have kept Western multinationals from operating. Chinese companies are also moving into the developed markets such as Canada, the United States, Australia, and Europe now.

Both the strategies and scale of China's foreign policy have been expanded. These transformations are indeed a reconstruction of China's identity in international relations. Though realism and liberalism can partially explain what China has been doing in international political economy since the early 1990s, social constructivism seems to offer a better theoretical framework to understand China's policy shift and adjustment. Identities and concepts like "responsible stakeholder" and "peaceful development" are new in international relations. If "anarchy is what states make of it," as Alexander Wendt has suggested, then new ideas such as "a harmonious world," "peaceful rise" and "responsible stakeholder" can also be created and practiced by states. China is not following a particular model that has existed; rather, it has borrowed from other models and is searching for a new development path—a peaceful one as a new player in the increasingly interdependent world. It is charting a new trail and creating a new identity while practicing it. In the process, it is bound to make mistakes and some of its practices may seem awkward, but these are growing pains. China seems to understand the importance of soft power in its national image building and has learned to enhance and project its growing power smartly. It appears willing to help other developing nations. A theoretical framework based on constructivism and smart power is most helpful to understanding the rationale, strategies and significance of China's new diplomacy in the developing world.

China's diplomacy has become more creative. For example, to promote relations with Portuguese-speaking countries, China has taken advantage of Macao's historical linkage with Portugal to reach out to several Portuguese-speaking nations. Trade-promoting offices have been set up in Macao and Portugal. Whereas China already has a productive relationship with countries like Brazil and Angola, this additional channel can only strengthen bilateral relations. For others such as São Tomé and Príncipe that still maintain formal relations with Taiwan, this is a new venue to explore future possibilities.

China is sometimes accused by Western countries of ignoring human rights abuses in countries like Sudan, Syria and Myanmar, but China does not wish to get entangled in civil wars and is not interested in lecturing others. No matter how the Western powers view China's growing influence around the world, for most developing countries, China serves as a practical and inspirational development model. Many of these countries hope that they can learn from China in reducing poverty and promoting growth without disrupting the existing political structure. On the other hand, many people tend to raise the bar a bit higher for China in matters such as human rights simply because of China's size and its importance in today's world. China is attempting to break the historical pattern of violence associated with the rise of a new power in the international system.

Chinese historian Zhang Baijia offered an interesting and perhaps a Chinese version of the constructivist perspective to look at the relationship between China and the outside world. He suggested that China should try to influence the world by changing China itself first. Reforming its own behavior is the main source of strength for China and its foreign policy, Zhang claimed.[1] Through reforming itself and changing its undesirable policies, a new identity—a more confident, peaceful, and responsible China—is created. As a rising global power, China's every move is closely watched by the international community. China must do more to promote sustainable development in developing countries.

---

1   Zhang Baijia, "*Gaibian Ziji, Yingxiang Shijie—Ershi Shiji Zhongguo Waijiao Jiben Xiansuo Chuyi*" (Change Self and Influence the World—An Analysis of the Basic Path of Chinese Diplomacy in the 20th Century), in Wang Jisi ed., *Zhongguo Xuezhe Kan Shijie* (World Politics—Views from Chinese Scholars), vol. 4 *Zhongguo Waijiao Juan* (China's Foreign Affairs) edited by Niu Jun (Beijing: Xin Shijie Chubanshe [New Century Publishing House], 2007), pp. 3–26.

It would be foolish for China to challenge the US supremacy or the US-dominated international system which has benefited China tremendously. China's soft power achievements using tools such as trade and investment, development and humanitarian aid, cultural influence and travel and tourism are built on a "very narrow base," according to a May 2008 study by the US Congressional Research Service.[2] Indeed, while China has used soft power to increase its economic and political leverage globally amid US preoccupation in the Middle East and a weakening US economy, China's success is modest and its influence remains limited. Most importantly, China still considers itself as a developing nation in the global South. With serious domestic challenges, China is neither interested nor ready to take the lead in world affairs although it has become more involved in different parts of the world.

The Chinese government and Chinese public have become more confident of themselves as China is playing an increasingly important role in global and regional affairs. According to a 1995 poll by the Horizon Group, a New York-based human resources management and consulting firm, when Chinese citizens were asked of their views of "the most prominent countries in the world," one third ranked the United States most prominent, and only 13 percent chose China. In 2003 the Horizon Group polled Chinese citizens again. This time, nearly 40 percent picked China as "the most prominent country in the world."[3] By 2008 even Americans had more faith in the future of China than in the United States. According to Gallup's World Affairs survey, dated February 11, 2008, four in ten Americans considered China to be the world's leading economic power; only 33 percent chose the United States. By contrast, in May 2000 the United States dominated public perceptions on this question, with 65 percent saying it was number one.[4]

In 2012, the belief that China is the world's top economy became more common in many parts of the world. Views about the economic balance of power shifted dramatically over time among the 14 countries surveyed by Pew Research Center each year from 2008 to 2012. In 2008, before the onset of the global financial crisis, a median of 45 percent named the United States as the world's leading economic power, while just 22 percent said China. In 2012 only 36 percent said the United States, while 42 percent believed China was in the top position.[5]

A more confident China has become more active in international affairs. In the past, "Whenever the issue of peacekeeping came up, China would either not participate or abstain" because peacekeeping did not fit China's idea of nations

2   P. Parameswaran, "China's 'Soft Power' Blitz No Major Concern: US Study," *AFP*, May 5, 2008.

3   Joshua Kurlantzick, "China's Charm: Implications of Chinese Soft Power," *Policy Brief*, No. 47 (June 2006), Carnegie Endowment for International Peace.

4   Lydia Saad, "Americans See China Crowding Out US as Economic Leader," *The Gallup Poll* (http://www.gallup.com), February 21, 2008.

5   "Global Opinion of Obama Slips, International Policies Faulted," Pew Research Center, June 13, 2012.

minding their own business, says veteran diplomat Wu Jianmin, who served as a junior diplomat at the UN in the early 1970s. Wu noted that in 2008 China had 8,000 peacekeeping troops overseas. The message seems to be that it is now acceptable to interfere in other countries' affairs, as long as there's a UN mandate. "We are a part of the existing international system," Wu says, "We are its beneficiaries. The international system is evolving and we are participating in it and constructing it."[6]

Indeed, China is gradually becoming more responsive to international demands to put diplomatic pressure on authoritarian regimes such as Sudan and North Korea. China's special envoy on Sudan Liu Guijin responded to foreign criticism that Beijing was shielding Khartoum from censure by saying that "China's basic policies on the Darfur question are not substantially different from those of Western nations. We agree that the international community should speak with one voice and exert equal influence on the Sudanese government and rebel forces … or, as Western nations prefer to say, exert pressure."[7]

Chinese diplomats do not mention "non-interference" now as frequently as before. Until the mid-1990s, China had shunned multilateralism in foreign policy for fear of becoming a target of attack by a united West. Today, through a combination of growing economic clout and increasingly sophisticated diplomacy, China has established solid and productive relationships throughout Southeast Asia, Africa, Latin America, the Middle East, Central Asia and other parts of the world. Chinese diplomats are crisscrossing the globe seeking energy deals. China has come to realize that growing hard power must be accompanied by soft power. And both hard power and soft power have to be used smartly. If others mistrust a country's intentions, more power will lead to less security for that country since it will fall into the classic security dilemma. In many media reports, China is portrayed as an economic success story for its rapid development and achievements in pulling millions of people out of poverty. Many people, notably some African and Latin American leaders, even applaud the Chinese model as a viable alternative to Western models for development.

China's traditional "non-interference" policy does not seem to be so sacred anymore since China has on many occasions already violated this principle. Beijing's initiative in the Six-Party Talks on North Korea's nuclear program is a prime example that China has departed from its traditional policy of "non-interference" in the internal affairs of other countries. China's involvement in Zambia's elections and some Pacific island nations' domestic politics casts doubt on its standard claim that it never interferes in the internal affairs of other nations.

Since its appointment of an envoy on Africa in May 2007, China has been more actively involved in the UN efforts to find a peaceful solution to the Darfur crisis. China has sent engineers and peacekeeping forces to Sudan as part of the

---

6   Anthony Kuhn, "China Alters its Role in World Economy, Diplomacy," *National Public Radio*, All Things Considered, March 31, 2008.

7   Ibid.

UN operations. The Sudan case suggests that the Chinese government cares so much about its international image that sometimes international pressure has the power to compel China to change its long-standing policy. On Darfur, international pressure apparently worked. China certainly did not wish to have the Beijing Olympics remembered as "genocide Olympics" as Hollywood activist Mia Farrow had labeled. China seems to understand that not all international criticisms of China are unjustified or evil. After all, a more confident and mature China needs to be more tolerant of and receptive to critical views, especially when they are raised in a constructive way.

From North Korea to Iran, from Sudan to Zimbabwe, China is moving to align its policy with those of other major powers. China has been actively involved in Afghanistan's post-war reconstruction and began to train Afghan police officers in 2012 ahead of the planned pullout of US-led troops in 2014. "There is a trend ... of China making decisions that reflect the international perspective more than the narrow Chinese perspective," observed David Zweig, an expert of Chinese foreign policy at the Hong Kong University of Science and Technology. He pointed to the way Beijing had worked closely with Western countries over Darfur since 2007. "China is learning on this," Professor Zweig added, "They want to be a responsible player" in world affairs.[8] Another such example is China's decision to turn around a ship full of arms that was bound for Zimbabwe in April 2008 amid international concerns that President Mugabe may use the weapons against opposition after his loss in the March 2008 election.

Theoretically, this book has argued that among various International Relations theories constructivism best explains China's new diplomatic behaviors. Granted, other theories are helpful in understanding China's specific policies. For example, realism can explain why China seeks to secure so many energy deals to satisfy its domestic needs; liberalism, on the other hand, can answer the question why China opts to cooperate with other countries especially in trade. However, to fully understand China's new diplomacy since the early 1990s and its attempt to rise peacefully during the global power transition, constructivism offers the most powerful insight into China's policy objectives and implementation. China is charting some new territory in international relations, with new norms and identity associated with its rise in the 21st century.

As a re-emerging great power, China has set an ambitious goal of rising peacefully without disrupting the international system or confronting the United States. Overall, China's development since the late 1970s has been steady and peaceful and US–China relations are strong, stable and cooperative despite lingering differences over issues such as human rights and trade. China's new identity as a peaceful, responsible and constructive great power is still in the making, and in the process China may well experience growing pains and setbacks, as evidenced in its deteriorating relations with several of its neighbors between 2010

---

8   Scott Baldauf and Peter Ford, "China Slammed for Arming Zimbabwe's Mugabe," *The Christian Science Monitor*, April 23, 2008.

and 2012. As illustrated in previous empirical chapters, China is not a full-blown great power yet. China has a lot of learning, experiment and adjustment to do in its new diplomacy. It's ultimately up to China itself to decide what kind of power it will become or how it will use its growing strength. But since China is working toward achieving its proclaimed objective and becoming a new great power in the international system, other countries should help China by encouraging it to follow internationally accepted norms and to balance its domestic interests and international obligations. Other powers especially the United States can do more to help shape the future of China.

Threat to the West or Model for the Rest?

Whether China's strategies are duplicable by other countries is questionable, and China has all along emphasized that it does not export any ideology or model. Still, China's new diplomacy around the world has generated heated discussions. Developing countries generally welcome China's more active role in international political economy. They like China's trade and investment. China's successful economic reforms also offer a useful example for them as they attempt to accelerate development. For many developing nations, China offers a welcoming alternative development model to the ones prescribed by the West; for some, China is also a potential political partner.

Africa is a continent that has benefited from China's aid and investment as well as China's development model. According to Obiageli Ezekwesili, the World Bank's vice president of the African region, Africa needs investments of some $22 billion annually to improve its infrastructure networks alone if it is to have global competitiveness. In addition, some $17 billion is required to maintain existing infrastructure.[9] China has intensified its support to Africa's economic development since the beginning of the 21st century. It has renewed its commitment to give more financial and technical assistance to the continent, help it train professionals, reduce tariffs on products from Africa and cancel debts. China's experience in lifting millions of people out of abject poverty in a short span of time is particularly appealing to many developing countries. "The fundamental lesson of China's transformation for Africa is embracing of reforms and integration into the market as a response to internal problems by finding solutions that enable citizens to take advantage of facilities that globalization offers," commented Ezekwesili.[10]

US response to China's new diplomacy is complex. The two countries' interests converge in certain aspects, such as stabilizing the global economy, promoting peace and stability in the Middle East and East Asia, combating poverty in the developing world, and fighting against piracy on high seas. The two countries are locked in

---

9   Xin Zhiming, "An Example for Africa: Top WB Official says Continent can Learn from China," *China Daily*, March 6, 2008, p. 13.

10   Ibid.

economic symbiosis and have expanded economic cooperation during the global financial crisis. The two countries' interests also diverge in other aspects. China's "no political conditions attached" trade and investment policy is often at odds with America's efforts to advance human rights and good governance in the developing world. Anxiety is discernible among American policy makers regarding China's expanding diplomatic role around the world. Despite its repeated assurance of a "peaceful development" policy, Beijing's long-term motivations are unclear. It has not articulated a clear long-term plan or strategy for the role it wants to play in the world, leading to some misgivings and apprehension. China has characterized the burgeoning relationships with developing countries as mutually beneficial, spurring their development and satisfying Chinese demand for energy and raw materials. But China's spending spree is also redrawing political alliances, and some analysts fear the United States is losing influence in Africa, Latin America, and many other regions. In July 2008, US Undersecretary of Defense for Policy Eric Edelman told the Senate Foreign Relations Committee that "China's full-court press to establish influence and connections in Africa and Latin America may be seismic in its future implications for the United States."[11] The United States began to "pivot" to Asia in its foreign policy in 2010 as President Obama claimed to be America's first "Pacific president."America's "strategic rebalancing" which includes stationing troops in Australia and beefing up alliances with Japan and the Philippines is an apparent attempt to counter China's growing influence in the Asia–Pacific region.

Some analysts have begun to talk about an "axis of oil" that links China with Russia, Iran, Sudan and Venezuela. These authoritarian regimes could pose the most serious threat to the United States and its democratic allies since the collapse of the Soviet empire, according to Joshua Kurlantzick, a scholar at the Carnegie Endowment for International Peace. Others such as Randall Schriver, a former US Deputy Assistant Secretary of State, are less pessimistic and argue that the growing Chinese reliance on the outside world for energy could actually drive China and the United States toward closer cooperation, since both powers want to keep shipping lanes open and encourage stability in oil-producing regions.[12]

Overall, China's new diplomacy has been moderately successful. China has promoted friendly relations with most developing countries, many of which are eager to trade with China despite some domestic opposition that imported Chinese goods and investment are crowding out local businesses. An increasing number of countries hold a more favorable view of China than the United States. China is broadening the menu of choices for developing nations as they attempt to achieve the long-delayed economic and social development.

Other emerging powers are following China's footprints in strengthening relations with the developing world. India is trying hard to catch up and copying many of China's practices abroad. In April 2008, India, mimicking what China

---

11   Craig Simons, "China's Influence among African Nations Spurs Concerns," *The Atlanta Journal-Constitution*, November 30, 2008.

12   "Galloping Demand Raises Big Questions," *Financial Times*, October 20, 2006, p. 4.

did in October 2006, hosted its first India–Africa summit in New Delhi, which was attended by leaders from a dozen African countries. Two documents, the Delhi Declaration and the Africa-India Framework for Cooperation, came out of the first India–Africa summit. The Delhi Declaration was a political document to cover issues of bilateral, regional and international interest to India and Africa, including positions on the reforms of the United Nations, climate change, WTO and international terrorism. The Framework for Cooperation focused the areas of multilateral cooperation on human resources, institutional capacity building, education, science and technology, agricultural productivity, food security, and the development of the health sector and infrastructure.

India once shared close ties with the African continent, and staunchly supported the African independence struggle against colonial rulers. The British colonial administrators imported Indian labor to build Africa's railroads (later many Indians held midlevel management posts). Now Africa is still home to 2 million Indians.[13] However, India's influence waned in recent decades as it focused on building closer ties with the United States and Europe. India's hosting of the summit was believed to be rectifying New Delhi's neglect of Africa. Indian companies have made robust investments in Africa in recent years, and India's trade with Africa increased from $5.5 billion in 2001–2002 to over $30 billion in 2007–2008.[14] Some of India's biggest names such as pharmaceutical company Cipla and oil giant ONGC have invested in Africa lately. The Indian government has invited 15,000 African students to its schools and plans to train 1,000 of African civil servants each year.[15]

China's active diplomacy compels other powers such as Japan to strengthen their ties with the developing world lest they are competed out. The Fourth TICAD convened in Yokohama from 28 to 30 of May 2008, marking the 15th anniversary of the TICAD process, which was first launched by Japan in 1993. This summit-level conference brought together representatives from 51 African countries, 74 international and regional organizations, the private sector, civil society organizations, notable individuals, as well as 34 partner countries, including the G-8 and Asian countries. In the opening session, then Japanese Prime Minister Yasuo Fukuda announced Japan's intention to double its ODA to Africa by 2012. According to Prime Minister Fukuda, Japan would offer up to $4 billion of ODA loans to assist Africa in infrastructure developments, and Japan would double its grant and technical cooperation for Africa over the next five years. The conference adopted the "Yokohama Declaration" which summarized the outcome of the TICAD process and confirmed the continuing political commitment of Japan and other partners to African development. Most importantly, the conference introduced a "Yokohama Action Plan" for the next five years and a "TICAD Follow-up Mechanism" for monitoring and assessment.[16] Whether China's development serves as a model or

---

13   "India Plays Catch-up in Africa," *Business Week*, May 26, 2008, p. 55.
14   "India-Africa Co-op Discussed Prior to Forum Summit," *Xinhua*, April 7, 2008.
15   "India Plays Catch-up in Africa," *Business Week*, May 26, 2008, p. 55.
16   *Japan Info*, Vol. 11, Consulate General of Japan in New York, June 2008.

threat depends on one's perspectives. But everyone is taking China seriously. The challenges from China are real; the biggest one for developing countries is how to turn the competition into an opportunity for development.

Challenges Ahead

China's new diplomacy has significant implications for international political economy and raises several serious challenges for China itself. If the developing world lacks energy and natural resources needed for China's rapid industrialization and modernization, will China still be interested in trade and cultural exchanges? Will China still build Confucius Institutes all across the world? How can China strike a balance between safeguarding its own national interests and becoming a more responsible and respectable global power? The following are some of the key challenges China faces in the years ahead:

Developing Alternative Energy Resources

China, India and other emerging markets are in the midst of exceptional economic boom and need cheap energy to keep growing and modernizing. William Chandler, an energy expert at the Carnegie Endowment for International Peace, estimated that if the Chinese were using energy like Americans, global energy use would double overnight and five more Saudi Arabias would be needed just to meet the world oil demand. India is not far behind. By 2030, the two counties will import as much oil as the United States and Japan do today.[17]

China's sustainable growth depends on three "Es," namely, economic growth, energy security, and environmental protection. The three variables are dynamically linked with one another. Energy security means security of supply—sustainability of access to global energy resources—and security of demand—efficiency of energy consumption and environmental protection. China's power is still largely generated by coal, the dirtiest source of electricity. China has some of the world's most polluted cities. Its rivers and air are also severely polluted. The environmental consequences of China's surging energy use cannot be underestimated.

High oil prices and environmental deterioration have become driving forces behind development of alternative energies. China began tapping into renewable energy in the late 1980s amid worries that pollution and related health and environmental issues caused by rapid industrialization could cause social unrest. It has strengthened research and development of alternative and renewable energies. In the long run, nuclear power will become one of China's main energy sources. China has built nine reactors and two more are under construction, with a further 19 having been proposed.[18] The Daya Bay and Qinshan are two big nuclear

---

17 Jad Mouawad, "The Big Thirst," *The New York Times*, April 20, 2008.
18 "Galloping Demand Raises Big Questions," *Financial Times*, October 20, 2006, p. 4.

power plants already in operation. China plans to develop more nuclear power, hydropower, solar power, wind power, tidal power and geothermal power.

While China is most commonly known for its voracious demand for energy with a spotty environmental record, it is quietly becoming a leader in developing renewable energy sources and technology. It has developed the new concept of "green GDP" and passed new environmental protection laws. With its energy needs growing exponentially and oil price setting new records, China is using every means possible to eke out extra kilowatts, by not just cutting oil deals with rogue states and building nuclear reactors but also putting into place some of the most aggressive renewable energy policies in the world. When the Renewable Energy Law took effect on January 1, 2006, the Chinese government announced a goal of having 10 percent of the country's gross energy consumption be renewable by 2020—a huge increase from one percent at the time.[19] China has also promulgated building codes mandating that all new construction dramatically improve energy efficiency. Renewable energies such as wind, solar, and biofuels are expected to grow into a $100 billion market over the next 15 years in China, making it a global powerhouse in renewables. "China is rapidly moving into a world leadership position in the industry," observed William Wallace, an adviser to the United Nations Development Program in Beijing.[20] In 2007 alone China spent $10 billion—about 7 percent of the world's total investment in green energy, making it the 2nd largest investor in renewable energy.[21]

Biodiesel from crops probably could never replace conventional diesel entirely, but this renewable fuel is environmentally cleaner and can be a bigger part of the energy mix in the future. China's new emphasis on renewables is a relief for those who worry about the environmental impact of China's energy consumption. Since China remains a large agrarian country, one obvious strategy is making biofuels and biogas out of the vast amount of agricultural and animal wastes, which can be used as a substitute for imported oil. Western countries can help China in this respect by providing technological and other assistance. Other emerging economies such as India, Brazil, Russia, Indonesia, and South Africa also have greater needs for energy. They are also forging closer ties with oil-rich regions. As China and other emerging economies continue to grow, it is imperative that they, with the help of developed countries, develop alternative energy sources.

Improving International Image

China's international image, especially in the Western world, remains poor despite much progress China has achieved. What is wrong? What can China do to rectify

---

19 Bay Fang, "China's Renewal: Hungry for Fuel, it Emerges as a Leader in Alternative Energy," *US News & World Report*, June 12, 2006, p. 37.

20 Ibid.

21 "Freeman Facts: Renewable Energy in China," *Freeman Report*, CSIS, Washington, DC, October, 2008.

the situation? China's economic impact on the rest of the world may prove to be a mixed blessing since it presents both opportunities and challenges to some developing nations. The political consequence of China's new diplomacy is more complicated. China's reluctance to pressure countries with poor human rights or governance record is not only detrimental to democratization in those countries but also hurts China's own prestige.

In particular, China can do a better job in explaining to the West and its neighbors why China (legitimately) needs to increase its military budget and what China's intentions are as its power continues to grow. China has long been tightlipped about its military strength and capacity, drawing criticism from others wary of its military modernization program. China has claimed its military upgrading is purely for defensive purposes, but many remain unconvinced.

Close neighbors are dearer than distant relatives. China's relations with Japan, the Philippines and Vietnam worsened after 2010. It may be too simplistic to blame China's more assertive diplomacy for all the troubles in its neighborhood, nevertheless China needs to improve relations with these countries and enhance its peaceful international image in the years ahead.

For a developing and energy-short country like China, a sharp rise in the price of oil or a sudden disruption of energy supply can have a devastating impact. Chinese naval expansion is directly linked to the Chinese need to protect its increasingly vital energy supply routes from the Middle East and Africa. If China can clearly explain how important these sea lanes are to China's economy and why China sent warships abroad to protect its interests, perhaps more people will have a better understanding of why China needs to upgrade its military, especially its navy. In August 2009 China's Defense Ministry launched its first official website (http://eng.mod.gov. cn) as part of an effort to be more transparent. Aimed at countering foreign fears about the PLA's secrecy, the dual-language website (Chinese and English) includes sections on China's defense policies and laws and news about military exercises, peacekeeping roles and international military exchanges. The PLA's other public relations efforts include naming a press spokesperson and busing foreign journalists and military delegations to bases near Beijing for observing military exercises and visiting facilities.

Former US Deputy Secretary of State Robert Zoellick's "responsible stakeholder" expectation of China seems to have been widely accepted as a yardstick for China's international behavior. Chinese Foreign Minister Yang Jiechi said that China would shoulder more responsibility for world affairs, but he cautioned that this was not just to please specific countries. "Frankly speaking, China, as a developing country, cannot undertake a level of obligation that goes beyond its capacity," he said. "I would like to emphasize that we are not taking international responsibilities to serve the interests of certain countries."[22] In fact, the downplaying of its capabilities has become a part of China's strategy. Proposed by former US national security advisor Zbigniew Brzezinski and others, the G-2 concept (with the United States and China

---

22   Kuhn, "China Alters its Role in World Economy, Diplomacy," March 31, 2008.

forming a team to lead the world out of the economic crisis and co-manage other world affairs) has gained some popularity in Western media since early 2009.[23] Not surprisingly, Chinese scholars and officials have dismissed it as premature.

Aiming to establish some 1,000 Confucius Institutes around the world by 2020, China is careful to point out that these cultural centers are not pushing any ideological agenda. "Confucius Institutes do not teach Confucianism (as a religion). They don't promote any particular values," says Zhao Guocheng, an Education Ministry official in charge of the institutes. "They're just an introduction to Chinese culture, and they're established at the invitation of foreign people who want to understand China."[24] The Confucius Institutes are now officially sponsored and supported by the Chinese government. Perhaps one day when other countries take the initiative to establish and expand such institutes to study Chinese, China's soft power will really be strong. A Confucian rule says, "Don't do unto others what you wouldn't wish upon yourself." Confucius' message on soft power was clear: Lead by moral authority, not force. Keep your own house in order, and others will follow your example. China must follow this golden rule in its new diplomacy.

China's lack of exchanges and contacts with NGOs, civic groups, and the ordinary citizens in many developing countries is a major cause of discontent and resentment. Already in Africa, Latin America and elsewhere, Chinese presence has triggered protests by those who felt marginalized by globalization and who have not benefited from China's expanding trade and influence. China must address this dislocation between elite and general populace seriously in order to become a more appreciated partner by the locals. The new diplomacy is not monopolized by the Chinese government and the Chinese public is increasingly involved in the process. In fact, Chinese businesspeople, educators, students, tourists, artists, entertainment and sports stars and other non-official individuals probably have done more than Chinese diplomats to promote China's presence and improve its image around the world. Chinese diplomats need to do more to reach out to ordinary citizens of their host countries instead of staying inside their "comfort zones" and focusing on small Chinese communities and the governments in their host countries. The societal level exchanges as a form of public diplomacy must be further promoted and expanded.

Perhaps the most difficult public relations challenge for China is its policy toward Taiwan, Tibet and Xinjiang, which is closely monitored by the international community. Any mishandling will immediately hurt China's image abroad.

Dealing with Taiwan, Tibet and Xinjiang

Taiwan, Tibet, and Xinjiang will continue to be sources of frustration for China for a long time to come. Though Beijing considers these regions as domestic affairs,

---

23   Zbigniew Brzezinski, "The Group of Two That Could Change the World," *The Financial Times*, January 13, 2009.

24   Anthony Kuhn, "China Tries to Export Culture as Influence Increases," *National Public Radio*, April 2, 2008.

how Beijing treats them will have international repercussions and will directly affect China's image abroad. No matter how Beijing defends its policies regarding these regions, viewed from the outside, they are all issues related to human rights and democratization. It is perhaps understandable why China pushed hard to squeeze Taiwan's international space, especially when Taipei's pro-independence government under Chen Shui-bian constantly provoked Beijing (and Washington) before May 2008. However, China's desire to isolate Taiwan as one major motivation for its new diplomacy also runs counter to its claim to be a peaceful and friendly growing power. People in Taiwan and elsewhere may ask: why are you so ruthless? Why can't we have more international space? At least some of China's diplomatic success may have been nullified by its tough handling of Taiwan.

To placate the Taiwanese public, the majority of whom still prefer the "no independence and no unification" *status quo*, the PRC government may have to change its strategy.[25] Instead of denying Taipei's international space, Beijing should confidently encourage and help Taiwan to continue to play some role in international economic and cultural affairs. The PRC should help Taiwan's application for membership in international organizations where statehood is not a requirement. Even in some international organizations that are strictly for sovereign states such as the WHO, where the health conditions of the Taiwanese public are not periodically reported, the Beijing government must be flexible and creative so as to allow Taiwan's interests to be represented. It makes sense for Taiwan to be included in these non-political forums since the condition of the 23 million people there is not a simple political issue. Taiwan's meaningful participation in international affairs, along with warming cross-Strait interactions, is conducive to the final solution of the Taiwan issue. Fundamentally, if China cannot resolve the Taiwan issue peacefully, then China's claim to be a peaceful power will not be validated.

To the satisfaction of many in and outside Taiwan, Taiwan eventually participated in the World Health Assembly (WHA) as an observer under the name "Chinese Taipei" in May 2009. This was the first time Taiwan had been invited to attend the official international gathering of the WHO after its expulsion from the UN in 1971. Undoubtedly, without Beijing's blessings, Taiwan would not have

---

25   According to a survey by Taiwan's Mainland Affairs Council (MAC) in December 2008, 91.8 percent Taiwanese surveyed prefer the *status quo* across the Taiwan Strait, broadly defined. It is the highest support for maintaining the *status quo* since Taiwan began to conduct surveys on cross-Strait ties in the 1980s. "Most People Welcome China Links, But Suspect China: Poll," *Radio Taiwan International*, December 26, 2008.

The MAC's March 2013 survey suggests that the overwhelming majority of the public (86.1 percent) still supported maintaining the status quo defined in a broader sense (including "Maintaining the status quo and deciding on independence or unification later," "Maintaining the status quo and unification later," "Maintaining the status quo and independence later," and "Maintaining the status quo indefinitely"). Polls conducted by pro-DPP groups often yield different results, showing a high percentage favouring independence.

been able to participate in any official WHO activities. Even President Ma Ying-jeou openly expressed his appreciation of Beijing's kindness.

By the end of 2008, the so-called "three direct links" across the Taiwan Strait—shipping, flight, and mail—had been realized. To reciprocate, the PRC has also demonstrated goodwill toward Taiwan. In September 2008, Taiwan's bid to participate in the activities of the UN special agencies failed, without surprise. But significantly, China's UN ambassador Wang Guangya suggested that though Taiwan could not become a member of the UN due to the widely accepted "one-China" principle, both the PRC and Taiwan could work out a creative solution for Taiwan's participation in international organizations. If the two sides work in a spirit of "building mutual trust, putting aside differences, seeking common ground and striving for a win-win result," they will surely find an appropriate solution (to Taiwan's international participation) through consultation, remarked Ambassador Wang.[26] This was the first time that a top Chinese diplomat had publicly supported Taiwan's international space. On New Year's Eve of 2009, President Hu Jintao proposed in a policy speech that the two sides of the Taiwan Strait should engage in efforts to promote military confidence building and discuss Taiwan's participation in international organizations.

Ma Ying-jeou proposed a "diplomatic truce" between Taipei and Beijing during his 2008 presidential campaign. All indications suggest that the PRC seems to have agreed to an end, at least temporarily, to the cut-throat competition between Taipei and Beijing for diplomatic allies. It seems that China has given a tacit consent to end the practice of buying diplomatic friends. China could buy practically all of Taiwan's cash-starved allies, if it went all out to do so. Taipei has no way to stop Beijing. Yet Beijing has gone out of the way to let Taiwan keep its existing allies. China will let Taiwan keep its small diplomatic club but probably will not tolerate it if Taipei ever tried to get a country to defect. Beijing may also end the honeymoon if Taipei continues to shy away from political dialogue on the basis of "one-China."[27]

The economies of Taiwan and the PRC have become increasingly interdependent. The two sides signed a total of 16 agreements during Ma's first term (2008–2012) including the historic ECFA in 2010. The two-way trade reached over $145 billion in 2010 and is expected to expand with the implementation of ECFA. According to President Ma, who was elected for a second term in 2012, all the 16 agreements were part of a broadly defined cross-Strait peace accord.[28] Despite significant improvements in cross-Strait relations, the final political resolution of the Taiwan issue remains remote.

---

26   "UNGA Decides Not To Include Taiwan Proposal on Agenda," *Xinhua*, September 17, 2008.

27   Joe Hung, "China May Stop Poaching Taiwan's Allies," *The China Post*, March 18, 2009.

28   "Ma Views All Cross-Strait Pacts As Basis for Peace," *Taiwan Today*, February 9, 2012.

While the Taiwan situation has noticeably improved since May 2008, Tibet and Xinjiang are likely to emerge as more serious challenges to the PRC in the near future. Tibetan protests against Chinese rule in March and April 2008 and the July 2009 deadly Han-Uyghur conflicts in Xinjiang highlighted China's dilemma and challenge in the two autonomous regions.

The Dalai Lama enjoys widespread popularity around the world. He has repeatedly said that he does not seek independence, but only genuine autonomy, for Tibet. The Chinese government remains skeptical and considers him the source of violence and instability in Tibet. China is also suspicious of the Dalai Lama's intentions of establishing an autonomous "Greater Tibet," which would cover other Tibetan-inhabited regions within China. The Dalai Lama demanded in his "five-point peace plan" in 1987 and the "seven-point new suggestions" in 1988 that the Chinese troops and military facilities be withdrawn from Tibet. He also demanded to stop the Han Chinese from settling in Tibet. The Dalai Lama's "Greater Tibetan region" would cover a quarter of China's territory, which is completely unacceptable to China.

The Dalai Lama and his supporters have accused China of carrying out "cultural genocide" in Tibet, while the Chinese government feels that its efforts to develop Tibet by pumping in billions of *yuan* every year go unappreciated. Despite the fact that Tibetan economy has been growing with massive financial support from the central government, China has been accused of having a poor human rights record and suppressing religious freedom in Tibet. Tibetans in and outside Tibet will continue to have different interpretations of Tibet's current status and its future.

The Dalai Lama retired from political life in early 2011 but remains an influential figure as the spiritual leader of Tibetans. With the aura of a Nobel Peace laureate, the Dalai Lama holds the moral high ground. Perhaps the biggest dilemma for the Chinese government is that whenever a dispute erupts between the Dalai Lama and the Chinese government, the international community especially the Western world will almost immediately, often indiscriminately, throw their support behind the Dalai Lama. In the Western public perception, China's communist government is always wrong. Due to China's and the West's different focus of human rights and their different perceptions of the current situation of Tibet as well as the Dalai Lama's uncontested popularity outside China, China faces an uphill battle in defending its Tibet policy. Over 100 self-immolations by Tibetans since 2010 in apparent protests of Chinese policies have made such a job even more difficult for the Chinese government.

Problems in Xinjiang are no less serious for China. Han-Uyghur tensions remained high after the July 2009 riots. The pro-Xinjiang independence group, World Uyghur Congress (WUC) headed by Rebiya Kadeer, remains active and defiant of the Chinese government. WUC's meeting held in Japan in May 2012 not only deepened suspicion between the Chinese government and WUC, but also sparked a new Japan–China row in the already strained relationship due to the Diaoyu/Senkaku island dispute, leading to China's cancellation of several high-ranking officials' visits to Japan.

Final Thought

By the early years of the 21st century, China had integrated itself into the international economic and political systems. China's close cooperation with the developing world in trade, business, energy, and cultural exchanges is a successful example of South-South cooperation in international political economy. This is particularly significant and mutually beneficial for China and other developing countries at a time when the global financial crisis had hit major industrial powers, which, as a result, could not offer the much-needed help to the developing world. Though China has become more cautious in its overseas investment in the wake of the 2008–2009 financial crisis, its affirmation to fulfill its commitment to Africa and other developing regions is real good news.

Expectations are high for China, especially during the global economic crisis. At the April 2009 G-20 summit, a few world leaders such as Australian Prime Minister Kevin Rudd and World Bank President Robert Zoellick suggested that China should play a leadership role in international political economy. However, China does not seem to be so ambitious and it will probably continue to contribute to the international community at its own pace. It is particularly sensitive to concerns from the United States and has attempted not to challenge or disrupt the US-dominated international system. Aware of the tragedies in history associated with global power transition, Chinese leaders seem to be determined to develop a peaceful path for China's rise. The fourth generation of the PRC leaders, under President Hu Jintao and Premier Wen Jiabao, developed the theory of "three harmonies (*san he*)"—*hexie shehui* (a harmonious society 和谐社会), *hexie shijie* (a harmonious world 和谐世界), and *heping fazhan* (peaceful development 和平发展), the theory that guided China's domestic and international policies in the early years of the 21st century. The fifth generation of the PRC leaders headed by Xi Jinping and Li Keqiang has restated China's intention to become a peaceful power.

China has largely succeeded in projecting an image of a responsible and constructive power in the world, despite some concerns about its increasing military budget and its human rights policies. From the 1997–1998 Asian financial crisis to the 2008–2009 global economic recession, China has behaved responsibly. China is not aimed at replacing the United States as the dominant power in the international system; rather, it seeks to establish a multipolar world in which it can play an increasingly more active role in international political economy as one of the greatest powers.[29]

US–China relations remain vital for China's diplomacy in the future. As the wars in the Middle East came to an end, the United States began to shift more attention to Asia in 2010 as part of its strategic rebalancing. Though the United States has long-standing strategic and economic interests in the Asia–Pacific region, the recent US "pivot" to Asia is often cast in terms of countering China's rise. Obviously the two powers need to better understand each other's intensions.

---

29 For a discussion on this thesis, see Jenny Clegg, *China's Global Strategy: Toward a Multipolar World* (Pluto Press, 2009).

In November 2012, President Barack Obama returned to Asia within days of his re-election, making stops in Thailand, Cambodia and Myanmar and attending the East Asia Summit. Viewed from Beijing, America's strategic rebalancing toward the Asia-Pacific region is real and US–China competition for influence will deepen in the years ahead.

The talk of a Pax Americhina or Chinamerica dominating the 21st century geopolitics is premature. China's overriding concern is continued domestic growth and stability. Due to the huge gap between the military and political might of China and the United States, China is likely to continue to steer clear of direct confrontation with the United States in international affairs. However, in terms of the scramble for oil, gas and other resources, competition among major powers such as China, the United States, Japan, Russia and India has already intensified. One way to avoid the potential conflict over scarce resources is for these countries to cooperate and develop renewable and alternative energies. China and the United States are joined at the hip economically. They have also become increasingly interwoven in security, energy, environment and other issues. As Foreign Minister Yang Jiechi aptly noted, "we can hardly find an area where US-China cooperation is not needed" today.[30] At the first Strategic and Economic Dialogue (SED) between China and the United States held in Washington in July 2009 and during his November 2009 visit to China, President Obama also called for closer cooperation and claimed that US–China relations will shape the 21st century.[31] Summit meetings between the two great powers have been frequent and leaders from both sides seem committed to this important relationship.

China is a country full of contradictions. It became the second largest economy in the world in 2010. Meanwhile, it is still the largest developing nation with a low per capita GDP. The Chinese government's priority is to promote continued growth at home, narrowing the income gap between regions and tackling various social problems. On the other hand, it continues to reach out and play a role in international political economy that is commensurate with its power. Willingly or unwillingly, China is being pushed to the center stage of global politics and economics. Not everyone will be impressed by China's new diplomacy, but what China has been doing will fundamentally change the global power structure and international political economy.

China's new diplomacy is a reflection of China's national interests. While addressing a national meeting of diplomats in July 2009 in Beijing, President Hu Jintao stressed that China would stick to the independent foreign policy of peace, pursue the path of peaceful development and develop friendly cooperation with all the countries in line with the Five Principles of Peaceful Coexistence.[32] The new

---

30   Yang Jiechi, "Broaden China-US Cooperation in the 21st Century," speech at the Center for Strategic and International Studies, Washington, DC, March 12, 2009.

31   "Obama: US-China relations to shape 21st century," *The Associated Press*, July 27, 2009.

32   "Chinese President Urges Diplomats to Serve National Interests," *Xinhua*, July 20, 2009.

CCP leader Xi Jinping reiterated China's effort to rise peaceful while meeting with a group of foreign experts in December 2012. Xi said China would continue to open the door to the outside for further development. China's development "is absolutely not a challenge or threat to other countries. China will not seek hegemony or expansionism."[33] President Xi accentuated China's desire for cooperation during his June 2013 summit with President Obama in California.

Peace and development have been the top objectives of Chinese foreign and domestic policies since the end of the Cold War. With the continued growth of its economy, China is expected to widen and deepen its global search for energy and other resources and to expand its political clout. It is actively projecting soft power and presenting a peaceful image abroad by promoting cultural, educational, sports, tourism and other exchanges at the societal level. There is good reason to believe that China's re-emergence to great power status will continue to be peaceful since it serves China's fundamental interests. However, China will be a half-baked "responsible stakeholder" in the 21st century world if it cannot help tackle "problem countries" such as Sudan, Zimbabwe, Iran, Syria, and North Korea in its foreign policy. Relations with these countries, together with Beijing's policies towards Taiwan, Tibet and Xinjiang, will be a litmus test of China's new role in the 21st century.

Though its new diplomacy has become more sophisticated, China is still learning to be a peaceful, responsible and respectable great power in the ever-changing world. Indeed there is much to learn. In addition to traditional diplomatic challenges, China also needs to pay more attention to the danger of non-traditional security threats such as infectious diseases, economic crises, terrorism, drug trafficking, cyber hacking, piracy, transnational crimes, and environmental degradation. As a major player in today's world, China will need to cooperate with other countries and deal with these new challenges in its foreign relations. One hopes that China's new diplomacy will continue to benefit not only China itself but also the rest of the world in the 21st century and beyond.

Questions for Discussion

1. What are the similarities and differences in China's new diplomacy in various parts of the developing world?
2. What are major challenges in China's diplomacy in the years ahead?
3. What kind of world order does China wish to establish?
4. How successful has China been in promoting its soft power? What are the major obstacles?
5. Why are Taiwan, Tibet and Xinjiang important for China's national interests? How do they affect China's foreign policy?
6. How would you evaluate China's new diplomacy? Why?

---

33 "China's Rise Is Peaceful, Xi Jinping Tells Foreign Experts," *The South China Morning Post*, December 6, 2012.

Bibliography

"Achieving the Millennium Development Goals in Africa: Working with China," Department for International Development (DFID), United Kingdom, November 2007.

Alden, Chris. *China in Africa* (London and New York: Zed Books, 2007).

Alden, Chris, Daniel Large, and Ricardo Soares de Oliveira (eds). *China Returns to Africa: A Rising Power and a Continent Embrace* (New York: Columbia University Press, 2008).

Americas Quarterly, Winter 2012, Special Issue on "China's Global Rise: Implications for the Americas."

Andrews-Speed, Philip and Roland Dannreuther. *China, Oil and Global Politics* (New York and London: Routledge, 2011).

Archibold, Randal. "China Buys Inroads in the Caribbean, Catching U.S. Notice," *The New York Times*, April 7, 2012.

Armony, Ariel C. and Julia C. Strauss. "From Going Out (zou chuqu) to Arriving in (desembarco): Constructing a New Field of Inquiry in China-Latin America Interactions, *China Quarterly*, Vol. 209 (March 2012): pp. 1–17.

"Asia Poised to Overtake US as Latin America's Top Trading Partner," *Fox News Latino*, April 19, 2012.

Asian Development Bank. *Asia 2050: Realizing the Asian Century* (Manila, Philippines: Asian Development Bank, 2011).

Bateman, Sam. "The Great Australian Defense Debate: Is China a Threat"? RSIS Commentaries 40/2009, Nanyang Technological University, Singapore, April 24, 2009.

Beckley, Michael. "China and Pakistan: Fair-Weather Friends," *Yale Journal of International Affairs*, Volume VII, Issue 1 (March 2012): pp. 9–22.

Bergsten, Fred C., Charles Freeman, Nicholas R. Lardy, and Derek J. Mitchell. *China's Rise: Challenges and Opportunities* (Washington, DC: Peterson Institute and CSIS, 2008).

Bergsten, Fred C., Bates Gill, Nicholas R. Lardy, and Derek Mitchell. *China the Balance Sheet: What the World Needs to Know Now About the Emerging Superpower* (New York, NY: PublicAffairs, 2006).

Bhadrakumar, M.K. "Cash-rich China Courts the Caspian," *Asia Times Online*, April 18, 2009.

Brady, Anne-Marie (ed.). *Looking North, Looking South: China, Taiwan and South Pacific* (Singapore: World Scientific Publishing, 2010).

Brautigam, Deborah. *The Dragon's Gift: The Real Story of China in Africa* (New York: Oxford University Press, 2011).

Broadman, Harry G. "China and India Go to Africa: New Deals in the Developing World," *Foreign Affairs*, March–April 2008.

Broadman, Harry G. *Africa's Silk Road: China and India's New Economic Frontier* (Washington, DC: World Bank Publications, 2007).

Brookes, Peter. "Into Africa: China's Grab for Influence and Oil," *The Heritage Foundation*, March 26, 2007.

Brown, David E. *Hidden Dragon, Crouching Lion: How China's Advance in Africa is Underestimated and Africa's Potential Underappreciated* (Strategic Studies Institute, US Army War College, September 2012).

Brown, Kerry. *Struggling Giant: China in the 21st Century* (London, New York and Delhi: Anthem Press, 2007).

Brzezinski, Zbigniew. "The Group of Two That Could Change the World," *The Financial Times*, January 13, 2009.

Buck, Karl. *China's Engagement in Latin America and the Caribbean — Expectations and Bad Dreams*. Geneva: Geneva Center for the Democratic Control of Armed Forces, 2006.

"Bush Says No Plans for New US Bases in Africa," *Reuters*, February 20, 2008.

Buszynski, Leszek. "The South China Sea: Oil, Maritime Claims, and U.S.-China Strategic Rivalry," *The Washington Quarterly*, 35:2 (Spring 2012): pp. 139–156.

Castaneda, Jorge. "The Forgotten Relationship," *Foreign Affairs*, Vol. 82, No. 3, May–June 2003, pp. 67–81.

Cha, Ariana Eunjung. "Asians Say Trade Complaints Bring out the Bully in China," *The Washington Post*, September 5, 2007.

Cha, Victor D. *Beyond the Final Score: The Politics of Sport in Asia* (New York: Columbia University Press, 2009).

Chan, Gerald, Pak K. Lee, and Lai-Ha Chan. *China Engages Global Governance: A New World Order in the Making?* (London: Routledge, 2012).

Chan, Steve. *China, the US and the Power-Transition Theory: A Critique* (London and New York: Routledge, 2008).

Chandler, Marc. "Latin America: Key Theatre in Sino-US Economic Rivalry," *Active Trader*, November 2005, pp. 52–57.

Cheek, Timothy. *Living with Reform: China since 1989* (London and New York: Zed Books, 2006).

Chen, Zhimin. "Nationalism, Internationalism and Chinese Foreign Policy," *Journal of Contemporary China*, Vol. 14, No. 42, February 2005, pp. 35–53.

"China and Southeast Asia," Policy Bulletin, *The Stanley Foundation*, October 16–18, 2003.

China, India, and the United States: Competition for Energy Resource (Abu Dhabi, UAE: Emirates Center for Strategic Studies and Research, 2009).

China Quarterly, Vol. 209 (March 2012), Special Issue on China-Latin America relations.

"China to Step up Trade with Pacific Island Countries," *Xinhua*, September 7, 2008.

"China's Foreign Policy and 'Soft Power' in South America, Asia, and Africa: A Study Prepared for the Committee on Foreign Relations, United States Senate," Congressional Research Service, Washington, DC, April 2008.

"China's Growing Role in UN Peacekeeping," Asia Report No. 166, *The International Crisis Group*, April 17, 2009, www.crisisgroup.org.

Chu, Shulong. "The US and China in the Early 21st Century: Cooperation, Competition or Confrontation"? Presented at the "Partnership for Peace: Building Long-Term Security Cooperation in Northeast Asia" conference, Shanghai, China, March 3–4, 2003.

Chu, Yun-han, Larry Diamond, Andrew Nathan, and Doh Chull Shin. *How East Asians View Democracy* (New York: Columbia University Press, 2008).

Chua, Amy. *Day of Empire: How Hyperpowers Rise to Global Dominance—And Why They Fall* (Doubleday Publishing, 2007).

Clegg, Jenny. *China's Global Strategy: Toward a Multipolar World* (Pluto Press, 2009).

Collins, Gabe and Carlos Ramos-Mrosovsky. "Beijing's Bolivarian Venture," *The National Interest*, September–October 2006, pp. 88–92.

"Comparing Global Influence: China's and US Diplomacy, Foreign Aid, Trade, and Investment in the Developing World," CRS Report for Congress, Congressional Research Service, Washington, DC, August 15, 2008.

Cowan, Geoffrey and Nicholoas J. Cull (eds). "Public Diplomacy in a Changing World," *The Annals of the American Academy of Political and Social Science*, Vol. 616 (Thousand Oaks, CA: Sage Publications, March 2008).

Daly, John C.K. "Premier Wen's Eurasia Tour: Beijing and Moscow's Divergent Views on Central Asia," *China Brief*, Vol. 7, No. 21, November 14, 2007, The Jamestown Foundation, Washington, DC.

Dannreuther, Roland. "Asian Security and China's Energy Needs," *International Relations of the Asia-Pacific*, Vol. 3, 2003, pp. 197–219.

Das, Dilip K. *The Asian Economy: Spearheading the Recovery from the Global Financial Crisis* (London: Routledge, 2011).

Deng, Yong. *China's Struggle for Status: The Realignment of International Relations* (Cambridge: Cambridge University Press, 2008).

Deng, Yong. "Remolding Great-Power Politics: China's Strategic Partnerships with Russia, EU, and India," *Journal of Strategic Studies*, Vol. 30, No. 4–5, August 2007, pp. 863–903.

Deng, Yong and Fei-Ling Wang (eds). *China Rising: Power and Motivation in Chinese Foreign Policy* (Lanham: Rowman & Littlefield Publishers, Inc., 2004).

DeYoung, Karen. "US to Cut 10 Percent of Diplomatic Posts Next Year," *Washington Post*, December 13, 2007.

Dillon, Dana and John Tkacik. "China's Quest for Asia," *The Heritage Foundation*, December 14, 2005.

Ding, Sheng. *The Dragon's Hidden Wings: How China Rises with its Soft Power* (Lexington Books, 2008).

Dirlik, Arif. "The Idea of a 'Chinese Model': A Critical Discussion," *International Critical Thought*, Vol. 1, No. 2 (June 2011): pp. 129–137.

Dittmer, Lowell and George Yu (eds). *China, the Developing World, and the New Global Dynamic* (Boulder, CO: Lynne Rienner, 2010).

Djoumessi, Didier T. *The Political Impact of the Sino-US Oil Competition n Africa* (London: Adonis & Abbey Publishers Ltd, 2009).

Dobell, Graeme. "China and Taiwan in the South Pacific: Diplomatic Chess Versus Pacific Political Rugby," *Policy Brief*, January 2007, Lowy Institute for International Policy, Sydney, Australia.

Dominguez, Jorge. "China's Relations with Latin America: Shared Gains, Asymmetric Hopes," Working Paper, *Inter-American Dialogue*, June 2006.

Dreyer, June Teufel. "The China Connection," China-Latin America Task Force, Center for Hemispheric Policy, University of Miami, November 8, 2006.

Dumbaugh, Kerry and Mark Sullivan. "China's Growing Interest in Latin America," Congressional Research Service, Washington, DC, April 20, 2005.

Dwivedi, Ramakant. "China's Central Asia Policy in Recent Times," *China and Eurasia Forum Quarterly*, Vol. 4, No. 4, 2006, pp. 139–59.

Economy, Elizabeth C. and Adam Segal. "The G-2 Mirage," *Foreign Affairs*, Vol. 88, No. 3, May–June 2009, pp. 14–23.

Eisenman, Joshua, Eric Heginbotham, and Derek Mitchell (eds). *China and the Developing World: Beijing's Strategy for the Twenty-first Century* (Armonk, NY: M.E. Sharpe, 2007).

Ellis, R Evan. *China-Latin America Military Engagement: Good Will, Good Business, and Strategic Position*, Strategic Studies Institute, US Army War College, 2011.

Engardio, Peter (ed.). *Chindia: How China and India are Revolutionizing Global Business* (McGraw-Hill, 2006).

Erikson, Dan. "China in the Caribbean: A Benign Dragon"? *Focal Point* (www. focal.ca), Vol. 4, No. 4, April 2005.

Erikson, Dan and Adam Minson. "China's Ties to Latin America: US Policy Implications," *Inter-American Dialogue*, January 2006.

Fang, Bay. "China's Renewal: Hungry for Fuel, it Emerges as a Leader in Alternative Energy," *US News & World Report*, June 12, 2006, pp. 37–40.

Farrow, Ronan and Mia Farrow. "The 'Genocide Olympics,'" *The Wall Street Journal*, March 28, 2007.

Fieser, Ezra. "Caribbean Nations Get Caught in China-Taiwan Tug of War," *The Christian Science Monitor*, March 5, 2012.

Fishman, Ted C. *China Inc.: How the Rise of the Next Superpower Challenges America and the World* (New York: Scribner, 2005).

Foot, Rosemary and Andrew Walter. *China, the United States, and Global Order* (Cambridge University Press, 2011).

Forero, Juan. "China's Oil Diplomacy in Latin America," *The New York Times*, March 1, 2005.

French, Howard. "China in Africa: All Trade and No Political Baggage," *The New York Times*, August 8, 2004.

Friedberg, Aaron L. "Bucking Beijing: An Alternative U.S. China Policy," *Foreign Affairs*, 91:5 (September/October 2012): pp. 48–58.

Friedman, Edward. "How Economic Superpower China Could Transform Africa," *Journal of Chinese Political Science*, Vol. 14, No. 1, Spring 2009, pp. 1–20.

Fujiwara, Kiichi and Yoshiko Nagano. *The Philippines and Japan in America's Shadow* (Singapore: National University of Singapore Press, 2011).

Fung, K.C. and Alicia Garcia-Herrero. *Sino-Latin American Economic Relations* (London: Routledge, 2012).

Gallagher, Kevin P., Amos Irwin, and Katherine Koleski, "The New Banks in Town: Chinese Finance in Latin America," *Inter-American Dialogue*, February 2012.

Garrison, Jean A. *China and the Energy Equation in Asia: The Determinants of Policy Choices* (Boulder, CO: First Forum Press, 2009).

Garver, John W. *China and Iran: Ancient Partners in a Post-Imperial World* (Seattle, WA: University of Washington Press, 2006).

Ghazvinian, John. *Untapped: The Scramble for Africa's Oil* (Harcourt, 2007).

Gill, Bates. *Rising Star: China's New Security Diplomacy* (Washington, DC: The Brookings Institution Press, 2007).

"Global Unease with Major Powers," The Pew Global Attitudes Project, June 27, 2007.

Goldstein, Avery. *Rising To the Challenge: China's Grand Strategy and International Security* (Stanford, CA: Stanford University Press, 2005).

Goldstein, Jonathan (ed.). *China and Israel, 1948–1998: A Fifty Year Retrospective* (Westport, CT: Praeger, 1999).

Gross, Donald. *The China Fallacy: How the U.S. Can Benefit from China's Rise and Avoid Another Cold War* (New York and London: Bloomsbury, 2013).

Gu, Xiaosong and Mingjiang Li. "Nanning-Singapore Corridor: A New Vision in China-ASEAN Cooperation," RSIS Commentaries, 114/2008, Nanyang Technological University, Singapore, October 24, 2008.

Guerrero, Dorothy-Grace and Firoze Manji (eds). *China's New Role in Africa and the South: A Search for a New Perspective* (Oxford, UK: Fahamu, 2008).

Hakim, Peter. "Is Washington Losing Latin America," *Foreign Affairs*, Vol. 85, No. 1, January–February 2006, pp. 39–50.

Hall, Ben and Geoff Dyer. "China Seen as Bigger Threat to Security," *The Financial Times*, April 15, 2008.

Hanson, Fergus. "China: Stumbling Through the Pacific," Lowy Institute for International Policy, Sydney, Australia, July 2009.

Hanson, Fergus. "Australia and the World: Public Opinion and Foreign Policy," *The Lowy Institute Poll 2008*, Sydney, Australia, October 2008.

Hanson, Fergus. "The Dragon in the Pacific: More Opportunity than Threat," Lowy Institute for International Policy, Sydney, Australia, June 2008.

Hanson, Fergus. "China and the South Pacific: No Cause for Panic Yet," PacNet #15, Pacific Forum, CSIS, March 4, 2011.

Hao, Yufan, C.X. George Wei, and Lowell Dittmer (eds). *Challenges to Chinese Foreign Policy: Diplomacy, Globalization, and the Next World Power* (Lexington: University of Kentucky Press, 2009).

Hao, Yufan and Bill K.P. Chou. *China's Policies on its Borderlands and the International Implications* (Singapore: World Scientific Publishing, 2011).

Hawksley, Humphrey. "China's New Latin American Revolution," *The Financial Times*, April 5, 2006, p. 13.

He, Wenping. "The Balancing Act of China's Africa Policy," *China Security*, Vol. 3, No. 3, Summer 2007, pp. 23–40.

Henderson, John and Benjamin Reilly. "Dragon in Paradise: China's Rising Star in Oceania," *The National Interest*, No. 72, Summer 2003, pp. 94–104.

Ho, Stephanie. "China Raises Profile, Concerns in Latin America," *Voice of America*, November 1, 2006.

Ho, Xuan-Trang. *China's Burgeoning Role in Latin America—A Threat to the US?* Political Affairs (http://politicalaffairs.net/article/articleview/712/1/78/), the Council on Hemispheric Affairs, February 24, 2005.

Hopkirk, Peter. *The Great Game: The Struggle for Empire in Central Asia* (London: John Murray Publishers Ltd, 1990).

Horta, Loro. "The Changing Nature of Chinese Business in Africa: The case of Cape Verde," *RSIS Commentaries*, S. Rajaratnam School of International Studies, Nanyang Technological University, Singapore, January 17, 2008.

Horta, Loro. "China on the March in Latin America," *Asia Times Online*, June 27, 2007.

Hsu, Jenny. "Nicaragua-Taiwan Ties Still Strong: Ambassador," *Taipei Times*, October 25, 2008.

Hu, Jinshan. 非洲的中国形象 (*The Image of China in Africa*) (Beijing: People's Publishing House, 2010).

Hua, Shiping and Guo Sujian (eds). *China in the Twenty-first Century: Challenges and Opportunities* (New York: Palgrave Macmillan, 2007).

Hunter, Alan (ed.). *Peace Studies in the Chinese Century* (Aldershot, UK and Burlington, VT: Ashgate, 2006).

Hyland, Tom. "Hard Power, Soft Targets," *The Age* (www.theage.com.au), November 11, 2007

Ibraimov, Sadykzhan. "China-Central Asia Trade Relations: Economic and Social Patterns," *China and Eurasia Forum Quarterly*, Vol. 7, No. 1, 2009, pp. 47–59.

Jacques, Martin. *When China Rules the World*, 2nd edition (New York: Penguin Books, 2012).

Jenkins, Rhys, Enrique Dussel Peters, Mauricio Mesquita Moreira. "The Impact of China on Latin America and the Caribbean," *World Development*, Vol. 36, No. 2, 2008, pp. 235–53.

Jia, Qingguo. "The Shanghai Cooperation Organization: China's Experiment in Multilateral Leadership," in Iwashita Akihiro (ed.), *Eager Eyes Fixed Eurasia: Russia and its Eastern Edge* (Sapporo: Slavic Research Center, Hokkaido University, 2007).

Jiang, Wenran. "China's Energy Engagement with Latin America," *China Brief*, Vol. 6, No. 16, August 2, 2006.

Jilberto, Alex E. Fernandez and Barbara Hogenboom (eds.). *Latin America Facing China: South-South Relations beyond the Washington Consensus* (New York and Oxford: Berghahn Books, 2012).

Jin, Liangxiang. "Energy First: China and the Middle East," *Middle East Quarterly*, Vol. XII, No. 2 (Spring 2005). www.meforum.org/article/694.

Johnson, Stephen. "Balancing China's Growing Influence in Latin America," The Heritage Foundation, Backgrounder No. 1888, October 24, 2005.

Johnson, Tim. "China, Latin America: A Dance of Two Strangers," *Miami Herald*, July 10, 2005.

Johnston, Alastair Iain and Robert S. Ross (eds). *New Directions in the Study of Chinese Foreign Policy* (Stanford, CA: Stanford University Press, 2006).

Kahn, Joseph. "China, Shy Giant, Shows Signs of Shedding its False Modesty," *New York Times*, December 9, 2006.

Kang, David C. *China Rising: Peace, Power, and Order in East Asia* (New York: Columbia University Press, 2007).

Karrar, Hasan H. *The New Silk Road Diplomacy: China's Central Asian Foreign Policy since the Cold War* (University of British Columbia Press, 2010).

Kawalski, Emilian. *Ashgate Research Companion to Chinese Foreign Policy* (Surrey: Ashgate, 2012).

Kerr, Pauline, Stuart Harris, and Qin Yaqing (eds). *China's "New" Diplomacy: Tactical or Fundamental Change?* (Basingstoke, UK: Palgrave Macmillan, 2008).

Kissinger, Henry. *Does America Need a Foreign Policy?: Toward a Diplomacy for the 21st Century* (Simon & Schuster, 2002).

Kissinger, Henry. *On China* (New York: Penguin Books, 2012).

Kissinger, Henry. "The Future of U.S.-Chinese Relations: Conflict is a Choice, not a Necessity," *Foreign Affairs*, 91:2 (March/April 2012): pp. 44–55.

Kleine-Ahlbrandt, Stephanie and Andrew Small. "China's New Dictatorship Diplomacy: Is Beijing Parting With Pariahs"? *Foreign Affairs*, January/February 2008.

Knight, Franklin W. "China in Latin America and the Caribbean," *The Jamaica Observer*, November 1, 2006.

Kuhn, Anthony., Julie McCarthy, Michael Sullivan, Peter Kenyon, Gregory Feifer, and Mike Shuster. "China and the World," *National Public Radio* Special Series, March–April 2008.

Kurlantzick, Joshua. *Charm Offensive: How China's Soft Power is Transforming the World* (New Haven, CT: Yale University Press, 2007).

Kurlantzick, Joshua and Joshua Eisenman. "China's Africa Strategy," *Current History*, May 2006.

Lam, Peng Er. *Southeast Asia between China and Japan* (Newcastle: Cambridge Scholars, 2012).

Lam, Willy Wo-Lap. "Beijing Learns to be a Superpower," *Far Eastern Economic Review*, May 2009.

Lam, Willy Wo-Lap. "China's Encroachment on America's Backyard," *China Brief*, Vol. 4, No. 23, November 24, 2004.

Lampton, David M. *The Three Faces of Chinese Power: Money, Might, and Minds* (University of California Press, 2008).

Lampton, David M. *The Making of Chinese Foreign and Security Policy in the Era of Reform* (Stanford University Press, 2001).

Lancaster, Carol. "The Chinese Aid System," *Center for Global Development Essay*, June 2007. http://www.cgdev.org.

Landau, Saul. "Chinese Influence on the Rise in Latin America," *Foreign Policy In Focus* (FPIF), June 23, 2005.

Lanteigne, Marc. *Chinese Foreign Policy: An Introduction* (London and New York: Routledge, 2009).

Leonard, Mark. *What Does China Think?* (New York, NY: PublicAffairs, 2008).

Lee, Margaret C., Henning Melber, Sanusha Naidu, and Ian Taylor. *China in Africa*. Current African Issues, No. 35 (Nordic Africa Institute, June 2007).

Li, He. "China's Growing Interest in Latin America and Its Implications," *The Journal of Strategic Studies*, Vol. 30, No. 4–5, August–October 2007, pp. 854–58.

Li, Mingjiang. "China's Rising Maritime Aspirations: Impact on Beijing's Good-Neighbor Diplomacy," RSIS, Nanyang Technological University, March 28, 2012.

Li, Xiaofei. *China's Outward Foreign Investment: A Political Perspective* (University Press of America, 2011).

Liu, Guoli. "China's Policy Toward Russia and Central Asia," unpublished manuscript.

Lum, Thomas, et al. "Comparing Global Influence: China's and US Diplomacy, Foreign Aid, Trade, and Investment in the Developing World," Congressional Research Service, Washington, DC, August 15, 2008.

Lynch, Colum. "China's Arms Exports Flooding Sub-Saharan Africa," *The Washington Post*, August 25, 2012.

Mahbubani, Kishore. *The New Asian Hemisphere: The Irresistible Shift of Global Power to the East* (New York, NY: PublicAffairs, 2008).

Mahbubani, Kishore. "Smart Power, Chinese-Style," *The American Interest*, Vol. 3, No. 4, March–April 2008.

Malik, Mohan. "China's Growing Involvement in Latin America," *PINR (Power and Interest News Report)*, June 12, 2006.

Manji, Firoze and Stephen Marks (eds). *African Perspectives on China in Africa* (Oxford, UK: Fahamu, 2007).

McCrummen, Sephanie. "Struggling Chadians Dream of a Better Life – in China," *The Washington Post*, October 6, 2007.

McGiffert, Carola, William S. Cohen, and Maurice R. Greenberg. "Smart Power in US-China Relations," Report of the CSIS Commission on China. Washington, DC: Center for Strategic and International Studies, March 2009.

McGregor, Andrew. "China's Oil Offensive Strikes: Horn of Africa and Beyond," *China Brief*, Vol. 7, No. 16, The Jamestown Foundation, Washington, DC (August 8, 2007).

McNally, Christopher A. "Sino-Capitalism: China's Reemergence and the International Political Economy," *World Politics*, Vol. 64, Issue 4 (October 2012): pp. 741–776.

Medeiros, Evan S. and M. Taylor Fravel. "China's New Diplomacy," *Foreign Affairs*, November/December 2003.

Men, Jing and Barton, Benjamin (eds). *China and the European Union in Africa; Partners or Competitors?* (Farnham: Ashgate, 2011).

Michel, Serge. "When China Met Africa," *Foreign Policy*, May–June 2008, pp. 39–46.

Mooney, Paul. "China's African Safari," *YaleGlobal*, January 3, 2005.

Moyo, Dambisa. "Beijing, A Boon for Africa," *New York Times*, June 27, 2012.

Nathan, Andrew and Andrew Scobell. "How China Sees America"? *Foreign Affairs*, 91:5 (September/October 2012): pp. 32–47.

Naughton, Barry. *The Chinese Economy: Transitions and Growth* (Cambridge, MA: The MIT Press, 2007).

Nolan, Peter. *Is China Buying the World?* (Cambridge: Polity Press, 2012).

Onuf, Nicholas Greenwood. *World of Our Making: Rules and Rule in Social Theory and International Relations* (Columbia: University of South Carolina Press, 1989).

Oppenheimer, Andres. "China Seeks Materials, Political Allies," *Miami Herald*, September 25, 2005.

Orban, Nadege. "Contemporary China: Confucius Returns," *RSIS Commentary 124/2007*, Nanyang Technological University, Singapore, November 19, 2007.

Organski, A.F.K. *World Politics* (Alfred A. Knopf, 1958).

Oviedo, Eduardo Daniel. "The New International Role of China and its Relations with Argentina in Time of Crisis," Paper presented at the 21st World Congress of Political Science, Santiago, Chile, July 12–16, 2009.

Pan, Guang. "China and Central Asia: Charting a New Course for Regional Cooperation," *China Brief*, Vol. 7, No. 3, February 7, 2007, pp. 4–7.

Pan, Philip P. *Out of Mao's Shadow: The Struggle for the Soul of a New China* (New York: Simon & Schuster, 2008).

Paz, Gonzalo, "Rising China's 'Offensive' in Latin America and the US Reaction," *Asian Perspective*, Vol. 30, No. 4, 2006, pp. 95–112.

Peerenboom, Randy. *China Modernizes: Threat to the West or Model for the Rest?* (Oxford and New York: Oxford University Press, 2007).

Pei, Minxin. *China's Trapped Transition: The Limits of Developmental Autocracy* (Cambridge, MA: Harvard University Press, 2006).

Percival, Bronson. *The Dragon Looks South: China and Southeast Asia in the New Century* (Westport, CT: Praeger, 2007).

Perlez, Jane. "China Competes with West in Aid to its Neighbors," *The New York Times*, September 18, 2006.

Perlez, Jane. "Chinese Move to Eclipse US Appeal in South Asia," *The New York Times*, November 18, 2004.

Perlez, Jane. "The Charm from Beijing," *The New York Times*, October 9, 2003.

Pokharna, Bhawna. *India-China Relations: Dimensions and Perspectives* (New Century Publications, 2009).

Polgreen, Lydia. "African Hopes Sink as an Investment Partner, China, Grows More Cautious," *The New York Times*, March 26, 2009, p. A6.

Powell, Gareth. "Building Confucius Institutes into a 'World Brand,'" *China Economic Review*, December 18, 2007.

Power, Marcus, Giles Mohan, and May Tan-Mullins. *China's Resource Diplomacy in Africa: Powering Development?* (London: Palgrave Macmillan, 2012).

"Prime Minister Launches Confucius Institute in New Zealand," University of Auckland news release, February 16, 2007.

Ramo, Joshua Cooper. *The Beijing Consensus* (London: The Foreign Policy Center, 2004).

Ratliff, William. "Pragmatism Over Ideology: China's Relations with Venezuela," *China Brief*, Vol. 6, No. 6, March 15, 2006, pp. 3–5.

Reilly, James. "China's Unilateral Sanctions," *The Washington Quarterly*, 35:4 (Fall 2012): pp. 121–133.

Roett, Riordan and Guadalupe Paz (eds). *China's Expansion into the Western Hemisphere: Implications for Latin America and the United States* (Washington, DC: Brookings Institution Press, 2008).

Rohter, Larry. "China Widens Economic Role in Latin America," *The New York Times*, November 20, 2004.

Ross, Robert S. "Taiwan's Fading Independence Movement," *Foreign Affairs*, March/April 2006, pp. 141–8.

Ross, Robert S. and Zhu Feng (eds). *China's Ascent: Power, Security and the Future of International Politics* (Ithaca, NY: Cornell University Press, 2008).

Rotberg, Robert I. (ed.). *China Into Africa: Trade, Aid, and Influence* (Washington, DC: Brookings Institution Press, 2009).

Rozman, Gilbert (ed). *China's Foreign Policy: Who Makes It and How Is It Made?* (Seoul, Korea: Asan Institute for Policy Studies, 2012).

Ruggie, John Gerard. *Constructing the World Polity: Essays on International Institutionalization* (London and New York: Routledge, 1998).

Saunders, Phillip C. "China's Global Activism: Strategy, Drivers, and Tools," Occasional Paper No. 4, Washington, DC: Institute for National Strategic Studies, National Defense University, 2006.

Schmitt, Gary J. (ed.). *The Rise of China: Essays on the Future Competition* (New York: Encounter Books, 2009).

Schonberg, Karl K. *Pursuing the National Interest: Moments of Transition in Twentieth-Century American Foreign Policy* (Praeger Publishers, 2003).

Shambaugh, David. "China's New Foray into Latin America," *YaleGlobal*, November 17, 2007.

Shambaugh, David. *Power Shift: China and Asia's New Dynamics* (Los Angeles, CA: University of California Press, 2006).

Shambaugh, David. "Coping with a Conflicted China," *The Washington Quarterly*, 34:1 (Winter 2011): pp. 7–27.

Shambaugh, David. *China Goes Global: The Partial Power* (Oxford University Press, 2013)

Shapiro, Charles. "The Role of China in Latin America: Diplomatic, Political, and Economic Consequences," Testimony before the US Senate Subcommittee on the Western Hemisphere, Peace Corps, and Narcotic Affairs, September 20, 2005.

Shaplen, Jason T. and James Laney. "Washington's Eastern Sunset: the Decline of US Power in Northeast Asia," *Foreign Affairs*, November–December 2007.

Sheives, Kevin. "China Turns West: Beijing's Contemporary Strategy Towards Central Asia," *Pacific Affairs*, Vol. 79, No. 2, Summer 2006, pp. 205–23.

Shen, Simon and Jean-Marc F. Blanchard (eds). *Multidimensional Diplomacy of Contemporary China* (Lanham, MD: Lexington Books, 2012).

Sheng, Lijun. "Is Southeast Asia Becoming China's Playpen"? *YaleGlobal Online*, January 11, 2007.

Shinn, David. "Chinese Involvement in African Conflict Zones," *China Brief*, Vol. 9, No. 7, April 2, 2009.

Shinn, David, and Joshua Eisenman. *China and Africa: A Century of Engagement* (Philadelphia: University of Pennsylvania Press, 2012).

Shirk, Susan L. *China: Fragile Superpower: How China's Internal Politics Could Derail its Peaceful Rise* (Oxford University Press, 2007).

Smith, Peter, Kotaro Horisaka, and Shoji Nishijima (eds). *East Asia and Latin America: The Unlikely Alliance* (London: Rowman & Littlefield, 2003).

Steinberg, David I. and Fan Hongwei. *Modern China-Myanmar Relations: Dilemmas of Mutual Dependence* (Singapore: ISEAS, 2012).

Storey, Ian. "Impeccable Affair and Renewed Rivalry in the South China Sea," *China Brief*, Vol. 9, No. 9, April 30, 2009.

Storey, Ian. "China's Inroads into East Timor," *China Brief*, Vol. 9, No. 6, March 19, 2009.

Storey, Ian. *Southeast Asia and the Rise of China: The Search for Security* (New York and London: Routledge, 2011).

Strauss, Julia C. and Ariel C. Armony. *From the Great Wall to the New World: China and Latin America in the 21st Century* (Cambridge University Press, 2012).

Sun, Jing. *Japan and China as Charm Rivals* (Ann Arbor: University of Michigan Press, 2012).

Sun, Xuefeng. "The Efficiency of China's Multilateral Policies in East Asia: 1997–2007," *International Relations of the Asia-Pacific*, Vol. 10 (2010): pp. 515–541.

Sutter, Robert G. *Chinese Foreign Relations: Power and Policy since the Cold War* (Lanham, MD: Rowman & Littlefield Publishers, 2012).

Sutter, Robert G. *China's Rise in Asia: Promises and Perils* (Lanham, MD: Rowman & Littlefield Publishers, 2005).

Sutter, Robert and Chin-Hao Huang. "China-Southeast Asia Relations: Summitry at Home and Abroad," *Comparative Connections: A Quarterly E-Journal on East Asian Bilateral Relations*, CSIS, December 2006.

Swaine, Michael D. and Ashley J. Tellis. *Interpreting China's Grand Strategy: Past, Present, and Future* (Santa Monica: RAND Corporation, 2000).

Swanstrom, Niklas. "China and Central Asia: A New Great Game or Traditional Vassal Relations"? *Journal of Contemporary China*, Vol. 14, No. 45, November 2005, pp. 569–84.

Syroezhkin, Konstantin. "China in Central Asia: from Trade to Strategic Partnership," *Central Asia and the Caucasus*, No. 3(45), 2007, pp. 40–51.

Tarling, Nicholas. *Southeast Asia and the Great Powers* (London and New York: Routledge, 2010).

Tarrazona, Neol. "US, China Vie for Philippine Military Influence," *Asia Times Online*, September 20, 2007.

Taylor, Ian. *China and Africa: Engagement and Compromise* (London: Routledge, 2006).

Taylor, Ian. *China's New Role in Africa* (Boulder, CO: Lynne Rienner, 2008).

Thompson, Drew. "China's Soft Power in Africa: From the 'Beijing Consensus' to Health Diplomacy," *China Brief*, Vol. 5, No. 21, 2005.

Thompson, Drew. "Think Again: China's Military," *Foreign Policy* (March/April 2010).

Trubowitz, Peter. *Defining the National Interest: Conflict and Change in American Foreign Policy* (University of Chicago Press, 1998).

Tull, Denis M. "China's Engagement in Africa: Scope, Significance and Consequences," *Journal of Modern African Studies*, Vol. 44, No. 3, 2006, pp. 459–79.

United Nations. "Ranking of Military and Police Contributions to UN Operations," April 2008.

United Nations. "United Nations Peacekeeping Fact Sheet," February 2008.

van Wie Davis, Elizabeth and Rouben Azizian (eds). *Islam, Oil, and Geopolitics: Central Asia after September 11* (Lanham, MD: Rowman & Littlefield, 2007).

Vang, Pobzeb. *Five Principles of Chinese Foreign Policies* (AuthorHouse, 2008).

Waldron, Arthur (ed.). *China in Africa* (Washington, DC: The Jamestown Foundation, 2008).

Walt, Vivienne. "China's Appetite for African Oil Grows," *Fortune*, February 15, 2006.

Wang, Gungwu and Zheng Yongnian (eds.) *China and the New International Order* (New York and London: Routledge, 2008).

Wang, Jisi. "China's Search for a Grand Strategy: A Rising Great Power Finds Its Way," *Foreign Affairs*, Vol. 90, Issue 2 (March/April 2011): pp. 68–79.

Wang, Jing. *Brand New China: Advertising, Media, and Commercial Culture* (Cambridge, MA: Harvard University Press, 2008).

Wang, Yiwei. "China's Rise: An Unlikely Pillar of US Hegemony," *The Harvard International Review*, Vol. 29, No. 1, Spring 2007, pp. 60–63.

Watson, Cynthia. "A Warming Relationship," *China Brief*, Vol. 4, No. 12, June 3, 2004.

Watson, Cynthia. "Adios Taiwan, Hola Beijing: Taiwan's Relations with Latin America," *China Brief*, Vol. 4, No. 11, May 27, 2004.

Welch, Matthew. "China vs. US: Who Is Better for Africa"? *The Global Post*, November 25, 2012.

Wendt, Alexander. *Social Theory of International Politics* (Cambridge: Cambridge University Press, 1999).

Wendt, Alexander. "Anarchy Is What States Make of It: The Social Construction of Power Politics," *International Organization*, 46 (1992), pp. 391–425.

Wesley-Smith, Terence. *China in Oceania: New Forces in Pacific Politics* (Honolulu, HI: The East-West Center, 2007).

Wesley-Smith, Terence and Edgar A. Porter (eds.) *China in Oceania: Reshaping the Pacific?* (New York and Oxford: Berghahn Books, 2010).

When China Met Africa, a documentary by Nick Francis and Marc Francis, Speak-it/Zeta Productions, 2010.

White, Hugh. *The China Choice: Why America Should Share Power?* (Australia: Black Inc., 2012).

Wild, Leni and David Mepham (eds). *The New Sinosphere: China in Africa* (London, UK: Institute for Public Policy Research, 2006).

Wilson, Ernest J. III. "Hard Power, Soft Power, Smart Power," in Cowan, Geoffrey and Nicholas J. Cull (eds), *Public Diplomacy in a Changing World*, The Annals of the American Academy of Political and Social Science, Volume 616 (Thousand Oaks, CA: Sage Publications, March 2008), pp. 110–24.

Wines, Michael. "China's Influence in Africa Arouses Some Resistance," *The New York Times*, February 10, 2007.

Winters, L. Alan and Shahid Yusuf (eds). *Dancing with Giants: China, India, and the Global Economy* (World Bank Publications, 2007).

Wu, Guoguang. *China's Challenge to Human Security: Foreign Relations and Global Implications* (New York and London: Routledge, 2012).

Yang, Jian. "China in the South Pacific: hegemon on the horizon"? *The Pacific Review*, 22(2), May 2009, 139–58.

Yang, Jiechi. "Broaden China-US Cooperation in the 21st Century," speech at the Center for Strategic and International Studies, Washington, DC, March 12, 2009.

Yang, Rui. "China's Soft Power Projection in Higher Education," *International Higher Education*, No. 46, Winter 2007.

Yueh, Linda (ed.). *China and Globalization* (New York: Routledge, 2012).

Zakaria, Fareed. *The Post-American World* (New York and London: W.W. Norton & Company, 2008).

Zakaria, Fareed. "Does the Future Belong to China," *Newsweek*, May 29, 2005.

Zambelis, Chris. "China's Persian Gulf Diplomacy Reflects Delicate Balancing Act," *China Brief*, Vol. XII, Issue 4 (February 21, 2012): pp. 3–6.

Zehfuss, Maja. *Constructivism in International Relations: The Politics of Reality* (Cambridge: Cambridge University Press, 2002).

Zhang, Biwu. *Chinese Perceptions of the U.S.: An Exploration of China's Foreign Policy Motivations* (Lanham, MD: Lexington Books, 2012).

Zhang, Guihong. "China's Pacific Strategy Unfurled," *Asia Times Online*, April 10, 2008.

Zhang, Qingmin. *China's Diplomacy* (Beijing: China Intercontinental Press, 2010).

Zhao, Hong. *China and India: The Quest for Energy Resources in the 21st Century* (New York and London: Routledge, 2012).

Zhao, Qizheng. 公共外交与跨文化交流 (*Public Diplomacy and Communication between Cultures*) (Beijing: Renmin University Press, 2011).

Zhao, Suisheng (ed.). *China and the United States: Cooperation and Competition in Northeast Asia* (New York: Palgrave Macmillan, 2008).

Zheng, Bijian. *China's Peaceful Rise: Speeches of Zheng Bijian 1997–2005* (Washington, DC: Brookings Institution Press, 2006).

Zheng, Yongnian. 中国模式及其未来 (*The China Model and Its Future*) (Singapore: World Scientific Publishing, 2011).

Zhu, Zhiqun. *US-China Relations in the 21st Century: Power Transition and Peace* (London and New York: Routledge, 2006).

Zhu, Zhiqun. "Beijing's Diplomatic Blitz Gathers Pace," *Asia Times Online*, February 24, 2009.

Zhu, Zhiqun. "Big Picture of China Lost in the Debates," *CNN.com*, October 29, 2012.

Zoellick, Robert. "Whither China? From Membership to Responsibility"? Speech at the National Committee on US-China Relations, September 21, 2005.

Zweig, David and Chen Zhimin. *China's Reforms and International Political Economy* (London and New York: Routledge, 2007).

Index